Justice at the Boundaries

Justice at the Boundaries

MEDIATING RECONCILIATION AND LEGAL
RECOGNITION IN TAIWAN'S INDIGENOUS COURTS

J. Christopher Upton

UNIVERSITY OF CALIFORNIA PRESS

University of California Press
Oakland, California

© 2026 by J. Christopher Upton

All rights reserved.

Cataloging-in-Publication data is on file at the Library of Congress.

ISBN 978-0-520-42331-2 (cloth)
ISBN 978-0-520-42332-9 (pbk.)
ISBN 978-0-520-42334-3 (ebook)

GPSR Authorized Representative: Easy Access System Europe, Mustamäe tee 50, 10621 Tallinn, Estonia, gpsr.requests@easproject.com

35 34 33 32 31 30 29 28 27 26
10 9 8 7 6 5 4 3 2 1

*To my family,
Jennifer Lynne Upton,
Juliet Catherine Upton,
and Miriam Clare Upton*

CONTENTS

List of Maps and Illustrations ix
Acknowledgments xi
Note to the Reader xvii

Introduction: Of Courts and Ancestral Spirits 1

1 · Born of Wood, Born of Stone 43

2 · Orders in the Court 79

3 · Ethereal Presences of the Ad Hoc Chambers 125

4 · One Community, Two Controversies 164

5 · Hybrid Practices and Legal Indigeneities 195

6 · Boundary Institutions and Beyond 225

Glossary of Terms in English, Pinyin,
and Chinese Characters 243
Notes 247
Bibliography 259
Index 287

MAPS AND ILLUSTRATIONS

MAPS

1. Map of Taiwan's Indigenous peoples   10
2. Map of field sites   29

FIGURES

1. Katratripulr demonstration   2
2. Hualien District Court   23
3. Hualien District Court interior   24
4. Hualien High Court   25
5. Electrical barrier fences   54
6. Hunters' release   74
7. Discussion of hunting convention   85
8. Homemade hunting guns   97
9. Hunting in the mountains   109
10. President Tsai Ing-wen's apology   114
11. Protest sign   115
12. Court site visit   167
13. Lawyer working under a tent   221
14. Display at Taoyuan International Airport   228

ACKNOWLEDGMENTS

These acknowledgments are an expression of my deep gratitude to those who invested in the research and writing of this book. Behind the words of this book is a remarkable social and cooperative undertaking involving many individuals and institutions. They opened their worlds and lives to me, sharing their knowledge, welcoming my questions, including me in events, and thinking through ideas with me. Without them, this book would not be possible.

I am profoundly grateful and humbled by the support of my many collaborators and friends in Taiwan. While I cannot thank most of them publicly, their wisdom and insights are present throughout the following pages. Many have become lifelong friends, and I feel immensely fortunate to have known and learned from them over the past decade of this research. I am especially thankful to the Institute of Ethnology at Academia Sinica and the National Museum of Prehistory, Taiwan, which served as my host institutions during the research. I am also indebted to the Taiwan Judicial Yuan for including me in judicial training events and facilitating introductions with judicial actors. I also owe my deep thanks to the talented lawyers and staff at the Legal Center of Indigenous Peoples, who generously shared their expertise and welcomed me into training programs and other initiatives. I am equally grateful to the judges and staff at the Hualien District Court and High Court for allowing me to observe proceedings and for their willingness to share their own insights and perspectives.

I am especially indebted to my many Indigenous collaborators, colleagues, and friends, particularly members of Dowmung and Tastas, who welcomed me and my family into their homes. Their generosity, patience, and knowledge have profoundly shaped this work. The insights they shared with me far exceed what I have been able to convey in these pages, and the modest results presented here reflect only a fraction of their deep contributions.

This book has been immeasurably enriched by the thoughtful conversations, critical feedback, and generous support of many colleagues and friends. I am especially grateful to Awi Mona, Lin San-jia, Chester Lee, Todd Wang, Chen Cai-yi, Qiu Gui, Sayun Tosu, Tsai Ting-yi, Lin San-yuan, Tang Wen-zhang, Paul Chang, Chang Hung-chieh, William Hsu, Wang Tay-sheng, Kurtis Pei, Lin Ping-chin, Tung Yuan-chao, Hu Chia-yi, Fu Jun, Lin Yih-ren, Lin Hao-li, Scott Simon, Jan Hoffman French, Paul Barclay, Bruce Miller, Dana Powell, Georgina Ramsay, and Robin Valenzuela. Scott Simon, Jan Hoffman French, and Robin Valenzuela read every word of the manuscript. Their incisive critiques, thoughtful insights, and generous guidance transformed and improved this book in countless ways. I owe special thanks to Fang Chun-wei at the National Museum of Prehistory, Taiwan, who has not only become a lifelong friend but also supported this research in numerous ways and assisted with translations in this book.

I presented materials drawn from this project at various conferences and institutions. These include the Conference on Indigenous Courts and Indigenous Rights in Taiwan and Globally, organized by the Center for World Austronesia and Indigenous Peoples (CWAIP) at National Tsing Hua University, Taiwan; the American Anthropological Association Annual Meeting in Seattle, Washington; the 3rd World Congress of Taiwan Studies Conference in Taipei, Taiwan; the National Museum of Prehistory, Taiwan; the Institute of Anthropology at National Tsing Hua University, Taiwan; Max Planck Institute for Social Anthropology in Halle, Germany; the Environmental Justice Center in Taipei, Taiwan; the Institute of Ethnology at Academia Sinica in Taipei, Taiwan; and the Ostrom Workshop Research Series at Indiana University-Bloomington. I am especially grateful to Jeffrey Nicolaisen and I-yi Hsieh for their insightful comments on a paper based on the introduction, presented at the International Center for Cultural Studies at National Yang Ming Chiao Tung University. I also appreciate comments from Justin Richland and Aomar Boum on a paper based on chapter 2 at the Law & Humanities Workshop for Junior Scholars at UCLA Law School. In addition, I thank the Law & Humanities Working Group at Temple University for their comments on a paper based on chapter 3, especially Edith Beerdsen, Brian Hutler, Meghan Morris, Carolina Angel, and Ben Heath.

This book is the product of several transformative moments and experiences. The first concerns my parents, John and Deborah Upton, who moved our family to southern Taiwan when I was a youth to undertake missionary work. My brother, my sister, and I grew up in a mixed neighborhood of Han Taiwanese, Amis, Paiwan, and Pinuyumayan peoples along the coast of Taitung County. This was a profoundly formative experience, shaped by long soaks in hot springs, abundant mangos, and deep friendships. It instilled an abiding love for all things Taiwan and a deep interest in Indigenous peoples and their rights.

A second moment came out of conversations I had with anthropologists serving as expert witnesses on habeas corpus cases I was handling at Guantanamo Bay. I mentioned to the lawyer with whom I was working on these cases, Terry Connor, that I was considering a transition from law practice to anthropology. I did not fully know what that entailed, but it felt like a natural progression. He put me in contact with Jan Hoffman French, a legal anthropologist at the University of Richmond, and our conversation proved life changing. Not long after, I packed up my office at the law firm and moved to Bloomington, Indiana, to begin graduate studies in anthropology. Since then, Professor French has remained a vital source of guidance, support, insight, and encouragement.

Another experience came through the extraordinary mentorship I received during my doctoral work at Indiana University-Bloomington. There, I had the privilege of studying with Sara Friedman, who steered my dissertation to completion with patience and insight. She devoted countless hours of offering advice, challenging my ideas, and encouraging me to sharpen my thinking. I am profoundly grateful for her steady support, wise guidance, thoughtful critiques, and unwavering generosity over the years of this research.

I am also deeply grateful to the other members of my dissertation committee—Carol Greenhouse, Brian Gilley, Ethan Michelson, and Marvin Sterling—whose critical insights, thoughtful feedback, and generous guidance were instrumental in shaping the research that underlies this book. At Indiana University-Bloomington, I received additional inspiration and support from Eduardo Brondizio, Hilary Kahn, and Sarah Osterhoudt, whose perspectives enriched my thinking and research in many essential ways. I am especially thankful to Beverly Stoeltje for her commitment to my professional and personal development, and for the many conversations that helped clarify and refine my ideas.

I also want to express my deep thanks to my colleagues in the Department of Anthropology at Temple University for their intellectual and moral support throughout the writing of this book. I also thank my wonderful students at Temple University, whose thoughtful engagement with ideas underlying this research in the classroom and consistent enthusiasm have been a continual source of motivation and inspiration.

At UC Press, I am especially grateful to Chad Attenborough for his insights, vision, and steady support throughout the writing process. His enthusiasm, professionalism, and thoughtful guidance were essential to bringing the manuscript to completion. I also thank the Press for securing such capable anonymous reviewers, whose critical questions, careful corrections, and insightful recommendations significantly strengthened the book.

I thank the J. William Fulbright Scholarship Board, National Science Foundation, Taiwan Fellowship, Native American and Indigenous Studies Fellowship, and Henry Luce Foundation/ACLS Program in China Studies, as well as stipends and travel grants from Indiana University-Bloomington, for providing the funds that made the research possible. I am deeply grateful for the time and space to reflect on issues that would be clarified in the writing of this book during a dissertation writing-up fellowship at the Department of Law and Anthropology at Max Planck Institute in Halle, Germany, and a postdoctoral fellowship at the Center for World Austronesia and Indigenous Peoples (CWAIP) at National Tsing Hua University in Hsinchu, Taiwan. I also thank the Department of Anthropology at the University of Virginia for supporting my research as a visiting scholar.

Finally, at the foundation of everything, my family has been a tremendous support and source of inspiration throughout the years of this research. My wife, Jennifer, and our daughters, Juliet and Miriam, have been my home base as I engaged in this research and ventured into many other professional and personal endeavors. Jenn made it possible for me to step away from law practice and relocate our family to Bloomington and then to Hualien, Taiwan, so that I could pursue a PhD in anthropology and complete this research. She has been my constant companion on this journey, joining me on field trips, assisting with data collection, developing ideas, and playing a vital role in editing the manuscript. Her presence opened doors that otherwise would have remained closed. The relationships she developed allowed me to gain deeper insight into Bunun, Truku, and Han Taiwanese social worlds, particularly the lives and experiences of women. My cultural understanding was greatly enriched by people inviting her and our daughters to events in the communities, meetings with local leaders, and everyday activities.

The presence of Juliet and Miriam made it possible for me to learn about details of daily life in Bunun, Truku, and Han Taiwanese communities that otherwise would have remained obscure: the worlds of children, the rhythms of school life, parenting practices, and the subtle dynamics of intergenerational relationships. Later, when we returned and they were older, I learned more about children playing sports, preparing for performances of songs and dances, and navigating friendships and preteen life. I am endlessly proud of their courage, kindness, and patience as we navigated this journey together as a family. There has been no greater inspiration to study anthropology than witnessing these young women grow and grapple with the complexities of personhood. They made this experience one of the most meaningful of my life.

Several chapters originated as articles and book chapters. These include "Courts of Being and Non-being: Taiwan's Indigenous Courts and Judicial Hybrid Practice," *Journal of Legal Anthropology* 6 (2): 25–51 (2022); "From Thin to Thick Justice and Beyond: Access to Justice and Legal Pluralism in Indigenous Taiwan," *Law & Social Inquiry* 47 (3): 996–1025 (2022); "Courts and Indigenous Reconciliation: Positivism, the A Priori, and Justice in Taiwan," in *Indigenous Reconciliation in Contemporary Taiwan: From Stigma to Hope*, ed. Scott Simon, Jolan Hsieh, and Peter Kang, 96–118 (Routledge, 2023); "Legal Indigeneities: Identity, Authenticity, and Power in Taiwan's Indigenous Courts," *International Journal of Taiwan Studies* 6 (1): 5–32 (2023); and "Codifying *Gaya*, Cultivating Hunters: Indigenous Hunting Self-Governance and Self-Discipline in Taiwan," *PoLAR: Political and Legal Anthropology Review* (forthcoming).

NOTE TO THE READER

PEOPLE'S NAMES

The names of individuals have been replaced with pseudonyms to offer anonymity as much as possible, while acknowledging that in various instances events are discussed that allow for identification to be made from public records. For ethical reasons, certain events, people, and place names are combined to ensure privacy. Exceptions are in cases of public figures or those who provided express permission to be identified.

TRANSLITERATION

Chinese-language terms are transliterated in Hanyu Pinyin, except for personal names and words that are customarily rendered in Wade-Giles, for example place names like *Kaohsiung* and *Taichung*. Japanese-language terms are transliterated in the modified Hepburn system. The romanization of Indigenous languages in Taiwan is widely used within Indigenous communities and recognized by the government, although there is no standard system for transliterating Indigenous words, personal names, or place names. I have endeavored to follow local conventions when using Indigenous terms.

TRANSLATIONS

All translations of interviews and Chinese sources are my own, except where an official English translation was available. I note issues with the official translations where relevant.

PHOTOS

Unless otherwise noted, all photos are my own.

Introduction

OF COURTS AND ANCESTRAL SPIRITS

ON MAY 3, 2013, thirty claimants from the Pinuyumayan community of Katratripulr gathered outside the Kaohsiung High Administrative Court in southern Taiwan, the Republic of China (ROC). They had traveled by bus to attend a hearing related to their lawsuit, which sought to prevent the relocation of an ancestral cemetery in nearby Taitung County.¹ At the suggestion of their lawyer, a non-Indigenous Han Taiwanese attorney who represented the community pro bono, they arrived at the courthouse dressed in Pinuyumayan attire. Their outfits featured intricately embroidered sashes, vests, and chaps with rich, woven patterns, along with floral headpieces and yellow bandanas emblazoned with the slogan "Defend the ancestral spirits and refuse to relocate the burials!" (*hanwei zuling, jujue qian zang* 捍衛祖靈、拒絕遷葬!) (figure 1).

Elders from the community performed a ceremony near the steps of the courthouse using betel nut, an important medium in Pinuyumayan cosmology for communicating with the ancestors and gods. The nut, a narcotic closely associated with Indigenous peoples, was split in half and placed on the ground as part of a ritual prayer for spiritual protection of their burial grounds. Nearby, Katratripulr activists waved banners and led chants advocating Indigenous peoples' rights, condemning the injustices of assimilationist policies that discriminated against their cultures and languages, and asserting their claims as the original inhabitants of Taiwan. Amid these activities, the community's lawyer held a press conference for Taiwan Indigenous Television, a national cable station serving Indigenous communities, to explain the dispute to reporters.

Today, Taiwan is home to 546,700 Indigenous persons, who make up nearly 2.3 percent of the population. The majority of Taiwan's population,

FIGURE 1. Katratripulr community members demonstrating outside the Kaohsiung High Administrative Court, 2013. Photograph by Lai Ping-yu, 2013.

approximately 95 percent, is ethnically Han Chinese, including the Hoklo, Hakka, and other groups with origins in mainland China (Executive Yuan 2016b). In response to growing calls for greater recognition of Indigenous peoples' cultures and languages, Taiwan introduced reforms to its national court system. In 2013, specialized Indigenous court divisions or units, called "ad hoc Chambers of Indigenous Courts" (*yuanzhuminzu zhuanye fating* 原住民族專業法庭), were established in the national courts of first and second instance (district courts and high courts, respectively) to handle certain criminal, civil, and administrative cases involving Indigenous persons, communities, and groups.[2]

The ROC Judicial Yuan (*sifa yuan* 司法院) created the Indigenous court units, which are the central focus of this book, with the aim of improving communication between Han Taiwanese state actors and Indigenous persons in the courtroom and addressing the disadvantaged position Indigenous peoples occupy within the national court system.[3] In aspiration, the new court units would help bridge cultural and linguistic divides between Indigenous and non-Indigenous actors across a wide range of legal matters. This initiative was part of a broader set of governmental efforts intended to strengthen constitutional multiculturalism in Taiwan, with aims related to Indigenous recognition and reconciliation, but with other state interests also in mind.

The Katratripulr trial staged a series of encounters between state actors and Indigenous peoples that underscored stark differences in state definitions of the legal process and Indigenous cultural values, knowledge, and law. At the trial, the Katratripulr community's lawyer stood to present his argument. He held in his hand two betel nuts and shook them as he spoke. One of the judges on the judicial panel, composed entirely of Han Taiwanese, asked about the significance of this gesture. The lawyer explained that an elder had asked him to shake the betel nuts, as the community believed it would call their ancestral spirits to help him make his argument. The judge fell silent, looking slowly around the room. His silence suggested discomfort about the idea of sharing the courtroom space with the spirits of Indigenous persons. This encounter, and similar ones in other cases, highlighted how courts of law operate at the intersection of state authority and Indigenous worldviews, serving as arenas where boundaries of difference and identity are negotiated and contested.

These observations highlight key concerns central to this book: the construction and negotiation of cultural, ethnic, legal, linguistic, ontological, racial, and territorial boundaries while the ROC state turns to multiculturalism in order to advance Indigenous recognition, enhance Taiwan's international standing, and secure its claim to sovereignty. The book asks: What is at stake in fixing the boundaries that divide Indigenous peoples and the colonizing society? How are these boundaries negotiated in forums designed by and for the colonizing state? In a context marked by multiple colonialisms and contested sovereignty, how might there be opportunities to advance Indigenous interests that are unavailable in more "settled" colonial contexts? By integrating boundary work theory with multicultural politics and rule-crafting processes, this book explores how Taiwan's ad hoc Chambers of Indigenous Courts have attempted to bridge, sometimes successfully and sometimes not, state and Indigenous understandings of culture, territory, and law.

Broadly, this book is concerned with new configurations of Indigenous courts, rights, identities, and sovereignty emerging in the Asia-Pacific region. Turning our attention to this region reveals new geographies of colonialism and the diverse consequences and effects of Indigenous rights struggles. The book focuses on the Indigenous context in Taiwan, an island nation in the western Pacific with a layered history of multiple colonialisms, whose sovereign status remains contested. The ROC government administering the islands of Taiwan lost its seat as the representative of China in the United

Nations in 1971 and maintains official diplomatic relations with only eleven countries and the Holy See, while carrying on unofficial relations with 110 others. It lives under the threatening shadow of its powerful neighbor, the People's Republic of China, which claims the island as part of its territory. In recent decades, the ROC has turned to Indigenous peoples' cultures, identities, and rights in order to pursue constitutional multiculturalism, with the aim of garnering international support and crafting a distinct Taiwanese identity. At the same time, a vibrant Indigenous movement has emerged in Taiwan that has called attention to the ongoing colonization of Indigenous peoples' lands and lives by the ROC government. This movement has demanded greater recognition for Indigenous languages, cultures, and sovereignties. The establishment of specialized Indigenous court units has been an important development in this context as a government initiative supported by Indigenous politicians and activists. These court units are seen by some as a step toward decolonization and reconciliation, offering an avenue not only to secure Indigenous rights but also to engage with human rights, strengthen democracy, construct national identity, and secure global recognition.

The exercise of power over others, the essence of the relationship between the colonizer and the colonized, is often expressed through the establishment and control of boundaries. Within this power dynamic, the colonizing society often determines which behaviors are acceptable, which forms of knowledge are legitimate, and what can and cannot be said. This book examines the processes of constructing and maintaining boundaries separating the ROC state (and its dominant Han Taiwanese society) and Indigenous peoples, alongside the practices developed to navigate these divides, through litigation. It is concerned with the ways in which state institutions, such as courts of law, understand and address Indigenous cultural and linguistic differences in legal disputes. The stakes are high, as judges interpret laws that define Indigenous status and shape the nature of the relationship between the state and Indigenous peoples. But judges are not the only actors in courtrooms. Indigenous plaintiffs, defendants, witnesses, and interpreters—as well as non-Indigenous lawyers, prosecutors, and staff—all play critical roles. By reformulating, transgressing, and blurring these boundaries, Indigenous actors and their allies transform courts into spaces that advance their own aims and integrate Indigenous perspectives on culture, territory, and law. This book examines how these processes emerge in the everyday operations of Taiwan's ad hoc Chambers of Indigenous Courts through constructing and deconstructing procedures and structures; through activities of categorization and interpretation; and through negotiations of inclusion and exclusion. It also investigates how these courtroom dynamics intersect with Indigenous peoples' broader struggles for self-determination and how they relate to Taiwan's own enactment of state sovereignty.

In brief, this book is about *boundary institutions*: the techniques and practices developed to create, maintain, and span boundaries of social worlds in the pursuit of a normative interest. The boundary metaphor, introduced by Fredrik Barth (1998 [1969]) a half century ago, refers to the social and symbolic boundaries that emerge when actors distinguish social categories and when they treat members of such categories differently. While Barth was primarily concerned with the reproduction of ethnic boundaries, this book is concerned with how such boundaries emerge in the first place and in the processes of making (and remaking and unmaking) cultural boundaries at the intersection of the state and Indigenous peoples.[4]

In exploring boundary institutions, I draw on boundary work theory (Gieryn 1999), which concerns work that discursively and materially shifts or sustains boundaries between different groups. Research on boundary work has been primarily focused on explaining how different social worlds can meet productively around scientific issues, addressing challenges of translation and negotiations to align mutual interests. Various studies explain how the stability of relations between science and nonscience is maintained through "boundary objects" (Star and Griesemer 1989), "standardized packages" (Fujimura 1992), and "boundary organizations" (Guston 1999, 2000, 2001), with applications to scientific evidence in U.S. courts (Ziaja and Fullerton 2015).

I am interested in the meetings of social worlds outside the relatively stable context of U.S. scientific and political institutions, choosing forums situated in the unstable and politically charged setting of state-Indigenous relations that strive to promote respect for the Indigenous "other" in a system where such respect has largely been absent. This requires recognizing that boundaries often involve intersections across multiple scales and that they are embedded in relations of power that privilege certain groups. Taiwan's Indigenous court units are not Habermasian ideal speech arenas in which all voices and perspectives can be expressed and carefully debated. Instead, they are highly formalized and constrained spaces in which only certain views and motivations are presumed to count. Yet the units are not static; they can be destabilized and pushed in new directions, which is, at least ostensibly, part of their purpose. Understanding boundary-spanning activities in such circumstances requires paying close attention to the techniques and practices developed to deal with problems of cultural and linguistic translation and negotiations of mutual (and sometimes conflicting) interests. This approach stresses the on-the-ground activities of local actors and exploratory ways of working to bridge social worlds, revealing the adaptive and unsettled operation of justice at the constructed boundary of the state and Indigenous peoples.

The ad hoc Chambers of Indigenous Courts are situated at the intersection of Taiwan's Han Taiwanese and Indigenous social and legal worlds. While these chambers often functioned as ordinary courts with few distinguishing features, Han Taiwanese judges also developed new practices and adapted old ones to incorporate Indigenous peoples' worldviews and perspectives, at times redefining what was possible in the legal system. Indigenous individuals, in turn, devised creative strategies to influence proceedings in their favor, asserting their identities as Indigenous and challenging dominant narratives about indigeneity, territory, and law. Lawyers, experts, and Indigenous elders and community members acted as cultural brokers in the courtroom, bridging gaps in knowledge and language. These activities and others indicated how the Indigenous court units were positioned as world-spanning institutions in the national court system.

The operations of Taiwan's Indigenous court units reveal that boundary institutions, as I use the term here, are characterized by features of hybridity, process, practice, and power. These units form hybrid spaces composed of artifacts, people, and rules in ever-shifting relations that mix facts, identities, norms, and values (see also C. Miller 2001). They involve processes designed to manage different activities and interests, in a context where behaviors, expectations, and roles may flux and flow. They entail the development of practices and ways of working to navigate the tensions created by spanning boundaries. Finally, they are entrenched in relations of power that, in contexts of ongoing colonialism, often prioritize the interests of the colonizing society over those of Indigenous peoples. This study of Taiwan's Indigenous court units examines how these dynamics play out in specific cases involving Indigenous persons and communities.

Examining the Indigenous court units leads me to think more broadly about innovations in Indigenous courts globally. Indigenous courts have taken on new importance in many colonial and postcolonial contexts at a time when ideas about recognizing and incorporating Indigenous justice practices, and their relation to Indigenous sovereignty claims, are more pervasive and embattled than ever. My study is also motivated by an empirical goal: to provide an ethnographic account of a system of Indigenous court units set within a national court system and identify the possibilities and pitfalls of relying on state court institutions to span Indigenous and non-Indigenous worlds.

This book aims to bring together new lines of inquiry and insights into the study of Indigenous court institutions. While a small body of ethnographic work beyond the Taiwan context has explored the structures, practices, and ideologies that characterize Indigenous courts and their jurisprudence, as well as how Indigenous actors invoke concepts of custom, tradition, and culture in legal proceedings (see Cooter and Fikentscher 1998a, 1998b; B. G. Miller 2001; Nesper 2007; Richland 2008), these studies have largely been focused on Indigenous-controlled courts. This book examines Indigenous courts within the national court system that are not controlled by Indigenous actors. Additionally, we know comparatively little about the everyday practices and processes through which actors in Indigenous courts navigate the tensions between Indigenous and non-Indigenous discourses of culture, territory, and law, particularly in the Asia-Pacific region. These dynamics are important because they suggest capacities for Indigenous reconciliation, but also because they may be bound up in other interests and programs, such as multicultural politics and constructions of national identity.

The book endeavors to fill these gaps or, at least, the gaps as I see them. To do so, I focus on the interactions of three classes of actors in Taiwan's Indigenous court units: Han Taiwanese judges who preside over cases; Indigenous defendants and claimants committed to local laws and cultural practices; and a class of mediating actors consisting of lawyers, witnesses, experts, interpreters, and elders and community members who engage with both judges and litigants through advocacy, argumentation, testimony, and translation. In the following chapters, I examine how judges understand and address Indigenous cultural practices in legal proceedings; analyze how Indigenous parties use courts to advance their own understandings of culture, territory, and law; and explore the role of intermediaries in bridging cultural and linguistic divides in the courtroom. By analyzing the interactions among these actors, I aim to shed light on the experiential dimensions of state governance of Indigenous peoples and to highlight the transformative potential of these interactions for both Han Taiwanese state actors and Indigenous persons and communities.

SHIFTING PERSPECTIVES ON INDIGENEITY

In 2017, I visited an Amis artist in her studio in southern Taiwan. She was experimenting with ways to incorporate maps into her artwork, and our conversation soon shifted to cartographic representations of Taiwan. She laid a map of the island on the table and made an observation. The typical north-facing orientation of the map, she said, obscured a key feature of Taiwan: its deep connections to Oceania. With that, she rotated the map clockwise so that west was now at the top. From this new perspective, the familiar narrative of Taiwan's ties to the Chinese mainland seemed less certain. Instead, the island appeared as part of a larger chain of islands settled by Austronesian peoples, connected southward to the Philippines and beyond and extending across the Pacific Ocean. Austronesian-speaking hunting-gathering societies have occupied Taiwan for millennia (Bellwood 1984, 113). These peoples are related linguistically and culturally to Austronesian groups across the Pacific and Indian Oceans. Peter Bellwood's "out-of-Taiwan" narrative suggests that Austronesian languages may have originated in Taiwan and then spread to the rest of the region, reaching as far as Hawai'i to the east and Madagascar to the west. Over thousands of years, Austronesian-speaking peoples in Taiwan have developed a profound, interdependent relationship with the land and surrounding waters, shaped by practices of hunting, fishing, agriculture, and gathering of forest products, among other cultural and historical practices.

In 2017, I began my research on the ad hoc Chambers of Indigenous Courts in Hualien City. Located on Taiwan's east coast, Hualien is a place of striking beauty. To the west, rugged, lush mountains rise sharply; while, to the east, low-lying coastal plains stretch toward the ocean. The Hualien coastline is shaped by broad floodplains that carry rainfall from the mountains to the sea, creating dramatic swirling eddies. With a climate that ranges from subtropical in the north to tropical monsoon in the south, Hualien's landscape is rich and verdant, home to rivers, fields, and forests that support a diverse range of flora and fauna. Hualien is also home to six Indigenous groups: the Bunun, Kavalan, Pangcah, Sakizaya, Seediq, and Truku. These communities take immense pride in their cultural heritages, legal traditions, and identities as the island's original inhabitants. Together, they make up about a quarter of the local population, giving Hualien County one of the highest concentrations of Indigenous peoples on the main island.

Like many other regions with Indigenous populations, Hualien's history is marked by violence, suppression, displacement, loss of sovereignty, erasure, and assimilation under imperial, colonial, and state regimes over four centuries.[5] The reverberations of harsh governance policies are still felt today in many Indigenous communities. These impacts are evident in persistent and, in some cases, growing inequalities in education, employment, health, and life expectancy. They also manifest in daily life as many Indigenous individuals under the age of fifty struggle to speak their mother languages fluently. Furthermore, they are reflected in laws and policies that define Indigenous status, excluding certain groups and restricting practices and rituals integral to shaping and expressing their personal, social, and cultural identities.

Oppressive governance practices and local efforts to resist them form an important part of local cultural memory for some Indigenous communities. I recall, as a boy, sitting in the home of our elderly Paiwan neighbor in Taitung, nibbling on dried fish snacks and listening intently to his stories. He spoke of being forced by Japanese military personnel, along with other men from his village, to march to a local beach during World War II. Showing me the scars on his legs, he recounted how he and the others were wrapped in barbed wire and made to lie in the surf at gunpoint, intended to deter U.S. naval forces from shelling the beach. The U.S. naval forces never arrived, having bypassed Taiwan on their way to Okinawa. Later, during my fieldwork, I heard stories from Bunun men, who shared memories of accompanying their fathers to collect the heads of dead soldiers after raids on military outposts (see also Simon 2012a). Younger Truku activists also spoke of how some elders made them feel "not Indigenous enough" because they spoke Mandarin and lacked full knowledge of their traditions, a result of decades of colonial policies that prohibited the teaching of Indigenous languages and restricted cultural practices. Anchored in past struggles, these memories and experiences were points for individuals and communities that stabilized, and sometimes destabilized, their identities as Indigenous.

These stories highlight the complexities of the boundaries separating Han Taiwanese and Indigenous peoples in Taiwan. As social scientists grapple with defining the cultural and linguistic boundaries of Indigenous groups, individuals within those communities often face their own struggles with identity classification. Some may not identify with the classifications forced upon them, and they may or may not pursue their own classification. As in other global contexts, the process of constructing indigeneity and ethnic categories in Taiwan has been a contested one. In recent decades, this process

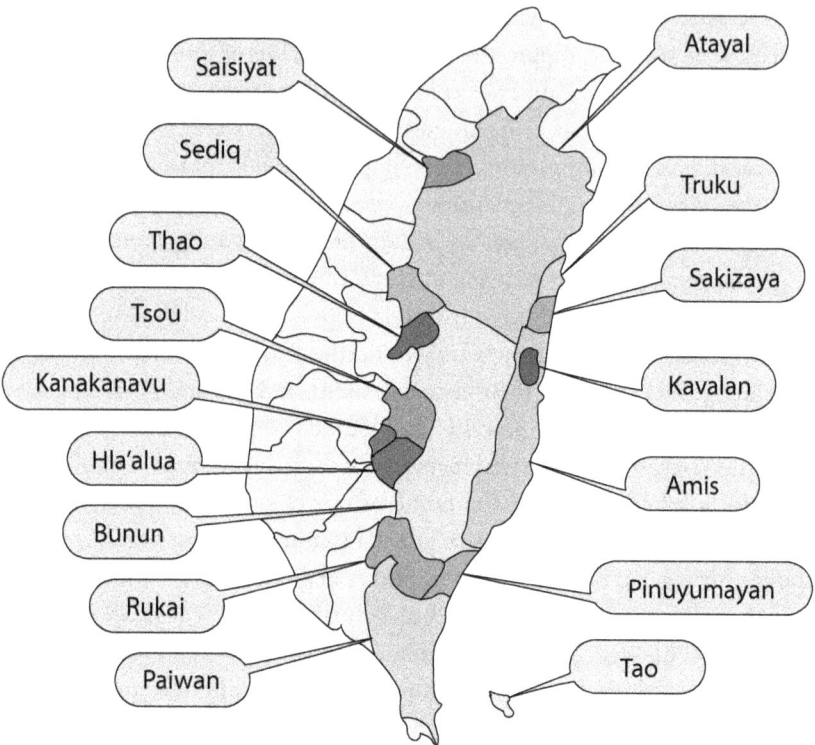

MAP 1. Spatial distribution of Taiwan's sixteen officially recognized Indigenous groups. Courtesy of the Taiwan Indigenous People's Knowledge Economic Development Association.

has gained new significance as the ROC government has increasingly turned to Indigenous peoples and their cultures to reach a global public and counter China's territorial claims to the island.

Official lines delineating who is "authentically" Indigenous, or *yuanzhumin* 原住民 (lit., "original inhabitants"), in Taiwan have their roots in imperial and colonial classifications and governance strategies dividing mountain-dwelling and plains-dwelling peoples.[6] Generally, the concept of indigeneity marks the descendants of Austronesian-speaking inhabitants who came to the islands some six thousand years ago. Taiwan's Indigenous peoples are remarkably diverse and remain divided by village, community affiliation, language, region, cultural practices, and degree of assimilation into Taiwan's Han Taiwanese society (see map 1). Currently, the ROC government recognizes only mountain-dwelling peoples as Indigenous, excluding plains-dwelling groups, known as *pingpuzuqun* 平埔族群, on the grounds that they are seen as having assimilated into Han Taiwanese society. Further, mountain-based Indigenous groups have resisted recognition of their plains-dwelling neighbors as Indigenous. A 2022 ruling by the Taiwan Constitutional Court, however, has possibly paved the way for *pingpuzu* recognition.[7]

To further complicate matters, issues of indigeneity intersect with claims of "native Taiwanese" (*benshengren* 本省人), a category used to distinguish the southern Chinese (Hoklo and Hakka) who began settling Taiwan over four hundred years ago from the Chinese "Mainlanders" (*waishengren* 外省人) who arrived with the ROC military and government in the late 1940s. Many Indigenous persons also identify themselves more strongly with their specific community (*buluo* 部落) or village (*cunluo* 村落) than with broader labels like Indigenous, Taiwanese, or their ethnic group. For instance, my friends in Dowmung village often referred to themselves as *tongmenren* 銅門人, a term distinguishing their community from another Truku community living in the same village. In addition, nontraditional Indigenous communities may include members of multiple ethnic groups. The Katratripulr community mentioned above, for example, was formed during the Japanese colonial period from two Pinuyumayan families and one Paiwan family (TIPP, n.d.).

Even as self-identification as Indigenous has grown, the concept remains contested. As I sat with a Pinuyumayan elder one afternoon, he expressed frustration with the categories imposed by anthropologists and policymakers, stating, "You talk too much about Indigenous, Puyuma, Paiwan. You should be talking about humans; we are all humans. Why draw lines?"[8] Similarly, lines demarcating Indigenous ethnic groups in the "name rectification movement" (*zhengming yundong* 正名運動) have been a source of intense local debate. A recent example is the complex process of delineating the Seediq and Truku from the broader category of Tayan (also called Atayal), to be discussed in chapter 1.

The cultural, ethnic, and linguistic boundaries at work, and being worked, in these cases are, therefore, fraught with complexity. A great deal is at stake in determinations of Indigenous status, as recognition can bring social welfare benefits, cultural and territorial rights, and political representation. From an Indigenous perspective, however, recognition is about much more than material gain or governmental support. It is about restoring communities, rebuilding sovereignty, and seeking justice and healing. It is about international human rights and democratic principles, as well as affirming enduring claims to land and being "here." It is about ecological balance, mutual respect, sharing, and fulfilling responsibilities.⁹

A key aspect of the formation and operation of the ad hoc Chambers of Indigenous Courts is the construction, maintenance, and troubling of lines of culture, ethnicity, language, and law that mark Indigenous peoples in relation to Taiwan's Han Taiwanese society. By creating forums to bridge these complex boundaries, what I am calling boundary institutions, the Judicial Yuan hoped to deepen judges' understanding of Indigenous peoples' cultures and special legal rights and empower Indigenous persons and communities to engage more meaningfully with the state legal system. For their part, Indigenous activists hoped that these units would foster greater respect for Indigenous peoples within the legal system and provide a platform for recognizing local Indigenous laws equally with state laws, with the long-term goal of establishing autonomous, Indigenous-controlled courts.

MULTICULTURAL PROGRESS AND ITS PROBLEMS

As recently as two decades ago, Indigenous persons in Taiwan seldom would have dared to wear their customary attire in public or openly acknowledge their Indigenous roots. Today, however, many proudly embrace their Indigenous identity. They draw on their cultures, languages, and social structures as sources of empowerment and as a means to promote decolonization and restore their sovereignty.

Indigenous peoples have figured centrally in the development of multiculturalism in government policy and the formation of a "multicultural Taiwan" national identity. Article 10 of the Additional Articles of the Constitution of the Republic of China (or ROC Constitution), amended in 1997, affirms cultural pluralism and commits to preserving and fostering the development of Indigenous languages and cultures. In 2001, then president Chen Shui-bian declared that the ROC is a "multi-ethnic and multi-cultural country. Multiculturalism is a basic national policy" (Tseng and Lim 2018, 97n7). Similarly, in 2016, then president Tsai Ing-wen's landmark apology to Indigenous peoples emphasized Taiwan's status as "a culturally diverse society." Multiculturalism has thus emerged as a crucial value in Taiwan, though one marked by tensions (Wang 2004). On the one hand, it is used as a tool for social justice that promotes diversity and respect for cultural difference; on the other hand, it is presented as a new national identity that emphasizes unity to resolve tensions between Chinese nationalism and Taiwanese consciousness. Indigenous peoples find themselves caught between these conflicting demands for diversity and unity, as their cultural practices and languages are conscripted by both approaches, even though, as Kerim Friedman (2018, 79) points out, Indigenous peoples may not have been the intended primary beneficiaries of Taiwan's multicultural policies.

Wang Li-jung (2004) notes that Indigenous (and, secondarily, Hakka) cultural policies represent the main components of "multicultural Taiwan." As I discuss in later chapters, invocations of Indigenous cultures in Taiwan's multicultural discourse have shifted over time. Initially, the ROC government emphasized that Indigenous peoples belonged to the tradition of Chinese culture and were one of the Chinese peoples. Indigenous cultures were enlisted to support various Chinese cultural movements. With the decline of Chinese nationalism in the 1990s, the use of Indigenous cultures shifted toward constructing a new Taiwanese national identity distinct from the Chinese on the mainland. Indigenous peoples represented the only clear category of non-Chinese people. Lin Chiang-yi, former head of the Department of Culture and Education in the Council of Aboriginal Affairs (later the Council of Indigenous Peoples, or CIP), put it succinctly, saying, "Only Taiwanese aboriginal culture can present a Taiwanese culture that is clearly different from Chinese culture" (quoted in Wang 2004, 307). Today, the role of Indigenous peoples in constructing a "multicultural Taiwan" is evident in many places, from legislation aimed at protecting Indigenous languages and cultures to displays of Indigenous peoples in the international terminal of Taiwan Taoyuan International Airport.

The rise of official multiculturalism in Taiwan coincided with efforts to elevate the status of Indigenous peoples through a range of laws, policies, and institutions. New legislation granted Indigenous groups limited autonomy over their ancestral territories and protected their cultural and ritual practices. Innovative educational initiatives supported the preservation and revitalization of Indigenous languages. Policies awarded Indigenous applicants extra points on college admission exams. Museums included exhibitions on Indigenous cultures. Roads were renamed to recognize the island's original inhabitants. National universities established research centers focused on the study of Austronesian-speaking groups in Taiwan and across Oceania. Envoys of Indigenous peoples traveled to Pacific islands sharing a cultural and linguistic lineage. Delegations of Indigenous youth participated in side events at the United Nations and engaged with UN bodies through their involvement in nongovernmental organizations, even as the ROC government was excluded from official UN participation. The CIP signed memoranda of understanding with Canada and New Zealand, and the ROC government (as Chinese Taipei) cofounded the Indigenous Peoples Economic and Trade Cooperation Arrangement in partnership with Australia, Canada, and New Zealand. President Tsai's apology also signaled the possible beginning of a new legal paradigm for Indigenous peoples.

Since the first decade of this century, multicultural approaches in Taiwan have taken on the character of a partnership between Indigenous peoples and the ROC government (Tsai 2019, 620). But even as Taiwan has emerged as one of the most progressive countries for Indigenous rights, Indigenous activists are still far from achieving their goal of recognition as peoples engaging with the ROC government on a nation-to-nation basis. Elizabeth Povinelli (2002, 184) identifies a "cunning" in multicultural discourses. Recognition of Indigenous identities and rights in Taiwan has related power dynamics: In the moment of acknowledging cultural difference and expression, the politics of multicultural recognition authorizes Indigenous identities and in so doing disciplines, regulates, and constrains them. Significant gaps remain between constitutional principles that protect Indigenous peoples and their actual implementation, and the spirit of multiculturalism has not been fully realized within Taiwan's legal system. Laws protecting Indigenous peoples conflict with one another. Judges frequently lack understanding of Indigenous social norms and legal rights. State authorities apply arbitrary and essentialized understandings of culture to limit the application of Indigenous peoples' rights, often justifying these restrictions in the name of protecting wildlife, forest resources, or social order. Prosecutors aggressively pursue charges against Indigenous persons for engaging in cultural and ritual practices. Legal proceedings are conducted in the language of Han Taiwanese society. Legal aid services to Indigenous peoples are inadequate and do not address the many challenges of accessing the court system. Local Indigenous laws, legal precedents, and jurisprudence are generally ignored in the national legal system, including in the ad hoc Chambers of Indigenous Courts.

PAIWAN *ALILI* INCIDENT AND COURT REFORM

Taiwan's ad hoc Chambers of Indigenous Courts emerged in response to demands by Indigenous activists and politicians who objected to the recurring criminal prosecutions of Indigenous persons engaged in cultural practices. Calls for court reform took on urgency in 2012 when prosecutors in Taitung charged a Paiwan elder with aggravated indecent assault for holding and gently patting the genitals of his nephew, a practice among the Paiwan called *alili* used to bless males of the younger generation.[10] Such an Indigenous practice, seen from the perspective of Han Taiwanese society, was deviant and vulgar, and raised the potential of criminal liability.

Locally known as the Paiwan Alili Incident (*paiwanzu alili shijian* 排灣族阿力力事件), the elder's prosecution drew condemnation from Indigenous leaders across Taiwan. At the trial, the Taitung District Court heard testimony from several witnesses, including the boy's grandmother, who explained the significance of the Paiwan practice to the court. She said, "We Indigenous people dote on our grandsons. Your grandfather touches you to see if you have grown up. We are Indigenous people; we touched our sons' little birds [*xiaoniao* 小鳥; a euphemism for penis] like this when they were young. This is an expression of love for your son. He [the grandfather] will pat his grandson's little bird like this." Based on her testimony and that of others, the judge concluded that the elder's conduct was not intended to excite or satisfy sexual desire, as required for aggravated indecent assault. The charges were, therefore, reduced to sexual harassment, but not dismissed. Ultimately, the boy's guardian withdrew the complaint, and the court determined that the prosecution could not proceed.

It is significant that the court did not recognize *alili* as a "traditional" Paiwan cultural practice. The legal aid lawyer representing the elder speculated that this may have been driven by a concern that such recognition would have had broader implications for Taiwan's social and legal order (M.-h. Lin 2013). If the court's reluctance stemmed from worries about the conflict between Indigenous norms and state law, and the potential far-reaching consequences of that conflict, it was not alone. For instance, Ronald Niezen (2003b) considers the tension between cultural relativism and human rights, whereby distinct laws created for different groups, such as Indigenous peoples, could potentially sanction human rights violations in the guise of protecting traditional cultural practices.

By not identifying *alili* as a "traditional" practice, the court sidestepped some of these conundrums. Instead, it treated the Paiwan practice as a mere fact illuminating the elder's mental state, ultimately finding that the necessary intent was lacking and dismissing the case on a technicality. Similar to Bruce Miller's (2023) insights about courts and Indigenous peoples in the

North American context, the case illustrates how state law diminishes Indigenous peoples. In this instance, the elder suffered a double diminution. Not only was his Paiwan practice deemed so deviant that it warranted criminal prosecution, but the court also reduced *alili* to a fact for legal processing and effectively erased his Indigenous identity.

The Paiwan Alili Incident marked a tipping point as Indigenous activists and legislators used the case to highlight how little the Taiwan judiciary understood Indigenous peoples' cultures and to demand the establishment of an Indigenous court. The case was the latest in a line of prosecutions of Indigenous persons for engaging in cultural practices and accessing resources on their ancestral territories.[11] Soon thereafter, the Judicial Yuan announced plans to establish an experimental system of Indigenous hearings, in district courts located in areas with large Indigenous populations, intended to make the national court system more attuned to, and respectful of, the cultural differences of Indigenous peoples.

In January 2013, the Judicial Yuan established ad hoc Chambers of Indigenous Courts in nine district courts, expanding the program in 2014 to include all district, high, and administrative courts on the island. The 2005 Indigenous Peoples Basic Law (hereafter "Basic Law"), an aspirational law that promised to meet the demands of the Indigenous social movement, provided the legal foundation for these specialized units. While the Basic Law's provisions suggested a robust Indigenous court institution applying local Indigenous laws and potentially managed by Indigenous persons, what ultimately emerged was an ad hoc system of Indigenous hearings set within the national court infrastructure.

Public announcements from the Judicial Yuan emphasized that the new system of hearings would ensure "respect" (*zunzhong* 尊重) for Indigenous peoples' cultures and secure their "judicial rights" (*sifa quanyi* 司法權益) (Judicial Yuan 2012b; Xiang 2012), indicating that these hearings would address Indigenous cultural differences and barriers they faced in accessing the court system. The hearings would be managed by specialized divisions consisting of units of specially trained judges. There is, however, little Indigenous representation within the units, because few judges and lawyers in Taiwan have Indigenous status. In their daily operation, the units apply state laws and legal procedures, rather than local Indigenous laws or justice practices. The official language of the units is Mandarin Chinese, not Indigenous languages. While judges in the district courts receive some training about Indigenous peoples and their rights, that training is limited, and appellate judges are not required to participate. The jurisdiction of the units is broad, and they rarely administer cases involving Indigenous cultural issues. Additionally, a ranking system in the courts means that Indigenous peoples' cases may be assigned to other units. References to the units in legal proceedings are rare, and there is no acknowledgment that courthouses sit on Indigenous territories. In the Indigenous communities where I worked, some individuals had heard of these specialized units, but there was little in-depth understanding of the units' purposes or operations.

These features gave the ad hoc Chambers of Indigenous Courts an ethereal presence in courthouses. In certain respects, the units appeared to be little more than a procedural mechanism for organizing an "Indigenous" docket, lacking any distinctive characteristics. Even those who regularly worked in the units sometimes expressed uncertainty about their actual presence in courtrooms. As explored in later chapters, ambiguity emerged as a central element of the ad hoc chambers. These ambiguities, however, also pointed to the units' purpose: to find ways, within the constraints of Taiwan's civil law tradition and amid the obscurities of national laws protecting Indigenous peoples, of building knowledge about Indigenous peoples and bridging the state legal system and Indigenous cultural practices. One official from the Judicial Yuan described the units as "courts of opportunity."[12] In his view, the case assignment procedures and training that constitute the units raised the probability, but did not necessarily guarantee, that Indigenous persons would encounter non-Indigenous state actors who were knowledgeable about their lifeways and who would work to accommodate their cultures and unique circumstances.

In spirit, Taiwan's ad hoc Chambers of Indigenous Courts potentially represent a step, albeit a cautious one, toward recognizing local Indigenous laws as equal to state law, an approach known as formal legal pluralism. Significant imbalances in power persist, however, because Han Taiwanese actors, language, laws, and understandings of justice and indigeneity dominate the units. Despite this, the units are normatively oriented toward promoting Indigenous recognition and rights. Further, the system of Indigenous court units intersects with broader government aspirations related to national identity construction and global recognition. As a result, while these units are shaped primarily by state law and procedure, they are also influenced by interconnections among indigeneity, Taiwanese identity, and Taiwan's international standing. I will return to these interconnections later, but first, let us consider how these units fit into adaptations of Indigenous courts globally.

INDIGENOUS COURTS AND THEIR OTHERS

Global contexts in which large Indigenous populations or substantial Indigenous lands are situated in a national territory sometimes encompass parallel or overlapping justice systems serving Indigenous communities. The interplay of social change, historical legacies, and cultural identities of Indigenous peoples has led to a diverse array of institutional structures, processes, jurisdictional parameters, and norms (Richland 2008, 12). For example, in the North American context, the Navajo judicial system includes courts that function similarly to the Anglo-American adversarial system in U.S. state and federal courts (Cooter and Fikentscher 1998a, 1998b). Other Native American tribes have established courts with narrower mandates, dealing with matters related to dimensions of tribal operations, such as the Gaming Enterprise Division of the Mashantucket Pequot Court (Newton 1998). Some Indigenous justice systems rely on nonadversarial methods of dispute resolution, whereby legal codes and jurisprudence take a back seat to local concepts of authority and relationship values in resolving disputes among community members (Cooter and Fikentscher 1998a, 1998b). Other systems blend these approaches, using criminal and civil procedures for disputes involving non-Indigenous individuals and mediation-style processes for disputes among Indigenous persons, as seen in the Peacemaker Courts in the Navajo court system (Tso 1989). In some cases, governments operate in partnership with Indigenous justice systems. For instance, Alaska Rules of Civil Procedure endorse local dispute resolution in civil cases by allowing parties to "agree to resolve disputes, subject to court approval, by referring them to tribal courts, tribal councils, elders' courts, or ethnic organizations" (Rule 100(i)(4)).

These examples reflect Indigenous-controlled justice systems and programs, in which elders or other community members are vested with the authority to resolve disputes. Ethnographic studies of Indigenous courts have shed valuable light on the roles that notions of custom, tradition, and culture play in contemporary tribal legal systems (Cooter and Fikentscher 1998a, 1998b; B. G. Miller 2001; Nesper 2007; Richland 2008). These studies also indicate the significance of interactions among the Indigenous peoples who engage with, shape, and contribute to these institutions, as well as the political implications of these engagements. They reveal the role of human agency accruing to particular Indigenous actors at particular moments as they engage with one another in the courtroom. Moreover, these studies indicate that invocations of tradition in Indigenous courts do not necessarily represent a definitive world of Indigenous normativity beyond the parameters of the specific actors, events, and disputes at hand (Burns et al. 2008, 314).

This book aims to build on these insights in the context of a model of Indigenous courts operating within the state legal system, where the goal is to address Indigenous cultural practices and conceptions of justice and where elders and other community members do not have the final authority to decide cases or impose punishment. In recent decades, these forms of Indigenous courts, representing a variety of approaches, have taken root in contexts around the globe. In Canada, for example, the Gladue (Aboriginal Persons) Courts operate as special courts for Indigenous criminal offenders that apply Canadian law but also work to take into account the harsh situations in which Indigenous people live in bail and sentencing hearings (Rudin 2009). In Australia, various states have introduced "Aboriginal courts," including the Koori Court in Victoria, the Murri Court in Brisbane, the Nunga Court in South Australia, Circle Sentencing in New South Wales, the Ngambra Court in the Australian Capital Territory, and the Darwin Community Court in the Northern Territory (LRC 2005). These urban-based courts use informal procedures, involve Aboriginal elders in the sentencing process, allow open dialogue about the crime, and consider offenders' broader circumstances (Forsyth 2009, 235). In New Zealand, Rangatahi and Pasifika (Youth) Courts and Mātāriki Courts invite the offender's family, subtribe, and tribe to address the court at sentencing (UNHRC Working Group 2013, 9).

Debates have arisen about whether these Indigenous courts should be classified as problem-solving courts, as forms of therapeutic jurisprudence, or as occupying a special category (LRC 2005, 145–46). Problem-solving courts are specialist courts that use their authority and processes to address underlying issues; these include drug courts and domestic violence courts (Freiberg 2004, 2). Labeling Indigenous courts as problem-solving courts, however, suggests that the "problem" lies with Indigenous peoples; that is, that they introduce some social problem that the court can resolve. This interpretation generally runs counter to the spirit of these courts and their recognition that the problem stems from the state legal system's failure to accommodate Indigenous peoples' needs. Therapeutic jurisprudence focuses on the healing potential of the law and seeks to promote the well-being of participants (King 2003, para. 1). This model encourages greater engagement in the court process and aims to foster respect between the judicial officer and the participants (King 2003, para. 19). Some commentators have concluded that Indigenous courts draw on principles of therapeutic jurisprudence (Freiberg 2004, 8). Other commentators have suggested that Indigenous courts occupy "a category of their own" (Marchetti and Daly 2004, 4). The active involvement of Indigenous community members plays a crucial role in reshaping legal processes, often in subtle ways. These processes can change the attitudes of judicial actors, empower Indigenous elders and community members, and encourage corrections in other arenas of the justice system.

During my fieldwork, local perspectives on the ad hoc Chambers of Indigenous Courts varied. Some judges working in the units viewed them as problem-solving courts, seeing Indigenous persons as lacking an understanding of state law, which the new units could correct. One judge explained, "The Indigenous court is just designed to be friendly to Indigenous people, to help them understand Taiwan law, not to help them or protect Indigenous culture, whatever culture means, or fill in gaps [in law]."[13] The Judicial Yuan, on the other hand, emphasized the therapeutic potential of the units, framing them as spaces for fostering respect between Han Taiwanese judges and Indigenous participants. Seeing the specialized units in therapeutic terms, however, overlooked their actual practice and missed their transformative potential. For example, this perspective failed to recognize that the units' jurisdiction was so wide, and their knowledge about Indigenous cultures and rights so limited, that they generally operated as ordinary courts, not as specialized units (see also Tang 2013, 19). State-centric approaches to indigeneity also tended to acknowledge Indigenous cultures only insofar as they did not challenge or offend Han Taiwanese society, as seen in the Paiwan Alili Incident. Moreover, framing the courts in terms of therapeutic justice presumed that judges could distribute rights equitably, even though many lacked a deep understanding of the social inequalities rooted in Taiwan's long history of colonization.

As explored in this book, the involvement of Indigenous defendants, claimants, elders, and community members had the potential to move law and legal proceedings in unexpected directions. Indigenous defendants and witnesses, for example, sometimes refused to testify in Mandarin Chinese, opting instead to use their mother tongue to emphasize their cultural distinctiveness and to control courtroom discourse about indigeneity. Similarly, Indigenous plaintiffs sometimes coordinated their attire and disregarded courtroom decorum to assert their identities as Indigenous persons, and not always intentionally. Communities also used site visits to challenge state narratives about national ownership of Indigenous territories. These activities shifted courtroom dynamics and reframed disputes in new ways, demonstrating how Indigenous involvement in cases could be transformational. They also indicated the considerable labor Indigenous individuals must undertake to accomplish these interventions, the fruits of which were never guaranteed. Moreover, these activities intersected with broader assertions of Indigenous identity and self-determination that extended beyond courtroom disputes. Indigenous communities issued hunting identification cards, built structures on ancestral lands, blocked roadways, unilaterally claimed territories, and established legal centers. These were not merely activities of resistance but acts of what Audra Simpson (2014) calls "refusal" and Justin Richland (2021) refers to as "insistence." Indigenous activists and communities refused to submit to the apparatuses of the state, engaging in strategic and generative activities aimed at redirecting the levels of engagement with the state and asserting their laws and practices to advance their self-determination.

Further, while Taiwan's civil law tradition generally limits court interpretation to existing laws, the absence of a tradition of judicial precedent meant that judges were not strictly bound by previous decisions in similar cases. This allowed judges more freedom to interpret statutes and develop innovative strategies. While some conservative judges maintained that their ability to adapt was constrained, more progressive-minded judges advocated "a new view of the law"[14] and a "different starting place"[15] in state-Indigenous relations. These judges turned to creative practices to integrate Indigenous worldviews and laws into established practices in legal proceedings. These exploratory activities took various forms and were central to the mission of the Indigenous court units: to find ways of securing recognition for Indigenous peoples within the confines of the national court system. Not all judges, however, engaged in these kinds of activities, and those who did participate did not always do so consistently. Additionally, while these practices sometimes benefited Indigenous individuals, they could also work against them. Nonetheless, these efforts indicated the strategies judges were exploring in order to strengthen Indigenous recognition in situations where structural support for such recognition was lacking.

In moments when Indigenous actors worked to get their identities and values acknowledged in courtrooms, and when judges explored ways to integrate Indigenous worldviews and laws, the Indigenous court units emerged as extraordinary institutions amid the otherwise ordinary circumstances of their typical operation. In these moments, the units engaged in the kind of work Marchetti and Daly (2004) observed in the Australian context: empowering Indigenous peoples and communities, generating knowledge about Indigenous cultures and laws, transforming judges and Indigenous persons, and altering the attitudes of the people involved. As a new court structure operating in a rapidly changing landscape of laws and policies related to Indigenous peoples, the Indigenous court units were still working to find their place in the court system. These moments of engagement suggested that the units could be more than mere problem-solving courts or forms of therapeutic jurisprudence. They could also be transformational spaces for empowering Indigenous peoples and changing the participants involved.

THE AD HOC CHAMBERS OF INDIGENOUS COURTS IN HUALIEN

I chose the ad hoc Chambers of Indigenous Courts in the District Court and High Court in Hualien City as my primary field sites owing to the relatively high volume and variety of Indigenous cases they handled. During previous visits to Taiwan, I had established contacts with judges and lawyers working in the Hualien courts, and the Judicial Yuan helped facilitate introductions to other legal actors in Hualien and around the island. Court proceedings in the units were typically open to the public, ensuring regular access to cases involving Indigenous persons and communities.

The Hualien District Court was among the first courts selected to create an ad hoc Chamber of Indigenous Courts, in 2013. Constructed during the Japanese colonial period (1895–1945), the building was a formidable structure of concrete, iron, and glass influenced by Western architecture (figure 2). Its white façade stood in sharp contrast to the blue Taiwan sky, with large, gold Mandarin Chinese characters announcing *taiwan hualian difang fayuan* 臺灣花蓮地方法院 (Taiwan Hualien District Court). A separate building housed the civil division. Behind the courthouse, the towering peaks of the Central Mountain Range rose dramatically. Situated near key government offices, including the Hualien County Government Office, Health Department, Local Tax Bureau, and Audit Office, the courthouse formed part of a larger complex of administrative buildings in downtown Hualien City. The Taiwan flag, representing the red earth, blue sky, and white sun of the ROC government, fluttered atop the building.

FIGURE 2. Hualien District Court, 2016.

For anyone who has watched television legal dramas like *Matlock*, *Perry Mason*, *Law & Order*, or *L.A. Law*, to step into the Indigenous court unit at the District Court would have been to enter a familiar setting, with the exception that there was no jury box (figure 3). The room was divided by a low wooden "bar" separating legal actors from the public. Beyond the bar, the judge's desk was elevated, commanding the space. In front of the judge was a lower desk reserved for the court clerk and the judicial assistant. A table on the left was designated for the prosecution and plaintiffs, and one on the right was designated for defendants, although courtrooms varied in this regard. Between the tables sat a small, single-seat desk for witnesses. Benches for persons waiting to testify ran along the front of the bar. Behind the bar, seating was arranged for the public, journalists, and judges in training. Their seats faced the judge, lawyers, and parties, giving the courtroom the air of a small theater. The walls were plain, white drywall, with a humming air conditioner operated by a bailiff using a remote control. Projectors hung

FIGURE 3. Interior of Hualien District Court, Civil Division, 2018.

suspended from the ceiling, beaming images and text behind the heads of the parties and their legal counsel.

Despite the official establishment of Indigenous court units, there were few references to Indigenous peoples' cultures or identities in the District Court. One exception was a sign in the waiting room, which featured information about the Legal Aid Foundation's Legal Center of Indigenous Peoples (*caituan faren falü fuzhu jijinhui yuanzhuminzu falü fuwu zhongxin* 財團法人法律扶助基金會原住民族法律服務中心). The sign depicted a Tsou woman dressed in formal attire, accompanied by the greeting "Aveovoeyu!" (Tsou: Hello). Beyond this, the only visible indicator of the units' presence appeared in the case numbering system. Many cases assigned to the units, particularly criminal ones, contained the Chinese character *yuan* (原) to indicate that the matter involved a person with Indigenous status.

The Hualien High Court (*taiwan gaodeng fayuan hualian fenyuan* 臺灣高等法院花蓮分院) was located just a short distance from the District Court and shared many of its features (figure 4). As in the District Court, representations of Indigenous peoples were generally absent in the building. One notable difference, however, was the visibility of Indigenous identities and cultural productions in its immediate vicinity. Unlike the District

FIGURE 4. Hualien High Court, 2017.

Court, which was part of larger complex of government buildings, the High Court stood somewhat apart. Across from the courthouse, the Hualien City Indigenous Culture and History Museum showcased exhibits on Indigenous cultures, arts, and histories, and regularly hosted festivals and performances in an open space along the road. Just across the traffic circle, the Hualien County Cultural Affairs Library displayed Indigenous artwork and featured books written by Indigenous authors. One might expect that such proximity to these displays of Indigenous cultures and crafts would influence the High Court to be more attuned to Indigenous issues. The reality was more complex. In both the Hualien District Court and the High Court, recognition of Indigenous peoples and their rights often depended on the individual judges and their personal attitudes toward Indigenous claims.

Many of the cases handled by the Indigenous court units in the Hualien District and High Courts were routine matters, like drunk driving, theft, fraud, and property disputes. A smaller subset of cases involved issues associated with Indigenous cultures and territories, including wildlife hunting, firearm use, and collecting of forest products and minerals. I initially anticipated that my research would focus primarily on hunting cases, because these issues were central to the Indigenous rights movement at the time. When I arrived, however, the Taiwan Supreme Court was reviewing an appeal by Bunun hunter Tama Talum (Wang Guang-lu 王光祿), who was challenging his conviction for illegal hunting. While Indigenous hunters were still being arrested, prosecutors in Hualien had begun deferring their cases or finding alternative solutions while awaiting the resolution of Mr. Talum's appeal. As a result, prosecutions of Indigenous hunting had largely stalled, although not entirely. In their place, disputes over Indigenous rights to land and resources began to dominate the units' dockets, and I spent the majority of my time observing these cases amid the array of more typical civil and criminal matters.

Taiwan courts engage with different assemblages of Indigenous peoples within their respective jurisdictions, sometimes including overlapping groups. The Hualien District Court primarily handled cases involving the Amis (Pangcah), Bunun, Kavalan, Sakizaya, Seediq, and Truku peoples, while the District Court in neighboring Taitung County typically dealt with cases involving the Amis (Pangcah), Bunun, Paiwan, Pinuyumayan, Rukai, and Tao peoples. The Hualien High Court was responsible for reviewing appeals from both jurisdictions. Judges had different approaches to Indigenous issues, a trend that became particularly apparent as I visited other Indigenous court units in Kaohsiung, Pingtung, Taipei, and Taitung. This was more than simple variation among decision-makers, which fifty years of scholarship in the Law and Society movement has amply demonstrated (Abel 2010). It shaped the character of the court units. Dealing with different assemblages of Indigenous peoples, with different cultures, languages, and experiences with colonialism, together with varying judicial approaches, meant that the specialized units took different forms. As one legal aid lawyer observed, "There is no single chamber of Indigenous courts, there are many different Indigenous court chambers across the island."[16] The Indigenous court units were, therefore, less preset organizations than an institutional framework adapted to the needs of the local context and shaped by the individual approaches of judges, even as nominal training attempted to establish some continuity across them.

Between 2017 and 2018, I spent seventeen months conducting research on the ad hoc Chambers of Indigenous Courts in the Hualien District and High Courts, with shorter research periods in the summers of 2015 and 2016. Over this time, I observed seventy court hearings related to more than fifty civil and criminal cases involving Indigenous individuals and communities. My family moved to Meilun District in Hualien City, living within walking distance of the Hualien District and High Courts, allowing me to participate in activities at one or both courthouses nearly daily. While most of the cases I observed were routine matters, interspersed were cases involving more culturally sensitive issues over hunting, firearms, and minerals. In this book, I focus primarily on disputes related to Indigenous cultures and identities, but I also draw on the many routine cases to examine how the Indigenous court units operated in practice.

I spoke with individuals involved in the Indigenous court units who represented various levels of the court system and who engaged with the specialized units in different capacities. I interviewed more than seventy individuals (thirty of these interviews were recorded and transcribed), speaking with judges, lawyers, defendants, claimants, anthropologists, witnesses, activists, politicians, legal scholars, government officials, and elders and community members.[17] Like many anthropologists, I found that the most meaningful insights did not come from formal interview sessions, which were often disconnected from the flow of ordinary life and constrained by scheduled times and recording devices (Bernstein 2008, 928). Instead, the material I found most valuable emerged from casual conversations, moments of unguarded thought, and commentaries on the everyday events that shaped their lives. I conducted these interviews and conversations in Mandarin Chinese, although some included English. Han Taiwanese legal actors spoke Mandarin Chinese, and most texts relating to and circulating within the specialized units were written in Chinese. Due to language policies in the ROC, most Indigenous persons also spoke Chinese, sometimes alongside their mother language, Taiwanese Hokkien (a variety of Chinese spoken by Hoklo immigrants from southern Fujian Province), or Japanese.

Beyond courtroom observation and interviews, I analyzed both historical and current legal cases, conducting documentary research in court, government, museum, newspaper, and personal archives.[18] Methodology, however, is more than just data collection. It involves continuous analysis and refinement of one's understanding of the people, places, and events encountered. In this case, my analytical approach allowed me to build on each piece of information gathered to expand upon an idea of "boundary institutions." This framework helped explain how actors in the ad hoc Chambers of Indigenous Courts made sense of and bridged Indigenous and non-Indigenous social and legal worlds in the administration of disputes over Indigenous cultural practices and territories.

A central component of my research was participant-observation in the Hualien ad hoc chambers, as well as in other ad hoc chambers and connected spaces (see map 2). To better understand how legal professionals learned about Indigenous peoples' cultures and rights, I joined training programs for judges organized by the Judicial Yuan and educational programs for lawyers arranged by the Legal Aid Foundation. I was fortunate to be affiliated with a law center in Hualien that served Indigenous communities, which gave me an opportunity to engage informally with a small group of dedicated lawyers defending Indigenous persons in cases related to land, natural resources, and wildlife hunting. Members of two Indigenous communities—Dowmung, a Truku community near Hualien City mentioned earlier, and Tastas, a Bunun community in neighboring Taitung County—had ongoing cases due to conflicts between their local law and state law. Through interactions at the courthouses and introductions from local contacts, I became acquainted with members of these communities. I spent an increasing amount of time in the communities, participating in daily activities such as agricultural work, hunting, gathering of forest products and minerals, cultural and ritual ceremonies, and church services, among other activities. As my research progressed, it took on a circular pattern: I would attend court proceedings, travel to visit the communities, and then return to the court to observe cases involving community members.

Dowmung, a Truku community of 852 people, is located in the Mugua River Basin, about a thirty-minute drive west of Hualien City. During the Japanese colonial period, Japanese administrators built a dam on the community's territory, with the river basin becoming a key source of hydroelectricity. When the island came under the control of the ROC government in 1945, the government continued to use the dam and, at the same time, implemented a forest development policy that led to extensive deforestation in the area. Since 2000, the ROC government has invested heavily in tourism in the Dowmung area to capitalize on its scenic mountain landscape. These efforts, however, have generated unrest within the community. Frustrated by the influx of busloads of tourists clogging their village streets and the tourists' disrespectful treatment of their territories, Dowmung residents protested and urged the Hualien government to protect their lands, but their efforts have largely been ignored (*The News Lens* 2015). Compared to many other rural Indigenous communities in Taiwan, Dowmung has faced particularly intense pressure from state-led development and control due to the region's rich and special natural resources (Dai 2015).

The mountain road leading to Dowmung was prone to damage from earthquakes, heavy rains, landslides, and typhoons, which were challenges

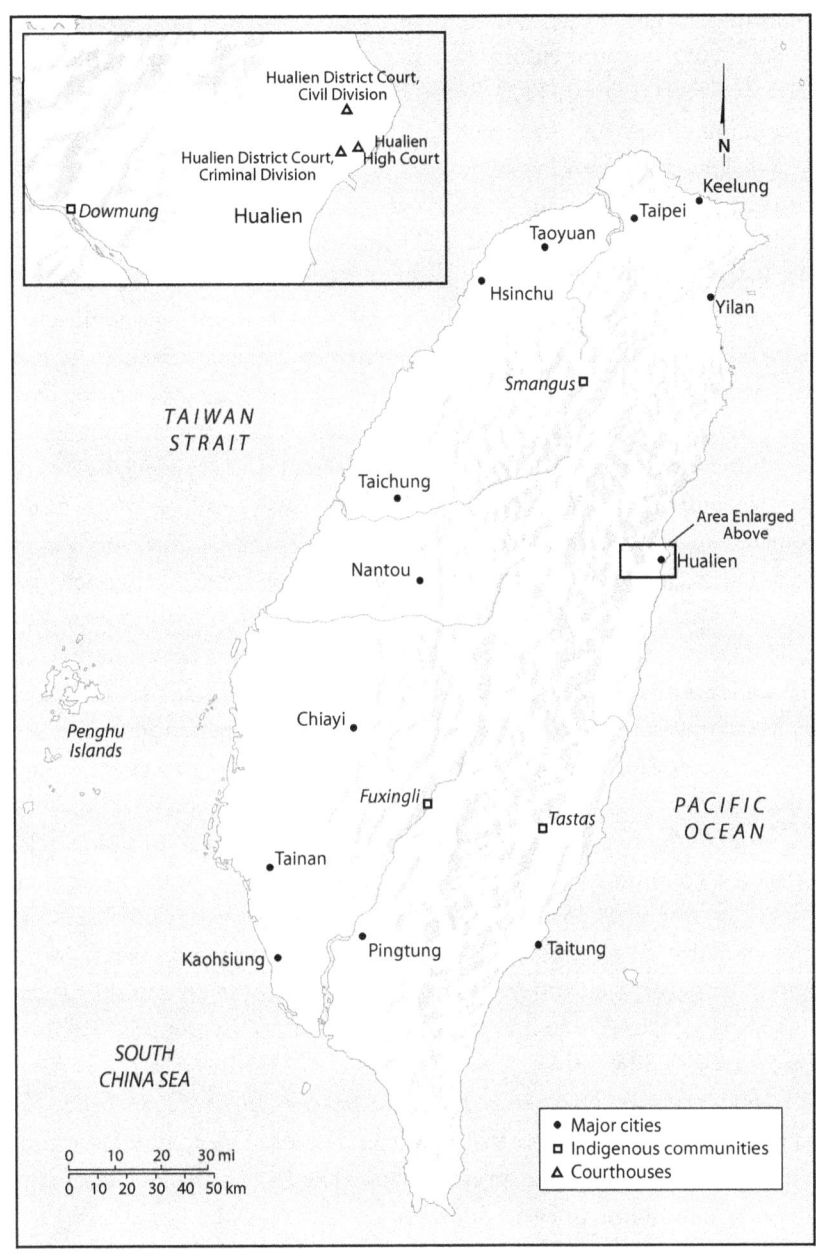

MAP 2. Field sites and other communities and locations mentioned in this book. Prepared by Bill Nelson Cartography.

I encountered on my first visit when a rockslide blocked the road to the village. Residents of Dowmung cultivated millet, sweet potatoes, and corn on the flat terraces overlooking the Mugua River. They also regularly hunted in the nearby mountains, following practices passed down through generations. These included the use of traps, hunting dogs, and homemade muskets to hunt mountain boar, sambar deer, flying squirrel, and Formosan muntjac. The Presbyterian church served as the heart of community life, with a smaller Catholic church at the opposite end of the village. According to residents, about 70–80 percent of the community identified as Christian, and they described how family clans historically assigned members to each church to maximize the collection of resources, such as bags of rice and medicines. Two small general stores offered food and other essentials for residents to purchase. Recently, the community had built a computer center, funded by a grant from the CIP, which housed six new computers and provided residents internet access, email, and social media connections. A multifunctional open-air center, used for community gatherings, also became the venue for intense negotiations over a convention that outlined local hunters' rights and responsibilities under Truku ancestral law, called Gaya (explored later in the book). When I first visited Dowmung in 2017, the community was embroiled in two cases related to their access to ancestral lands and natural resources (also described in detail in later chapters).

Tastas is a Bunun community of 330 people located farther south, just across the Taitung County border. Originally, the community lived in the Dalun River Basin to the west, but in 1933, Japanese colonial authorities relocated the community as part of a broader policy of moving Indigenous groups to areas where local police could monitor them more easily. The community called themselves Tastas in reference to a nearby waterfall; in the Bunun language, the word *tastas* mimics the sound of water crashing on the rocks below. Japanese colonial authorities referred to the group as "Takimi," Japanese for "falling water."

Some Tastas residents worked in a nearby town, running small shops or laboring in the expansive rice paddies along the river. I spent most of my time with local hunters, engaging in conversation and joining them on their trips into the mountains to hunt animals. At the time, the community was embroiled in a high-profile criminal case involving one of its residents, Mr. Talum, mentioned earlier, who had been arrested and prosecuted for providing meat for his ailing mother. His conviction in the Taitung District Court had been upheld in the Hualien High Court, and he was awaiting the Supreme Court's decision on his appeal. Reforms to ROC laws allowed

Indigenous persons to engage in hunting under limited circumstances, but when I accompanied Tastas hunters in the mountains, the "law" governing wildlife hunting and land use often had less to do with formal statutes or codes than it did with local interpretations by law officials, a process Sally Merry (2006) calls vernacularization. Concepts of law and rights did not always filter down as efficiently as one might expect, and locating the "law" in such circumstances became a complicated affair.

PLURALISM, RULES PRODUCTION, AND POSITIONED RESEARCH

In 2017, Rakaw, an elder in Dowmung, oversaw the construction of a hunters' lodge that the community intended to use as a cultural center where they could pass down Truku language and culture to future generations. While the community maintained that the center was built on their ancestral territory, local authorities disagreed, arguing that it was constructed without authorization on land that had been nationalized. Prosecutors in Hualien filed criminal charges against Rakaw, and the case was assigned to the ad hoc Chamber of Indigenous Courts in the Hualien District Court. Throughout the trial, courtroom discussions were dominated by ROC national laws, but other normative orders also emerged as Rakaw, witnesses from Dowmung, and legal aid lawyers drew on Gaya, international human rights, and jurisprudence of other nations to support their arguments.

The multiple, overlapping legal orders and jurisdictional powers in Indigenous cases, including Rakaw's case, reflect a familiar situation of legal pluralism (Merry 1988). A useful idea for studying multilayered legal fields, legal pluralism describes how societies contain multiple normative orders and legal discourses, some of which are maintained by institutions other than the state. It includes relationships between state law and unofficial forms of law (e.g., agreements, codes of conduct, customs) and between legal orderings (e.g., local law, common law, and statutes) and nonlegal orderings (e.g., guidelines and norms), and how law responds to social complexity and issues over time. It draws attention to the numerous modes of conflict management outside the courts and to the general social context of the law, particularly the powerful role of the state. This concept has become so widespread that it is common for scholars to argue that legal pluralism exists in virtually every society (Tamanaha 2007, 1).

Recent scholarship has sought to document a more complex power relationship between legal orders in colonized societies, highlighting the hybridization that occurs across legal orders. This position, known as interlegality, focuses on the ways in which legal orders intersect, overlap, and blend, emphasizing the porousness of law and how the life of law involves an intersection of legal orders, particularly between national law and local Indigenous law (De Sousa Santos 1987). Andre Hoekema (2017, 72) describes interlegality as a phenomenon in which "local law actors involved in situations with different legal orders adopt elements of a dominant legal order, national and/or international, and elements of the frames of meaning inherent in these orders, into the practice of their local legal order, and/or the other way around." In this sense, interlegality is both the activity of adopting elements of other forms of law and a broader outcome of the hybridization of legal orders.

Legal pluralist approaches are valuable because they highlight that state law is not the only relevant or effective legal order in people's lives. They reveal how legal orders superimpose, interpenetrate, and mix into one another and, importantly, how this involves non-neutral processes that promote the expression of some interests and disputes while suppressing others. Moreover, they draw attention to the concrete activities of local actors who navigate and maneuver across legal orders. These considerations are relevant to the ad hoc Chambers of Indigenous Courts not only because of the presence of legal pluralism in Taiwan, but also because these units were established as institutions charged with finding ways to bridge Indigenous and non-Indigenous understandings of culture, territory, and law.

State law served as a central framework in the operation of the ad hoc Chambers of Indigenous Courts. ROC statutes, codes, constitution, and legal procedures held a privileged position around which local Indigenous laws and justice practices were organized. The centrality of state law, however, could become unsettled. Indigenous defendants and litigants invoked their own legal traditions, such as when Rakaw invoked Gaya during a judge's site visit to the cultural center (discussed later). Lawyers appealed to international legal frameworks, such as human rights law. Experts, including anthropologists, explained the cultural significance of Indigenous norms and practices. Indigenous witnesses sometimes refused to speak Mandarin Chinese, insisting on using their mother languages in court. Community members performed rituals on the courthouse steps, while activists waved banners and contested nationalist narratives about land and rights. Judges worked to incorporate Indigenous worldviews and norms into applications of national laws and legal procedures.

These observations indicate the approach to law taken in this book: Law, whether in the form of state legislation or local Indigenous law, does not preexist its application. Law is determined only after it is set out, by examining its applications, consequences, interpretations, and negotiations, a phenomenon Jan Hoffman French (2009) calls "postlegislative negotiation." This perspective emphasizes the ongoing, open-ended work after a law is enacted, and the diffused nature of these activities. The concept of postlegislative negotiation, as I see it, is a particular instantiation of a phenomenon that applies widely to systems of social rules. The implementation and maintenance of social rules, including customs, laws, norms, regulations, and taboos, calls for adaptation, adjustment, and cumulative experience. I regard these productive practices as *rule-crafting* processes, highlighting the making and interpretation of rules as social constructions and the inevitability of their reformulation and transformation. Social rules are crafted things in that they are shaped by applications, context, and relations of power through a dialectical interplay of regulated domains and across realms of the regulated and unregulated. Viewing rules in this way helps explain how normative systems change as people touched by them use them in a variety of ways, and highlights the role of various actors at different levels who are engaged in making, interpreting, and negotiating norms.

The processes in and around the ad hoc Chambers of Indigenous Courts bring this feature of norms and rules into relief. An ensemble of governmental and nongovernmental actors and institutions is at work in crafting Indigenous peoples' rights in Taiwan. ROC government officials pass legislation and enact policies that define the scope of Indigenous protections. Judges interpret these laws and policies, sometimes serving as allies of Indigenous peoples in their bids for justice, while at other times adopting narrow interpretations that work against them. Police make decisions about investigations and arrests. Prosecutors determine which criminal charges to pursue. Lawyers craft arguments to advance legal interpretations that benefit their clients. Indigenous parties and elders describe cultural practices and local laws in courts and in their communities. Anthropologists provide social scientific evidence about Indigenous cultures through reports and testimony. Churches serve as central sites in the Indigenous recognition movement. Media reports inform the public on Indigenous issues. Spiritual forces, as seen in the Katratripulr case, may also intervene and influence disputes. Just as these actors emerge as crucial agents in articulating the rights of Indigenous peoples, they can also reinforce the dispersal of state power and of categories that dominate discourses of indigeneity (Foucault 1991).

In considering the legitimating role of lawyers and anthropologists, I should also address my own position as a legal advocate and an anthropologist. For several years, I practiced law at an international law firm in the United States, where I was a member of legal teams that litigated antitrust suits in U.S. federal courts, negotiated financing arrangements for infrastructural projects in East Africa and Europe, and handled human rights cases, including representing detainees at Camp Delta in Guantanamo Bay Naval Base. These experiences shaped my field research in various ways, sometimes facilitating the research and sometimes presenting challenges. Judges, lawyers, and government officials in Taiwan were often generous with their time, and our meetings frequently involved an exchange of ideas about trial procedures, human rights, and Indigenous issues in Taiwan and North America. By contrast, prosecutors in Hualien were more hesitant to engage with me because I was associated with Indigenous activism. I used this proximity to Indigenous activists and communities to better understand their perspectives and motivations, while also taking solace in the fact that prosecutors in other jurisdictions were more open to communication.

As both an advocate and an anthropologist, I was often positioned as a mediator between the realms of law and culture. Judges asked about ethnographic methods and social scientific concepts, like "culture," that often arose in Indigenous cases but were seldom clearly defined. Meanwhile, anthropologists consulted on how to frame their reports and testimony in ways that would make social scientific knowledge more accessible and persuasive to legal actors. At a legal aid center, lawyers invited me to serve as an intermediary between the center and a committee of Indigenous elders who advised the center. Similarly, members of a hunters' association in Dowmung invited me to participate in efforts to codify Gaya.

Conducting this research also meant critically examining my own identities as a legal advocate and an anthropologist through the lens of each discipline, which yielded productive moments of reflection, opportunities to reencounter my chosen fields and myself. I could explore my identity as an advocate through the lens of anthropology, and my research as an anthropologist through the lens of law practice. These reflections yielded surprising insights and became points of engagement for anthropological problems. One example came in my transition from law practice to anthropology.

Although I had practiced law for many years, I had never identified myself as a "lawyer." In my world of law, a lawyer was someone like the fictional character Atticus Finch in *To Kill a Mockingbird*: a whole-system-viewing, justice-driven advocate for the powerless and marginalized. I was not that. My colleagues at the law firm identified more as businesspersons than as lawyers. The "goods" we produced were high-quality billable hours. Concepts like social justice were remote and often subject to ridicule (cf. Riles 2006, 61). This was a view of law framed in terms of the pragmatics of the law business. I did not become a "lawyer" until I attended graduate school and encountered colleagues in the social sciences who insisted that this was the category I occupied.[19] Similarly, I was struck by the difficulty some legal practitioners had in translating anthropologists' "huge stories," as one lawyer put it, into something usable for law.[20] Yet these same practitioners were quick to produce their own fictive stories about Indigenous peoples and about me (for instance, that I was a United Nations observer) to support their positions for or against Indigenous parties. This led me to wonder whether the "lawyers" with whom I worked in Taiwan, and other actors like "judges," "hunters," and "Indigenous persons," saw themselves in terms of those categories and associated meanings. It also led me to wonder about the kinds of stories that legal actors could, or were willing to, hear and the production of many kinds of narratives circulating in legal disputes, from recitations of facts to statutes themselves.

My decision to focus on cases involving disputes over Indigenous cultural practices and land shaped my research in several respects. These cases arose most often in the criminal courts. As a result, many of the cases discussed in this book involve criminal matters, although I also address civil and administrative cases. Criminal prosecutions related to Indigenous cultural practices also tended to focus on activities associated with men, like hunting, making firearms, and gathering forest products and minerals. Cultural practices involving or affecting Indigenous women were comparatively absent from public view in the courts. For example, cases involving family matters or sexual violence were typically closed to the public (Lee 2015, 60n455; Lin 2010, 175n85), and I did not observe proceedings on these topics. This is not to say, however, that Indigenous women were themselves absent. On the contrary, they were extremely active in cases administered by the ad hoc Chambers of Indigenous Courts, frequently appearing as claimants in civil suits, witnesses, unofficial translators, or supporters in the audience, as is evident in cases discussed in this book.

My field research also required me to address the fact that my family was part of Taiwan's colonial encounter. My parents served as Protestant missionaries in Taiwan from the mid-1980s to the early 1990s. We lived in a mixed neighborhood in Taitung County that was home to Han Taiwanese, Amis, Paiwan, and Pinuyumayan peoples. Western Christian missionaries have been present in Taiwan since the seventeenth century, frequently focusing their conversion efforts on Indigenous populations. The adoption and localization of Christian spirituality has also been a strategy for Indigenous peoples to resist assimilation into Chinese culture, and today over 80 percent of Indigenous peoples identify themselves, at least nominally, as Christian. My family, like other missionary families in the area, worked in part with Indigenous communities. Mindful of this background, I tried to configure my research in ways that my Indigenous collaborators and their communities identified as valuable and beneficial. These activities included maintaining a website that documented pollution left by Han Taiwanese tourists, collecting old traps in the mountains, and giving presentations on international human rights and Indigenous issues in North America. The activity my collaborators identified as most important, however, was explaining the enduring significance of Indigenous practices, languages, and lands to ROC officials, prosecutors, lawyers, police, and judges. Always cautious not to present myself as speaking for these communities, this became an important part of my interactions with state actors involved in the ad hoc Chambers of Indigenous Courts.

INDIGENOUS COURTS AS BOUNDARY INSTITUTIONS

This book emerged from a desire to understand the development and operation of Taiwan's system of ad hoc Chambers of Indigenous Courts. I set out to explore how these specialized units grappled with ideas about indigeneity and Indigenous rights in a context of multiple colonialisms where the sovereign status of the state was contested, and where the pursuit of multiculturalism has led to reconciliatory efforts while also being mobilized in support of other state interests. As I hope to demonstrate in this book, the activities making up the daily life of Taiwan's specialized units were entwined with larger processes of articulating indigeneity, promoting Indigenous recognition and rights, engaging with international orders like human rights, strengthening democratic institutions, constructing national identity, and enhancing global recognition for the state. More broadly, I am interested in what the daily activities in Taiwan's ad hoc chambers reveal about geographies of colonialism and Indigenous rights struggles in the Asia-Pacific region.

I have thus far outlined the basic situation in regard to Indigenous peoples in Taiwan, court reforms establishing ad hoc Chambers of Indigenous Courts, and my position in studying these developments—points I will expand upon in later chapters. I will now summarize the book's main contributions, in its integration of boundary work theory with multicultural politics and rule-crafting processes through analysis of Indigenous courts situated in the national court system, and highlight some insights this analysis offers from the perspective of Taiwan's Indigenous legal and political scene.

Toward a more dynamic view of frameworks linking social worlds that moves beyond the U.S. context and the idealized relationships between policymakers and scientists that have occupied much of boundary work theorization, I work with the concept of *boundary institutions*. This term is meant to recognize the diverse actors, techniques and practices, and power dynamics in institutions designed to mediate between the state and Indigenous societies. My approach to boundary institutions draws from anthropology, Indigenous studies, and post/colonial theory. *Boundary*, as I intend the term here, emphasizes that boundaries are not inherent or fixed but are actively produced and maintained through social practices. They are "leaky," as Ilana Gershon (2019, 405) phrases it, in ways that facilitate circulation but also raise contestations about what should pass through or be transformed. They may appear differently depending on participants' positions and may involve the intersection of multiple boundaries at multiple scales. *Institutions* shifts the focus from assumed fixed organizations or objects to the techniques and practices involved in creating, maintaining, and spanning boundaries. These activities, in turn, operate as sites of knowledge and power.[21] The model of boundary institutions developed here, therefore, emphasizes the elaborations of activities intended to differentiate and bridge social worlds. It critically assesses these activities through a lens that foregrounds how they are shaped by and embedded in relations of power and knowledge.

A first point concerns management of *hybridities* in boundary institutions. Hybridization may seem like an odd feature to emphasize for an institution defined by separation, but a great deal of work in the ad hoc Chambers of Indigenous Courts involved managing hybridities, their possibilities, and their scope. The specialized units formed hybrid spaces of multiple relations among artifacts, people, and rules, sometimes mixing and sometimes selecting among facts, identities, norms, and values. Participants in the ad hoc chambers included Han Taiwanese officials, judges, prosecutors, lawyers, police officers, experts, and clerks, as well as Indigenous claimants, defendants, witnesses, elders, audience members, journalists, and spirits. Managing distinctions between participants' identities as Han Taiwanese, as Indigenous, or as communities or villages often reified ethnic and racial differences but sometimes troubled them. Participants would, at times, emphasize their Han Taiwanese or Indigenous identities, but at other times stressed their shared ROC citizenship or broader Taiwanese identity. At still other times, they highlighted a common humanity that transcended national or ethnic considerations. The courtroom space was also marked by the circulation of multiple legal and normative orders, including state laws, local Indigenous laws, international human rights, jurisprudence from other nations, and religious principles from Buddhism and Christianity. Participants sometimes worked to maintain these legal and normative orders as distinct, but at other times they highlighted points of commonality or attempted to weave them together. In this way, the specialized units became spaces where Han Taiwanese and Indigenous worlds intermingled and sometimes merged.

The second point regards *process*. When creating the ad hoc Chambers of Indigenous Courts, the Judicial Yuan anticipated that, through incremental experience and future program development, the units would promote respect for Indigenous peoples within the national court system. The agency hoped that the units would encourage judges to develop strategies for securing Indigenous peoples' legal rights within Taiwan's civil law tradition and build a repository of case decisions to ensure consistency across the judiciary. The units did not remain static but were in an ongoing process of adaptation. Changes were occurring at the level of institutional structure, in forms of interaction, and in the expectations and incentives of participants (cf. Parker and Crona 2012, 281–82). The Judicial Yuan established the specialized units quickly, omitting certain steps and providing little instruction to courts about their implementation. At the same time, ROC laws protecting Indigenous peoples were changing rapidly, requiring new jurisprudential interpretations and flexibility from those involved. In addition, court procedures were changing, such as the introduction of new programs to strengthen legal representation and interpreter services for Indigenous persons. The pace of change was so fast that certain strategies, like delaying cases, became an important tool for lawyers representing Indigenous clients. Participants in the specialized units also did not always occupy fixed or well-defined roles. Even within the courtroom, a space seemingly defined by clear roles, participant processes could introduce or remove actors and collectives depending on the issues at hand (Arpin et al. 2016, 17). Thus, the specialized units were dynamic and generative spaces, accomplishing more than resolution of disputes and experiencing flux and flow with new developments and proficiencies in managing cases.

A third point concerns *practice*. Boundary institutions emphasize the everyday techniques and practices developed to navigate the "landscape of tensions" (Parker and Crona 2012) inherent in spanning boundaries to achieve a normative end. For anthropologists, institutions are not readymade, complete, and established sets of rules and incentives; instead, they are fluid combinations, continuously changed, supplemented, and reassembled through the work of various actors (Clifford 1988; Farmer 2004; Ho 2009; Moore 1986; Nader 1972; Niezen 2003a). They involve emergent, process-driven activities, habits, norms, procedures, and roles that are molded and transmitted by various conduits, including cultures, routines, and social structures. In giving priority to practices as constitutive of boundary institutions, practice-centered approaches provide valuable insights into how actors make decisions that are informed by broader social practices from other domains, while still allowing space for creativity in unpredictable moments of social action (Bourdieu 1977, 1990; Comaroff and Roberts 1981; Moore 1978). In the ad hoc Chambers of Indigenous Courts, judges experimented with new techniques to incorporate Indigenous norms and perspectives into established legal practices, such as integrating Indigenous worldviews into the application of criminal law. Indigenous litigants and their supporters, in turn, developed their own strategies to assert their interests and positions in legal proceedings. For example, they sometimes stressed their cultural and linguistic distinctiveness through coordinating their attire or speaking in their mother language, while at other times, they de-emphasized these differences by blending identities or stressing commonalities. Over the brief life of the specialized units, a range of creative and exploratory practices emerged to bridge state-Indigenous divides. While some of these practices helped strengthen Indigenous recognition in the courtroom, in the hands of others they could also work against Indigenous participants.

A final point regards *power*. Attention to relations of power, or to the ways in which subtle but pervasive exercises of power shape participation and practice, brings into relief issues of authority, control, and coercion (Abu-Lughod

1990; Coulthard 2014; Richland 2008; Rifkin 2011). Power relations may take many forms, including structural arrangements, hegemonic forms, perceptions of legitimacy, and priorities of action. In courts, for instance, judges serve as decision-makers and gatekeepers of evidence (Ziaja and Fullerton 2015). The hegemony of state law and procedures over other normative orders and justice practices often furthers the interests of the colonizing society (Comaroff and Comaroff 1991; Greenhouse 2005; Merry 2000; Nader 1990). Furthermore, control over determinations about "authentic" Indigenous identities frequently limits and distorts Indigenous recognition (Povinelli 2002). Examining relations of power, therefore, uncovers the hegemonic ideologies and structures, and the reproduction of systemic inequalities, at work in boundary institutions. It also underscores the reality that not all participants participate in the same ways, or even voluntarily. Yet power is not always coercive or repressive; it can also be productive (Foucault 1982). Attention to power relations reveals participants' activities of refusal and resistance to the inequities and power imbalances within boundary institutions. This is particularly significant for the ad hoc Chambers of Indigenous Courts, highlighting the labor that Indigenous peoples must undertake to challenge the enduring colonial power structures embedded in the specialized units through assertions of their identities, cultures, and rights as Indigenous persons.

THE CHAPTERS AHEAD

The book begins at the boundary of Han Taiwanese and Indigenous worlds in Taiwan. Chapter 1, "Born of Wood, Born of Stone," explores the shifting meanings of indigeneity in the Taiwan context. It examines the connections between Taiwan's Indigenous peoples and Austronesian-speaking peoples across Oceania. It describes the efforts of Dutch, Spanish, Chinese, and Japanese powers to exert control over portions of Taiwan and the implementation of measures to categorize and manage the Indigenous population. I also consider late-twentieth-century developments that opened a space and, in some respects, created an incentive for the ROC government to turn to Indigenous peoples' identities and rights as a means of affirming Taiwan's place on the world platform and as a symbol for an independent Taiwan. Finally, I examine the legal definitions of the term *Indigenous* under ROC law and explore the meaning of indigeneity as it travels from global legal orders into local forms of self-identification.

Chapter 2, "Orders in the Court," turns its attention to the legal and normative orders that circulate in and around disputes in the ad hoc Chambers of Indigenous Courts. I begin by considering the role of Gaya in wildlife hunting among the Truku in eastern Taiwan. I then examine the regime of legal protections carved out for Indigenous peoples in ROC law, identifying three movements of rights development since the ROC took control of Taiwan in 1945. Finally, I describe the regime of international human rights protections for Indigenous peoples and how state actors in Taiwan have incorporated these global norms into the legal system. Woven into these discussions are ethnographic descriptions of individuals' experiences living with, under, and against these orders: a Pinuyumayan elder's experience living through Taiwan's transition to the ROC, hunting muntjac deer in the mountains with Bunun men, Indigenous demonstrators reacting to President Tsai's landmark apology to Indigenous peoples, and lawyers crafting legal arguments based on international human rights to support Indigenous claims.

Chapter 3, "Ethereal Presences of the Ad Hoc Chambers," focuses on the system of ad hoc Chambers of Indigenous Courts. It describes the history, structure, and personnel working in these specialized units. I begin by tracing the developments that led to their establishment. Next, I examine the units' structure and the ambiguities that have led to disagreements about their presence in national courthouses. Then I consider the judicial actors who administer the units, the advocates representing Indigenous defendants and litigants, and the style of proceedings in the units. I conclude by addressing the spatial, economic, and linguistic obstacles that Indigenous persons and communities must overcome to access the units.

Chapter 4, "One Community, Two Controversies," offers a detailed analysis of two cases involving members of the Truku community in Dowmung. These cases provide a ground-level view of how the ad hoc Chambers of Indigenous Courts handled disputes over Indigenous culture, territory, and natural resources. In examining these cases, I adopt a phenomenological approach to capture the powerful atmosphere of the disputes. I do not confine myself to the courtroom space. Instead, I engage in what I call a *mobile ethnography of justice*, following each case, the circulation of conceptions of law and indigeneity, and the courts themselves as they traveled beyond the courtroom into other spheres of social and legal action, such as lawyers' offices, judicial chambers, and the streets of Indigenous villages.

Chapter 5, "Hybrid Practices and Legal Indigeneities," studies the specific practices developed by participants in the ad hoc Chambers of Indigenous

Courts to bridge divides between the state and Indigenous peoples. I begin by examining the techniques employed by Han Taiwanese judges to incorporate Indigenous peoples' cultures and perspectives into legal processes. I then turn to the performances of indigeneity that Indigenous actors used to compel courts to recognize their identities and legal rights as Indigenous persons. With the new and hastily implemented system, it was up to local actors to maneuver and innovate to make the specialized units meaningful, relevant, and concrete realities in the court system. In this discussion, I emphasize the role of intermediary actors who facilitated interactions between Han Taiwanese legal actors and Indigenous litigants and defendants, and the transformative potential of these practices.

Chapter 6, "Boundary Institutions and Beyond," concludes by stepping back to consider again the connections between indigeneity and sovereignty in Taiwan. It reflects on the possibilities and limitations for Indigenous recognition in situations of multiple colonialisms and contested sovereignty, and the role of the Indigenous court units in mediating state-Indigenous divides. Taiwan's complex history and uncertain future puts it in a unique position to think reflexively about how both the ROC state and Indigenous communities must engage in sovereignty making through opportunistic efforts and the practical and symbolic value of making space for Indigenous sovereignty and self-determination. Thus, the Taiwan experience presents an opportunity to reimagine sovereignty and the character of state-Indigenous relations more broadly.

ONE

Born of Wood, Born of Stone

MY TRUKU FRIENDS SHARED a story about their origins. In ancestral times, there was an enormous tree in a place called Bunohon, located in the central mountain range of Taiwan. The tree was unique, with one side made of wood and the other of stone. The spirits of this extraordinary tree became gods. One day, a god and a goddess emerged from the trunk of the tree, and together they had many children. Their descendants thrived, and food was abundant. Whenever they wanted meat, they had only to call for a wild boar and it would come. By plucking a single hair from the boar, cutting it into pieces, and cooking it, they would have all the meat they needed. After many generations, however, Bunohon became too small for the group, so they migrated to new lands. But once they left Bunohon, they had to learn to farm, and life became much more difficult (see also Wang 2008, 13–14).

This "born of wood, born of stone" origin story, like many other origin stories, was as much about contemporary circumstances as it was about the past. Four centuries of foreign encroachments have left a profound and lasting impact on Taiwan's Indigenous peoples. Imperial, colonial, and state powers worked to integrate the diverse Indigenous polities they encountered into Chinese, Japanese, and later Chinese (again) societies. Some Indigenous groups resisted these intrusions and were isolated through the construction of boundary trenches and guard lines. Other groups accepted foreign rule. Still others were complicit in colonial projects. Over time, foreign powers systematically dispossessed Indigenous peoples of their lands and exploited their natural resources. In the late twentieth century, new opportunities for Indigenous recognition emerged, but efforts to secure Indigenous peoples' rights through legislation and policy have been fragmented and inconsistent. While indigeneity has become an important legal and political category promising improvement in Indigenous peoples' lives, Indigenous territories have not been returned, their cultures and languages continue to face pressures, and many communities remain marginalized economically and socially. Thus, Taiwan's Indigenous peoples today experience colonialism as an enduring structure and ongoing process.

Indigeneity is a concept central to the creation and operation of Taiwan's ad hoc Chambers of Indigenous Courts, one that the units are tasked with managing as they handle disputes involving Indigenous individuals and communities. In this chapter, I explore the meanings and mobilizations of the category of "Indigenous" in Taiwan. I begin by examining the historical connections between Taiwan's Indigenous peoples and the diverse groups of Austronesian-speaking peoples across Oceania. I then consider the actions of foreign powers, such as the Dutch, Spanish, Chinese Ming and Qing dynasties, Imperial Japan, and, most recently, the ROC, as they sought to exert control over parts of Taiwan and engage with the diverse Indigenous polities residing there. Shifting to more recent history, I discuss Taiwan's dismissal from the United Nations and its transition to democracy, a period in which Indigenous peoples' identities and rights became pivotal for affirming Taiwan's place on the world platform and an important symbol representing an independent Taiwan. I then analyze the legal definitions of *Indigenous* under ROC law. Finally, I trace the idea of indigeneity as it travels from global legal orders into local forms of self-identification. This discussion illustrates how understandings of indigeneity in Taiwan have shifted in response to historical and political developments, where the concept has acquired different meanings for different groups and has been strategically deployed to advance different agendas.

AUSTRONESIAN PEOPLES AND COLONIALISMS OF TAIWAN

The main island of Taiwan, along with its surrounding smaller islands, has been known by many names throughout history. In the fourteenth century, it was referred to as Taiwan in Mandarin Chinese; Portuguese explorers called it Ilha Formosa (beautiful island) in the sixteenth century; and in the seventeenth century, it was known as Tayouan in the region now called Tainan (Andrade 2008). The original names of territories on the island, however, would have come from the Austronesian-speaking peoples who have inhabited them for at least six thousand years. Today, the forty-two languages and dialects spoken by Indigenous peoples in Taiwan belong to the Malayo-Polynesian family group, also known as the Austronesian family group. Spread across Southeast Asia and Oceania, this language family is one of the most widely distributed in the world. With an estimated three hundred million speakers, Austronesian peoples span a vast oceanic region. The Austronesian languages spoken in Taiwan are the most varied among all Austronesian localities, leading some scholars to argue that Taiwan was the origin point of the Austronesian diaspora (see Bellwood 1984).

Scholars have noted, however, that grand narratives presenting Taiwan as the homeland of Austronesian-speaking peoples can be problematic, both for Austronesian peoples—like Polynesians, who may be conceptualized as immigrants to their native lands and thus as similar to other citizens (Arvin 2019, 170–71)—and for Taiwan's Indigenous peoples, which they potentially portray as merely genetic repositories for other Austronesian groups (Munsterhjelm 2014, 135). For their part, my Bunun and Truku collaborators identified more with the mountains than with the image of seafaring Austronesian peoples.

For millennia, a diverse array of Indigenous polities coexisted, often in tension, on the islands of Taiwan, varying widely in their social structures, scales of organization, languages, means of production, and governance. At this time, the notion of "Austronesian peoples" was not a historical or self-aware, culture-bearing category. These diverse polities in Taiwan lived off the plentiful deer resources in the forests and swidden cultivation of rice and millet (Allee 1994, 32–33). They engaged in frequent conflicts with one another, organizing occasional alliances, long before and during the arrival of European, Chinese, and Japanese powers. Indeed, for many communities living in places like the Yilan Plain in northern Taiwan or on the Puli Plateau in central Taiwan, the concept of an "outsider" would have extended not only to Europeans, Chinese, and Japanese peoples but also to other groups now identified as "Austronesian."

Both the Chinese and Europeans arrived in Taiwan during the seventeenth century, marking a period of profound change. The earliest evidence of Chinese settlement on the main island dates back to the 1590s (Allee 1994, 23), although Chinese migration to the Penghu (Pescadores) Islands, located in the Taiwan Strait between the mainland and Taiwan, may have started as early as the late eleventh century. These early Chinese settlers primarily inhabited the island's southwest coast, and their numbers remained relatively small until the mid-seventeenth century.

In the early 1540s, Portuguese sailors passing along northwest Taiwan were captivated by the island's natural beauty and called it Ilha Formosa (Hsu 1980, 10). European interest in Taiwan remained limited, however, until the seventeenth century. In 1622, representatives of the Dutch East India Company attempted to build a fort in the Penghu Islands, but their efforts were thwarted by Ming dynasty forces two years later. Undeterred, the Dutch returned in 1624, establishing a fort on the southwestern coast of Taiwan, near present-day Tainan City. This location was strategically important, serving as a key outpost for the company between their main East Asia base in Batavia (Jakarta) and their trading post in Deshima, Japan (Allee 1994, 24).

Products such as deerskins, dried venison, and rattan, sourced from local Indigenous groups, became valuable trade items for the Dutch East India Company. The company also recognized the potential for cultivating crops like sugarcane on the island. To support this, it implemented policies that encouraged Chinese laborers from Guangdong and Fujian Provinces on the southeastern coast of China to come to Taiwan and work on rice farms and sugar plantations (Hirano, Veracini, and Roy 2021, 227). These Chinese settlers were primarily concentrated around the Dutch fort, with their settlement extending southward into the northern part of today's Kaohsiung City. During the period of Dutch control of southwestern Taiwan, the Chinese population may have grown to between forty and fifty thousand (Allee 1994, 24). Tonio Andrade (2008) argues that it was the Europeans, rather than East Asian states, who created the conditions for large-scale Chinese migration to Taiwan, thereby extending Chinese agricultural practices and social patterns to the island. This influx of Chinese settlers, facilitated by the Dutch, had significant consequences for Indigenous peoples. As the Chinese population grew, local Indigenous groups' access to traditional hunting grounds became increasingly limited, and the thriving trade in deerskins severely depleted a food resource that was vital for these communities.

When Dutch traders arrived in Taiwan, they encountered lowland Indigenous groups living in southwestern Taiwan, including the Siraya, Taivoan, Makatau, Pangsola-Dolatok, and Lungkiau (Wang 1980, 35–38). The establishment of a Dutch enclave brought the traders into direct contact with the Siraya, with whom they quickly established trade. The Dutch sent missionaries and representatives to neighboring Indigenous groups, appointed chieftains in communities that lacked formal leadership, imposed taxes, and restricted movement, in addition to encouraging Chinese migrants to cultivate the land. Dutch traders also brought with them the matchlock gun, a weapon prized for its superiority over Chinese-made firearms. Indigenous hunters eagerly traded for these guns, passing them down through generations (Martin 2006, 42).

The Dutch East India Company signed treaties with neighboring Indigenous polities that, in principle, respected certain aspects of their sovereignty (Andrade 2008, 185–86). These treaties allowed villages to retain rights to their lands and ensured that their territories could not be alienated without their consent. When Chinese or company officials cut timber or farmed on Indigenous lands, they were required to pay a fee to the Dutch East India Company that was meant to be passed on to the communities. Fishing and hunting licenses were subject to similar fees. In practice, however, these revenues rarely reached their intended Indigenous recipients.

The Dutch were the first and only European power to establish a long-term presence and government on Taiwan. The Spanish, by contrast, established a small outpost on the northern tip of the island, near present-day Tamsui, between 1626 and 1642. Viewing the Dutch presence in southwestern Taiwan as a threat to their interests in the Philippines, the Spanish aimed to seize control of northern Taiwan. Their plan was to attract Chinese traders to the region, revive trade with the Japanese (which had ceased the previous year), and use Taiwan as a base for missionary efforts in China and Japan (Hsu 1980, 12). The Spanish population in Taiwan never exceeded five hundred, and their efforts were mostly unsuccessful. Their main focus was on converting the Indigenous population to Christianity, although they only managed to establish good relations with eight Indigenous groups (Allee 1994, 24n16; Wang 1980, 14). Spanish interest in Taiwan began to wane after a revolt in Tamsui in 1636 (Borao Mateo 2009, 86). In 1642, the Dutch expelled the Spanish from the island, sending them back to their colony in the Philippines.

During the period of Dutch control, southwestern Taiwan became a key gateway for maritime trade, connecting China, Europe, Japan, South Asia, and Southeast Asia. The Dutch played an active role in managing these trade routes, but meanwhile China was experiencing a dramatic upheaval. In 1644, Manchurian forces began their invasion from the northeast, overthrowing the Ming dynasty. In search of safety, thousands of Chinese immigrants from the coastal provinces of China fled to Taiwan. At the time, forces loyal to the Ming court retreated southward to resist the Manchurian advance. Among these Ming loyalists was General Zheng Cheng-gong (Koxinga), a military leader who commanded a network of traders, pirates, and mercenary armies operating from Japan to Southeast Asia. In 1661, Zheng's naval fleet and forces laid siege to the Dutch East India Company's headquarters in Taiwan. After a year of conflict, a treaty was signed in 1662, and the Dutch were forced to leave the island. With the Dutch departure, the treaty rights previously established with Indigenous groups expired.

Taiwan became the final stronghold from which Zheng and his heirs organized their resistance against the Manchurian Qing forces. Zheng and his successors controlled portions of the island until 1683, when the Qing finally took control. During those decades, Chinese settlement continued to expand rapidly, and the population may have doubled to around one hundred thousand (Allee 1994, 24). Migration was the primary driver of this growth, with Chinese settlements spreading across a larger portion of the island, although they remained primarily concentrated in the southwest. Magistrates in the Zheng regime acted as landlords, responsible for registering land and collecting taxes. Policies were implemented to minimize conflict between the occupying army, Chinese settlers, and Indigenous peoples by prohibiting interference with already cultivated fields. The primary purpose of these policies, however, was to encourage land reclamation, ensuring that those who converted lands opened by the military into productive farmland were granted ownership rights, which also helped increase tax revenues (Shepherd 1993, 93). Despite these measures, resentment toward Zheng's occupying forces simmered among the Indigenous population. During the brief period of Zheng family rule, three major Indigenous uprisings occurred (Wang 1980, 39).

In 1683, the Qing took control of the southern and western parts of Taiwan, making the area a prefecture of Fujian Province (Andrade 2008, 260). Qing rule would last for more than two centuries. During this time, hundreds of thousands of impoverished Chinese migrants from coastal southeastern China defied the Qing court's ban on travel to Taiwan and made their way to the island in search of better opportunities. As a result, Chinese settlements in the south continued to grow in the late seventeenth and early eighteenth centuries. This expansion put increasing pressure on lowland Indigenous groups, such as the Siraya, Taivoan, and Makatau, forcing many to migrate eastward into the mountains or southward (Wang 1980, 39). Those who remained became intermixed with Chinese settlers and were gradually Sinicized.

The expansion of Chinese settlements in central Taiwan often came at the expense of Indigenous lands. In areas like Nantou and Chiayi, Chinese settlers faced fierce resistance from Indigenous groups living in the mountains. These conflicts led to five major Indigenous uprisings in the early eighteenth century, notably in Nantou, Pingtung, and Chiayi (Wang 1980, 41). In response, the Qing government implemented a policy in 1739 that prohibited Chinese settlers from entering the territories of mountain Indigenous groups. This restriction remained in place until 1875.

As the Chinese population expanded and became dominant across Taiwan's western plains, a process of assimilation gradually blurred distinctions between Chinese settlers and lowland Indigenous groups. Indigenous communities were generally divided into three categories, based on their level of acculturation to Chinese society and relationship with the Qing state. "Cooked savages" (*shoufan* 熟番) referred to those groups who had submitted to Qing rule, adopted settled agriculture, and lived peacefully with the Chinese. A transitional category, "transformed savages" (*huafan* 化番), included groups that were in the process of being "cooked" but had not yet fully assimilated. These two categories of cooked groups contrasted with the "raw savages" (*shengfan* 生番) or mountain-dwelling groups who retained their own political institutions and remained resistant to Chinese society and Qing authority (Tavares 2005, 364).

To maintain order on the frontier, the Qing government sought to ensure peaceful relations between Chinese settlers and mountain Indigenous groups by establishing a strict boundary line beyond which Chinese settlement was legally prohibited, with guard posts erected along major routes leading into Indigenous territories. More will be said about this boundary, but efforts to constrain Chinese settlement in Indigenous territories proved largely futile. The boundary line was pushed farther into the interior four times during the mid- to late eighteenth century, demonstrating the difficulty of restricting Chinese expansion into Indigenous lands in the mountains (Allee 1994, 27).

The "raw" and "cooked" distinction used by the Qing to classify Indigenous groups was based not on cultural, ethnic, or racial characteristics, but primarily on the political relationship between the Qing and these groups, largely serving tax and administrative purposes (Bekhoven 2016, 215). Indigenous groups classified as "cooked" had formally submitted to Qing rule and paid taxes to Qing authorities. By contrast, "raw" groups did not pay taxes and lived beyond the boundary trenches dug by the Qing to prevent Chinese encroachment and headhunting attacks by mountain-based Indigenous groups (Shepherd 1993, 16–17). By the nineteenth century, the classification "cooked savage" became synonymous with "plains savage," while "raw savage" was equated with "mountain savage." These territorial classifications, however, did not align with reality. For example, some groups living on the plains of the east coast were classified as "raw savages," while some mountain villages that were loyal to the Qing were considered "cooked savages" (Bekhoven 2016, 215).

Patterns of subethnic Chinese settlement began to take shape in the early eighteenth century. Hokkien-speaking migrants from Fujian were often the first to settle in new frontier areas, while in other regions Hakka-speaking migrants from Guangdong led the way. Even in areas where the Hakka had already established settlements, they were sometimes displaced by the more numerous Hoklo and forced to move to more marginal areas (Allee 1994, 27). This competition for territory led to tensions and conflicts between the two groups. While the rapid growth of the Chinese population during this period inevitably generated conflicts with Indigenous groups, particularly those living in the mountains, it also created disputes between Han Chinese subgroups as they sought to establish themselves on new frontiers in Taiwan.

After the Second Opium War (1856–60), the Qing opened several ports in Taiwan to Western traders, including those in Keelung, Tamsui, Anping (now part of Tainan City), and Takau (now Kaohsiung City). In response to growing global demand for camphor and tea, these products became major cash crops exported from Taiwan. Northern Taiwan, which was the primary source of these goods, quickly surpassed the southwest as the island's political and economic hub. By the mid-nineteenth century, foreign powers, particularly the British and Japanese, began to challenge Qing control over Taiwan. In response, the Qing strengthened the island's defenses and made significant investments in economic and infrastructural development. Following the Sino-French War (1884–85), during which French forces attempted to seize Keelung and Tamsui, the Qing formally declared the portions of Taiwan under its control a province of the empire in 1885.

After more than two centuries of Chinese settlement, Taiwan's Chinese population had grown from an estimated one hundred thousand during the Zheng regime to over three million by 1887 (Wang 1980, 43). By this time, most of the island's western plains had been brought under intensive cultivation. The Qing were forced to address the mountain territories after Japan sent an expedition to Taiwan in 1874, ostensibly to punish Indigenous groups who had killed a boatload of Ryukyuan seamen blown ashore in southern Taiwan. Viewing this as a sign of potential Japanese claims to the island, the Qing lifted its ban on Chinese settlement in Indigenous mountain territories in 1875 (Allee 1994, 29).

This move was part of a broader effort to assert full control over Taiwan. To manage the conquest of resistant Indigenous groups, the Qing established a Bureau of Pacification and Reclamation (*fukenju* 撫墾局) and a General Bureau of Camphor Affairs (*naowu zongju* 腦務總局) to oversee camphor production and its taxation (Tavares 2005, 366). Under a policy of "open the mountains, pacify the Indigenes" (*kaishan fufan* 開山撫番), Chinese settlers quickly moved into the mountains, motivated by the commercial demand for camphor and tea. They encountered fierce resistance from mountain-based Indigenous groups, leading to twenty major uprisings between 1875 and 1895 (Wang 1980, 43). Qing efforts to subdue these groups were largely unsuccessful, resulting in several humiliating defeats (Allee 1994, 29). By the end of Qing rule, the government had not fully pacified the mountain Indigenous groups, but the trend of expanding Chinese settlement into Taiwan's rural, mountainous regions was firmly underway.

In 1894, the First Sino-Japanese War broke out between the Qing and the Empire of Japan after Japan invaded Korea. The conflict ended in 1895 with the Treaty of Shimonoseki, under which the Qing ceded Taiwan and the Penghu Islands to Japan. In response, some political elites in Taiwan rejected this outcome and declared the establishment of the Republic of Taiwan. Without strong leadership or international backing, the movement quickly crumbled, and within six months Japanese forces decisively defeated the republic and dismantled its militias (Barclay 2020).

In their administration of Taiwan, the Japanese encountered a patchwork of Indigenous groups and developed varying relationships with them. These policies evolved over time, often shaped opportunistically and applied unevenly. Viewing Taiwan as a critical part of its regional strategy, Japan sought to bring all of its peoples and territories under Japanese sovereignty and control over the course of two decades. Some Indigenous groups, eager to collaborate with the new regime, played key roles in supporting Japanese efforts. Paul Barclay (2005, 2017) describes how some Pinuyumayan communities near Beinan, led by Tata Rara, and the Seqalu, represented by Bunkiet, helped the Japanese establish a foothold on the Hengchun Peninsula in southern Taiwan and in what is now Taitung County. Other groups were not initially classified as Indigenous when the Japanese arrived. Tony Tavares (2005) recounts how the Saisiyat, for example, emerged as a distinct group following the Nanzhuang Incident (*nanzhuang shijian* 南庄事件) in 1902. This violent confrontation led to the group's reclassification from a "cooked" (assimilated) group to a "raw" (unassimilated) group in the eyes of Japanese authorities.

The Japanese initially continued the Qing practice of categorizing Indigenous peoples into "cooked" groups in the plains and "raw" groups in the mountains. By 1915, however, most had abandoned efforts to distinguish plains Indigenous groups as differences between them and local Chinese communities became increasingly blurred through acculturation and intermarriage (Templeman 2018, 464–65). The Qing policy of "open the mountains, pacify the Indigenes" had facilitated significant Chinese settlement in the mountains, which also influenced how Indigenous groups were classified under Japanese rule. Some remote, mountain-based communities were reclassified and brought into the fold of Japanese administrative control. In the first fifteen years of Japanese rule, large numbers of Pinuyumayan, Amis, Saisiyat, and some Paiwan peoples were brought under "normal administration" and subjected to the taxation system. Although these groups were still recorded as culturally Malayo-Polynesian in census records, their status as "savage villages" was abolished and they were reorganized into "townships." This reclassification reflected their growing engagement with surplus production, the use of money, and their perceived economic advancement equivalent to that of the Hakka and Hoklo agriculturalists in the region. Barclay (2017, 147) notes that these classifications often mirrored the extent of the Qing's administrative influence as of 1895.

Japanese authorities viewed mountain Indigenous groups as uncivilized and excluded them from the legal system. The government adopted a policy of indirect rule, denying these groups land rights and appointing chiefs to manage them (Awi Mona and Simon 2011, 50). At the same time, Japan encroached on mountain territories by establishing police stations and schools in villages (Wang 1980, 44). Japan's annexation of Taiwan also granted it a near monopoly over global camphor supplies. In 1899, the government established the Taiwan Camphor Bureau, which required that all camphor wood be sold to it. Additionally, the government formed the Office of Pacification and Reclamation to oversee Indigenous groups and open frontier land for the camphor industry. While the government established a legal framework for Chinese property rights over farmlands, it treated all other land as "unclaimed," giving itself the right to grant land concessions in the forests. In some cases, however, the government acknowledged Indigenous peoples' rights to compensation for camphor lands (Simon 2015a, 81–82). These policies generated unrest and led to violent resistance by Indigenous groups, particularly the Atayalic groups living in the camphor-rich northern forests of Taiwan.

Initially, the Japanese focused primarily on pacifying the Chinese population, giving little attention to the mountain regions. Then, in 1896, tensions flared between the Truku and the Japanese who had seized Truku lands in search of camphor and violated Truku women. This led to the Xincheng Incident (*xincheng shijian* 新城事件) in which the Truku killed thirteen Japanese soldiers. A decade later, in 1906, another conflict erupted over a wage dispute between Truku camphor miners and Japanese administrators. The dispute escalated, resulting in the decapitation of twenty-five Japanese merchants and officials. In response to these uprisings, Japanese forces launched a brutal military campaign against the Truku in 1914, known as the Truku War (*tailuge zhanzheng* 太魯閣戰爭), to suppress the resistance and reassert control over the region.

In response to these incidents and others, the Japanese adopted and adapted the Qing boundary strategy by constructing a defensive-guard-line system, surrounded by land mines and later electrified, to protect Chinese settlements. By 1900, this guard line extended from Yilan to Nantou, encircling the settlements of Atayal, Seediq, and Truku peoples (Chen 2000) (figure 5). Between 1903 and 1908, the line was pushed inland into Indigenous mountain territories seventy-five times. In 1907, another guard-line system was built in the northern part of Hualien (Wang 1980, 45). In the southern regions, however, the Japanese did not implement the guard-line system. Instead, they established a network of police stations to manage Indigenous communities. By 1909, there were approximately 123 stations in operation, overseeing the activities of mountain Indigenous groups (Wang 1980, 45).

The Japanese allowed trade with subdued mountain groups and encouraged them to move within the boundaries of the guard line or near the guard stations that monitored entry into Indigenous territories. In the 1920s, the Japanese abandoned the guard-line system and introduced a new policy of village settlement and Indigenous reserved lands (Japanese: *banjin shoyôchi* 蕃人所要地). This policy required nomadic groups to settle in permanent villages and adopt agriculture. They were also compelled to establish tribal councils with chiefs who would represent their communities to Japanese administrators (Simon 2017, 238). The reserve land system, which Scott Simon (2011, 26) notes was inspired by U.S. Indian policies, designated lands for the exclusive use of mountain Indigenous groups. The primary aim of these policies, however, was to reduce Indigenous territories and restrict their movements, thereby facilitating the production of camphor and other forest resources in the mountains (Simon and Awi Mona 2013, 103).

The reorganization of mountain Indigenous settlements fueled deep resentments, culminating in a violent revolt in 1930. Led by Mona Ludaw, the Seediq launched an attack on a Japanese police station in Wushe, central

FIGURE 5. "Yyire Entanglements, Bonbon Valley, Formosa." This postcard, depicting the electrical barrier fences used in the Japanese war against the northern tribes of Taiwan, was likely issued during the 1910–14 campaign. Courtesy of Lafayette Digital Repository.

Taiwan, killing over a hundred policemen and their families. This event, known as the Wushe Incident (*wushe shijian* 霧社事件), prompted an aggressive response from Japanese authorities, who sent more than two thousand troops and police into the mountains and enlisted warriors from other Indigenous groups (who outnumbered the Japanese forces) to crush Mona Ludaw and punish Seediq communities, even resorting to aerial bombings in an effort to flush Mona and his allies out of the mountains (Simon 2015a, 88).

By 1930, Japan had successfully pacified mountain Indigenous groups through intermittent warfare and forced resettlement onto small reserves, completing the first comprehensive, large-scale colonization of the entire island (Moser 1982, 24). Since around 1900, Japanese ethnologists and officials had been refining classifications of Indigenous groups in the mountain regions on the basis of perceived cultures and linguistic similarities (see Kyōko 2003). By 1935, a nine-group classification system had emerged (Awi Mona and Simon 2011, 50). The system was formalized in a landmark survey by Utsushikawa Nenozō, Mabuchi Tōichi, and Nobuto Miyamoto, *The Formosan Native Tribes: A Genealogical and Classificatory Study Vol. 1* (1935), which identified the Amis/Pangcah, Atayal/Tayan, Bunun, Paiwan/Payuan,

Pinuyumayan/Puyuma, Rukai, Saisiyat, Tsou, and Yami/Tao. This classification system became the basis for determining Indigenous status, a framework that has continued to influence the Taiwan national government's recognition of Indigenous groups from its postwar inception to the present day.

In conjunction with this classification scheme, Japanese authorities extended the household registration system into remote Indigenous communities. The system had a category for "Formosan tribes" (Japanese: *takasagozoku* 高砂族), which included unassimilated Indigenous communities living in the high mountains known to the Japanese as "barbarian areas" (Japanese: *banchi* 蕃地) and the adjoining "lowland areas" (Japanese: *hirachi* 平地) (Templeman 2016; see also Brown 2004, 54). Kharis Templeman (2018, 465) notes that just as these communities were being associated for the time as larger groupings of "tribes," Indigenous status also became increasingly linked to place of residency, and the township-level distinction of barbarian areas and lowland areas became more firmly set in place.

In 1937, the outbreak of the Second Sino-Japanese War followed growing tensions after the Japanese invaded Manchuria in 1931. In the wake of this conflict, Japanese policy toward Taiwan's population, including Indigenous groups, shifted to one of acculturation through imperialization campaigns (Japanese: *kōminka* 皇民化), which lasted from 1939 to 1945. During this period, Japanese authorities encouraged Indigenous persons to adopt Japanese names, speak Japanese, worship at Shinto shrines, and serve in the Japanese military (Simon 2015a, 89–90). As Taiwan became a key base for Japan's southward ambitions in the Pacific Islands and Southeast Asia, the development of heavy industry intensified. By 1941, when the United States declared war on Japan, Taiwan boasted one of the most modern industrial and transportation infrastructures in Asia outside of Japan.

During World War II, Japanese administrators conscripted Indigenous men into the military, some of whom joined voluntarily. These men were deployed as laborers and soldiers in combat zones across the Philippines, New Guinea, the Solomon Islands, and other parts of the South Pacific where they suffered devastating casualty rates. For some Indigenous men, serving in the Japanese military was seen as a badge of honor, while others endured bitter and traumatic experiences (Huang 2001). In addition, the Japanese forced Indigenous women to participate in the "comfort women" system of wartime sexual slavery. Chou Ching-yuan (2009, 120–24) documents the use of caves in Hualien County as comfort stations where young Truku women were raped and abused by Japanese soldiers.

Japanese control of Taiwan ended with Japan's defeat in World War II. After Japan's surrender in 1945, Taiwan came under the control of the ROC, led by Chiang Kai-shek's Kuomintang (KMT) government. Shortly before the takeover, the Nanjing-based KMT government officially incorporated Taiwan as a province of the ROC in accordance with the 1943 Cairo Declaration. During the early period of KMT rule, the ROC regarded Taiwan as a "border area." With the Chinese Communist Party victory in 1949, however, the KMT retreated to Taiwan, where the government had to redefine the island as the center of a "free China" and the true home of Confucian culture (Chun 1994). National discourse during this time was deeply China-centered, with the assumption that the KMT would eventually reclaim the Chinese mainland, a view still reflected today in street names like *guangfulu* 光復路 (lit., Recovery Road). Kerim Friedman (2018, 90) notes that this China-centered focus meant that Indigenous peoples during this period were "doubly marginalized," seen as not following Chinese cultural norms while their perceived ties to the land of Taiwan rendered them peripheral to the geographic center of an imagined Chinese nation.

The KMT policies toward Taiwan's Indigenous peoples were, in many ways, just as harsh and devastating as those of the Japanese colonial regime (Tai 2015, 2052). From 1949 to 1987, the KMT ruled the island under martial law and enforced a program of "White Terror" (*baise kongbu* 白色恐怖) aimed at suppressing political dissidents. This campaign oppressed both native Taiwanese (*benshengren*) and Indigenous groups. The KMT promoted a vision of Chinese nationalism that excluded alternative nationalisms, among them Indigenous national aspirations, insisting that Taiwan had only one culture and ethnicity, Han Chinese, as it emphasized the unity of Chinese on the mainland and on Taiwan (Bekhoven 2016, 211).

The KMT government continued a policy of different property rights regimes for Han Taiwanese and Indigenous peoples, the latter now referred to as "mountain compatriots" (*shandi tongbao* 山地同胞). Fearing that the remote mountaintops might become communist strongholds, similar to the situation in Cuba during the Cold War, the government restricted Indigenous peoples' access to their territories and established a permit system for entry into these areas. In 1966, the KMT reorganized Indigenous reserves, now renamed "mountain reserves" (*shandi baoliudi* 山地保留地). Under this new system, land was registered in individual names rather than as collective property of Indigenous bands, and Indigenous persons were allowed to rent or sell their land only to other Indigenous individuals, not to non-Indigenous persons (Simon 2011, 26). This reorganization effectively dismantled Indigenous collective land ownership, and it further weakened band political structures that had already been weakened by forced resettlement during the Japanese colonial era (Awi Mona and Simon 2011, 51).

As the KMT solidified its control over Taiwan, Mandarin Chinese was made the mandatory language of instruction in schools, and Indigenous languages were banned from being spoken or taught (Chen 1998, 65–66). In 1958, textbooks were standardized and Indigenous children were forced to follow the same curricula as their Han Taiwanese peers. Indigenous names were also changed to Chinese names, and Indigenous persons were required to adopt Chinese naming conventions. This practice persisted until 1995, when reforms allowed Indigenous individuals to return to using their own names. During the 1980s, textbooks often depicted Indigenous peoples in a derogatory light, portraying them as primitive and as headhunters, in contrast to the "civilized" and "superior" Chinese. From the perspective of some Indigenous groups, the shift from Japanese to Chinese rule, especially during the period of martial law, was merely a change in the identity of colonial rulers, whereby Sinicization replaced Japanization (Chiu 2000, 117).

At the same time, Indigenous peoples slowly gained a voice. In 1950, the KMT-controlled ROC government granted thirty mountain townships "local autonomy" (Simon 2010, 731). The electoral system in these townships was structured around a hierarchy of offices, including a township magistrate, council members, and village heads. Only Indigenous persons were eligible to run for office. While this system helped preserve Indigenous communities, Scott Simon (2009, 414; 2010, 731) notes that it also effectively established a system of indirect rule, whereby Indigenous municipalities were responsible for implementing policies set by government officials. In addition to granting local autonomy to some mountain townships, the ROC also created a quota for Indigenous representation in the Taiwan Provisional Assembly, reserving three seats for Indigenous groups in 1951 (Schafferer 2003, 76). In 1962, the ROC signed the International Labour Organization's *Convention Concerning the Protection and Integration of Indigenous and Other Tribal and Semi-Tribal Populations in Independent Countries* (ILO No. 107), which aimed to protect the human rights of Indigenous peoples. This move was partly driven by a desire to demonstrate to the international community that Taiwan treated Indigenous peoples better than the PRC, which had suppressed an uprising in Tibet three years earlier (Simon 2011, 17).

As calls for liberalization intensified, Chiang Kai-shek's rigid authoritarianism gradually gave way to a softer form of governance under his son, Chiang Ching-kuo. During this period, government policies and economic development models gave rise to relatively equitable income distribution, education levels rose, and a prosperous civil society developed. New political parties formed, and significant political and constitutional reforms followed, including direct elections of legislators and the president, the creation of an independent judiciary, and the establishment of a free press. In 1987, after nearly four decades, the KMT lifted martial law, and Taiwan held its first full parliamentary elections in 1992, followed by its first direct presidential election in 1996 (Lim 2011). In this environment of political transformation, the foundations of a growing Indigenous rights movement began to take root.

As Taiwan democratized in the late 1980s, Indigenous communities experienced rapid social and economic change. In 1983, only 6 percent of Indigenous persons lived outside their village communities. By 2009, that figure had risen to 39 percent (Huang and Liu 2016, 299). Today, more than half of Indigenous individuals reside in urban centers (Hale 2020). Many of these urban migrants live in industrial districts, working semi-skilled jobs in sectors such as assembly-line production, construction, truck driving, and service industries (Huang and Liu 2016, 299–300). Meanwhile, those who remain in village communities often live in marginal areas with limited arable land and few employment opportunities.

Despite recent migration to urban areas and efforts to address the trauma of colonialism, Indigenous peoples continue to lag behind Taiwan's Han Taiwanese society in key metrics, including education, employment, income, health, and life expectancy. Although Taiwan now has a twelve-year compulsory education system, nearly 60 percent of Indigenous persons in rural areas aged fifteen and above have only a junior high school education or less (Lee et al. 2011, 62; see also Lo et al. 2023, 2554). Indigenous students also experience higher dropout rates, more academic deferrals, and poorer academic outcomes than their Han Taiwanese peers (Hou and Huang 2012, 80; Nesterova 2019, 159). Unemployment rates among Indigenous peoples are one and a half to three times higher than in the rest of Taiwan society (Chiu 2005, 1), and more than 85 percent of rural Indigenous people fall into the lowest income brackets (Huang and Liu 2016, 304). Their household incomes are 40 percent lower than the national average (Munsterhjelm 2002), and employment opportunities are further threatened by the influx of foreign laborers competing for jobs (Lee et al. 2011, 62). Indigenous peoples' average life expectancy is 72.2 years,

8.2 years lower than the national average of 80.4 years (Ciwang and Hsieh 2023, 123), and their mortality rate is 14 percent higher than that of the broader population (Juan, Awerbuch-Friedlander, and Levins 2016, 3). Among the leading causes of death, rural Indigenous peoples are more likely to die from accidents or liver disease, a disparity likely linked to high alcohol consumption in these communities (Huang and Liu 2016, 305). Some scholars argue that these health disparities are a direct consequence of historical trauma stemming from colonialism, compounded by ongoing discrimination, exclusion from ancestral lands, and the criminalization of cultural practices such as hunting (Ciwang and Hsieh 2023, 136). These trends have led some researchers to conclude that "the general well-being gap between indigenes and the majority remains huge, and in some areas it is expanding" (Huang and Liu 2016, 304).

Significant threats to the preservation of Indigenous languages, lands, and cultures continue to persist. Five decades after the ROC government banned the use of Indigenous languages, many Indigenous persons under fifty years of age speak their mother tongue either not fluently or not at all (Sterk 2020a, 69). For younger generations, speaking Mandarin Chinese—the primary language of school education and mass media for nearly fifty years—has become the norm. Meanwhile, some older Indigenous persons who were educated during the Japanese occupation still speak Japanese (Tsukida 2011, 291). Indigenous lands remain under threat as well. Recent CIP regulations exclude territories located on private lands, effectively stripping Indigenous communities of their rights to these areas (Charlton, Gao, and Kuan 2017, 145–46). Legal protections of Indigenous cultural practices are ambiguous and inconsistently applied by Taiwan courts. Despite ongoing efforts to decriminalize cultural practices such as hunting, many Indigenous persons consider these activities highly risky due to the possibility of arrest (see also Simon and Awi Mona 2015, 12). In a sobering assessment of the situation, Indigenous poet Monanen Malialiaves warns that, with the domination of Chinese culture and language in Taiwan and the media, Indigenous identities may vanish and become fully Sinicized within just twenty to thirty years (quoted in Maziere 2011).

TRANSPOSITIONS, TRENCHES, AND TRANSFORMATIONS

Taiwan's colonial history spans more than four hundred years, centuries marked by the expanding reach of multiple foreign powers. Over the course of this history, Indigenous peoples endured various forms of control, including indirect rule, assimilation, settler colonialism, and other intrusions into their lives and territories. Some critiques of Taiwan's colonial experience have emphasized elements of "internal colonization" or "recolonization" (Chiu 2000; Allen 2005; Jacobs 2019). Bruce Jacobs (2019) observes, for example, that while Chinese migrants to Taiwan played a role in suppressing Indigenous peoples, they themselves were frequently subjected to foreign rule, first by the Dutch, then by the Qing, and later by the Japanese. Likewise, when the KMT government assumed control of Taiwan, it systematically oppressed not only Indigenous peoples, but also the Chinese settlers who had arrived before 1895. The concept of recolonization moves in a similar direction, emphasizing the continuity of power structures across colonial regimes. For instance, the swift transition from Japanese to ROC control in Taiwan illustrates how similar forms of domination persisted despite changes in rulers (Chiu 2000). These analyses use colonialism as a framework for understanding how external powers maintained control over local populations for their own benefit, often perpetuating layers of exploitation and oppression that overlapped different groups.

Other scholars have applied the concept of settler colonialism as they examine how various foreign powers imposed domination in Taiwan (Hatfield 2022; Hirano, Veracini, and Roy 2021; Shih 2011; Sugimoto 2018; Weitzer 1990). Hirano et al. (2021), for instance, focus on the processes of dispossession and resource extraction from Indigenous lands carried out by Dutch, Chinese, and Japanese settlers. Tomonori Sugimoto (2018) likewise examines forms of settler colonial incorporation and inheritance during the KMT period and the post-authoritarian era in which academics, particularly anthropologists, played a crucial role. Drawing on the work of theorists like Patrick Wolfe (2006) and Lorenzo Veracini (2011), these accounts highlight how external powers transformed Indigenous territories into settler homelands, often through tactics of forced relocation, confinement to reservations, and the imposition of foreign property systems. Beyond these direct acts of dispossession, settler colonialism also aimed to reshape Indigenous lives by classifying Indigenous groups, imposing settlers' languages, forcing adoption of foreign names, erasing Indigenous identities from history, and incorporating them into settler narratives of the nation. The effects of these processes have manifested in persistent disparities in health and income, as well as in reforms that undermined Indigenous institutions and practices, further entrenching colonial domination.

These accounts capture the diverse and complex colonial experience in Taiwan, where power dynamics, lived experiences, and opportunities for resistance unfolded in unique ways across time and space. A historical perspective that takes these temporal and spatial differences into account highlights the fractures and distinctions between and within the categories of colonizer, settler, and Indigenous person. For example, Chinese settlers from Fujian and Guangdong, who arrived in Taiwan in the eighteenth and nineteenth centuries to sublet land and repay the costs of their passage, often lived in nearly constant anticipation of communal violence, both from other Han Chinese migrants and from Indigenous groups (Allee 1994; Meskill 1979). Before and during the incursions of the Dutch, Chinese, and Japanese, Indigenous groups engaged in their own forms of political aggression; intervillage warfare and headhunting were universal, and alliances formed occasionally across communities (Shepherd 1993, 7). Some Indigenous groups also navigated colonial rule to their advantage, using it to gain power and wealth at the expense of rival Indigenous groups or leveraging colonial trade and resources to strengthen their positions within local power structures (Barclay 2017).

Rather than diminishing the critique of colonialism, attention to the ruptures and contradictions within colonial encounters strengthens it. It illuminates the depth of colonial impacts on various aspects of life, highlighting its differential and contradictory effects across race, ethnicity, class, gender, sexuality, and other factors. It also reveals the violence perpetuated by social scientific frameworks intent on categorizing and controlling its scope. Here, I briefly consider the colonial encounters in Taiwan in relation to the physical boundaries that separated Indigenous and non-Indigenous worlds (and marked separations within Indigenous worlds), the transformations in global order, and Taiwan's democratization. These issues are connected to indigeneity and the experiences of Indigenous peoples today.

Examining the physical boundaries constructed to manage Indigenous populations—along with the efforts to facilitate communication across these boundaries—offers valuable insights into recent initiatives, such as the ad hoc Chambers of Indigenous Courts, intended to bridge cultural and linguistic divides between Indigenous and non-Indigenous peoples, that also form another colonial instrument through which the legitimacy of Han Taiwanese control has been secured. Historically, both Qing and Japanese officials established boundary lines to separate Indigenous groups from Chinese settlers, creating a physical divide. These boundaries, however, were not always rigid, as some groups were brought across the line.

Over the course of Qing rule, the boundary separating Indigenous peoples from Chinese settlers transformed from a loosely defined, permeable frontier into a clearly demarcated, state-controlled divide. Barclay (2005, 326) identifies three phases in the development of this boundary, which extended from early Qing rule and into the early years of Japanese administration. Initially, the boundary consisted of makeshift lines and mixed settlements, often marked by stone stelae. Following a rebellion in 1721, the Qing deepened and fortified this boundary by constructing six-foot-deep trenches that stretched from Pingtung in the south to Keelung in the north. Workers piled the soil dug from the trenches on one side of the boundary line, creating mounds that, from a distance, resembled the backs of oxen. These trenches became known as "earth-oxen trenches" (*tuniugou* 土牛溝), remnants of which remain visible today in Taoyuan County (NCAO 2017). Qing officials established these trenches not only to prevent further conflicts between Chinese settlers and Indigenous peoples, but also to block bandits and fugitives from escaping into the mountains. Further, the trenches ensured that Chinese settlers, along with Indigenous groups who had assimilated into Chinese society, would not join forces with Indigenous communities beyond the trenches in resistance to Qing rule (Shepherd 1993, 16).

As previously mentioned, the Qing later introduced a legal barrier to prevent further Chinese encroachment into mountain territories. This led to the emergence of a buffer zone between the legal line and the fortified boundary demarcating mountain territories. Occupied by plains Indigenous groups, this buffer zone was a strategic part of the Qing's policy, using plains Indigenous peoples to defend against attacks by mountain Indigenous groups while also restraining Chinese settlement in the mountains. Finally, following the 1875 campaign to "open the mountains, pacify the Indigenes," and with the assimilation of plains Indigenous groups into Chinese society, the boundary consisted simply of the fortified line demarcating mountain territories.

During Japanese rule, conflicts between settlers and Indigenous peoples were driven by various factors, many of which stemmed from Indigenous efforts to defend their hunting grounds, fields, and forests from encroachment by camphor harvesters. To ensure a steady supply of camphor, the Japanese revived and expanded upon the Qing practice of boundary lines. In 1900, Japanese authorities began building an "aboriginal border," deploying Japanese and Chinese troops armed with mortars along the camphor frontier (Barclay 2017, 97–105). From 1903 to 1909, Japanese police forces were concentrated along fortified guard lines in the north, enclosing Atayal, Seediq, and Truku settlements, regions where camphor harvesting was most active. This effort involved clearing trails, constructing guardhouses, digging bunkers, building relay stations, and installing wire fencing within a two-hundred-meter-wide strip of scorched earth (Japanese: *aiyūsen* 隘勇線) intended to provide guards (many of whom were Chinese) clear visibility. In some areas the wire was electrified and land mines were planted. By 1912, the line included 756 guard stations and stretched 226 miles. Acting as a moving cordon, Japanese forces steadily advanced the guard line until 1915, pushing deeper into Indigenous territories. The strategy was to cut off trade by prohibiting crossings across the line without a permit and to relocate surrendered villages "inside the line" (Barclay 2003, 231).

In the late 1910s, Japanese authorities began to shift their approach to managing mountain Indigenous communities. Weary from the nearly incessant fighting along the guard line, the government delegated the resolution of Indigenous disputes to rural district police officers, their Indigenous wives, and local chiefs. This period, which Barclay (2017, 47) describes as a time of "native authority," saw the boundaries of state sovereignty blur along the guard line. Local chiefs and the families of Indigenous women married to Japanese police officers or to Chinese settlers played pivotal roles as intermediaries between the government and Indigenous communities. Barclay (2005; see also Barclay 2017, 120–26) highlights the significant contributions of Indigenous women in this intermediary role. Many served as "interpreters" (*tongshi* 通事), bridging cultural and linguistic divides between the Japanese officials and Indigenous peoples. These women thus acted as vital cultural brokers in the administration of Indigenous communities living in the mountains. In exchange for their cooperation, the government offered these intermediaries rewards such as stipends, medals, badges, and even trips to Taipei and Tokyo. These intermediaries, however, were never entirely dependent on the government. Barclay compares this dynamic to Richard White's (1991) concept of the "middle ground" in North America, noting that power was balanced so long as Indigenous peoples occupied a middle position between the Japanese government and Chinese bandits in the mountains. This delicate balance unraveled with rising tensions that culminated in the Musha Incident of 1930, bringing the period of "native authority" to an end.

The creation of physical boundaries across the landscape was a notable feature of the colonial encounter in Taiwan. Structures like earth-oxen trenches and electrified fences were designed not only to restrict the movement of Indigenous peoples and prevent them from reclaiming their territories, but also to reinforce state security by limiting interactions between settlers and Indigenous peoples and among Indigenous groups. Amid the tensions and conflicts that emerged along these boundary lines, intermediaries played a crucial role, serving as bridges for communication and negotiation between the state, settlers, and Indigenous peoples.

The divides between Indigenous and non-Indigenous peoples that the ad hoc Chambers of Indigenous Courts aim to manage and bridge today have their roots in these logics of separation and integration of Indigenous peoples. As in earlier conflicts along the boundary line, intermediaries played a pivotal role in the specialized Indigenous court units. Indigenous elders and community members, many of whom were, once again, women, served as key figures in these processes, working alongside Han Taiwanese lawyers, experts, and other legal professionals. Together, they strove to foster understanding across cultural and linguistic divides in disputes over Indigenous practices and lands.

The historical conditions that ultimately led to the specialized Indigenous units are complex, but two key developments in the late twentieth century arguably paved the way for new understandings of indigeneity and Indigenous peoples' rights that eventually contributed to the establishment of the units. First, in 1971, the UN General Assembly dismissed "the representatives of Chiang Kai-shek" as representative of the "State of China" (United Nations 1971).[1] In the wake of this decision, many countries severed diplomatic ties with the ROC (Su 2006, 51). As mentioned earlier, the ROC now maintains official diplomatic relations with only 11 of the 193 United Nations member states, along with the Holy See. This change left Taiwan in an ambiguous position: While the ROC was a state-like entity maintaining de facto control over Taiwan and its surrounding islands, pressure from the PRC prevented it from seeking recognition as "Taiwan" and blocked other states from considering that possibility (deLisle 2011, 2019).[2] In this context, compliance with international law and norms has provided an opportunity for Taiwan to affirm its place on the world platform. Promoting international human rights, including the rights of Indigenous peoples, became an important avenue through which Taiwan sought to strengthen its international standing and legitimacy (Gao, Charlton, and Takahashi 2016, 69).

Second, Taiwan's democratization in the 1980s coincided with the rise of a global Indigenous rights movement. Inspired by this international movement, and emboldened by new possibilities for expression and organization under democracy, activists launched an Indigenous rights movement focused on advocating a pan-Indigenous identity and international human rights (Allio 1998). Key early initiatives included the creation of publications like *Mountain Greenery* (*gaoshanqing* 高山青), an underground newspaper run by Indigenous students at National Taiwan University in 1983, and the founding of organizations such as the Alliance of Taiwan Aborigines in 1984. These early efforts to secure Indigenous rights were primarily driven by urban interest groups and focused on working within the state structure. Over time, state laws and policies began to strengthen formal recognition for Indigenous peoples while increasingly engaging with international legal frameworks and institutions.

Several significant developments in the 1990s and beyond marked important strides in recognizing Indigenous peoples and their rights. In 1994, Indigenous activists successfully lobbied lawmakers to change their legal status to "Indigenous" in constitutional revisions. The Executive Yuan established the Council of Aboriginal Affairs in 1996, a ministerial-level body responsible for overseeing Indigenous affairs. In 2005, the Legislative Yuan passed the Indigenous Peoples Basic Law, a comprehensive piece of legislation that outlined numerous rights for Indigenous peoples, predating the United Nations Declaration on the Rights of Indigenous Peoples (UNDRIP) by two years. Further steps were taken in 2009 when the Legislative Yuan incorporated the International Covenant on Civil and Political Rights (ICCPR) and the International Covenant on Economic, Social and Cultural Rights (ICESCR) into Taiwan's domestic law. In 2013, the Judicial Yuan established ad hoc Chambers of Indigenous Courts in the national courts. In 2016, President Tsai Ing-wen issued a formal apology on behalf of the ROC government to Taiwan's Indigenous peoples. Her administration also created the Presidential Office Indigenous Historical Justice and Transitional Justice Committee (*zongtongfu yuanzhuminzu lishi zhengyi yu zhuanxing zhengyi weiyuanhui* 總統府原住民族歷史正義與轉型正義委員會), tasked with addressing Taiwan's history of discrimination and erasure of Indigenous identities. During this period, Indigenous representatives also began to participate in the UN Permanent Forum on Indigenous Issues, engaging in what Ronald Niezen (2003b) describes as "global indigenism" (see Simon 2016).

The UN's dismissal of Chiang Kai-shek's representatives and the country's transition to democracy created both an opening and, in respects, an incentive for the ROC to embrace international norms and Indigenous peoples' identities. As Taiwan distanced itself from the notion of an idealized China, Indigenous rights came to symbolize an independent Taiwan, shaping the state's identity and countering the PRC's claims that Taiwan is "part of China" (Schubert 2016; Ku 2012). In this context, new legal frameworks and institutions not only served to bolster Taiwan's global position, but also helped construct a distinct Taiwanese identity. Despite this shift, the ROC government has maintained tight control over the definition of *Indigenous*, including determining who legally qualifies as an Indigenous person.

LEGALITIES OF INDIGENOUS STATUS IN TAIWAN

To determine who qualifies as "Indigenous" under ROC law, we must turn to the 2001 Status Act for Indigenous Peoples (Status Act) and the 2005 Indigenous Peoples Basic Law. These laws provide different approaches for defining "Indigenous" status, and they reveal the enduring influence of colonial categories and frameworks in contemporary ROC legal definitions.

The Status Act, passed in 2001, is the official law regulating Indigenous status in Taiwan. Article 2 of the act provides the following definition of *Indigenous people*:

> The term "Indigenous people" herein includes native Indigenous peoples of the mountain and plain-land regions. Status recognition, unless otherwise herein provided, is as provided in the following:
>
> - Mountain Indigenous peoples: permanent residents of the mountain administrative zone before the recovery of Taiwan, moreover census registration records show individual or an immediate kin of individual is of Indigenous peoples descent.
> - Plain-land Indigenous peoples: permanent residents of the plain-land administrative zone before the recovery of Taiwan, moreover census registration records show individual or an immediate kin of individual is of Indigenous peoples descent. Individual is registered as a plain-land Indigenous peoples in the village (town, city, district) administration office.

The phrase "recovery of Taiwan" refers to the transfer of Taiwan from Japan to the ROC at the end of World War II in 1945 (Gao 2014, 8n6). As such, the Status Act situates Indigenous peoples within the historical context of Japanese rule and the early modern period. Additionally, it preserves earlier Japanese classifications, distinguishing between Indigenous peoples living in "barbarian areas" and those in "lowland areas" by categorizing them as "Mountain Indigenous peoples" and "Plain-land Indigenous peoples."

The 2005 Basic Law offers an alternative framework for defining Indigenous peoples. Initial versions of Article 2.1 linked the concept of "Indigenous peoples" to territory, performance, difference, and self-identity:

> The term "Indigenous Peoples" means peoples, under the State's jurisdiction, who usually live within (or maintain attachments to) geographically distinct ancestral territories; who tend to maintain distinct social, economic, and political institutions within their territories; who typically aspire to remain distinct culturally, geographically and institutionally rather than assimilate fully into national society; and who self-identify as Indigenous Peoples.

Early versions of Article 2.2 also rehearsed distinctions between "barbarian" and "lowland" Indigenous groups by defining *Indigenous Persons* as "nationals who are registered either as Mountain Region Indigenous Peoples or as Plain Region Indigenous Peoples and thereby obtain legal Indigenous status, being evidenced by the household registration records of aforesaid Indigenous Persons" (Tagliarino 2017, appendix n24).

Subsequent amendments to the Basic Law eliminated references to these categories and emphasized tradition, self-identity, and approval by the CIP. In its current formulation, Article 2.1 defines *Indigenous peoples* as follows:

> Indigenous peoples: refer to the traditional peoples who have inhibited [*sic*] in Taiwan and are subject to the state's jurisdiction, including Amis tribe, Atayal tribe, Paiwan tribe, Bunun tribe, Puyuma tribe, Rukai tribe, Tsou tribe, Saisiyat tribe, Yami tribe, Tsao tribe, Kavalan tribe, Taroko tribe and any other tribes who regard themselves as Indigenous peoples and obtain the approval of the central indigenous authority upon application.

Article 2.2 likewise defines *Indigenous persons* as including "any individual who is a member of any of indigenous peoples."

Scholars have noted that the definitions of *Indigenous peoples* in the Status Act and Basic Law create difficulties that demonstrate continued colonization of Indigenous communities (Bekhoven 2018, 216–17). First, the ROC government unilaterally determines the criteria for who qualifies as Indigenous, imposing its view through the application of legal categories. Additionally, beyond continuing to rely on a classification system that no longer serves any purpose, there is a lack of clarity regarding the specific criteria and principles used to determine Indigenous status. No laws, regulations, or internal documents exist to define how "Indigenous peoples" should be recognized. Rather, the CIP evaluates petitions on the basis of precedents set during earlier colonial periods, without any clear regulatory framework. Scott Simon (2023b, 14) observes that by defining Indigenous peoples as "traditional" communities subject to the "central indigenous authority," the ROC engages in a "legalistic sleight of hand" that reinforces state control over Indigenous institutions and populations while simultaneously promising autonomy and self-determination.

Through the efforts of Indigenous activists and their lobbying activities in the name rectification movement, the number of formally recognized Indigenous groups in Taiwan has expanded from the initial nine mountain-based peoples to sixteen groups today. These groups are primarily concentrated in the mountainous central and eastern regions of the island, as well as on the outer island of Orchid Island. They include the Amis (called Pangcah in Hualien), Bunun, Hla'alua, Kanakanavu, Kavalan, Paiwan, Pinuyumayan, Rukai, Saisiyat, Sakizaya, Seediq, Tao, Tayan (also called Atayal), Thao, Truku, and Tsou. The ROC government distinguishes these groups from plains-dwelling Indigenous peoples, or *pingpuzu*, who primarily reside on the western side of the island. *Pingpuzu* groups include the Babuza, Basay, Hoanya, Ketagalan, Luilang, Makatao, Pazeh/Kaxabu, Papora, Qauqaut, Siraya, Taivoan, Toakas, and Trobiawan. As mentioned earlier, a recent decision by the Taiwan Constitutional Court has opened a path for *pingpuzu* recognition, but it left the determination of group recognition to the CIP. To date, no *pingpuzu* group has received official Indigenous status, although the Tainan County government has recognized the Siraya as Indigenous. County governments lack authority, however, to grant *pingpuzu* groups the rights and privileges associated with official Indigenous status under national law.

Only individuals belonging to the sixteen state-recognized Indigenous groups are eligible for Indigenous status. Article 2 of the Status Act stipulates that an individual's Indigenous status is determined on the basis of a household registration record. This record must indicate that the individual is of Indigenous descent or that their parents or other immediate kin are registered as Indigenous persons (Bekhoven 2016, 220). Under this system, Indigenous communities do not have control over who is granted Indigenous status; instead, it is determined by historical records dating back to the Japanese period, when authorities, as part of a broader program to control the island's population, marked individuals as Indigenous on census documents.

The household registration system presents several issues of concern (Bekhoven 2016, 220). First, it assumes the reliable maintenance of records across a regime change that occurred over seventy years ago. It also raises the question of whether Indigenous persons at the time willingly accepted or sought to avoid being classified as Indigenous by Japanese authorities. Additionally, the system relied on paternal lineage to determine Indigenous status, excluding individuals whose mothers were Indigenous. Another flaw is its assumption that plains-dwelling peoples had fully assimilated into Chinese society and were therefore no longer Indigenous. Further, the registration system has created tensions within ROC state law. The Status Act establishes one standard based on this registration system, while the Basic Law offers a different standard rooted in self-identification. The Legislative Yuan has not amended the Status Act to align it with the Basic Law, leaving it unclear whether the two documents present different standards or whether the Status Act outlines a specific test under the Basic Law.

In 2022, the Taiwan Constitutional Court introduced new questions into determinations of Indigenous status in cases of mixed marriages.[3] Article 4 of the Status Act grants Indigenous status to individuals with only one Indigenous parent, based strictly on surname (Lin 2022). The 2022 case involved a young girl with the surname *Wu* whose father was Han Taiwanese and whose mother was Truku. When her father attempted to register her Indigenous status, the local government rejected the request because she used her father's Chinese surname rather than her mother's Indigenous name. The Constitutional Court concluded that this provision violated the ROC Constitution, in that it obstructed her equal access to claim an Indigenous identity based on gender. The Court argued that, in practice, children often take their father's surname, meaning that children with an Indigenous father could obtain Indigenous status, while those with an Indigenous mother could not. The CIP is presently drafting legislation to address the Court's concerns.

The ROC government has thus retained a firm grip on the criteria by which groups and individuals are recognized as Indigenous. This power imbalance mirrors earlier forms of colonial control over Indigenous affairs and lands. The legal framework surrounding Indigenous status continues to uphold classification systems rooted in past practices of Indigenous subjugation. Decisions regarding the status of Indigenous groups rely on ambiguous standards and apply precedents set during earlier periods that defined who was authentically "Indigenous." Similarly, the determination of Indigenous status for individuals remains tied to a problematic household registration system. More broadly, ambiguities remain in the legal definitions of what it means to be "Indigenous."

INDIGENEITIES: FROM GLOBAL TO LOCAL

The *Oxford English Dictionary* defines *Indigenous* as "born or originating in a particular place; *spec.* (now often with capital initial) designating a people or group inhabiting a place before the arrival of (European) settlers or colonizers" (OED 2022). This definition raises as many questions as it answers. What does "originating in" mean? What are the expectations of authenticity? How can one prove that one is legitimately Indigenous? The definition also seems to presume an encounter with European colonization, but what about encounters with non-European powers? These questions highlight how the concept of indigeneity is shaped by various factors, including historical context, notions of race and ethnicity, political activism, and personal or collective self-definition.

Scholars of Indigenous studies have interrogated indigeneity as a complex and dynamic concept, examining the ways it has been defined, deployed, and transformed across different histories and experiences of colonization, dispossession, and resistance. Some scholars have emphasized Indigenous peoples' relational ties to land and place, whereby land constitutes a source of knowledge and life that sustains Indigenous thought and identity (L. B. Simpson 2014). Others have stressed the political dimensions of Indigenous identity grounded in assertions of sovereignty and self-governance, thinking critically about the politics of recognition and insisting on Indigenous political orders (Coulthard 2014; A. Simpson 2014). Some have emphasized the importance of Indigenous knowledge production and self-determination in defining Indigenous identity through centering Indigenous voices and methods (Smith 1999), while others have shown how Indigenous cosmologies may incorporate fluid definitions of who qualifies as Indigenous, critiquing reductive logics, like blood quantum, that undermine expansive identity claims (Kauanui 2008). Some scholars, in particular some Native feminist theorists, have highlighted the entanglements of indigeneity with interconnected systems of colonialism, heteropatriarchy, and racism that serve settler interests (Arvin 2019; Rifkin 2014). Others have observed how indigeneity has been deeply shaped by colonial encounters, emerging in bureaucratic, international, and legal forums as a category to name Indigenous peoples (Simon 2012b). Finally, scholars have emphasized how the global dimensions of indigeneity serve as a source of identity through shared experiences of suffering (Marsden 1994; Niezen 2003b).

These approaches and others indicate how indigeneity sits within a contested web of concepts and understandings of Indigenous identity, and part of this book is a search for what it means to be Indigenous in the Taiwan context. This includes the ways it has been defined by state laws and policies and how these definitions perpetuate structures and processes of colonialism through their applications in court proceedings, but it also includes articulations by individuals at the local level and how local processes are connected to an emerging global Indigenous politics that is not always or necessarily bound to how the state, courts, or other legal apparatuses define them. To this end, I trace the concept of indigeneity from global orders to local forms of self-identification in Taiwan.

At the global level, states have responded to the concept of indigeneity in different ways. Some states, such as China, India, Indonesia, and Myanmar, have rejected the idea of indigeneity within their borders, while others, including Brazil, the Philippines, and Taiwan, have inscribed it in their constitutional documents. Over the years, various international frameworks have been proposed to define the criteria for identifying Indigenous peoples. None of these, however, can claim universal acceptance.

In 1972, UN special rapporteur José R. Martínez Cobo provided an oft-cited definition of *Indigenous peoples* grounded in relational, historical, and political factors:

> Indigenous populations are composed of the existing descendants of the peoples who inhabited the present territory of a country wholly or partially at the time when persons of a different culture or ethnic origin arrived there from other parts of the world, overcame them, by conquest, settlement or other means, reduced them to a non-dominant or colonial condition; who today live more in conformity with their particular social, economic and cultural customs and traditions than with the institutions of the country of which they now form part, under a state structure which incorporates mainly national, social and cultural characteristics of other segments of the population which are predominant. (Cobo 1972)

In his final report on the problem of discrimination against Indigenous peoples, Cobo emphasized that Indigenous peoples share "a historical continuity with pre-invasion and pre-colonial societies that developed on their territories" (Cobo 1986). This definition appears to apply only to a limited group of Indigenous peoples, mostly in the Americas, Australia, and the Pacific (Van De Fliert 1994, 4).

In 1986, the UN Working Group on Indigenous Peoples broadened the definition of *Indigenous peoples* to add a line encapsulating the principle of self-identification, stating that "any individual who identified himself or herself as Indigenous and was accepted by the group or the community as one of its members was to be regarded as an Indigenous person" (Sandberg McGuinne 2014).

In 1989, the International Labour Organization's *Convention Concerning Indigenous and Tribal Peoples in Independent Countries* (ILO No. 169) provided a broad definition of indigeneity. It described Indigenous peoples as those "whose social, cultural and economic conditions distinguish them from other sections of the national community, and whose status is regulated wholly or partially by their own customs or traditions or by special laws or regulations" and "who are regarded as indigenous on account of their descent from the populations which inhabited the country, or a geographical region to which the country belongs, at the time of conquest or colonization."[4]

The World Bank, a global multilateral development institution, does not define the term *Indigenous*. Instead, in Operational Directive 4.20, it offers an operational definition based on the presence of certain characteristics, which may vary in degree:

> Indigenous peoples can be identified in particular geographical areas by the presence in varying degrees of the following characteristics: (a) close attachment to ancestral territories and to the natural resources in these areas; (b) self-identification and identification by others as members of a distinct cultural group; (c) an indigenous language, often different from the national language; (d) presence of customary social and political institutions; and (e) primarily subsistence-oriented production. (World Bank 2003)

The 2007 UNDRIP provides the most recent description of Indigenous peoples. Rather than offering a specific definition, Article 33 emphasizes the importance of self-identification, asserting that Indigenous peoples themselves determine their own identity as Indigenous:

1. Indigenous peoples have the right to determine their own identity or membership in accordance with their customs and traditions. This does not impair the rights of Indigenous individuals to obtain citizenship of the States in which they live.
2. Indigenous peoples have the right to determine the structures and to select the membership of their institutions in accordance with their own procedures.

Self-identification is, therefore, the prevailing conceptual framework for understanding indigeneity at the global level.

Some scholars of indigeneity emphasize how Indigenous peoples share common experiences of oppression and marginalization. David Marsden (1994, 41) writes, "Indigenous peoples are marginal peoples, dispossessed or threatened minorities." Ronald Niezen (2003b, 13) similarly observes, "A common experience of those who identify themselves as Indigenous ... is a sense of illegitimate, meaningless, and dishonorable suffering," a shared experience of "collective suffering." While indigeneity is a self-defined category, it is not necessarily defined by individuals, but rather by the collective consent of the global Indigenous community. Framing indigeneity as a fixed category based on shared suffering, however, risks reintroducing old problems as it de-emphasizes differences across contexts. It seems that rather than a single category, there exists a range of "Indigenous" persons across the globe (Merlan 2009). Furthermore, the connections between global Indigenous identity and domestic policymaking are complex and not always clear. National legal systems can present significant legal hurdles for advancing Indigenous interests (see Echo-Hawk 2010). As noted earlier, the ROC government has maintained exclusive control over Indigenous status and has excluded certain groups through an arbitrary classificatory scheme. In this regard, Scott Simon (2012b, 227) suggests that the term *Indigenous* might be understood not as an ethnic category, but as a legal classification.

Defining Indigenous peoples at the global level has been a complex process, and locally, within Indigenous communities, it can also be complicated. In July 2015, I attended a ceremony in Taitung celebrating the release of four Pinuyumayan men from police custody (figure 6). The ceremony took place on the lawn of the Paposong community center, which incidentally was located directly across the street from my childhood home. The men arrived wearing white shirts and colorful floral headdresses, while young Pinuyumayan women, dressed in customary attire, carried trays of betel nuts and distributed bottles of water to the guests. Members of the audience wore vests adorned with Pinuyumayan iconography, some also donning floral headpieces. It was a hot day, and organizers had set up a tent for shade, with tables and chairs underneath. Speeches were delivered as the men stood at the head of the table, and at the conclusion of the ceremony the crowd cheered and raised a toast to their release.

The background to the event was that, months earlier, the four men had applied for permission to hunt in preparation for the Mangayaw, or Hunting Festival. This three-day festival is the most important event of the year for the Pinuyumayan, comparable in significance to Lunar New Year for the Han

FIGURE 6. Pinuyumayan hunters celebrating their release from arrest, 2015.

Taiwanese. It serves as a key annual ritual for passing down ancestral knowledge and involves taking young men from the village into the mountains to hunt. As required by ROC hunting regulations at the time, the men submitted application forms that included their names, addresses, and a description of the activities they planned to undertake. According to community members' accounts, the community was performing a ceremony to prepare the men for the hunt when police raided the event. Officers read aloud the men's names from their hunting applications and arrested them, accusing them of possessing unregistered firearms and ammunition. Media accounts later suggested that the men were actively hunting at the time of their arrest (Hsiao 2015). Regardless, the community was outraged, feeling they had complied with the law only to be persecuted for engaging in their cultural practices.

Toward the end of the celebration, a Pinuyumayan elder pulled me aside. He arranged two plastic chairs, and we sat down in the shade of a tree. Expressing his frustration with the situation and its common occurrence, he said, "There is a technical term for this in English: 'Fucking bullshit.'"[5] We sat for long time, discussing the men's arrest and other issues facing the

Pinuyumayan people. I began to ask questions about Pinuyumayan cultural and ritual practice, and he became visibly annoyed. "You talk too much about Indigenous, Puyuma, Paiwan," he said. "You should be talking about humans; we are all humans. Why draw lines?"[6] To him, indigeneity and the ethnic categories tied to it were arbitrary classifications imposed by outsiders, specifically policymakers and anthropologists. These kinds of labels, in his view, distracted from a more vital truth that we, as human beings, were connected by a common humanity.[7] He believed that such constructed notions of ethnic and racial difference were at the heart of the men's arbitrary arrest and, more broadly, central to the subjugation of Indigenous peoples.

While some Indigenous persons were ambivalent about the concept of indigeneity and its underlying intentions, others actively participated in constructing Indigenous ethnic categories. They regarded these identities as potent sources of empowerment and meaning, even as the boundaries of group distinctions remained subject to contestation. The complexities surrounding the definition of the Truku ethnic group offer an example. Approximately thirty thousand Truku people live across four townships in Hualien. Like the broader concept of indigeneity, the ethnic label *Truku* was both complex and contentious, with roots tracing back to earlier Japanese classifications. When the Japanese colonized Taiwan, administrators created a system that categorized Indigenous peoples on the basis of social characteristics. At the turn of the twentieth century, Japanese scholars identified the "Atayal" as a distinct ethnic group, and by 1911, Japanese administrators officially adopted the term. Because the group was widespread and exhibited significant variation, Japanese scholars proposed dividing them into three subgroups: Səqoleq, Tsəʔoleʔ, and Sədeq. The Səqoleq and Tsəʔoleʔ referred to themselves as the Atayal, Tayal, or Tayen, which in their local language meant "human," "true human," or "people of the same tribe" (Wang 2008, 7–8). The Sədeq, whose name also means "human" in their local language, were further subdivided into west and east groups.[8]

This system of classification became the dominant way of understanding the Atayal. Later, scholars attempted to refine the system by combining principles of place of origin and political administration, creating a more complex framework of social divisions (Masau Mona 1984, 8–9). These principles, however, did not correspond to one another, resulting in a confused system in which, at times, lower-level subdivisions encompassed higher-level categories (Wang 2008, 9). The "Atayal" ethnic group was thus a construct shaped by Japanese efforts to categorize and manage Indigenous peoples. It resulted in a shifting category built around criteria that did not correspond with the dynamic social divisions in local communities (Wang 2008, 10).

In 1999, the east Seediq group launched the Truku Name Rectification Campaign (*tailugezu zhengming yundong* 太魯閣族正名運動) to separate themselves from the *Atayal* classification (Wang 2008, 12). The campaign involved many groups and institutions, including the local Presbyterian church, the Truku Cultural Development Association, the Truku Economic Affairs Association, Wanrung Work Station, and the Association for the Promotion of the Truku Name Rectification. Indigenous activists situated the name rectification effort within the sphere of Taiwan politics, making it part of the 2003 election for Hualien County head. This political positioning, however, shifted the campaign's focus toward what would be acceptable to Han Taiwanese society, rather than what was most important to the local communities themselves (Wang 2008, 12–13).

In 2004, activists succeeded in securing ratification of the name *Truku* with the Executive Yuan. This did not, however, settle the debate. The Truku Economic Affairs Association, composed of teachers and school officials, argued that the name should be *Seediq* rather than *Truku*. They also contended that the group should include the west Seediq in Nantou County. One representative questioned, "How can a tribe with the same culture, language and way of life be split in two? It makes no sense" (Ko 2004). Other members of the association claimed that the decision was politically motivated rather than ethnically driven. As one member stated, "It's a bid to woo the 13,000 Truku that live in Hualien County. They don't really care what the 7,000 Seediq in Nantou County think.... It is the saddest day in the history of the tribe" (Ko 2004).

The Truku Presbyterian Church disagreed, arguing that "Truku" was the correct name for the group. One church representative stated,

> It's a sacred moment, and it is for us the highest honor ... [and] today we are proud to call ourselves Truku.... We'll continue to negotiate with our brothers, the Sedeq in Nantou, and work toward holding a peace ceremony with them in the near future. (Ko 2004)

The name dispute created significant divisions in local communities as people debated origin stories, group names, customs, and historical memories in an effort to articulate the ethnic category of Truku (Wang 2008, 13–21). Today, the concept of Truku remains an uncertain category. One of my Truku collaborators, gesturing toward the distant mountains, remarked, "Maybe we are Truku. Our ancestors are from over there, in the mountains.

Maybe we have close relations to them." His words highlighted the persistent ambiguities surrounding the community's identity and its distinction from the neighboring Seediq.

Following the success of the Truku Name Rectification Campaign, activists began to revive "Truku culture" by reclaiming cultural practices and rituals. Rituals involving Gaya and Utux (ancestral spirits) soon became a field in which to congregate and rediscover their cultural heritage. The Truku Presbyterian Church, however, viewed ancestral worship as incompatible with Christian teaching and sought to suppress these practices. What was a fertile ground for cultural rediscovery quickly began to erode under the church's pressure (Wang 2008, 29–31).

While the Presbyterian church sought to limit ancestral worship, developments ten years later revealed a more complicated story. During my field research, a Truku elder from Dowmung was named as a defendant in a case over the construction of a hunting lodge, which I will discuss in detail later. This elder served as a deacon in the local Presbyterian church while continuing to engage in ancestral worship. In Dowmung, Christian beliefs and Truku cultural practice intermingled. For example, the local Presbyterian minister referred to Jesus Christ as a "hunter" (*lieren* 獵人) in her weekly messages, linking the Truku cultural practice of wildlife hunting to "hunting" for human souls, a cultural adaptation to Christ's call for his followers to be "fishers" of men. These activities suggested that what has emerged as "Truku culture" is richly complex.

CONCLUSION

The meaning of *Indigenous* and the term's mobilizations in the Taiwan context have resulted from many efforts to articulate the relationship between land, Indigenous peoples, and settler populations. These efforts have involved activities of classification, interpretation, and narration refracted through colonial categories, governance structures, global-order realignments, political regime changes, Indigenous movements, local politics, and personal self-identification. At times, the drive to define *indigeneity* focused on highlighting the distinctiveness of Indigenous peoples, sometimes identifying an incommensurability between Indigenous lifeways and those of the colonizing society. At other times, such differences were blurred to serve particular political or social agendas.

Indigenous identity is central to the creation and operation of the ad hoc Chambers of Indigenous Courts. The Judicial Yuan established the specialized units with the hope that they would help articulate the meaning of indigeneity in ROC law, build knowledge about Indigenous peoples' cultures and circumstances, and bridge divides between the state and Indigenous communities—and do so in a manner that was sensitive to the needs and desires of Indigenous peoples after centuries of dispossession, marginalization, and erosion of their cultures, languages, and lands. As we will see in the chapters to come, judges and other legal actors in the units often relied on state laws defining *indigeneity*, interpreting these laws through the lens of state legal process and Han Taiwanese understandings of what it meant to be Indigenous. Some of these actors were interested in exploring new ways of integrating Indigenous perspectives and values into legal proceedings, while others were less inclined to do so. Expectations about indigeneity and what counted as "authentically" Indigenous could also become unsettled. Indigenous claimants, defendants, elders, witnesses, interpreters, and audience members sometimes challenged dominant assumptions and narratives about Indigenous identities, their relationships to land, and their cultural practices. Through multifaceted situational and strategic performances of indigeneity, they pushed judges and other legal actors to recognize their identities as Indigenous persons and to secure their rights. In the process, they could move court proceedings in directions that advanced their own interests and aspirations.

TWO

Orders in the Court

LAW IS A KEY FEATURE of discourse and practice in the ad hoc Chambers of Indigenous Courts. Debates and discussions in the specialized units often focused on ROC laws and legal procedures, but local actors also insisted on the recognition and application of alternative orders of law and knowledge. Cases involving Indigenous cultural practices and relationships to land sat at the intersection of multiple legal orders, including local Indigenous laws, national statutes and regulations, international treaty and customary laws, and Buddhist and Christian religious precepts (see also Simon and Awi Mona 2015). This chapter examines the various legal and normative orders circulating in and around disputes in the ad hoc chambers and the processes used to make these orders authoritative, intelligible, and relevant in specific cases and in everyday life.

The coexistence of multiple legal and normative orders, some commonly recognized as "law" and others not, creates a situation of legal pluralism (see Merry 1988). This pluralism can be understood in two ways: empirical legal pluralism, or the existence of self-contained parallel systems of norms, and official or formal legal pluralism, in which local law is recognized as equal to state law (Hoekema 2017). In Taiwan, local Indigenous laws generally exist as normative orders in parallel to the state system, without formal recognition from the state, suggesting a situation of empirical legal pluralism. The picture, though, is more complicated than that. The Judicial Yuan now encourages judges to find strategies for incorporating Indigenous perspectives into the application of state laws. Indigenous communities have also worked to codify their local laws in ways that resemble state law. Additionally, the ROC has incorporated international human rights instruments, some of which protect Indigenous peoples' cultures and lands, into its domestic law, giving them the status of state law. These developments and others suggest that while the present legal situation of Indigenous peoples in Taiwan is one of empirical legal pluralism, there are signs of movement toward formal legal pluralism in certain arenas as well as the possible future creation of autonomous Indigenous courts.

Understanding the different legal and normative orders circulating in and around disputes in the ad hoc chambers is important, not only because these orders regulate daily life in Indigenous communities, but also because conflicts among these orders sometimes give rise to disputes that find their way into the specialized units. A key function of the units was to bridge divides between these different legal orders through training for judges and creating a space where Indigenous voices and perspectives could be heard. The specialized units engaged in boundary-spanning activities through navigating the ambiguities of legal pluralism, a process that had the potential to open new spaces for Indigenous recognition even as it forced Indigenous peoples to seek legitimacy through state norms and the national court system. In the following discussion, I will examine these legal and normative orders in detail, combining legal analysis with ethnographic examples representing how individuals and communities experienced law in their daily lives. By approaching law as something embedded in social relations in specific places and moments, I aim to offer a textured understanding of how law works in people's lives. This perspective emphasizes the significance of "untidy" moments often overlooked in formal approaches to law, focusing on the applications, interpretations, and negotiations through which law finds its meaning and relevance in disputes and in life.

I begin by considering the importance of local law in Taiwan's Indigenous communities, with a particular focus on the Truku people. I describe the significance of Gaya in the daily lives of Dowmung community members and examine recent efforts to "codify" Gaya. Next, I turn to the regime of ROC laws designed to protect Indigenous peoples, their cultures, and their lands. I interweave ethnographic examples describing how Indigenous individuals have experienced state laws and their transformations over time. These examples include a Pinuyumayan elder's experiences during Taiwan's transition to ROC rule, hunting muntjac deer in the mountains with Bunun men, and the reactions of Indigenous demonstrators to President Tsai's apology to Indigenous peoples. Finally, I examine international human rights protections for Indigenous peoples, and how state actors in Taiwan have worked to integrate these international norms into ROC laws and legal processes. In this discussion, I share my experience of working with Han Taiwanese lawyers to develop legal arguments based on human rights norms to support Indigenous peoples' claims.

LOCAL ORDER: GAYA AND HUNTING

In the mountains west of Hualien City, much of daily life in Dowmung is organized around Gaya. Gaya is the sacred Truku law, passed down orally from the ancestors, that governs relationships between people (e.g., property rights, reciprocity, sexuality, sharing meat and alcohol) as well as between people and animals (e.g., trapping and hunting). Elusive of precise definition, Gaya is the conceptual way of life taught by the ancestors, setting out codes of conduct and moral standards. It embodies values of respect, reciprocity, and social obligation, and, to an extent, determines property relations (see also Simon 2015b, 699; Simon and Awi Mona 2015, 6). When speaking Mandarin Chinese, members of Dowmung often described Gaya as *fa* or "law," but many Truku speakers also used the term to refer to "culture" (Simon 2023b, 4). In many ways, Gaya encapsulates a holistic way of life for the Truku (Simon 2012a, 173). Fernando Pecoraro, a Catholic priest who developed a Truku-French dictionary, captured this holistic feature of Gaya in the following way: "Effectively, GAYA is at the center of the life of the Taroko (Truku), the source, criteria and the judge of their entire personal or social life from birth to death—and after! GAYA is certainly the most sacred reality for the Taroko" (Pecoraro 1977, 70, quoted in Simon 2012a, 173).

Interpretations of Gaya norms can vary across Gaya groups. A Gaya group typically consists of one or two close relatives, along with other distant relatives or marriage affinities. Members of the group worship, farm, and follow taboos together, sharing kinship bonds, economic ties, and territories. Gaya affects the entire group, with the ancestors demanding respect from their descendants and meting out punishments not only to individuals but to other members of the Gaya group. Enforcement of Gaya occurs in this life rather than in the afterlife. As a result, Dowmung hunters who violate Gaya risk misfortune, such as falling off a mountain or being bitten by a poisonous snake, while those who abide by Gaya are rewarded with successful hunts (see also Simon 2015b, 699; Wang 2008, 28). Therefore, successful hunting is a sign of moral righteousness in and of the community. Penance for violations depends on the nature of the offense and its severity, and may involve slaughtering a chicken, duck, or pig and offering the blood to the ancestors.

Hunting is an integral part of Truku cultural identity and an inseparable aspect of Gaya ethics. In Dowmung, during my field research, only six or seven families were actively engaged in wildlife hunting, with a total of about twenty-five hunters. While hunting was normatively a men's activity due to the divisions of labor in Truku society (Simon 2013), women also played important roles in hunting-related activities, such as serving as porters. Dowmung hunters targeted a variety of game in the mountains, including boar, serow, sambar, muntjac, flying squirrel, and macaque. Gaya provided explicit guidelines concerning the treatment of game animals (*Samat*) and set clear rules for what constituted appropriate and prohibited hunting practices. These included taboos against speaking about bad news or engaging in inappropriate behavior, killing pregnant animals, hunting during periods of mourning or celebration, overhunting, wasting meat or other natural resources, failing to retrieve traps, and stealing the game of other hunters, among others. Sharing was a central ethic in hunting; if a family did not hunt, others were expected to share meat with them. Each family unit had its own hunting grounds, although they regularly granted permission for others to hunt on their land. Dowmung hunters were deeply attuned to the animals on their hunting grounds, taking care to maintain healthy animal populations.

Gaya constituted a vibrant and adaptive repertoire of customs, morals, rituals, and taboos that governed daily life in Dowmung. It was not, however, the only source of normativity. Gaya interacted with ROC laws and regulations surrounding hunting. Police patrolled the mountains to search for poachers, prosecutors aggressively pursued criminal charges against hunters, and Han Taiwanese judges wielded significant power in interpreting the scope of hunting rights and practices. Additionally, Gaya intersected with Christian precepts that sometimes pushed against reclamation of Truku ancestral practices (Wang 2008, 29–31) but, at other times, incorporated elements of Christianity, such as referring to the Ten Commandments as the "ten Gaya" (Simon 2013, 224). Gaya also interacted with Buddhist principles embedded in Taiwan's animal rights movement, which prohibited the taking of life, as well as international human rights norms that offered broad protections for Indigenous cultural practices. Within the community itself, there were varying interpretations of Gaya norms (see also Simon and Awi Mona 2015, 7–9). Further, ancestral knowledge embedded in Gaya contended with other forms of knowledge, such as scientific principles and methodologies that informed state regulations and wildlife conservation efforts. The intersections of state order and Gaya shaped Gaya in yet another way: by molding Gaya in the image of state law.

. . .

When I began my fieldwork, the Forestry Bureau of the Council of Agriculture (now the Forestry and Nature Conservation Agency) had recently launched a hunting self-governance pilot program with the Tsou in Chiayi County and was working with other Indigenous groups to establish similar initiatives. These programs aimed to close the gap between state laws and Indigenous daily practices by allowing Indigenous communities to self-manage hunting and animals on their territories, while also addressing the diverse stakeholder interests in wildlife conservation (Lo and Lu 2021, 115).

A key component of these programs was the preparation of "hunters self-governance and self-discipline conventions" (*lieren zizhu guanli zilü gongyue* 獵人自主管理自律公約). In the past, Forestry Bureau personnel had drafted conventions outlining the rules allowing Indigenous communities to self-regulate hunting, but local hunters found these proposals unsatisfactory and refused to participate. As attitudes toward Indigenous rights changed, the bureau revised its approach and began encouraging Indigenous hunters to draft their own conventions. By 2018, the bureau had established eight pilot projects with the Amis, Bunun, Paiwan, Pinuyumayan, Tayan, and Tsou (NDHU 2020, 1n2). Dowmung, however, was not yet part of a bureau pilot program. Past interactions with the local government had eroded trust in working with state agencies, but they had heard about the success of the Tsou program. Inspired by this, the Dowmung community decided to organize a hunters' association and draft a hunting convention on their own, leaving open the possibility of participating in a pilot program in the future.

In 2018, a friend from Dowmung invited me to attend a village meeting about drafting the hunting convention. The convention would establish rules for how local hunters may engage in hunting on Dowmung territories. It would interweave multiple forms of law and knowledge by incorporating Gaya, state hunting regulations, procedures for scientific monitoring, and potential partnership activities with the Forestry Bureau. He explained to me that the convention had two main objectives. First, it would enable the community to internally regulate hunting activities on their territories more efficiently and in alignment with Gaya. Second, it would provide legal protection for Dowmung hunters, shielding them from arrest and prosecution in

Taiwan courts. As he put it, "We will be able to show the convention to the judge and say, 'Look, here are our rules. Our hunter followed Gaya.' This convention will help protect the hunters."[1]

That evening, thirty-eight members of the community, thirty-four men and four women, gathered at the multifunctional center for the meeting (figure 7). They sat on plastic chairs in the cool of the evening at the open-air center, passing around betel nut. Each person was given a copy of the draft convention, which was printed on pink paper, entitled "Articles of the Dowmung Hunters Self-Governance and Self-Discipline Convention" (*tongmen buluo lieren zizhu guanli zilü gongyue tiaowen* 銅門部落獵人自主管理自律公約條文). A large tile mural of a Truku man carrying a hunting firearm, accompanied by his hunting dog, hung on the wall at the front, reminding everyone about the centrality of hunting in Truku cultural life. Two elders stood beneath the mural and explained the convention through a crackling microphone. They read the Mandarin Chinese text aloud and then translated it into Truku for the audience. They had used the Tsou hunting convention as a model and had worked with two Han Taiwanese ecologists, whom they had also invited to the meeting, to draft the document. They had not, however, consulted legal professionals about its admissibility in Taiwan courts or its potential effect in negotiating with the Forestry Bureau. When I asked if they had sought legal advice, my friend replied, "Why? They do not know Gaya. With this document, we may not need them anyway."[2] In his view, the convention would override the ROC laws regulating hunting; there was no need to involve lawyers.

At the core of the Dowmung hunting convention was an effort to inscribe the oral tradition of Gaya. Leaders in the hunters' association believed that by collecting, coming to a consensus about, and documenting the dictates of Gaya—in effect, codifying Gaya—they could protect hunters by making the local law legible to Han Taiwanese state actors. Additionally, they believed that inscribing Gaya would help the association encourage hunters to adhere to Gaya norms in the face of competing normative frameworks. One component of this process concerned the form through which the hunting convention presented Gaya. Annelise Riles (1998) draws attention to the significance of form and aesthetics in legal documents. In her study of international legal instruments negotiated at UN conferences, she argues that attention to form reveals important insights into how laws are produced and gain legitimacy. Practices, such as standardized structures and bracketing, illustrate that the form and aesthetics of a legal document are as crucial as its content in the

FIGURE 7. Gathering at the Dowmung multifunctional center to discuss the hunting convention, 2018.

negotiation and production of legal documents. Riles's work highlights the importance of form, not just meaning, when it comes to how legal documents are created and accepted.

The Dowmung hunting convention imitated the form of ROC national laws and regulations. Gaya, which is transmitted orally in Truku language, was inscribed in the language of Taiwan's Han Taiwanese society, Mandarin Chinese. Like national laws, the convention organized Gaya and other norms into numbered chapters and articles, mirroring the format of ROC laws. Twenty-three articles defined the relationship between Gaya and hunting, the qualifications of hunters, their rights and obligations, Gaya rules for hunting practice, safety protocols, punishments for violations, and the process for promulgating the convention. It also incorporated provisions for reporting hunting results and partnership activities with the Forest Bureau Division Office. Empty brackets in the text indicated topics requiring further negotiation. These brackets functioned as more than editorial marks: They were a diplomatic way of avoiding disagreement, and they signaled openness to many possibilities. Red font marked proposed language in need of further discussion. The text was organized into three columns: article number, article content, and an "Explanation (Origins)" column, which provided a history and rationale for each article, much like a legislative history.

Members of the hunters' association remarked that attending to the form of the document would give Gaya legitimacy and credibility on par with ROC state law. My friend stated, "Our culture has been distorted. There is so much misinformation spread about our community. We need our law, Gaya, to be seen like law for us to get recognized."[3] Disagreements arose within the Dowmung community, however, over the convention's articulation of Gaya norms. A particularly contentious issue was who would manage the hunter identification cards issued by the hunters' association. Some members argued that hunters should control their own cards, allowing individuals the freedom to decide when, how, where, and what to hunt. Others believed that this approach was inconsistent with Gaya because it ignored the familial aspects of hunting. They argued that the leader of each family clan, not the individual, should control the identification cards and that the leader should decide hunting matters. These debates continued over several meetings and rose to the level of people shouting, making accusations, and walking out in frustration. At one point, a man stood up, pointed angrily at the speakers, and shouted, "This is not our tradition! The leader decides hunting!" In the end, the association adopted the family-based approach, with family clan leaders managing the hunter identification cards.

Tensions in the community arose in yet another way. Recent studies show a decline in adherence to Gaya (Tai et al. 2011, 40). Similar to Paul Nadasdy's (2002) observations in the North American context, tensions arose between Gaya and the language of national rights. For some community members, Gaya set the rules for the "proper" way to relate to animals and the land. Some younger men, however, were less inclined to follow Gaya norms. They hunted animals in ways that others found troubling. They hunted on land without permission, often using vehicles like jeeps, and hunted at night using headlamps to locate game animals, rather than relying on ancestral knowledge. They hunted animals indiscriminately, and they overhunted. The language of hunting rights in ROC law offered an alternative normative framework allowing them to think of and act toward animals and landscapes in new ways. They turned to claims based in national law of having the "right" to behave differently. Some community members did not accept this kind of rights-based argument as legitimate and believed that codifying Gaya would give leaders authority to enforce these norms in hunting activities. The regime of ROC laws, intended to protect and preserve Indigenous cultural practice, also provided an alternative discourse justifying behaviors inconsistent with it.

The practical effect of efforts to codify Gaya on interactions with Taiwan's state police or courts remained unclear. In my conversations with judges, I encountered varying opinions about the conventions. One district court judge remarked, "I would subpoena the drafter of the convention and add the convention to the resources used for evaluating Indigenous hunting practices."[4] A high court judge expressed a similar view: "I would use the convention. I trust their statement. But not every judge will do this."[5] Other judges, however, felt more was needed. One high court judge observed, "This is a very good attitude to solve the problem. When we make hunting decisions, we must respect Gaya and bring some of Gaya into the law. But it is just a convention for themselves. It would be better if it became a state rule or if it was a Council of Indigenous Peoples rule. That would put some authority behind it."[6] There was thus no guarantee that the Dowmung hunting convention would have the desired effect of protecting hunters from arrest or criminal prosecution. It was also unclear that local leaders would be able to encourage younger hunters to abide by Gaya if they refused to participate in the hunters' association.

Leaders in Dowmung had endeavored to self-manage hunting activities on their territories through drafting a convention that converted the Truku oral tradition of Gaya into a document resembling state law. The document they prepared drew upon the standardized conventions and structures of ROC law, even mirroring its negotiation practices, formalizing Gaya norms that were previously interpreted flexibly across Gaya groups. The leaders considered this approach necessary not only to secure recognition for Gaya by Han Taiwanese state actors, but also to foster respect for Gaya norms internally in the community. This second goal is important because it showed that local leaders did not see themselves as merely submitting to the ROC state. Rather, they were strategically appropriating the authority of national law to further their own goals. Sally Merry (2000) observes how Indigenous peoples may appropriate and repurpose state laws and knowledges toward other ends. Working in the Hawaiian context, she explores how law, a key institution of colonial control, was appropriated by Native Hawaiians to secure their survival and liberation. Hegemony may, in this sense, be reconfigured in the service of justice. In a similar vein, Dowmung leaders, forced to seek legitimacy through state norms, co-opted and reconfigured the form and content of ROC laws to challenge the disruptions caused by ongoing structures of colonialism and stave off further encroachments on their territories and lifeways.

STATE ORDER: LAWS OF ONE TO LAWS OF MANY

Legal protections for Indigenous peoples in Taiwan lack the backing of treaties or other nation-to-nation agreements that appear in other colonial contexts. Instead, Taiwan's framework for Indigenous rights developed incrementally and has culminated in a fragmented accumulation of rights and privileges. Many of these protections are rooted in earlier colonial governance structures and shifting state priorities. Similar to the legal definition of *Indigenous*, the ROC government has maintained firm control over what is considered an acceptable and "authentic" expression of Indigenous identity and behavior.

Three distinct phases are discernible in the development of Indigenous rights following Taiwan's transfer to the ROC in 1945 (see also Chang 2016). The first phase (1945–94) focused on the construction of a "One Chinese" national identity, which sought to suppress and erase Indigenous cultural distinctiveness. A second phase (1994–2016) emerged after Taiwan's transition to democracy in the 1990s, during which the state began to promote a new national identity based on multiculturalism, incorporating Indigenous identities and rights. In the past decade, a third phase (2016–present) has begun to take shape, characterized by a cautious shift toward Indigenous autonomy and self-governance. These phases have resulted in a system of legal protections for Indigenous peoples that is marked by contradictions, lacunae, and inconsistencies with the realities of Indigenous daily life. While this system often privileges ROC state interests, it also suggests that new possibilities for Indigenous recognition and rights are on the horizon.

Salt at the Table of Building a Nation

In 1945, control of Taiwan shifted from Japan to the ROC, and the KMT government imposed its legal system brought from the Chinese mainland on both the native Taiwanese and Indigenous populations. The highly centralized and paternalistic KMT regime took the position that there was little or no difference between Indigenous peoples and Chinese settlers. KMT policymakers sought to construct an image of the island's inhabitants as a single Chinese cultural ethnicity, effectively erasing the cultural differences between Chinese settlers and Indigenous peoples (e'Akuyana 2009, 306; Wang 2004). The hegemonic discourse promoted by the KMT thus framed Taiwan's population, including both Indigenous and native Taiwanese peoples, as "Chinese" (Chun 1996).

Cultivating a sense of Chinese identity was a crucial political strategy for the KMT as it transitioned to power (Rigger 2002). The KMT implemented a similar process of erasure concerning Taiwan's Japanese past, replacing any sense of Japanese identity with a Chinese one. This involved removing references to Japan from monuments and textbooks and framing Taiwan's history as a process of being either taken away from or returned to China (Greene 2016, 22). These efforts were not just about reconfiguring the legacy of Japan or Indigenous history; they were also aimed at constructing a sense of Chinese-ness that erased intra-island cultural differences to position Taiwan as the new home of China.

A 1986 case in the Taipei District Court illustrates this mindset of Indigenous cultural erasure. In its ruling, the court noted that there was no term for "Indigenous" in Mandarin Chinese. Lacking a formal term, the court instead described the accused Indigenous individual as someone "born in the backwoods" (*chushen qiongxiangpirang* 出身窮鄉僻壤).[7] Even after amendments to the ROC Constitution in 1994 and 1997, which introduced the terms *yuanzhumin* (Indigenous people) and *yuanzhuminzu* (Indigenous peoples), a significant development that I will discuss in detail later, traces of this earlier mindset persisted. As late as 2003, the Chiayi District Court reminded two Tsou defendants that they were now part of "civilized society" (*wenming shehui* 文明社會) and must adhere to national law.[8] Constructions of Indigenous peoples as uncivilized, "backwoods" persons lingered as the judiciary worked to sweep them into the fold of the "civilized" Chinese state (Chang 2016, 3).

But understandings of Indigenous peoples also began to shift. In 1950, the ROC government granted thirty mountain townships "local autonomy," and in 1951, the government signed ILO No. 107, which was the only existing international standard at the time that was focused on Indigenous peoples. Changing perceptions of Indigenous peoples were also apparent in the practice of reserving seats for Indigenous representatives in elected assemblies, which was designed to give Indigenous peoples a voice in national politics. In 1950, Indigenous representatives from highland and lowland electorates were introduced to popularly elected councils in counties with Indigenous townships. In 1951, Indigenous representatives were also included in indirect elections to the Taiwan Provincial Assembly. In 1972, when the ROC government held "supplementary elections" to replace legislators who were dying or had become incapacitated, one of the thirty-six seats was reserved for an Indigenous representative, elected by the entire Indigenous electorate across the island. In 1980, two Indigenous representatives, one highland and one lowland, were included in the Legislative Yuan. The number of reserved seats increased over the following decades: four in 1989, six in 1991, and eight in 1996 (Templeman 2018, 469n6). In 2005, the number of legislative seats was reduced from 225 to 113, and the number of reserved Indigenous seats was cut to six, three for highland and three for lowland representatives, where it remains today (Simon 2016, 10).

. . .

In April 2018, I traveled with a friend to a remote Pinuyumayan community in the mountains of Taitung County in southern Taiwan. We rattled up the winding roads in my small Toyota, heading to interview the father of one of our mutual friends (Father) about the challenges facing the Pinuyumayan people. Father was a respected elder who operated a fish farm near the community's territory, land that had been taken by the Japanese and later claimed by the KMT government. Now, much of the land lay unoccupied. Barking dogs greeted us as we arrived and made our way to Father's fish farm. After exchanging greetings, we walked the premises with Father. The fresh, earthy scent of petrichor filled the air, mingling with the mountain breeze. Father pointed out various plants growing along the edges of the farm before leading us to a pond where speckled koi swam lazily in the water.

Sitting in the shade and eating bananas, Father explained the deep connection the Pinuyumayan (formerly called Puyuma) people have to their land:

> Our culture is deeply connected to our land. Historically, we held our land as a community. We treated it as a resource open to the entire nation. If you worked hard, then you could use a bigger portion of the land. But we also moved a great deal because we practiced slash-and-burn agriculture. You know, two main values among the Puyuma originate from our relationship to

> the land: sharing and taking responsibility for others. Our land was an open resource for everyone. Our relationship to land is inclusive, not exclusive. We shared it with one another and took care of one another using its resources. If a newcomer came to our community, we would share our land with them and make sure they would be taken care of.[9]

He took a sip of tea and continued.

> If another group wanted to live on our land, they would need to pay annual tribute, often in the form of rice or millet. If they did not pay tribute, then we would defend our land, sometimes by headhunting. During our grandfathers' generation, the Japanese made us stop the tribute system because they saw this system as challenging their authority as the new power over the island. Then, the ROC government destroyed our social structure by creating a rival leadership system to challenge the traditional leadership system. And so, we lost both our land and our social structure. It was not until decades later that we began to have the room to revitalize our culture and rediscover our land.

Father reflected on the complexity of what constitutes "traditional" land:

> Puyuma territory was originally located farther north in the mountains. We were moved to this village by the Japanese, and they relocated, among other groups, the Bunun people to our original territory. When they moved us here. This placed us close to other Indigenous groups, like the Paiwan and Amis, which created new kinds of conflicts with these groups.

He pulled out old maps created by Japanese administrators and shared an Indigenous perspective on Taiwan's transfer to the ROC. He emphasized that it was not a "return" of Taiwan to China, as the KMT claimed, but rather the establishment of a new colonial authority by the ROC government.

> When colonists came, they brought with them the concept of property and ownership. They made us register our land and divide it up. The introduction of these ideas about private property created many new conflicts within my community that were never there before. It was also the source of many conflicts with the colonial powers. Recently, we have had a conflict concerning a dairy farm and tourist attraction, which is located on Puyuma territory. When the ROC government acquired Taiwan from the Japanese in 1945, the government told the Puyuma people that this land was state property and was not our land because they won the war against Japan, and they took over the land rights from the Japanese government. We told the government that this is our land, but they do not listen. They told us they could not believe us because we only have oral history, not written history, to prove it is our land.

He pointed emphatically at the maps.

> But just looking around at the place names in this region, they are all Puyuma names made into Mandarin Chinese language. Our history and relationship to this land can be seen everywhere. Even the Japanese accepted our oral history, but the ROC did not. Our elders reminded the ROC government that they only came to Taiwan because they were also defeated by the Chinese Communists, so by their own thinking it was wrong for them to take this land. We told them the Japanese came and robbed our land. We asked the government, are you robbers, too? When they finally agreed to allow us to buy the land back, they classified it as reserve land, which makes the land nearly valueless because you cannot do anything with it. As a result, many Puyuma people simply abandoned their land.

He gestured widely to the space around us. "Nobody lives here. They are all gone."

As we walked the premises once more, Father passionately defended Indigenous peoples' original claims to land, using a culinary analogy to make his point.

> Indigenous people are the original owners of the land, so we believe our opinions should be respected. We want to share with the immigrants who have come to our island, but they should not forget that we are the original inhabitants of the island. Colonial powers, like the ROC, should consult us and ask our permission regarding the use of our land. We are not a majority in Taiwan, like the Han Chinese, but a critical minority. We are like salt at the table: A little has a powerful impact on the entire meal.

When the KMT took control of Taiwan in 1945, its policymakers pursued a nationalist agenda grounded in an essentialized conception of Chinese-ness that erased Indigenous peoples' cultural distinctiveness and reimagined Taiwan as the new epicenter of Chinese society. Even as the concept of indigeneity emerged as a social and legal category, government agencies continued to perpetuate earlier prejudices, treating Indigenous peoples as barbaric and uncivilized "others." This process played out in Indigenous peoples' lives, some of whom still remember the Japanese administration, Taiwan's transition to KMT rule, and the period of White Terror. Indigenous individuals, like Father, experienced these policies firsthand and witnessed how they upset local systems of order and introduced new conflicts by placing Indigenous communities into unfamiliar relations of contact. Father and others in the community responded to these policies by pointing out to the new KMT government the irony that it claimed authority after having just lost a war.

This account requires a somewhat generous reading, since the KMT took control of Taiwan in 1945 and did not lose the Chinese Civil War until 1949. Further, Father's account paints a picture of Pinuyumayan social structure as one of egalitarianism and shared resources, but the historical and ethnographic record indicates a history of age-ranked societies, inherited wealth, and surplus extraction by political leaders, forming something resembling a kingdom. His description of Pinuyumayan societies as egalitarian, meritocratic, and communal likely reflects settlements as they appeared in the recent past, but Father's larger point was that the ROC government should reflect on its own history and struggles when engaging with Indigenous peoples. In this regard, the oppressive policies imposed by the KMT government later became a source of moral capital for Indigenous communities, who used them to emphasize their own ethics, grounded in equity and sharing, and to distinguish themselves from the repressive regime. To the extent that the ROC now uses international human rights and Indigenous peoples' rights as moral capital to distinguish itself from the PRC (deLisle 2019), Indigenous peoples would appear to be pioneers in this tactic in their responses to the KMT's oppressive practices.

Refrigerators, Rights, and Regulating Difference

With the decline of Chinese nationalism in the 1990s, government engagements with Indigenous peoples began to change. In the period leading up to democratization, national discourse had gradually shifted toward constructing a Taiwanese identity distinct from the mainland Chinese. As noted earlier, Indigenous peoples played a key role in this discourse, as they were the one clear category of non-Chinese people on the island. With democratization and the emergence of a global Indigenous rights movement, growing group consciousness among segments of the Indigenous population fueled new demands for Indigenous group-based autonomy and rights.

In 1994, Indigenous activists successfully convinced lawmakers to inscribe the term *Indigenous people* (*yuanzhumin* 原住民) into the ROC Constitution. Shortly after, while participating in international meetings in Geneva, Indigenous activists from Taiwan observed other Indigenous groups holding up signs with the letter *s* to demand recognition of Indigenous people as *peoples*, not just as individuals.[10] These activists returned to Taiwan and insisted on this change because it affirmed Indigenous peoples' right to self-determination. In 1997, lawmakers amended the term in the ROC Constitution to the plural *Indigenous peoples* (*yuanzhuminzu* 原住民族).[11] These developments signaled a shift in government policy toward greater recognition of Indigenous cultures and lands within the ROC legal framework.

The legal recognition of Indigenous peoples' cultures and lands gained momentum after the Democratic Progressive Party (DPP) took control of the ROC government in 2000, marking the first regime change since Taiwan's transfer from Japan to the ROC. Under the leadership of Chen Shui-bian's new liberal DPP government, the early years of the new century saw a significant expansion of legal protections for Indigenous peoples. As the ROC shifted toward recognizing Indigenous cultural and linguistic distinctiveness, however, it maintained its control over these cultures and lands by enacting and interpreting laws through a Han Taiwanese lens (Chang 2016, 4–11). Between 2000 and 2016, the government passed numerous legal measures that acknowledged Indigenous peoples' existence but insisted that the power to classify and address their differences remained firmly in the hands of the Han Taiwanese–controlled ROC state. In this framework, the state acted as the principal set of institutions through which Indigenous peoples were made legible in law, policies, and politics. Correspondingly, the emerging regime of Indigenous rights privileged state interests and Han Taiwanese perspectives.

Before the 2000 presidential election, Chen Shui-bian, then a candidate for the DPP, signed a "nation-to-nation" partnership agreement with leaders of the Indigenous movement (Kuan 2010, 9; Awi Mona 2007, 100). In 2000, Chen converted this agreement into a comprehensive "White Paper on Aboriginal Policy," which promised to recognize the sovereignty of Indigenous peoples and to promote Indigenous self-government, negotiate land treaties, return ancestral lands, and strengthen Indigenous political participation (Simon and Awi Mona 2013, 102; Simon 2009, 415). Within a span of five years, from 2000 to 2005, the DPP government introduced several legal reforms aimed at protecting Indigenous groups. In a first phase, the government framed Indigenous peoples as marginalized groups in need of social welfare support, focusing on issues of education, status, and employment. Legislative measures during this phase included the 1998 Education Act for Indigenous Peoples, the 2001 Indigenous Peoples Employment Protection Law, and the 2001 Status Act for Indigenous Peoples. A second phase of reforms were centered on safeguarding Indigenous peoples' cultures and access to natural resources, primarily through amendments to existing laws. These measures included amendments to the Firearms, Ammunition, and Knives Control Act (Firearms Act) in 2001, the Name Act in 2002, the Wildlife Conservation Act in 2004, and the Forestry Act in 2004. In 2005, the government passed the Indigenous Peoples Basic Law, building on the foundation laid by Chen's earlier partnership agreement and "White Paper."

While ROC laws expanded protections for Indigenous peoples, they also enabled state institutions to extend their influence into Indigenous communities. Throughout this process, the ROC government has maintained control over the content and scope of Indigenous peoples' rights. This piecemeal approach created a complex and uncertain legal terrain, characterized by inconsistencies and contradictions, with significant gaps between constitutional principles and their legislative implementation. Here, I focus on the ROC laws that shaped the discourse around Indigenous rights during my fieldwork, specifically the Firearms Act, Wildlife Conservation Act, Forestry Act, and Indigenous Peoples Basic Law.

Indigenous Hunters' Firearms and Ammunition. In general, ROC law prohibits the possession and use of firearms. In 2001, the Legislature amended Article 20 of the Firearms Act to decriminalize the manufacture, possession, and use of firearms and ammunition by Indigenous persons (Simon and Awi Mona 2015, 12). Under these amendments, Indigenous individuals could, upon approval by local authorities, manufacture and use firearms as part of their cultural practices. This approval was contingent upon a formal application and registration process for each individual firearm.

Article 20 mandates that Indigenous peoples' firearms must be "self-made" (*zizhi* 自製), a requirement rooted in the era of White Terror, reflecting fears that powerful firearms could be used for attacks on police or to organize political uprisings. This stipulation also froze Indigenous "tradition" into a nostalgic, imagined past. For example, Bunun men in Tastas noted that they had never been taught to hunt with self-made firearms; instead, their fathers and grandfathers taught them to hunt with Japanese rifles. In this regard, it is important to note the pervasiveness of firearms in Indigenous territories historically and just how radical legal restrictions on gun use must seem to Indigenous groups whose ownership rates in the recent past rivaled those of Texans in the United States (see Lin 2016, 236).

The self-made firearms they were now required to build often consisted of welded pipes with wooden gunstocks attached (figure 8). Since there was no market for gunpowder or musket balls, they had to produce these items themselves. Some hunters remarked that these self-made firearms were more primitive than the matchlock guns their ancestors had acquired from the Dutch in the mid-seventeenth century. They also pointed out that the firearms were dangerous to use, were difficult to repair, and caused more suffering for the animals they hunted. Keeping gunpowder dry in the wet forest environment was a constant challenge. If it became wet, the gunlock could ignite unevenly, leading to dangerous explosions. Hunters showed me photographs of severe injuries to hands, fingers, eyes, and faces caused by such explosions. Additionally, the "self-made" requirement was ambiguous. Did each individual hunter need to make their own firearm, or could someone in the community with the necessary skills make them? One high court judge observed, "Few Indigenous people really make their guns. It puts them in a position where they have to lie to the court and say, 'Yes, I made this gun,' when it is unreasonable to demand that they, individually, made a gun."[12]

Taiwan courts later added a condition to the Firearms Act, stipulating that Indigenous peoples' self-made firearms must also be muzzle-loading. This meant that users must manually insert musket balls into the barrel before each shot. Article 20 itself, however, refers generically to *lieqiang* 獵槍 (hunting guns) without specifying the type of firearm. In 2008, a Paiwan man in Pingtung made three homemade breech-loading rifles (loaded from the rear of the gun) in his workshop using an electric welder and grinding machines. He then used these rifles to hunt and kill a muntjac. Prosecutors charged him with possessing firearms and hunting in violation of the Firearms Act and Wildlife Conservation Act. The Pingtung District Court ruled that Indigenous peoples traditionally used muzzle-loading firearms and found the man guilty of violating Article 20 by making breech-loading firearms that were not, in the court's view, part of Indigenous tradition.[13] He was sentenced to three years in prison, with three years' probation, and fined 100,000 New Taiwan Dollars (NTD). The Kaohsiung High Court upheld the conviction, interpreting Article 20 as applying only to firearms made in the "traditional style" (*chuantong fangshi* 傳統方式), which it understood to mean muskets exclusively (Hsiang and Pan 2013).[14] A year later, however, the Taiwan Supreme Court overturned the man's conviction, emphasizing that the Indigenous Peoples Basic Law requires the ROC government to protect Indigenous peoples' cultural practices and observing that Article 20 did not distinguish among types of firearms.[15]

FIGURE 8. Bunun hunters' homemade firearms, 2016.

The Supreme Court's ruling would appear to mark a significant advancement in Indigenous peoples' right to maintain and use firearms for cultural practice. Legal decisions do not, however, remain idle (Sapignoli 2017). After the decision, government agencies interpreted the Court's ruling narrowly. In 2015, the National Police Agency approved the use of modified muskets using Hilti black powder caps and steel balls purchased at hardware stores, which are commonly used today by younger Indigenous hunters in their thirties and forties (Yi 2016).

Currently, Indigenous persons are permitted to use only self-made muskets or modified Hilti muskets when hunting. Meanwhile, the ROC has been considering new regulations that would prohibit hunters from making their own firearms and require them to purchase factory-made gun parts and ammunition from the government. Indigenous activists have had mixed responses to the proposal. Some have seen this as a positive step toward safety, ensuring that hunting firearms are more reliable and safer to use. Others expressed concerns that the proposal would impose a financial burden on hunters, who would be forced to buy costly materials, potentially increasing firearm costs by two to ten times (Lin 2023). Still others worried that the factory-made gun parts would result in weaker firearms, putting hunters at risk when facing aggressive animals like mountain boars. These concerns have resulted in the rumored growth of an underground firearms market.

Hunting Wildlife and the Case of Tama Talum. Like firearms, wildlife hunting is generally prohibited in Taiwan. In 2004, the Legislature amended Article 21–1 of the Wildlife Conservation Act to allow hunting under specific circumstances, namely for the "traditional cultural or ritual hunting, killing or utilization needs of Taiwan aborigines." This provision offered a narrow set of protections, restricting Indigenous hunting to ceremonial and public ritual activities. In 2017, the CIP and Council of Agriculture issued a joint interpretation that expanded Indigenous hunting rights, for the first time permitting hunting for "self-use" (*ziyong* 自用) purposes (Everington 2017).

Article 4 of the act divides wildlife into two general categories: "protected species" (which includes "endangered," "rare and valuable species," and "other conservation-deserving wildlife") and "general wildlife" that falls outside those categories. It allows Indigenous hunters to hunt unprotected species but prohibits hunting of protected species, except in cases where the population exceeds the land's carrying capacity or for educational purposes. In practice, many Indigenous groups continue to hunt protected species, including the mountain hawk-eagle, pangolin, macaque, and muntjac.[16] No population of protected species has been given an "exceeding carrying capacity" status. Local understandings of animal population numbers and the "carrying capacity" of an area often differ from official statistics. Moreover, while the practice of hunting for the transmission of cultural knowledge would ostensibly qualify as "educational purposes," Indigenous persons continue to be prosecuted for hunting wildlife.

The act regulates hunting by requiring Indigenous hunters to apply in advance, detailing the hunting method, target species, bag limit, hunting season, and location. Local authorities review hunters' harvests of animals to ensure that applicants followed the authorizations provided to them. Failure to adhere to the regulations can result in fines and the confiscation of hunting equipment. Indigenous hunters argued, however, that these regulations lacked congruence with local practices, which held that ancestral spirits, not hunters, determined the types and quantities of animals to be hunted. Additionally, under the regulations on the "Use of Wildlife Management Measures for Indigenous Peoples' Traditional Cultural and Ritual Hunting and Killing Needs," hunting was limited to designated areas and prohibited in national parks, many of which are located in Indigenous territories. Authorized hunting techniques included the use of firearms, as discussed above, but certain techniques commonly used by Indigenous hunters, like trapping and snaring, were constrained. Further, enforcement of these regulations has been uneven and problematic, with police abusing their authority and making arbitrary arrests, as seen in the case of the Pinuyumayan men mentioned earlier.

A 2013 case involving a Bunun hunter from Taitung, Tama Talum, raised important questions about the scope of Indigenous hunting rights. At the request of his ailing ninety-two-year-old mother, Mr. Talum went hunting in the mountains to gather meat she was accustomed to eating. He traveled with a group of men, but when they decided to return home, he ventured deeper into the mountains on his own. There, he hunted and killed a muntjac deer and a serow to bring back to his mother. When the men returned to the village, they reported illegal logging activities they had seen in the mountains to the local police. Two officers, one of whom was Bunun, set up an ambush to catch the loggers. Instead, they encountered Mr. Talum walking home. Mistaking him for one of the loggers, they stopped him. Upon realizing he was not involved in logging, they told him not to run away and explained they simply wanted him to sign a form before allowing him to leave. He agreed to approach them. When they learned that he had been hunting for personal use, rather than for cultural or ritual purposes, and discovered an illegal rifle in a nearby ditch, they arrested him.

The Taitung District Prosecutors Office charged Mr. Talum with violating Article 21–1 of the Wildlife Conservation Act and Article 20 of the

Firearms Act. His case gained public attention thanks to the efforts of his daughter and members of the Taitung Bunun Youth Group (*dongbuqing* 東布青), established by twentysomething Bunun activists in 2015. Lawyers from the local legal aid center took on his defense. Despite their efforts, the Taitung District Court found Mr. Talum guilty, sentencing him to three and a half years in prison and imposing a fine of NTD 70,000.[17] In its ruling, the court noted the significance of hunting culture among Indigenous peoples and acknowledged the local Indigenous laws governing hunting practices, but it confined Indigenous culture in a cage. In the court's view, Indigenous hunters were required to follow a written, state-created schedule reflecting practices in the distant past. The court's decision left little room for the possibility of cultural change or diverse understandings of cultural practice within Indigenous communities. One of the legal aid lawyers representing Mr. Talum observed:

> The judge believed Indigenous peoples can have guns, but that it should just be homemade primitive ones, not modern ones, and that they should hunt only like they did hundreds of years ago. The judge had a very narrow idea about culture in that the law protects Indigenous culture, but the judge read his own ideas into it and did not understand it.[18]

The Hualien High Court upheld the District Court's decision, and the Taiwan Supreme Court rejected Mr. Talum's request to overturn his conviction.[19] A remarkable turn of events transpired, however, on the day Mr. Talum was to be taken to prison. The prosecutor-general, Yen Da-ho, filed an extraordinary appeal to the Supreme Court challenging Mr. Talum's conviction. Focusing on the issue of firearms, Prosecutor-General Yen argued that the lower courts' rulings reflected a narrow interpretation of the law that discriminated against Indigenous cultural development. He contended that the courts' interpretations of the "self-made hunting guns" requirement "implied Indigenous peoples are not permitted to build more advanced firearms than those manufactured by their ancestors in the past, that they can only use outdated handmade firearms for hunting forever. The result of this is discrimination against Indigenous cultural development" (Yi 2016; *Apple Daily* 2017).

Following Prosecutor-General Yen's extraordinary appeal, the Taiwan Supreme Court suspended further proceedings and referred the case to the Constitutional Court for an interpretation of the laws governing wildlife hunting. In 2021, the Constitutional Court issued its ruling, upholding the constitutionality of the current regulatory framework limiting Indigenous hunting practices, while also determining that certain elements of the hunting application process imposed unreasonable restrictions on hunting and that regulations regarding self-made hunting firearms were insufficiently standardized.[20] In effect, the Constitutional Court's ruling upheld Mr. Talum's conviction and, in doing so, appeared to set a limit on the expansiveness of Indigenous hunting rights. It also left open an important question about the role of the Indigenous Peoples Basic Law in securing Indigenous peoples' rights.

Two weeks after the Constitutional Court's ruling, President Tsai Ing-wen granted a rare pardon to Mr. Talum, fulfilling a campaign promise to Indigenous peoples to resolve his case (Simon 2021). Some Indigenous activists saw Mr. Talum's case as the beginning of a new phase in the fight for Indigenous hunting rights in Taiwan. As one activist put it, "His case opened the pressure pot and made all the boiling about Indigenous hunting issues that has been kept hidden visible."[21] While President Tsai's pardon exempted Mr. Talum from punishment for his alleged violations, it did not erase or expunge the record of his convictions. As a result, Mr. Talum and his legal team continued to fight in the courts for his and other Indigenous peoples' hunting rights. Ultimately, on March 14, 2024, the Supreme Court reversed its earlier decision and overturned Mr. Talum's convictions (Hsieh and Mazzetta 2024).[22]

Forests, Forest Resources, and Smangus Village. The Forestry Act is designed to protect Taiwan's forests and forest resources. Article 15 guarantees Indigenous peoples' access to "traditional territory" and the natural resources on these territories. Article 56–3 stipulates, however, that this access is contingent upon it being related to "traditional living needs and activities." The act does not define what constitutes "traditional territory" or what is meant by "traditional living needs and activities." Indigenous persons must also obtain prior approval from local authorities before collecting forest products from "conservation forests," a category encompassing a wide range of forestlands, many of which overlap Indigenous territories.

A 2005 case involving three Tayan men from Smangus village in Hsinchu raised questions about the legal protections surrounding Indigenous peoples' interactions with forest landscapes. After a typhoon caused a landslide that blocked the roadway connecting Smangus village to the nearest township approximately three hours away, members of the community began repairing the road. During this process, they discovered a fallen beech tree buried under the mud and moved it to the side of the road. A month later, when they returned to continue their work, they found that Forestry Bureau personnel had cut the tree into pieces and taken away the most valuable sections, leaving only the trunk behind. A week later, the village appointed three men to collect the remaining wood and bring it back to the village, where it would be used for decorations. As the men were gathering the wood, however, patrolling police arrested them.

The Forestry Bureau argued that the fallen beech tree was national property. Accordingly, when the men attempted to transport the tree trunk to Smangus village, it constituted theft of forest resources under Article 52 of the Forestry Act (Abas 2009). The three Smangus men countered that they were engaging in cultural practices in accordance with Tayan law, called Gaga, at the request of their community. Further, they argued that the beech tree was located within Smangus "traditional territory," as defined in Article 15. The Forestry Bureau disagreed, pointing out that the site of the incident was twelve kilometers away from the village, which they argued invalidated the men's argument about "traditional territory."

The lower courts rejected the defendants' cultural claims and refused to consider the legitimacy of Smangus territory or ownership of resources under Gaga. The Hsinchu District Court convicted the men, imposing a fine of NTD 160,000 each and sentencing them to six months in prison, suspended.[23] In a striking statement, the court's decision framed Indigenous peoples' interactions with forest landscapes as lawless:

> It may be seen that although the use of land by Indigenous peoples should be highly respected, it must still be applied in a manner and scope determined by law. It is not completely unregulated by law. Therefore, there is no basis for the defense of freedom from punishment of the defendants in this part.

Within the same statement emphasizing respect for Indigenous use of land and resources, the only recognizable "law" was state law.

The Taiwan High Court upheld the men's conviction, sentencing them to three months in prison with an NTD 71,000 fine.[24] The men's defense, that they were sent to collect the wood by community leaders, raised the question of whether they had the requisite intent for theft under the law. The High Court found that such an intent was present, stating, "It is universal legal common sense that you do not take for yourself the products of another's land without consent of the owner." This statement was striking for two reasons. First, it required the court to disregard the community's claim that the tree was located on Smangus territory. Second, it assumed, without considering Tayan notions of property, that private ownership of property is a universally applied principle, and one that is interpreted uniformly across cultural groups. The High Court's decision neither investigated nor considered Gaga.

The Taiwan Supreme Court sent the case back to the Taiwan High Court, stressing in its ruling the need to respect Indigenous peoples' cultures, beliefs, and values, as well as the principle of cultural pluralism.[25] On remand, the High Court reversed the men's convictions, explicitly referencing Gaga and local understandings of spirituality in its decision: "Due to the reverence for the customary law (gaga) and reverence for their ancestral spirits (rutux), who control the reward and punishment of their descendants, everyone will abide by the rules."[26] Following the High Court's reversal, Smangus chief Icyh described the community's experience, saying, "We have had a tough fight in these four years. Like a shrimp fighting against a whale. We hope this is a beginning for the government to respect our rights and culture" (*The China Post* 2010). Like other court decisions considered above, this verdict appeared to set a precedent for future cases involving Indigenous rights, as it represented a successful assertion of Indigenous autonomy and a partial recognition of Indigenous practices. The courts did not, however, take territorial land right claims into account (Awi Mona and Huang 2021, 215).

Indigenous Rights at the Eleventh Hour. The 2005 Indigenous Peoples Basic Law is the most comprehensive legal instrument to date protecting Indigenous rights in Taiwan (Simon and Awi Mona 2015, 11). Passed two years before the UNDRIP, the Basic Law was adopted by a KMT-dominated Legislature that was hostile to the DPP, which was then in control of the executive branch. Indigenous voters have formed an important part of the KMT's electoral base, and Indigenous legislators within the KMT party drafted and supported the law. Indigenous support for the KMT stems from the popularity of service centers (*fuwuzhan* 服務站) established by the KMT government in earlier decades, which provided essential goods, such as rice, oil, and matches, to Indigenous communities (Hale 2020). Through these provisions, together with decades of KMT one-party rule, the KMT managed to establish deep roots in Indigenous communities that have persisted even as Taiwan democratized. The Basic Law drafted by the KMT was not, however, self-executing. As a result, voting for its passage did not immediately commit the KMT to its implementation (Charlton, Gao, and Kuan 2017, 137; Bekhoven 2016, 227n139).

Passed at the eleventh hour of the 2005 legislative term, the law received little attention from either KMT or DPP legislators. After its passage, members of the DPP-controlled Executive Yuan reviewed the law and found that it conflicted with other existing laws. A potential constitutional issue would have arisen, however, if the Executive Yuan asked the Legislature to review the law and it refused. To avoid this, President Chen Shui-bian directed Premier Hsieh Chang-ting not to request a legislative review. As a result, the version of the law that passed, despite its multiple conflicts with other ROC laws, was the version that remained.

Article 1 of the Basic Law describes its purpose as "protecting the fundamental rights of Indigenous peoples, promoting their subsistence and development and building inter-ethnic relations based on co-existence and prosperity." The law includes provisions for establishing a Tribal Council system to promote the independent development of Indigenous communities (Art. 2–1). It promises that the government will guarantee the equal status of Indigenous peoples and facilitate the implementation of their autonomy (Art. 4). Additionally, the law commits the state to protect and promote the development of Indigenous peoples' knowledge of biological diversity (Art. 13).

Article 19 protects specific Indigenous cultural activities, stating in relevant part:

> Indigenous persons may undertake the following non-profit seeking activities in Indigenous peoples' regions and the sea areas be promulgated by the central Indigenous competent authority:
>
> 1. Hunting wild animals.
> 2. Collecting wild plants and fungus.
> 3. Collecting minerals, rocks and soils.
> 4. Utilizing water resources.
>
> [...] The activities in Paragraph 1 can only be conducted for traditional culture, ritual or self-consumption.

The article protects Indigenous cultural activities under four conditions: (1) they are carried out by "Indigenous persons," (2) they take place within "Indigenous peoples' regions," (3) they are conducted for "non-profit seeking" purposes, and (4) they involve "traditional culture, ritual or self-consumption."

The first condition of Article 19 relates to the definition of what it means to be an "Indigenous person," the complexities of which we considered earlier. Regarding the second, the Basic Law defines *Indigenous peoples' regions* as "areas approved by the Executive Yuan upon application made by the central Indigenous authority where Indigenous peoples have traditionally inhabited, featuring Indigenous history and cultural characteristics." Identifying these regions, however, has been a complicated process, and the ROC government has been slow to develop clear regulations for delimiting such territories. Further, difficulties have arisen as Indigenous communities access natural resources on lands that they consider their own but that have not been formally recognized as Indigenous territories. The third condition stipulates that cultural practices must be for "non-profit seeking" purposes. This means that food and substances collected by Indigenous persons cannot be used for economic gain, such as trade or commercial activities. But there exists a long history of demands for natural resources and commercial activities on Indigenous territories, including trade with the Dutch for deerskins in the 1700s, participation in the camphor export trade in the 1890s through the 1900s, and, more recently, a robust industry in the 1970s and 1980s for mountain products (*shanchan* 山產) sold to Han Taiwanese consumers. Such "non-profit" requirements, in effect, caricaturize Indigenous peoples as noncommercial, self-sufficient societies that never existed, contributing to a myth of the noneconomic Indigenous person as a variant of the "noble savage" trope.

The fourth condition merits particular attention because it protects activities carried out for "traditional culture, ritual or self-consumption" purposes. This provision is broader than similar provisions in earlier ROC laws protecting Indigenous practices. For instance, Article 21–1 of the Wildlife Conservation Act does not contain an exemption for "self-use" in hunting, although the joint agreement issued by the CIP and Council of Agriculture, in part, remedied this. Similarly, Article 15 of the Forestry Act does not define "traditional territory," which, as a rule, belongs to the ROC state. The Basic Law adopts a broader understanding of "Indigenous land," encompassing both "the traditional territories and reservation land of Indigenous peoples" (Art. 2). While the Basic Law offers more expansive protections for Indigenous peoples than other ROC laws, it remains more restrictive than international norms. Simon and Awi Mona (2015, 11) observe a progressive narrowing of Indigenous rights in Taiwan as practices, such as hunting, trapping, and gathering, shift in meaning as they move from global norms to state laws.

As a "basic law," the Indigenous Peoples Basic Law is not a self-executing legal instrument. Instead, it requires the enactment or amendment of other laws to bring its principles into effect. Until changes in law are made, it remains primarily a guiding philosophical document. For concrete implementation, the Basic Law requires the ROC government to establish a promotion committee to coordinate matters related to its provisions (Art. 3). It also requires the allocation of budgets to support Indigenous autonomy, infrastructure, economic development, and land development (Arts. 5, 15, 18, 21). Additionally, the government is tasked with reviewing all existing laws, regulations, and administrative measures to ensure that they align with the principles of the Basic Law, making necessary corrections within three years of its enactment (Art. 34). By 2019, the Indigenous Peoples Basic Law Promotion Committee had met eleven times and had worked to develop and increase budgets aimed at advancing the law's principles (Executive Yuan 2019).

While there has been limited progress in bringing the Basic Law into action through legislative amendments or repeals of outdated laws (Gao, Charlton, and Takahashi 2016, 68–69), a range of actors have been actively working to implement its principles in practice, what French (2009) calls "post-legislative negotiation." Indigenous activists used the Basic Law to support their claims to protect cultural practices and access resources on ancestral territories. Discussions about the Basic Law circulated through Indigenous villages and appeared on Facebook posts addressing issues faced by communities. Lawyers representing Indigenous clients invoked the Basic Law's principles in court cases. Training sessions for judges assigned to the ad hoc Chambers of Indigenous Courts included discussions about the Basic Law's content.

In other words, although the ROC Legislature was slow to implement the Basic Law, this did not mean that the Basic Law was idle. Nevertheless, from the perspective of some legal actors, the Legislature's inaction enshrouded the Basic Law in ambiguity, leaving its legal status unclear. In Mr. Talum's case, the Taiwan Supreme Court sought clarification from the Constitutional Court on whether the Basic Law or domestic statutes took precedence in cases of conflicting laws (Focus Taiwan 2017). The Constitutional Court did not address this question in its ruling, which suggested that the Basic Law was subordinate to other state laws (Simon 2021). In later chapters, I will describe how judges in Taiwan struggled to make sense of the Basic Law, diverging widely in how they addressed the law in cases involving Indigenous cultural practices and territories.

. . .

In October 2018, I joined a group of Bunun men on a hunt in the Central Mountains. The men were from across the border in Taitung County. Among them was Dahu, an elder and an expert hunter with a sharp sense of humor. More than once, I found myself the target of his playful teasing, especially when I made too much noise or lagged behind on the rugged terrain, both of which happened often.

We arrived at the base of the mountain in a stripped-down blue van just before nightfall, carrying homemade muskets, headlamps, rubber rainboots, mesh backpacks, and bottles of water, typical gear for hunting at night. One of the men walked off and returned with a factory-made rifle, a hunting firearm prohibited by Taiwan law, that had been hidden in a tree hollow. Under ROC regulations, the men were required to submit a hunting application to the local Forest District Office. When I asked about this, Dahu replied, "We never apply to go hunting. Why should we? This is our land. But it is important that we follow Samu in hunting and using hunting territories."[27] Here in the mountains, local Bunun law, or Samu, took precedence over ROC laws.

Dahu and I donned our rainboots and headlamps and walked toward the mountain. Pointing up, he said, "Bunun people think of the mountain as a refrigerator. When we need something, we go up the mountain to get it. But the law only allows hunting for ceremonial use, not daily use. This does not fit our traditional practices." Comparing the mountain to a refrigerator was more than a creative way of conceptualizing hunting grounds through the lens of modern technology. It conveyed the productivity of these grounds and Bunun people's deep sense of familiarity with and dependency on them. Restrictions on access to hunting territories, imposed through land appropriation and state regulations, have had a deep impact on Bunun cultural identity and their connections to the land. In his poem "Closed Refrigerator," Bunun poet Salizan Takisvilainan (2012) mourns the loss of Bunun hunting territories in the mountains, writing, "Wearing hunting outfits, we go to the mountains, who took the refrigerator and closed it up?"

The men carefully inspected their homemade muskets, showing me with pride the craftsmanship of their firearms. They explained the special precautions they must take when using them. Dahu pointed to the gunlock and said,

> Look, this is a part of a basketball. I cut a basketball, and I put the rubber across the gunlock to keep the power dry. We have to keep the gunpowder dry, otherwise it may ignite unevenly and explode the lock. It could explode your hand or shoot the gunlock back into your eye. This has happened to people. Very dangerous.

He then held up a small metal ball and continued: "We must make our own musket balls. We do it by melting down lead sheets we buy at the store, the hardware store. We mold them into balls." He explained how hunters select among softer and harder lead sheets to manufacture musket balls with an appropriate density for their firearms and how they make musket balls of different sizes to hunt different animal species.

Dahu reflected on this for a moment and said, "It makes no sense that the law makes us use these homemade muskets. This is not our tradition. My father's gun was a Japanese rifle, not a musket. We have had to learn to use muskets, as if this is our tradition."

The men had chosen to hunt at night for two reasons. First, laws and regulations that appeared clear on paper often took new forms in practice, and darkness provided some cover from the equivocations of law on the books and law in reality. Second, headlamps made it easier to spot and harvest wildlife. The eyes of certain nocturnal animals, like muntjac, reflected light from their headlamps, allowing the hunters to spot them in the dense mountain underbrush.

Smiling, Dahu turned to me and said, "We will take the easy road for you." I looked up, wondering where this "road" was and how it could possibly be easy. Our path seemed to go straight up the mountain, with no clear trail in sight. We turned on our headlamps and began our ascent (figure 9). While the men seemed to bound effortlessly up the mountainside with their gear, I struggled behind, carrying only an empty backpack. The incline seemed impossible. I tripped over roots and wrestled through branches as we made our way up, the loose dirt beneath my boots offering little support. Large rocks tumbled past me, racing down the steep slope. Before long, I was covered in dirt, drenched in sweat, bruised, out of breath, and regretting my decision to join another hunting trip. Thankfully, the men slowed their pace to let me catch up.

This was more than just a hunt; it was a time for telling stories and sharing memories. The men spoke of how their ancestors managed the landscape, of

FIGURE 9. A Bunun man hunting at night in the mountains, 2018.

traveling with their fathers to collect the heads of fallen Japanese soldiers, of learning their culture and language, and the challenges of teaching the same to their children. They shared stories about the ethics and rules of hunting, the ways they had adapted their practices over time, and victorious hunts and near-death experiences. These stories filled hours as we hiked. As we walked, the men explained the social significance of hunting for the Bunun people. Dahu said,

> Hunting is so important. It is not only a way of getting meat but also a way of building a man's reputation in the community by showing courage, diligence, and generosity. It is so important that a man's gun becomes like his best friend. If a man is a good hunter, he will be respected in the village and have high standing.

As we walked, the men also explained the norms that guide hunt activities. Over generations of learning to coexist with the mountainous environment, the Bunun have developed systems of rules and taboos guiding conduct called

Samu. Each family clan has its own system of Samu. Certain Samu are based on signs or omens from animals, something perhaps better described as "thinking with" animals.[28] For example, if a *qusqus* bird (or sometimes another small bird or mammal) is seen flying away from the mountain, or if it crosses a hunter's path from left to right, it is interpreted as a sign of danger ahead, and the hunt should stop. Sneezing or flatulence can also be interpreted as cautionary signs.

Dreams play an especially important role, being seen as predictive of fortune or misfortune in the mountains. Before going hunting, family members share their dreams. In these dreams, animals symbolize people and people symbolize animals. For instance, if a hunter dreams of a car full of people driving off a mountainside to their death, it is considered a good omen because it means the hunter will have a successful hunt and catch many animals the next day. On the other hand, dreaming of the death of an animal is a bad sign, indicating that someone may be injured, possibly fatally, during the hunt.

Other Samu provide ethical guidelines for hunting. For example, hunting during the mating season is prohibited, and pregnant or young animals must not be hunted. Animals must be treated with respect, and hunters should avoid causing unnecessary suffering. The men explained that they do not catch an animal; rather, the ancestors provide the animal to them. Because the animal is considered a blessing from the ancestors, no part of it should be wasted. One hunter shared a story about his father who found a rotting animal covered in maggots caught in a trap. After harvesting the animal, his father collected the maggots in a bowl, cooked them, and ate them.

According to Samu, individuals must hunt any animal presented to them because it is a gift from the ancestors. This belief conflicts with ROC regulations requiring hunters to identify the species and number of animals they intend to hunt. In the mountains, such decisions are left to the ancestors. Just as no meat may be wasted, Samu dictates that all meat must be shared. Sharing is a core ethical principle for the Bunun. Men are expected to share meat with anyone who asks, believing that this generosity will be rewarded by the ancestors, who will provide more animals on future hunts.

The men explained that younger people in the community were not interested in hunting. Given the dangers involved, including exploding firearms, treacherous terrain, arrest by police, and encounters with mountain boars and venomous snakes, it is perhaps unsurprising that they were reluctant to learn their hunting practices. Instead, they preferred to get jobs in shops serving tourists in the neighboring town or working in the trucking industry. Dahu expressed sadness that his son had moved to Taipei to work in a factory, rarely returning home. His son's life was very different from his, and he feared that his son would never come to understand Samu or the interconnected relationships of people, wildlife, and land that were central to Bunun cultural life. Dahu's concerns about his son's lack of interest in hunting and the potential collapse of the Bunun ethical system may also have reflected larger anxieties about the decline of gerontocratic power structures in Bunun society, a pattern observed in other Indigenous communities (Simon 2012a).

We spent eight hours hunting in the darkness. The beam of our headlamps made our journey feel personal, intimate even, much more so than it might otherwise have in daylight. We stayed close, the light forming a small, transportable room that moved with us as we wound around the mountainside. The men killed four muntjac deer. They cut the liver out of the first and handed it to me to eat. It was warm and wet in my hands and tasted bitter as I swallowed it. I carried their harvest in my mesh backpack, struggling to find my footing on the loose rocks and tangled vines. As we walked, the smell of the muntjacs surrounded me. I could feel their warm bodies, sense their blood trickling down my back, and hear their last breaths.

We arrived at the base of the mountain at daybreak. Turning off our headlamps, we watched the sun rise across the mountainside. I could see waterfalls and rock outcrops we had passed in the night. I thought about the stories Dahu and the other men had shared at those spots. Exhausted, I dropped my backpack heavy with muntjacs on the ground, grateful to finally relieve my aching shoulders. The men arranged the animals into a row on the ground. They began telling more stories, this time about how they had killed each animal. Dahu recalled my stumbles through the darkness and mimicked them for the group. We all laughed, then climbed into the van. As we drove away, he grinned and said, "Okay, let's go home. Maybe those Forestry Bureau police are still up there looking for us."

Pluralism, Reconciliation, and Tsaqi *Apologies*

Efforts to implement the principles of the 2005 Indigenous Peoples Basic Law have been slow, with the mandatory three-year timeframe largely disregarded. In some areas, however, progress has been made, suggesting tentative movement toward formal legal pluralism. In 2008, the Council of Agriculture and CIP issued a joint ruling allowing Tayan people from the Smangus and Cinsbu communities in Hsinchu County to use natural resources on their ancestral territories for cultural, ritual, or personal purposes. In 2014, the Legislature restored the rights of five Indigenous towns to elect their own representatives after they had been placed under the control of non-Indigenous mayors following the merger of some city and county levels (Jennings 2014). In 2015, the Legislature amended the Basic Law by adding Article 2–1, which established a legal basis for creating Tribal Councils. The Legislature also prepared a "Draft Law on the Establishment of Tribal Public Corporation," allowing Indigenous communities to incorporate as "tribal public corporations" (*buluo gongfaren zuzhi* 部落公法人組織) and operate as semiautonomous entities with the power to govern certain internal affairs. In 2016, the CIP introduced the *Regulations for Indigenous Peoples or Tribes Being Consulted, Obtaining Their Consent and Participation*, which required Indigenous communities to be involved in decisions about development planning, land use, research, and regulation. In 2017, the CIP issued *Regulations for Demarcating Indigenous Peoples Land or Tribal Land Area*, laying a legal foundation for defining Indigenous ancestral territories, although controversially excluding territories on private lands (Charlton, Gao, and Kuan 2017, 145).

A landmark moment occurred in 2016, when President Tsai Ing-wen, whose paternal grandmother was Paiwan, formally apologized to Taiwan's Indigenous peoples on behalf of the ROC government for their oppression and exploitation over the past four hundred years. Her apology took place on August 1, Indigenous Peoples' Day in Taiwan, which commemorates the day that the government amended the Constitution to recognize "*yuanzhumin*" people. In her address, Tsai pledged her administration's commitment to promoting Indigenous self-governance, saying, "In the future, the ideals of Indigenous self-government will be realized step by step" (Tsai 2016). Following this, Tsai's administration established the Presidential Office Indigenous Historical Justice and Transitional Justice Committee to address cultural, governance, language, and land rights issues. Among its various initiatives, the committee has proposed legislation such as the "Draft Act Governing Indigenous Historical Justice and the Restoration of Indigenous Rights," calling on the government to formally acknowledge the historical injustices committed against Indigenous peoples and strengthen protections for Indigenous cultural and land rights. President Tsai's apology, together with these legal, policy, and regulatory changes, suggest that Taiwan may be on the cusp of a new era for Indigenous rights, one oriented, albeit cautiously, toward pluralism and strengthening Indigenous self-governance (Chang 2016, 11).

· · ·

At 9:30 a.m. on August 1, 2016, President Tsai Ing-wen stood alongside Capen Nganaen, a Tao elder from Orchid Island, at the Presidential Office Building in Taipei and issued a formal apology to Taiwan's Indigenous peoples. This apology was momentous because it obligated the ROC government to confront difficult and uncomfortable truths about the historical mistreatment of Indigenous peoples and the character of state-Indigenous relations in Taiwan, issues that could challenge the state's authority over territory and citizens. By making this apology, Tsai did what no other leader in Asia had done before, becoming only the fourth state leader in the world to offer a formal apology to Indigenous peoples.

"It's bullshit" (Paiwan: *Tsaqi*). I was sitting with a group of demonstrators under a large tent watching Tsai's apology in real time on their smartphones. The comment came from the Paiwan man seated next to me, his eyes transfixed on the screen of his phone. The night before, they had slept outside, participating in a larger two-day occupation of Ketagalan Boulevard, named after the Ketagalan people of northern Taiwan, which leads to the Presidential Office Building. Several hundred Indigenous demonstrators had gathered the day before to make their presence known during Tsai's apology. They waved banners and Styrofoam cutouts of hunting firearms, sang songs, and took turns giving speeches through crackling microphone systems, all in an effort to voice their demands and views.

Earlier that evening, police in riot gear forcibly dismantled a tent set up by demonstrators in the middle of Ketagalan Boulevard, leaving them exposed to the rain. The atmosphere was charged, and the evening grew increasingly tense. Several other clashes with police occurred and demonstrators found themselves surrounded by police on all sides. In one location, ten demonstrators were dramatically encircled by what looked to be over one hundred police officers. By the end of the night, the ratio of police officers to demonstrators was roughly three to one, with many more police likely waiting in the line of police buses parked along the boulevard (Hioe 2016).

The demonstrators were not protesting Tsai's apology itself but demanding genuine representation and concrete action on the unequal treatment of Indigenous peoples. One demonstrator put it this way: "Our voice has not been heard. We have been excluded from everything. The government must take this seriously and give us a voice."[29] If Tsai's apology was an attempt to address these concerns, the heavy-handed actions of police outside the Presidential Office Building stood in stark contrast. This was a vivid reminder of the diverse actors, interests, and practices that make up the projected image of a unified

FIGURE 10. Two Paiwan men share a smartphone to watch President Tsai Ing-wen's apology, 2016.

state. If it was a reminder of the state's disunity, that did not mean that it was a falsity, as the demonstrators who encountered police experienced firsthand.

We sat huddled together on red plastic stools, watching Tsai's speech on our smartphones or on mounted television screens (figure 10). The atmosphere was mostly quiet, with everyone concentrating on her words and watching her body language. Occasionally, someone mumbled or grunted in response. As Tsai finished her speech, an Amis man near me summed up his thoughts: "Some good, some bad. I am happy she is setting up plans and dealing with nuclear waste, but she did not describe what she means by Indigenous self-government, which is the most important issue, or how she plans to strengthen the Basic Law."[30]

Other demonstrators had a different perspective. The Paiwan man who said "*Tsaqi*" made his comment as Tsai called for action, saying, "I call upon all citizens to seize the opportunities offered by this day—to join together, work hard, and build a country of justice, a country of true diversity and equality." I wondered how such calls for action, although well-meaning, might be received from an Indigenous standpoint. The man's comment suggested he saw it as part of a political agenda, one that sought to use Indigenous

FIGURE 11. Protest sign on Ketagalan Boulevard during President Tsai Ing-wen's apology, 2016.

cultures to concretize a Taiwanese national identity that, in the end, left them out.

Soon the place was buzzing again. Invited speakers took turns sharing their thoughts on Tsai's speech. One demonstrator grabbed me by the arm and insisted I follow her. She led me out from under the tent to a large red sign hanging between two trees, proclaiming, "Indigenous peoples are not Chinese peoples" (figure 11). Pointing emphatically at the sign, she said, "This is what Tsai needs to remember."[31]

GLOBAL ORDERS: INDIGENOUS PEOPLES AND HUMAN RIGHTS

The rise of a global Indigenous movement in the late twentieth century had a significant influence on the Indigenous movement in Taiwan. It introduced a set of discourses, practices, and institutions facilitating the emergence of a new, pan-Indigenous category (*yuanzhumin*), and inspired Indigenous communities to advocate for economic, labor, and cultural rights and self-determination. The integration of international human rights instruments into ROC law, some of which included robust protections for Indigenous peoples, became a crucial tool for activists seeking to secure Indigenous recognition in the state's legal system. Moreover, human rights norms also helped accomplish other state goals, such as improving Taiwan's global standing and distinguishing Taiwan from mainland China.

Applying human rights norms to Indigenous cases proved challenging because Indigenous human rights in ROC law remain ambiguous and judges hold different opinions on their relevance and applicability. This complexity is reflected in Taiwan's treatment of the UNDRIP and the Two Covenants Act, which incorporates the International Covenant on Civil and Political Rights (ICCPR) and International Covenant on Economic, Social and Cultural Rights (ICESCR) into ROC law. It is also evident in the diverse ways judges address Indigenous human rights in court. Some judges embraced these norms, actively incorporating them into their decision-making, while others rejected their relevance in the ROC legal system. Still others expressed support for Indigenous human rights claims but conveyed a feeling of exhaustion from the sheer volume of invocations of human rights across many kinds of cases.

Human Dignity and Historic Injustice

The foundation for many core international human rights instruments resides in the dignity of the human being (Piechowiak 1999, 5). For example, the preamble to the Universal Declaration of Human Rights affirms that "the inherent dignity ... of all members of the human family is the foundation of freedom, justice and peace in the world." Similarly, both the ICCPR and the ICESCR emphasize that their respective rights "derive from the inherent dignity of the human person."[32] This concept of dignity, rooted in a Kantian belief in the intrinsic worth of all human beings, is a key element linking the rights pronounced in human rights instruments to human persons.

Indigenous human rights locate their normative foundation on a different footing. Two of the most significant international instruments protecting Indigenous peoples are ILO Convention No. 169 and the nonbinding UNDRIP. Both of these instruments ground their rights in historic circumstances. Addressing the earlier ILO No. 107, the preamble to ILO No. 169 states:

> Considering that the developments which have taken place in international law since 1957, as well as developments in the situation of indigenous and tribal peoples in all regions of the world, have made it appropriate to adopt new international standards on the subject with a view to removing the assimilationist orientation of the earlier standards[.]

The preamble to the UNDRIP similarly states: "Concerned that indigenous peoples have suffered from historic injustices as a result of, inter alia, their colonization and dispossession of their lands, territories and resources, thus preventing them from exercising, in particular, their right to development in accordance with their own needs and interests[.]"

By grounding Indigenous human rights in historical circumstances, these instruments disrupt the conventional narrative of human rights as deriving from an inherent and shared trait of humanity. Taking the UNDRIP as the current benchmark for Indigenous rights, these instruments anchor such rights in a particular set of historic circumstances or experiences, positioning them outside the body of human rights generally rooted in human dignity. Grounded in historical circumstances and encompassing a set of collective rights viewed as at odds with the individualistic norms underpinning the theory and practice of international human rights, Indigenous human rights rest on an unsettled normative foundation (see Engle 2010).

This observation tracks an ontological shift within international law and UN agencies, where the language of human rights has focused on individuals, or people, while Indigenous rights have emphasized collectives, or peoples. This shift is also evident in the ROC Constitution through a 1997 amendment, mentioned earlier, that changed language referring to Indigenous "people" to "peoples" (Shih 1999). Human rights discourse generally prioritizes the welfare of individuals over the interests of the group or state, maintaining that rights "belong to any individual as a consequence of being human, independently of acts of law" (Piechowiak 1999, 3). Indigenous rights, by contrast, are of a collective character and are based on a set of rights that include self-determination, cultural knowledge, land, governance, autonomy, and special consideration by the state in policymaking, a vision of rights considerably removed from notions of individualism (Mazel 2009, 149). Indigenous rights, based on "historically grounded communities rather than simply individuals or (inchoate) states," challenge the individual/state "perceptual dichotomy" that has dominated human societies and shaped international legal standards (Anaya 2000, 48). Assertions of collective rights also challenge notions of state sovereignty, as they intrude upon matters of social and political organization within the presumed sphere of state authority.

In Taiwan, efforts to integrate international norms protecting Indigenous peoples into the legal system have revealed resistance to recognizing Indigenous peoples' rights to land and self-governance. The government has instead focused on securing rights related to cultural practices, such as hunting (Gao, Charlton, and Takahashi 2016). From the perspective of the ROC state, elevating cultural values has been seen as more closely aligned with liberal notions of individual rights, whereas granting autonomy to Indigenous groups outside of state structures posed a direct challenge to state sovereignty (see also Simon and Awi Mona 2023). This is evident in the ROC's handling of human rights instruments protecting the rights of Indigenous peoples, including the UNDRIP, as well as the ICCPR and ICESCR.

One Declaration, Two Covenants, and Exhausting Human Rights

The adoption of UNDRIP by the UN General Assembly in 2007 sparked renewed interest in Indigenous rights and human rights in Taiwan. One week after its adoption, officials from the CIP declared that the Basic Law was consistent with the principles of the UNDRIP and pledged to continue efforts to strengthen it (Wang 2007). The ROC government, however, has yet to express its position on or to endorse the UNDRIP. Instead, it has passively acknowledged that the UNDRIP shares many common principles with the Basic Law (Covenants Watch 2016, para. 125). Notably, President Tsai's 2016 apology to Indigenous peoples made no reference to the UNDRIP.

In 2009, the Taiwan Legislature ratified the ICCPR and ICESCR. On the same day, it passed the Act to Implement the International Covenant on Civil and Political Rights and the International Covenant on Economic, Social and Cultural Rights (commonly known as the Two Covenants Act), which incorporated the human rights protections outlined in both covenants into domestic law (Tsai 2015, 296; Chen 2019). Although the ROC government had signed the covenants in 1967, when it still held a seat in the United Nations, ratification had proven elusive until 2009.

Under the Two Covenants Act, government agencies are required to uphold the human rights guarantees in the two covenants, refrain from violating human rights, protect citizens from violations by others, and actively promote the realization of these rights (Art. 4). The government must also ensure coordination across state institutions and agencies to advance and implement human rights (Art. 5), establish a human rights reporting system (Art. 6), allocate a budget to support the implementation of the covenants (Art. 7), and review all laws, regulations, and administrative measures to identify and correct those that are incompatible with the covenants within two years after the law's enactment (Art. 8).

The ICCPR and ICESCR contain provisions that protect the rights of Indigenous peoples. Article 27 of the ICCPR guarantees ethnic minorities the right to "enjoy their own culture," with the Human Rights Committee clarifying in General Comment No. 23 (1994) that this includes Indigenous cultural practices. Similarly, Article 15 of the ICESCR protects the rights of all individuals "to take part in cultural life," and the Committee on Economic, Social and Cultural Rights emphasized in General Comment No. 21 (2009) that Indigenous cultural practices should be protected on an equal basis. A series of interpretations by international committees have applied these provisions to specific disputes involving Indigenous peoples' cultural practices and territories.[33]

Granting the ICCPR and ICESCR the status of domestic law would appear to mark a step forward in securing Indigenous peoples' rights, but the ROC legal system lacks clear regulations outlining how these international treaties relate to other domestic laws (H.-c. Chang 2018, 13). Article 141 of the ROC Constitution provides some guidance, stating that the government should respect treaties and the Charter of the United Nations to promote international cooperation, justice, and peace. Grace Tsai (2015, 305) observes that the wording of Article 141 indicates that "the Covenants should enjoy a superior status over other domestic laws, and new legislation should not contradict the Covenants." In practice, however, applying the covenants to specific cases has proven more complicated.

In the first five years following Taiwan's ratifications of the ICCPR and ICESCR, Taiwan Supreme Court decisions referenced the two covenants in 207 cases, reflecting an increase in their application compared to their use pre-ratification (Covenants Watch 2016, para. 9). In 2016, the Supreme Court formally recognized Articles 2 and 3 of both covenants and incorporated the interpretations of their respective committees into domestic law.[34] As a civil law tradition, however, judicial decisions are not bound by the doctrine of stare decisis, meaning that prior rulings do not hold binding authority in subsequent cases, whether in the same court or in lower courts (Chiu and Fa

1994, 7; Simon and Awi Mona 2015, 13). As a result, lower courts were not formally required to adhere to the Supreme Court's decisions.

Judicial approaches to applying the ICCPR and ICESCR in court varied. Some judges cited these international instruments in cases involving Indigenous peoples.[35] For instance, one district court judge noted that "there are lots of decisions using international human rights laws and relying upon EU and Human Rights Council interpretations, particularly in Taitung and Hualien."[36] Other judges were more hesitant and found reasons to exclude them. One high court judge cited concerns about the lack of normative specificity in these covenants. Rejecting their application, he said, "They are abstract. They are not specific about the particular issue or the fact of the culture."[37]

Some lawyers and Indigenous activists speculated that judges' reluctance to apply human rights norms in cases involving Indigenous persons stemmed from the fact that, as one lawyer opined, "they are unfamiliar with how to interpret domestic laws in ways that fulfill Taiwan's human rights obligations."[38] Another lawyer believed the hesitation was rooted in the fact that "it has been too long between the time of Taiwan being the UN representative for China and the time of implementing international norms into domestic law."[39] Experience had led some lawyers and activists to conclude that human rights–based arguments were not worth making. One lawyer explained, "You cannot really use them [the ICCPR and ICESCR]. The judges will not hear them."[40] Judges, for their part, expressed frustration with lawyers, with one Hualien High Court judge noting, "Many of the lawyers practicing in the court do not know about human rights; they are not well trained."[41] The views of both lawyers and judges highlighted that the application of human rights depended largely on the individuals involved, including their knowledge of human rights law and their willingness to engage with human rights–based arguments. One Paiwan activist succinctly summarized the human rights situation in Taiwan courts, saying, "We make Basic Law and human rights arguments in many cases, maybe most, but it depends on the judge about whether they are effective or not."[42]

Indigenous persons also engaged with the discourse of Indigenous human rights in different ways. Some Indigenous activists saw human rights as a vital tool in their struggle for recognition and self-determination. Others were more skeptical, viewing human rights and international law as distant, irrelevant, and even disempowering. For example, one Truku elder—commenting on international protections for endangered species, some of which were hunted by Indigenous peoples—expressed frustration, saying,

"Animals have more rights than people. They are more protected than people."[43] A Bunun elder and Presbyterian minister shared a similar critique of the disparity between the treatment of Indigenous hunters and of animals: "Dogs and cats kill animals, which is okay, but if an Indigenous person hunts something, they are criminals. They are less than these animals."[44]

In conversation, some judges expressed exhaustion with the frequent use of human rights–based arguments. One high court judge remarked, "Everybody wants to argue human rights. No matter what the issue, human rights issues come up. Human rights come up in Indigenous cases, murder, labor, juvenile, housing, on and on, in lots and lots of cases."[45] Comments like this suggested a degree of "human rights fatigue" among judges, an exasperation with arguments grounded in human rights ideas having few discernible limits and appearing to be motivated more by legal opportunism than principled advocacy. This fatigue may also signal the emergence of a new understanding of human rights norms, one that is more complex than the potent horror at the cruelties in the early to mid-twentieth century that inspired their creation.

. . .

In 2017 and 2018, I worked informally with lawyers at a law center in Hualien that provided free legal services to Indigenous communities in eastern Taiwan. Wanting to contribute, I decided to offer something cherished by lawyers at large, international law firms in common law contexts: a series of legal memoranda. These memoranda would analyze how international tribunals have interpreted Indigenous human rights in disputes involving cultural and land rights. My hope was that lawyers at the center could use this information to develop new kinds of legal arguments in support of Indigenous claims and possibly predict how courts in Taiwan might rule on similar issues. After a few weeks of research at the local library, I completed several memoranda and handed them to a friend at the law center. My well-meaning attempt at an intervention, however, missed the mark. Puzzled, my friend asked me, "Why did you write these? We can read the statutes. Why do we need these documents?" Taiwan's civil law tradition, as mentioned earlier, largely limits court interpretations to existing statutes and regulations, not case law or jurisprudence interpreting these laws. The exhaustive analyses I put together had little relevance to the daily activities in a small, overworked law center.

I shared my disappointment with a lawyer in private practice who represented Indigenous clients in Taiwan courts. He offered to read the memoranda and explained that my expectations about human rights–based arguments got things out of order, saying:

> You must understand how to build Indigenous cases. Ambiguities in the legal framework allow for moving between different laws. Human rights law, constitutional law, Basic Law, domestic statutes, local ordinances, and rules. But sometimes judges do not like those arguments. They just want me to give the easiest law to analyze. I first give the judge the most directly related law and then as the trial develops, I will put in arguments showing that the issue is bigger than just this case. That the judge is solving a significant issue impacting all of the island. And then I expand to something international, like human rights. But starting with human rights will not work. Judges are not receptive to this approach.[46]

In his view, building an argument grounded in human rights was a gradual, strategic process that required careful timing to be effective. It involved expanding the scope of a dispute step-by-step, from a narrow focus on the immediate issues to a broader frame that connected the case to wider implications for Indigenous peoples, nationally and potentially globally. Human rights, he explained, were the aspirational end point of legal argumentation, not the starting point.

A few weeks later, I met with another lawyer who was defending several Truku men in a criminal case I will discuss later. The men's cultural activities in collecting semiprecious stones were not explicitly protected under ROC law. Believing that Indigenous human rights might provide a compelling set of arguments, he asked to see the memoranda. Drawing on the memoranda, he argued at the next hearing that the ROC government had incorporated the ICCPR and ICESCR into domestic law through the Two Covenants Act, and that Article 141 of the ROC Constitution and the 2016 Taiwan Supreme Court ruling obligated courts to give these two covenants priority over other domestic laws. He contended that these covenants protected the men's right to engage in cultural activities and that, based on this, the judge should acquit them. The judge, however, interpreted the law differently, stating:

> The ICCPR and ICESCR are on the same level of Taiwan's law. They are not above it. They are on the same level. So, you cannot argue that they supersede Taiwan law. And Taiwan law deals specifically with this situation. The ICCPR and other human rights are too general to be useful in Taiwan.

The judge concluded his remarks by saying, "You cannot use the ICCPR in Taiwan." On this basis, he dismissed the lawyer's arguments grounded on Indigenous human rights.

CONCLUSION

Disputes over Indigenous cultural practice and land in Taiwan involved the intersection of multiple legal and normative orders. These included local Indigenous laws, national statutes and regulations, international treaty and customary laws, and Buddhist and Christian religious precepts. The meaning of these legal and normative frameworks emerged through their applications, interpretations, and negotiations—what I have called rule-crafting processes.

ROC laws regulating the lives and identities of Indigenous peoples intersected with vibrant Indigenous orders, such as Gaya, and with international human rights norms that activists used to support Indigenous claims to cultural, civil, and political rights. State law generally functioned as an ideological frame through which these other legal and normative systems were interpreted and applied in specific cases. In doing so, it privileged the perspectives and interests of the ROC state and Han Taiwanese society. It also had potent material and symbolic power. Indigenous persons sometimes invoked state law logics to justify actions that conflicted with local norms, and communities sometimes worked to reconfigure their oral traditions in the form and image of state law. Judges, in turn, flexibly interpreted international human rights norms, sometimes giving priority to domestic laws and, at times, excluding human rights considerations altogether.

Indigenous persons were not passive actors in this process. They adhered to local Indigenous laws, even when doing so exposed them to the risk of arrest and prosecution. They crafted counternarratives to challenge ROC nationalist claims over their lands and territories. They adapted cultural activities to preserve their practices in the face of inconsistent legal interpretations of their rights. They also co-opted the form and substance of state laws to resist the disruptions caused by ongoing colonialism and to protect their territories and ways of life from further encroachment. Additionally, they organized protests and demonstrations to hold the ROC government accountable for its exploitation and mistreatment of Indigenous peoples, demanding that it honor its commitments to Indigenous recognition and rights.

The ad hoc Chambers of Indigenous Courts have emerged as key institutions for navigating these complex intersections of legal and normative orders and for finding ways to implement Indigenous peoples' rights in a manner that respects their cultures, their relationships to lands, and Taiwan's human rights obligations. The nature of these specialized Indigenous court units, however, has been ambiguous. They are administered by non-Indigenous judges, who generally apply ROC laws and legal procedures in court proceedings conducted in Mandarin Chinese. The next chapter explores the many ambiguities surrounding these units and examines how, amid these uncertainties, they sometimes generated spaces for new forms of engagement that could, at times, be transformative for the participants involved.

THREE

Ethereal Presences of the Ad Hoc Chambers

Field notes. August 11, 2016.

Mr. Wu and I sat in a conference room at the Judicial Yuan's headquarters, located in the government district of Taipei City, Taiwan's capital. Mr. Wu, a deputy director at the Judicial Yuan, was responsible for overseeing the ad hoc Chambers of Indigenous Courts in the ROC national court system. As we sipped tea, he outlined several factors that led to the establishment of the ad hoc chambers in 2013. These included "ensuring the multicultural development of Indigenous peoples," addressing "the disadvantages Indigenous persons faced in the national court system," and growing awareness that domestic laws impinged upon "cultural activities that serve as significant sources of identity and meaning for Indigenous peoples." With these concerns in mind, the Judicial Yuan first established the ad hoc chambers in nine district courts located in areas with large concentrations of Indigenous peoples and later expanded the program to all district and appellate courts across the main island. Curious about what set these specialized units apart from others, I asked Mr. Wu to explain. He paused. After a moment's reflection, he said, "They are courts of opportunity." In these courts, he explained, case assignment procedures and special training for judicial actors increased the probability that Indigenous persons would encounter Han Taiwanese state actors who were knowledgeable about and respectful of Indigenous lifeways and who would work to accommodate Indigenous peoples' cultural differences and unique situations. As I left the Judicial Yuan headquarters, I reflected on Mr. Wu's framing of the units in terms of probabilities of generous encounter. Later that afternoon, I shared the idea of the specialized units as "courts of opportunity" with a lawyer who represented Indigenous clients in Taiwan courts. The lawyer, unimpressed, snorted, "The Indigenous court units do not exist yet. Everything is just the same. You just treat the case the same as any other case."

MR. WU'S DESCRIPTION OF TAIWAN'S ad hoc Chambers of Indigenous Courts as "courts of opportunity" and the lawyer's dismissal of their presence surprised me at the time, but I came to understand their remarks as emblematic of the many ambiguities surrounding these specialized units. This chapter focuses on the ad hoc chambers themselves, examining their history, structure, personnel, and proceedings. It situates these court bodies in the context of recent legal reforms in Taiwan aimed at improving Indigenous peoples' position in the national legal system, while also highlighting the significant uncertainties surrounding their operations and the challenges involved in managing cases related to Indigenous issues.

Ambiguity emerged as a central characteristic of the units, a byproduct of political compromises and reflecting broader uncertainties surrounding indigeneity and Indigenous rights in Taiwan. In general, *ambiguity* refers to the quality of being open to multiple interpretations or remaining inexact (Augé 1998, 30). Anthropologists have explored the concept of ambiguity from various directions. Some have examined it as a productive tension between national discourse and everyday practice, noting how it can both reinforce national identity and challenge state power (Herzfeld 1987). Others have analyzed it as a form of hegemony, whereby ambiguity itself becomes the preferred, rehearsed category (Brković 2015, 2017; Green 2005). Still others have focused on the potential of ambiguity to create protective spaces for marginalized or vulnerable persons (Newman 2019).

This discussion contributes to these conversations by considering the ambiguities working in and through Taiwan's ad hoc Chambers of Indigenous Courts as these institutions attempt to span Han Taiwanese and Indigenous worlds through the administration of court cases. Ambiguities in the specialized units manifested in many ways, through disagreements over the chambers' real presences, hazy institutional purposes, the lack of Indigenous representation, gaps in knowledge about Indigenous cultures and rights, procedures indistinguishable from those of ordinary courts, inconsistent applications of laws meant to protect Indigenous peoples, varying attitudes among legal actors toward Indigenous claims, court procedures that disadvantaged Indigenous litigants, and the overall inaccessibility of the units. These issues reproduced other ambiguities in the ROC government's engagements with Indigenous peoples, but they also created openings for new forms of interaction that had the potential to be transformative. As I show in later chapters, the resolution of these ambiguities did not lie in the routine workings of the units but in a variety of exploratory and creative practices developed by judicial, Indigenous, and intermediary actors involved in cases related to Indigenous practices and lands, a feature reflecting the ad hoc chambers' work as boundary institutions.

FROM CONCEPTION TO INCEPTION

On May 15, 2012, the ROC Ministry of Justice hosted a symposium titled "Assessing the Feasibility of Setting Up a Special Indigenous Court" (*pinggu shezhi yuanzhuminzu zhuanye fating zhi kexingxing* 評估設置原住民族專業法庭之可行性), at the Academy for the Judiciary in Taipei. The event brought together Han Taiwanese and Indigenous scholars, lawmakers, judges, and lawyers from across the island to explore the possibility of establishing an Indigenous court for Taiwan's sixteen state-recognized Indigenous peoples. During the symposium, the majority of participants agreed to focus their efforts on court reform by creating a specialized court institution dedicated to handling cases involving Indigenous individuals and communities, rather than pursuing additional legislative enactments or reforms, to strengthen existing legal protections for Indigenous peoples (Judicial Yuan; 2018a, 2). The idea of establishing Indigenous courts was inspired by similar institutions created in the national court systems of Canada, New Zealand, and the United States. This initiative was driven by a growing recognition that Indigenous peoples held different views about culture and law from the Han Taiwanese, exemplified in the Paiwan Alili Incident discussed earlier. In aspiration, specialized courts that were knowledgeable about Indigenous peoples' cultures, practices, and legal concepts would be in a better position to protect their rights and ensure respect for their differences (see also Bekhoven 2018, 217n899).

Following the symposium, on May 30, 2012, the Judicial Yuan enacted a set of rules in the *Measures for the Annual Assignment of Judges in Civil and Administrative Litigation Cases and Special Courts* (hereafter "Judicial Assignment Measures"). These rules provided for assignments of judges that would establish a system of Indigenous court divisions or units within the national court system, effectively forming the ad hoc Chambers of Indigenous Courts (Judicial Yuan 2018a, 2). Amendments to Article 13 of the Judicial Assignment Measures granted local courts authority to create the ad hoc chambers, stating, "To protect the judicial rights of Indigenous peoples, the Judicial Yuan may order courts to establish Indigenous courts or specialized divisions." Additionally, amendments to Article 14 outlined the general procedures for creating the ad hoc chambers. These procedures included the appointment of judges by the chief judge in consultation with a committee of judges and setting three-year terms for the appointments.

In September 2012, Taiwan published its first report on the implementation of the International Covenant on Civil and Political Rights. In this report, the ROC government represented that it intended to establish Indigenous courts at the earliest opportunity, stating, "The government shall adequately evaluate and establish the Indigenous peoples' court or tribunal with the respect for traditional customs, culture, and values of Indigenous peoples" (Executive Yuan 2012, para. 359). According to the report, these specialized courts would take into consideration the uniqueness of Indigenous peoples' situations and show respect for their cultural values and traditions.

On October 8, 2012, following the release of the report, the Judicial Yuan issued a formal directive to the district courts in Taoyuan, Hsinchu, Miaoli, Nantou, Chiayi, Kaohsiung, Pingtung, Taitung, and Hualien, instructing them to create a specialized division of Indigenous court units that would commence operation on January 1, 2013 (Judicial Yuan 2012c). A year and a half later, on June 13, 2014, the Judicial Yuan sent another directive instructing the remaining district, high, and administrative courts, excluding Kinmen and the Taiwan Supreme Court, to establish special divisions of Indigenous court units, scheduled to begin operation on September 3, 2014 (Judicial Yuan 2014). In just seven and a half months, the Judicial Yuan had made and implemented a decision to create ad hoc Chambers of Indigenous Courts. The program was expanded nationwide eighteen months later, establishing the units in all district, high, and administrative courts.

Some individuals involved in the process commented on the rushed manner in which the Judicial Yuan established the ad hoc chambers. One participant noted that early plans envisioned a more deliberate three-stage process.[1] Under these plans, the ROC government would first survey and document local Indigenous laws and justice traditions across the island. Next, it would determine the historical boundaries of Indigenous communities, with the idea that the specialized units' jurisdictions would align with these boundaries. Finally, as the ad hoc chambers were being established, the government would amend all relevant laws and regulations to ensure consistency with the Indigenous Peoples Basic Law. Instead of following these steps, the Judicial Yuan bypassed the initial stages and created the ad hoc chambers in a matter of months, without any attendant legislative amendments. Some insiders I spoke with interpreted this rush as a political move by then president Ma Ying-jeou, whose administration had pledged to preserve and promote Indigenous cultures and safeguard their legal rights, but it was not a real measure to support Indigenous peoples.[2]

The Judicial Yuan publicly announced the ad hoc chambers in 2012, highlighting two key objectives for these new judicial institutions: (1) to "respect" (*zunzhong* 尊重) Indigenous peoples' traditional customs, cultures, and values; and (2) to safeguard Indigenous peoples' "judicial rights and interests" (*sifa quanyi* 司法權益) (Judicial Yuan 2012b). Press releases from the Judicial Yuan emphasized that the specialized units would "respect Indigenous cultures and protect civil rights" (Xiang 2012). Government reports further stated that the units would "establish an effective mechanism to protect the judicial rights of Indigenous peoples" (Judicial Yuan 2017b). The Council of Indigenous Peoples summarized the purpose of the ad hoc chambers as follows:

> In terms of the traditional customs of Indigenous peoples and domestic laws, when these come into contact, the special units can demonstrate respect for pluralistic cultures, traditional customs, and values, and provide Indigenous peoples a proper legal evaluation to implement the provisions of Article 30 of the Indigenous Peoples Basic Law. (Council of Indigenous Peoples 2015)[3]

In addition to fostering greater respect for Indigenous cultures within the judiciary, commentators analyzing the ad hoc chambers noted that the specialized units would allow judges to develop expertise in the unique legal protections afforded to Indigenous peoples, address their marginalized position within the national court system, and ensure consistent handling of cases involving conflicts between local Indigenous laws and state law across the judiciary (see D.-m. Chen 2012; Tsai 2015, 303). One district court judge familiar with the process also observed that, over time, the units would help build a repository of case law to which future judges could refer when adjudicating cases involving Indigenous peoples, their cultural practices, and their lands.[4] Even though Taiwan's civil law tradition prioritizes statutes over case law, judges sometimes looked to case law for reasons of mental economy and to avoid reversal.

STRUCTURE AND AMBIGUITY

The legal foundation for Taiwan's ad hoc Chambers of Indigenous Courts is rooted in Article 30 of the Basic Law, which states, "For the purpose of protecting Indigenous peoples' rights and access to the judiciary, Indigenous peoples' court or tribunal may be established." By design, the ad hoc chambers are impermanent judicial bodies (Hsu 2015, 94–95). They are classified as "specialized courts" (*zhuanye fating* 專業法庭) under Articles 14 and 34 of the Court Organization Act, which are special court divisions established for the betterment of work in response to societal changes. Other examples of specialized courts include electoral courts and labor courts. This kind of court body is distinguished from "specialized district courts" (*zhuanye difang fayuan* 專業地方法院), which consist of independent courts established on a permanent basis and require certification demonstrating competence in subject matter, such as the Intellectual Property Court.

The ad hoc chambers' jurisdiction is primarily based on the "identity" of individuals as Indigenous, rather than on the "type" of case involving matters related to Indigenous peoples' cultures or territories. Cases are assigned to the ad hoc chambers according to the following procedure: (1) all criminal cases involving an individual with Indigenous status; (2) civil cases involving a litigant with Indigenous status, a *buluo* (community), or an Indigenous group, provided that the case involves one of a prescribed set of legal issues; and (3) cases involving an individual with Indigenous status, a *buluo*, or Indigenous groups outside the prescribed categories, but where the party has petitioned the court to have the case adjudicated by the specialized units (Judicial Yuan 2012b). In the Taiwan court system, the assignment of Indigenous cases to the specialized units thus occurs as an ethnoracial jurisdictional grounding and is unique in the system (Tang 2013, 19).

The ad hoc chambers are intimately bound to the Taiwan national court system. They do not operate from separate buildings or facilities, but instead share courtrooms and other resources in national courthouse buildings. Cases involving Indigenous individuals are adjudicated on the basis of existing ROC statutes, regulations, and codes, rather than Indigenous legal systems (see also Tsai 2015, 303). The administration of these cases is predominantly handled by Han Taiwanese legal professionals, not Indigenous persons. During my fieldwork, only two judges and four lawyers nationwide had Indigenous status (see also Hsu 2015, 92), highlighting the limited representation of Indigenous persons in the ROC legal system. The language of law in court proceedings is Mandarin Chinese; Indigenous languages are secondary and accommodated through a special interpreter program.

Specialized training for judges and prosecutors serves as the cornerstone of the ad hoc chambers. District court judges assigned to the specialized units are required to complete twelve hours of mandatory training,[5] a requirement that does not apply to judges at the appellate level (see Tsai 2022). This training includes lectures by legal scholars on Indigenous peoples' unique rights; visits to Indigenous villages and the sites of significant cases, like Smangus village (mentioned earlier); mock trial exercises; and presentations on recent research into Indigenous practices, including topics like homemade firearms (Judicial Yuan 2018a, 19–22). Prosecutors serving in the ad hoc chambers participate in a similar training program. Beyond this basic training, however, the Judicial Yuan provides little guidance on how local courts should implement or operate the specialized units, leaving much of the process to individual courts' discretion.

In practice, participants observed that the mandatory training for judges assigned to the specialized units provided only about six hours of substantive instruction. Due to the infrequency of cases involving issues related to Indigenous cultural practices or territories, judges often lacked incentive to pursue additional training, opting instead to focus on other areas of law. One judge estimated that only half of those assigned to the ad hoc chambers pursued further training beyond the first year.[6] Additionally, the Judicial Yuan's training sessions often relied on the same experts, limiting the diversity of voices and perspectives on Indigenous peoples' cultures and rights. The training also lacked any assessment, such as examinations or other measures to ensure competency, unlike the programs for judges in the "specialized district courts." Recognizing these deficiencies, activists pushed for reforms to strengthen this training. In 2018, the Judicial Yuan introduced a voluntary certification program that allowed judges to apply for a certificate indicating their specialization in Indigenous legal rights and cultures. At the time of my fieldwork, only one judge had applied for a certificate. As a result, while many government actors regarded specialized knowledge about Indigenous cultures and rights as a defining feature of the ad hoc chambers, the consensus among participants was that such institutional knowledge was significantly lacking.

For some judges, the training had an ironic effect: compelling them to acknowledge that they *did not* know about Indigenous peoples' cultures or their rights. That is, more than productively instilling any in-depth knowledge about Indigenous peoples, the training had generated in these judges an awareness that they knew little about the subject and were ill-equipped to make informed decisions. To remedy this, some judges turned to self-education. As one high court judge observed, "There is some training for judges, but it does not necessarily mean they have any special knowledge about Indigenous people. In this region, there are more Indigenous cases, so judges must personally and by themselves do research about Indigenous people."[7] Other judges turned to outside experts, such as academics and local elders. A district court judge observed: "In cultural cases, like hunting, we will use experts from their particular village. Their culture is very complex. It is important that we ask experts from the particular village, not the community but their village."[8] Another district court similarly noted, "The biggest challenge is understanding the culture. So, we will use officials from tribes and elders to explain traditional practices. To find an expert witness, we ask the tribal government to provide a recommendation. We also have a list of people for each tribe."[9]

For these judges, the training provided by the Judicial Yuan was enough to highlight its own inadequacies and indicate that additional steps were necessary. There was, however, no formal protocol in place to guide the next steps. As discussed below, administrative procedures sometimes hindered using local experts. Moreover, the involvement of experts did not always resolve the issue, as their testimony sometimes challenged judges' assumptions about Indigenous cultural practices and ways of life.

The ad hoc chambers are one among several types of specialized divisions within the Taiwan national court system, which are ranked according to priority. Article 2, Paragraph 1, Section 4 (referencing Schedules 1 and 2) of the Judicial Assignment Measures sets out the categories of judicial assignments, which differ depending on whether the case involves civil or criminal matters. In the civil courts, judicial assignments are divided into eight categories: labor, election, medical, engineering, intellectual property, family, debt, and Indigenous units. In the criminal courts, there are nine categories: medical, financial, intellectual property, sexual assault, juvenile, military, Indigenous, criminal compulsory, and transitional justice units. Articles 14 and 36 of the Court Organization Act allow courts to establish specialized units based on their needs; as a result, the collection of units in particular courts differs around the island. These units are ranked hierarchically, meaning that cases involving Indigenous persons can be assigned to higher-priority units. As Ting-yi Tsai (2022, 80–81) notes, the ad hoc Chambers of Indigenous Courts are ranked lower than other specialized units. Consequently, in certain circumstances, Indigenous persons' cases may be assigned to high-ranking units. For example, Tsai provides a hypothetical case of a soldier with Indigenous status accused of sexual assault. Under this ranking system, the case would be assigned to the military unit rather than the Indigenous unit (or the sexual assault unit), despite involving an Indigenous person (and a sexual assault).

When I began my field research, I was struck by how much the ad hoc Chambers of Indigenous Courts in the Hualien District and High Courts looked and functioned like ordinary courts. I had expected something different, based on my understanding that these units were intended to be specialized. In each courtroom, I encountered proceedings administered by Han Taiwanese judicial actors with little knowledge about Indigenous peoples and who could not speak Indigenous languages. State laws and procedures applied, and the dominant language in the courtroom was that of Han Taiwanese society. The broad jurisdiction of the units meant that they rarely addressed cultural or territorial issues specific to Indigenous peoples. Furthermore, there was no dedicated space for the specialized units. Instead, they were constituted anew each time in courtrooms by the presence of an assigned judge and parties with Indigenous status.

This may not be dissimilar to other types of specialized courts elsewhere in the Taiwan court system, such as the family court divisions. Significant claims, however, were being made for the ad hoc chambers, creating expectations that their presence would be discernible in some respect. No art, artifacts, images, or other symbols of Indigenous peoples inhabited the courthouse buildings, an absence that stood out in contrast to the many representations of Indigenous peoples that adorned other local public buildings. For example, signs in the hospital in Hualien were written in Pangcah, Indigenous artwork was displayed in the Hualien County Cultural Affairs Library, and larger-than-life portraits of Indigenous persons adorned the walls of the Hualien train station to promote tourism. In the courtroom, judges made no announcements that a specialized unit was in session. Likewise, lawyers typically did not refer to the units in their oral arguments or court filings. Often, the only overt marker of the ad hoc chamber's existence was the presence of the Mandarin Chinese character 原 (*yuan*, signifying *yuanzhumin* or Indigenous person) in the docket numbers of cases.

The ad hoc chambers manage a significant volume of Indigenous cases each year. To provide a sense of numbers, Taiwan district courts resolved 9,230 criminal cases involving Indigenous persons in 2014 (out of 200,111 criminal cases total; or 4.61%); 10,831 in 2015 (out of 204,465; or 5.3%); and 11,106 in 2016 (out of 208,478; or 5.33%).[10] Over the same years, Taiwan high courts resolved 415 criminal appeals involving Indigenous persons (out of 17,116 criminal appeals total; or 2.42%), 500 (out of 16,058; or 3.11%), and 551 (out of

15,953; or 3.45%). The average number of days it took to resolve cases involving Indigenous persons in the district courts was 53.68 days in 2014, 55.11 days in 2015, and 66.28 days in 2016. In the high courts, the average number of days it took to resolve appeals involving Indigenous persons was 90.64 days in 2014, 94.16 days in 2015, and 100.24 days in 2016. Regarding civil matters, Taiwan district courts resolved 672 civil matters involving Indigenous persons in 2014, 731 in 2015, and 709 in 2016, and high courts resolved 26, 62, and 85 civil appeals involving Indigenous persons during the same years. Many of these cases concerned routine legal matters, like torts, criminal fraud, and criminal negligence. A smaller number addressed sensitive matters connected to Indigenous peoples' cultures and territories, such as hunting, firearms, fishing, gathering of minerals and forest products, and access to ancestral lands.

Disputes handled by the ad hoc chambers in the criminal division of the Hualien District Court were predominantly routine matters, such as drunk driving and drug possession, with little connection to issues associated with Indigenous cultures or lands (see also Tsai 2022). One case from my fieldwork exemplifies the everyday cases that occupied much of the chamber's time. It involved a young Indigenous woman charged with heroin possession. Following case assignment procedures, her case was assigned to the ad hoc Chamber of Indigenous Courts. During her testimony, the young woman explained to the judge, a Han Taiwanese person in their early thirties, that she had started using drugs two years earlier. After her family kicked her out of the house, she moved in with a friend who was also abusing drugs and who kept her dependent. She pleaded with the judge to keep her in jail, given that she had no place to go. In response, the judge asked why she had not sought a loan from a bank to rebuild her life. The woman explained that she was unable to obtain a loan. The judge, seeming surprised, insisted that getting a loan was straightforward: She only needed to visit a bank and ask. The woman's defense lawyer interjected, explaining that banks require collateral to approve loans, something the young woman did not have. The judge dismissed this explanation and ended the proceeding by setting a date for rendering the decision—which, predictably, was conviction. What stood out, in this proceeding and others like it, was the absence of meaningful discussion about the young woman's Indigenous status or cultural background. There was no reference to, or examination of, the systemic challenges, living conditions, or historical trauma faced by Indigenous communities that could help explain her struggles with drug abuse (see Ciwang and Hsieh 2023). The case was treated as no different than any other.

Between 2012 and 2015, the criminal division of the Hualien District Court handled over two thousand drunk driving cases and more than three hundred drug cases involving Indigenous persons, far outnumbering the cases seen as addressing Indigenous cultural practices or land-related issues. Those included only seventeen cases involving firearms, sixteen related to wildlife hunting, and fifteen about the gathering of forest products or minerals. As some legal actors and Indigenous activists noted, however, the line distinguishing "routine" cases from those involving Indigenous cultural or territorial issues was not always clear. It was also a contested line.

Generally, three types of cases emerged in the specialized units: (1) cases in which participants did not treat the dispute as involving an Indigenous cultural or territorial issue; (2) cases where participants explicitly framed the dispute as involving such issues; and (3) cases where one group of participants argued that Indigenous cultural or territorial issues were at stake, while another group disagreed. This discussion, and those in the following chapters, draws on examples from all three categories, as each sheds light on the contested understandings of law, culture, and land between state and Indigenous perspectives. Importantly, the fact that participants did not treat a case as involving an Indigenous cultural or territorial issue did not mean that no participants regarded it as involving such an issue; at times, they strategically chose not to raise the issue. Moreover, when participants invoked Indigenous culture or relationships to land, this did not necessarily reflect a broader Indigenous worldview. Instead, such invocations were often shaped by the specific actors, events, and circumstances of the dispute. Ultimately, the relevance of Indigenous culture and land in disputes was frequently influenced by the legal issues at play, the procedures of the court, and the assumptions and motivations of the participants (see also Tsai 2022).

Some judges expressed concern that the ad hoc chambers' broad jurisdictional scope distracted the courts from addressing Indigenous "cultural" issues and hindered focusing on matters related to the colonial situation or transitional justice. One high court judge remarked, "Judges generally do not pay attention to [cases involving Indigenous culture] really, because they are just mixed in with all the other cases. There is no time or motivation to separate these cases out from all the others."[11] This was underscored by one judge who reported to me that when he saw the *yuan* character in the criminal docket, he tended to assume that it was "another drunk driving case" involving an Indigenous person.[12] His assumption reflected a Han Taiwanese stereotype of Indigenous persons as chronically unemployed and frequently intoxicated

(Ciwang and Hsieh 2023, 136). Thus, while the ad hoc chambers' wide jurisdictional scope advanced the goal of securing Indigenous peoples' judicial rights by providing them with access to courts, it appeared simultaneously to work against another stated goal, that of respecting their cultural differences.

Under courtroom procedures, lawyers with little or no special training in Indigenous peoples' issues or rights were expected to raise matters related to Indigenous culture. These lawyers, together with their Indigenous clients, were the primary actors through whom courts came to regard disputes as involving Indigenous cultures or territories. Indigenous parties themselves, however, often declined opportunities to raise issues related to their cultures, owing to the uncertainty about how these issues would be treated by Han Taiwanese judges and lawyers. This uncertainty was not misplaced, as judges' attitudes toward Indigenous claims varied significantly, ranging from deep skepticism to thoughtful consideration of their circumstances and cultures. For example, as discussed in later chapters, one high court judge described core Indigenous rights instruments, like the Indigenous Peoples Basic Law, as "dangerous." Other judges were more sympathetic, like the high court judge who remarked, "These [Indigenous] courts send a clear signal that we must respect Indigenous cultures. We must look at the Constitution and multicultural provision and the Indigenous Peoples Basic Law."[13]

These features gave the ad hoc Chambers of Indigenous Courts an almost ethereal presence in the Hualien courthouse. Public pronouncements from the Judicial Yuan about their establishment notwithstanding, local judges, lawyers, and Indigenous people disagreed about the units' real presence in Taiwan courtrooms. Some believed not only that the ad hoc chambers were present, but that they played an important role in protecting Indigenous peoples' rights and access to justice. Others, however, questioned whether the specialized units were there at all, perceiving them as little more than ordinary courts under a different name.

Disagreements about the ad hoc chambers were a recurring theme during my field research. As I traveled across the island to visit various chambers, I frequently encountered conflicting views about the presence and effectiveness of the specialized units, sometimes while standing in courtrooms where the units were ostensibly in operation. These conflicting descriptions and perspectives could not be neatly categorized by institutional role (judge, lawyer), court level (district court, appellate court), identity (Indigenous, Han Taiwanese), or geographic location (eastern Taiwan, western Taiwan). For example, one district court judge asserted confidently, "The specialized

Indigenous courts are definitely there working to help Indigenous people,"[14] while another district court judge confided, "There are no special Indigenous court units."[15] Similarly, returning to the vignette at the start of this chapter, Deputy Director Wu insisted that the specialized units were present in both the district and high courts, whereas the lawyer who represented Indigenous clients dismissed this claim, stating, "Everything is just the same." In Dowmung, opinions were equally divided. Some community members regarded the ad hoc chambers as a "good development" that does "many good things for Indigenous peoples,"[16] while others dismissed them as a hollow initiative designed to secure future Indigenous votes. Still others had never even heard of the units. A Han Taiwanese legal scholar likewise expressed skepticism, remarking, "There is not enough to call them 'special Indigenous courts.' They are a different court in name only."[17]

These differences in opinion underscored the ambiguous position of the ad hoc Chambers of Indigenous Courts in the Taiwan national court system. Local actors recognized that much was at stake in determining whether the specialized units functioned as genuinely distinct judicial bodies or merely as a mechanical case assignment procedure creating an "Indigenous docket" of cases within the existing system. This distinction was critical, because the units were tasked with taking into consideration the uniqueness of Indigenous peoples' situations and promoting respect for Indigenous peoples and their cultures in the court system. Beyond this function, the units were also seen as advancing constitutional multiculturalism and symbolized a step toward formal legal pluralism (see also Simon and Awi Mona 2015, 6).

COURT COMPOSITION AND PERSONNEL

As previously mentioned, the ad hoc Chambers of Indigenous Courts are administered by specially trained judges in the civil and criminal divisions of Taiwan's district courts and high courts, as well as by specially trained prosecutors in the criminal divisions. Several features of these legal actors bear highlighting, which I discuss here in detail: The vast majority of judges and prosecutors are non-Indigenous, they receive limited training on Indigenous peoples' cultural issues and legal rights, and, in the case of prosecutors, they appear to be increasingly hostile to Indigenous rights claims. For some of these judges and prosecutors, their work in the specialized units may be their first meaningful encounter with Indigenous persons or their rights issues.

Judges

Article 81 of the Constitution of the Republic of China establishes a career judiciary (see also Chiu and Fa 1994, 14). Law graduates from Taiwan universities can qualify for this career path by taking the Civil Service Special Examination for Judges and Prosecutors (Judicial Officer Exam), which has a low success rate of approximately 4 percent. If they pass the examination, they then undergo two years of training at the Judicial Training Institute, divided into three periods (Chang 2014, 158). The first stage involves six months of law school–like instruction, followed by sixteen months of clerkships in courts or internships in administrative agencies, and, finally, a one-and-a-half-month period to write a thesis on a legal issue.

As a result, career judges can enter the judiciary as early as their twenties. This procedure has tended to produce judges who are academically accomplished but often lack life experience. This emphasis on academic achievement over life experience, along with the appointment of younger judges, has given judges a reputation of lacking substantive knowledge about real-world circumstances (see also Kennedy 2007, 8), something perhaps illustrated in the judge's assumptions about the ease of obtaining loans mentioned earlier.

Judges assigned to the ad hoc Chambers of Indigenous Courts are selected by the chief judge of the local court in consultation with a committee of judges. In practice, courts often assign younger judges to the specialized units. Assigning a block of cases, such as those involving Indigenous matters, to newer judges ensures that they carry a workload comparable to more senior judges. Importantly, no prior specialization or experience in Indigenous issues is required for participation in the ad hoc chambers. It is notable that Taiwan undergraduate law programs also generally do not offer courses on Indigenous cultures or legal rights, nor does the Judicial Officer Exam include questions on these topics. As a result, judges appointed to the specialized units rarely bring substantive knowledge about Indigenous peoples or the laws protecting their cultural practices and territories to the units.

During my fieldwork, I encountered only one judge who acknowledged having Indigenous ancestry (his mother was Pangcah), although he did not formally claim Indigenous status. As noted above, my collaborators in the Taiwan judiciary estimated that, out of the approximately 1,220 judges nationwide (Song 2000), perhaps only two or three judges had Indigenous status.[18] The Judicial Yuan, in special reports prepared for me, stated that they do not maintain records or statistics on the number of judges with

Indigenous status. Instead, they offered an assurance that "all [judges] have considerable respect for the diverse cultures of all ethnic groups, understanding, and inclusion."[19] In short, ethnic representation among the judges managing the ad hoc chambers was overwhelmingly Han Taiwanese.

The criminal division of the Hualien District Court assigned nine judges to the ad hoc Chamber of Indigenous Courts, a large number in comparison to other jurisdictions. This reflected the high volume of Indigenous cases that the court handled annually. The judges included both women and men, many of whom were relatively junior in status. None of them were Indigenous. While they all had participated in the mandatory training program provided by the Judicial Yuan, only half pursued additional voluntary training on Indigenous cultures and rights beyond the first year.

The Hualien High Court assigned three judges to the ad hoc chamber. Unlike their counterparts in the Hualien District Court, these judges were not required to attend the Judicial Yuan training program. Many elected not to participate, although some shared with me that they had undertaken independent study on Indigenous cultures and legal protections.[20] One High Court judge explained:

> Judges in the district courts receive special training in Indigenous issues, these judges are the special Indigenous court division. But at the appellate level all judges get these cases, there are three of us, it doesn't necessarily mean they have any special knowledge about Indigenous people. No, judges in the appellate court do not necessarily know about Indigenous people or have specialized knowledge. In the Hualien appellate court, there are more Indigenous cases, so judges personally and individually go research about Indigenous people.[21]

For these and other reasons, judges in the Hualien District Court sometimes questioned the commitment of High Court judges to the ad hoc chambers. One judge remarked, "High Court judges are not good students. They do not study hard. They do not care so much about these [Indigenous peoples'] cases."[22] This disparity in training and knowledge between District Court and High Court judges assigned to the specialized units had significant implications, particularly given that the Hualien High Court reviewed appeals de novo (afresh) from across eastern Taiwan, the region with the highest concentration of Indigenous peoples on the island.

Judges assigned to the ad hoc chambers in the Hualien District and High Courts described different jurisprudential orientations. District Court judges tended to frame civil and criminal disputes in terms of understanding the local situation and finding mutually acceptable resolutions. Their comments suggested an open-mindedness to solutions that would resolve disputes, including innovative ways of addressing Indigenous matters. High Court judges, by contrast, tended to focus on broader regional issues and adhered more closely to Supreme Court jurisprudence. While they were not entirely closed off to the idea of new solutions, their comments suggested a more conservative interpretation of the law and Indigenous claims. There were, of course, exceptions. For example, one High Court judge in Tainan invested considerable personal time in studying Indigenous peoples' cultures and rights and developed innovative ways of approaching these cases, such as engaging with Kantian notions of human dignity, which I will discuss later.

These different jurisprudential orientations were no secret. Lawyers were aware of them and adjusted their arguments accordingly. Among lawyers and Indigenous activists, the general perception was that lower-court judges, like those working in the Hualien District Court, were more receptive to claims related to Indigenous peoples' cultures and lands. Some attributed this to the presence of younger judges, who were seen as more progressive in their thinking. The High Court judges, by contrast, were viewed as more conservative and less inclined to entertain such claims.

The composition of the ad hoc chambers was shaped not only by judicial selection and appointment processes, but also by the system of judicial reassignment. In Taiwan, judges have the option to apply for reassignment to a different court at the same level every two years, or to a different level, such as being designated a supporting judge for a higher-level court, every three years. Judges typically seek reassignment for reasons such as living conditions, family issues, case type, and career advancement. These reassignment procedures posed a unique challenge for the specialized units, as the territorial jurisdiction of courts placed judges in certain assemblages of Indigenous peoples. When judges transferred from one jurisdiction to another, they took with them the knowledge they had acquired about the Indigenous groups in that region. Courts in counties with the highest concentrations of Indigenous peoples, including Hualien and Taitung Counties, were located in the least developed parts of the island. For more urban-minded judges, these areas offered undesirable living conditions and limited opportunities for career advancement, factors that frequently motivated them to seek reassignment.

During my fieldwork, several disputes in the Hualien ad hoc chambers were disrupted by rotations of judges, as judges transferred from Hualien to more urban areas and were replaced by new judges, even amid ongoing trials. Local lawyers recognized that judicial reassignment posted a significant challenge to the effective functioning of the specialized units. One lawyer framed the problem this way:

> Nobody wants to be in Hualien. Every few years, judges can apply to transfer. So many judges go back to the big cities. So, all the judges in the case today are new. And that makes a difference because Indigenous cultures in different areas are different. So, we lose expertise when judges move from one area to another.[23]

Another lawyer shared a similar observation: "Judges will rotate every September. Many judges want to go back to the cities. They do not want to stay in the countryside. Judges will want to leave, [and] apply to leave in September."[24]

Judicial rotation also takes place internally within Taiwan courts. Under Article 12 of the Judicial Assignment Measures, judges serve three-year terms on "specialized courts," such as the ad hoc chambers, after which they may request to either remain in their role or rotate to a different assignment. Judges shared with me that cases involving Indigenous cultural practices and territories, which themselves involve different issues, could be complicated and required significant knowledge and specialization that was infrequently used. As a result, an appointment to the ad hoc chambers was not always viewed as an interesting or career-advancing assignment. For these and other reasons, judges often sought to rotate off the ad hoc chambers. Again, such rotations led to an institutional loss of knowledge and expertise. One Judicial Yuan representative explained:

> Rotation of judges is a big problem. You have to realize that the Indigenous courts are not popular among judges, not considered important. They do not handle big issues. Taiwan's Indigenous people are only 2 percent of the population. And to be an expert it takes a lot of work and a waste of time. Internally in courts, there are rotation standards, so a judge will serve [in the Indigenous court unit] and then rotate to another area.[25]

A legal scholar likewise noted:

> Not that ideal to create a type of court. The judges rotate. They are assigned for a while and then go back to the mainstream [of court practice]. They are just a term-judge, not a real judge. There is a constant transition phase for the

court. They just created a division and judges rotate through. And judges do not want to go there because [they are] quite marginal and difficult cases.[26]

Prosecutors

Special prosecutors are assigned by local prosecutors' offices to the ad hoc Chambers of Indigenous Courts within the criminal divisions of Taiwan courts.[27] Like judges, aspiring prosecutors must pass the highly competitive Judicial Officer Exam and complete the two-year training program at the Judicial Training Institute. Prosecutors are selected on the basis of their exam results, their performance during training, the availability of positions, and personal preferences (Chang 2014, 155n38). Prosecutors' offices are organized into two teams of attorneys: investigative prosecutors, who handle pre-prosecution tasks such as case investigation and deciding whether to bring charges, and trial prosecutors, who oversee all proceedings once prosecution begins, including arguing motions and conducting trials (Wang 2011, 10).

Like judges, prosecutors are required to participate in a mandatory special training program to serve in the ad hoc chambers. These programs are similar to those provided for judges, although my judicial collaborators knew little about the specific training provided to prosecutors. During my fieldwork, the Hualien District Prosecutor's Office was reluctant to discuss the training provided to prosecutors or discuss the ad hoc chambers in general. Local legal actors described a distance between prosecutors and the other legal actors formally or informally associated with the ad hoc chambers. While many people had ready estimates of judges and lawyers having Indigenous status and debated their roles in the specialized units, discussions about the involvement of special prosecutors in the ad hoc chambers were much less common. When discussions of prosecutors did arise, local lawyers and Indigenous activists expressed concern that despite the Judicial Yuan's mandatory training, prosecutors were becoming increasingly antagonistic toward Indigenous claims. One lawyer observed: "District court judges are increasingly sympathetic and understanding of Indigenous issues, but prosecutors continue to strongly insist on Han Chinese understandings of justice and law. There is a huge gap between the judges and prosecutors developing."[28] A frequently cited example of this divide was the Hualien District Prosecutor's Office filing a controversial brief opposing the use of or reference to local Indigenous law in court proceedings, insisting that ROC law alone should govern. Incidents like this fueled concerns among lawyers and activists about the adequacy of training provided to special prosecutors and their role in the ad hoc chamber system.

In the criminal division of the Hualien District Court, trial prosecutors were assigned to specific courtrooms, just as judges were. Through the regularity of courtroom practice, prosecutors often developed rapport with judges assigned to the courtroom. Lawyers representing criminal defendants, including Indigenous persons accused of criminal offenses, viewed this procedure as giving prosecutors an advantage in that it provided them an opportunity to learn the judge's preferences and develop a professional relationship. In their view, this dynamic made defending criminal cases particularly challenging, with some lawyers expressing concern about what they saw as a "teaming up" of judges and trial prosecutors against defendants. One lawyer explained, "Often the judges and the prosecutors are aligned against criminal defendants. In the Taiwan legal system, it is two against one. It is not fair to criminal defendants."[29]

Prosecutors in Hualien often had a complicated relationship with Indigenous communities, illustrated by a 2018 investigation conducted by the Hualien District Prosecutor's Office. The case involved allegations that an elderly Pangcah woman had cooked a pangolin, a protected species under the Wildlife Conservation Act, for personal consumption. Acting on the report, police visited the woman's home to search for evidence, including the animal's remains and tools used for its capture, but found nothing. The woman explained that she had received pangolin meat as a gift from a customer who frequently stayed at her bed-and-breakfast. While she admitted to cooking and eating the meat, she insisted that she had neither hunted nor killed the animal.

Following the investigation, the prosecutor's office summoned the woman to discuss the case and the possibility of criminal charges. She arrived with a lawyer, a decision that irritated the prosecutor overseeing the investigation. The prosecutor asked, "If you claim you did nothing wrong, then why do you need to get a lawyer?" The woman explained that she was afraid of the prosecutor's office and did not want to go to the meeting alone. The question angered her lawyer, who accused the prosecutor of attempting to intimidate his client. He also questioned the prosecutor's understanding of criminal processes and criticized the latter's lack of awareness of the fear that prosecutorial investigations instilled in Indigenous communities. The lawyer reminded the prosecutor that his client was being forced to participate in a criminal system that was not her own and did not reflect Pangcah understandings of justice. Ultimately, no charges were filed against the woman.

Other Court Personnel

Rounding out the legal actors populating the ad hoc Chambers of Indigenous Courts are a judicial assistant, clerk of court, and bailiff, who are present in courtrooms during legal proceedings. These individuals play a role in the operation of the specialized units, contributing to the administration of justice for Indigenous persons. Judicial assistants are assigned to specific judges, while court clerks are assigned to a courtroom; consequently, they frequently work together. The division of labor is such that judicial assistants support judges by maintaining case files, obtaining documents, and managing the courtroom projector. Court clerks handle tasks such as collecting identification cards from litigants and witnesses, obtaining witness affidavits, and transcribing oral statements projected onto courtroom walls or screens, the wording of which often became the focus of intense and lengthy debates among lawyers. Meanwhile, the bailiff, a law enforcement officer, ensures order and security in the courtroom, rotating with other bailiffs every fifteen to thirty minutes.

During my fieldwork, I got to know a bailiff at the Hualien District Court. I explained to him that I was researching the ad hoc Chambers of Indigenous Courts. Puzzled, he replied, "There are no Indigenous courts or special Indigenous court units, just the courts. Why would Indigenous people get a special court?"[30] His remarks reflected the many ambiguities surrounding the specialized units, something I would encounter throughout my research.

In summary, it is important to emphasize the near-total absence of Indigenous representation in the personnel of the ad hoc Chambers of Indigenous Courts. Judges, prosecutors, and other court staff working in the units were overwhelmingly of Han Chinese descent. Indigenous persons appeared in the specialized units predominantly as the subjects of state authority—as litigants, defendants, and witnesses—rather than as administrators or decision-makers in this system. As Jane McMillan (2011) reminds us, however, the ontological conflicts that arise from the imposition of a justice system rooted in colonization cannot be resolved simply by increasing Indigenous representation in the court. Beyond representation, there was also a profound lack of institutional knowledge about Indigenous peoples' cultural practices and legal rights.

Amid these critiques, it is important to note the steps the Taiwan judiciary has taken to improve Indigenous recognition and institutional knowledge about Indigenous peoples in the ad hoc chambers. For example, the judiciary has experimented with Indigenous sentencing circles, incorporating local communities and families into decision-making and dispute resolution processes, as it has done in Chiayi County. Taiwan courts may also invite Indigenous elders and other local representatives to serve as expert witnesses, providing testimony about their cultural practices and relationships to land. Further efforts have extended to legal education and judicial training. The law college at National Taiwan University, Taiwan's leading law program, temporarily offered a course on Indigenous peoples' rights. The Judicial Yuan (2017, 35) also identified as a future priority the inclusion of questions about the Indigenous Peoples Basic Law on the Judicial Officer Exam, signaling a move toward integrating Indigenous issues into judicial education and evaluation.

LEGAL REPRESENTATION AND RE-PRESENTATION

Lawyers representing Indigenous individuals and communities in legal proceedings played a crucial role in the operations of the ad hoc Chambers of Indigenous Courts. In Taiwan, there are two primary pathways to becoming a lawyer. The first is passing the bar examination, which trends toward a low passage rate, around 10 percent in 2017 and 2018. Alternatively, judges and prosecutors can apply to the Ministry of Examination for certification as lawyers (Chiu and Fa 1994, 15). Unlike many other countries, Taiwan does not have professional law schools at the graduate level. Instead, aspiring lawyers pursue undergraduate law degrees through specialized university programs, though Taiwan has been developing alternative tracks, such as graduate law institutes, to diversify legal education opportunities (T. C.-h. Chen 2012, 34). Bar examination passage rates are low, and most law graduates do not become lawyers.

Lawyers who pass the bar examination must complete a one-month pre-practice training program at the National Bar Association Lawyers Training Institute (T. C.-h. Chen 2012, 38). After this initial training, they undertake a five-month apprenticeship under the guidance of a senior attorney before becoming eligible to join a local bar. While the introduction of separate examination processes for judges, prosecutors, and lawyers has increased the number of individuals passing the bar, it has also resulted in a reduction in the pre-practice training required for lawyers (T. C.-h. Chen 2012, 64–65).

Unlike judges and prosecutors assigned to the ad hoc chambers, local lawyers are not required to undergo specialized training to represent Indigenous individuals in the specialized units. As previously mentioned, only a small number of lawyers in Taiwan have Indigenous status. During my fieldwork, out of approximately seven thousand lawyers nationwide, there were perhaps five or six lawyers with Indigenous status.[31] Coupled with the fact that undergraduate law programs did not offer courses on Indigenous peoples' cultures or rights, this meant that many lawyers representing Indigenous clients often lacked the cultural and legal knowledge needed to advocate effectively. For these reasons, legal representation in the units was largely a re-presentation of standard forms of argument, evidence, and texts applied throughout the national court system.

Although Taiwan has experienced significant economic development, many Indigenous groups remain on the social, economic, and geographic margins of Taiwan society. This marginalization has created persistent barriers that hinder Indigenous peoples' access to legal counsel and the court system. In response, the Judicial Yuan, in collaboration with other government agencies, has implemented initiatives aimed at ensuring that Indigenous communities have access to legal representation while also enhancing lawyers' training to address Indigenous peoples' specific legal needs.

In 2004, legislative reforms led to the passage of the Legal Aid Act, aimed at providing legal assistance to those unable to afford legal representation through the establishment of a Legal Aid Foundation (LAF) (*caituan faren falü fuzhu jijinhui* 財團法人法律扶助基金會). Under the act, Indigenous persons may qualify for free legal assistance. Acknowledging the cultural, linguistic, and socioeconomic challenges faced by Indigenous persons and communities, the LAF partnered with the CIP in 2013 to launch the Legal Aid for Indigenous Peoples Program (*yuanzhuminzu falü fuwu zhuanan* 原住民族法律服務專案). Under this arrangement, the CIP would subsidize legal aid to ensure that individuals with Indigenous status could access free legal representation regardless of their income level (Legal Aid Foundation 2019, 18; Taiwan Association for Human Rights 2013, 25). Free legal representation for Indigenous peoples, however, came with a dubious distinction. Under Article 31 of the Code of Criminal Procedure, only two groups in Taiwan qualify for free legal representation regardless of income: Indigenous persons and mentally incompetent persons. This provision has been criticized for its discriminatory undertones. As one high court judge remarked, "This article is ridiculous. The law says they must appoint a lawyer for

Indigenous people and mentally impaired people. You can see the discrimination here."[32]

The LAF operates through twenty-two branches staffed by small teams of lawyers and legal professionals. Most cases involving Indigenous persons, however, are handled by private attorneys registered with the LAF. According to Article 37 of the Attorney Regulation Act, attorneys should participate in legal aid, legal services for the public, or other charitable activities. This creates a strong incentive, if not an obligation, for private lawyers to offer legal aid services. In 2019, 4,352 attorneys applied to become LAF legal aid attorneys (Legal Aid Foundation 2019, 41), many of whom were solo practitioners or part of small law firms (Hsu, Chiang, and Chang 2020, 29). Lawyers shared a variety of motivations for taking on cases involving Indigenous clients: Some wanted to contribute to public service; others sought to ensure a steady workflow, explore a new practice area, or pursue a personal interest in certain issues. While some of these lawyers worked pro bono (without charge) through the LAF program, others provided their services at a reduced fee, often referred to as "low bono."

Although many legal cases involve similar fact patterns and procedural issues, those involving Indigenous persons often present unique challenges that place additional demands on lawyers. These challenges may include the need to hire third-party services, such as expert witnesses or interpreters, and incurring expenses related to travel to and from Indigenous communities in rural and remote areas. While these activities may seem minor, they can play a crucial role in shaping case outcomes and can significantly impact the quality of legal representation (see also Herrera 2014, 8).

Lawyers also face practical challenges that can make it particularly difficult to handle cases involving Indigenous clients. These cases sometimes require specialized knowledge of Indigenous peoples' cultures and relationships to land and of the special laws protecting them, such as the Indigenous Peoples Basic Law, the Wildlife Conservation Act, and the Firearms Act. Acquiring this expertise requires lawyers to invest their own time and resources. To support lawyers interested in providing legal aid to Indigenous individuals and communities, the LAF offers specialized training. In 2018, the LAF conducted eight training sessions across the island (Legal Aid Foundation 2018b, 30), several of which I attended. These sessions included lectures on legal protections for Indigenous people, mock trial exercises, and visits to Indigenous villages, among other activities. The relatively low number of cases addressing matters of Indigenous cultures or lands, however, provided little incentive for lawyers to dedicate the time and resources needed to build expertise in these areas. As one lawyer candidly remarked, "I want to help Indigenous people and spend time on the cases, but I must pay the rent, I must pay the staff. For practical reasons there is pressure to focus on the cases that pay more rather than the legal aid cases."[33]

In a similar vein, research indicates that lawyers often prefer to provide pro bono services in areas that are substantively, and often geographically, removed from their usual practice settings. This preference is driven partly by a desire to avoid conflicts of interest and partly by a desire for novelty (Abel 2011, 307). Many of the pro bono lawyers with whom I worked did not specialize in Indigenous rights or issues. Instead, their primary areas of practice were corporate litigation, landlord-tenant disputes, family law, and other civil or criminal matters. For some, their interest in taking on Indigenous cases stemmed precisely from the opportunity to engage with issues outside their typical areas of expertise. Some of these lawyers participated in the voluntary training sessions offered by the LAF and others did not.

While general litigation skills were often valuable, many pro bono and low bono lawyers representing Indigenous individuals and communities had little practical experience in handling complex cases involving Indigenous cultures or territories. The duties of competence and diligence under Article 26 of the Code of Ethics for Lawyers notwithstanding, there were few economic or professional incentives for these lawyers to develop a deep understanding of such matters. As a result, while legal aid ensured free legal counsel for Indigenous persons and low bono services provided reduced-cost representation, these guarantees did not necessarily translate into high-quality representation. Lawyers offering these services often lacked the resources, training, or motivation to provide Indigenous clients the same level of advocacy afforded to higher-paying clients.

For these reasons, in 2018 the LAF established the Legal Center of Indigenous Peoples (LCIP) in Hualien, under the leadership of Dr. Awi Mona, a Seediq legal scholar and the first Indigenous person in Taiwan to earn a doctorate in law. The center, staffed by both Indigenous and Han Taiwanese legal professionals, was part of a broader initiative to deliver high-quality, culturally sensitive legal services to Indigenous communities. The LCIP focused on complex issues tied to Indigenous land rights and cultural practices, including hunting, fishing, and the gathering of forest products and minerals. In addition to providing free legal services to Indigenous individuals and communities in the region, the center played an important role in legal education and advocacy. It organized annual seminars on developments in domestic Indigenous rights and offered free workshops to train local lawyers in effectively litigating cases involving Indigenous cultural practices and territories. The LCIP's efforts also extended into Indigenous villages, where staff delivered presentations on legal developments, advised community members on their rights, and assisted with completing legal forms. As I explore later, these activities reflected what Greg Johnson (2014) describes as "bone-deep Indigeneity"—displays of Indigenous identity through managing the failures of state governance, such as using the national court system to secure Indigenous peoples' interests and rights.

These initiatives have improved Indigenous peoples' access to lawyers in the Taiwan legal system, but they have not adequately addressed the lack of substantive expertise among lawyers in handling cases involving Indigenous cultural practices and territories. The creation of a special law center, the LCIP, underscores the widespread gap in knowledge among lawyers in Taiwan regarding Indigenous peoples' cultures and rights. It was not merely that Indigenous individuals and communities found themselves in a disadvantaged position in terms of the lack of Indigenous representation in the ad hoc chambers; they were also disadvantaged by the uniqueness of their cases and the kinds of conflicts that arose between their cultural practices and the state legal system, issues that required a level of legal expertise and cultural understanding that many lawyers lacked. The Taiwan judiciary has been gradually coming to realize that improving access to legal counsel is only one part of the solution. The quality of legal representation, rooted in a deep understanding of Indigenous peoples' cultures, connections to land, and special legal rights, is also critical for the effective operation of the ad hoc chambers.

STYLES OF PROCEEDING AND CONCEDING

Taiwan's system of law reflects a blend of historical influences, incorporating elements of Imperial Chinese law as well as civil law and common law traditions (Chiu and Fa 1994; Martin 2019). Rooted in Confucian philosophy, Chinese legal concepts emphasize harmony between human actions and the natural order. These ideas have been reinterpreted and integrated into the modern civil law framework in Taiwan, which has been shaped by Japanese and German influences. Since the 1950s, Taiwan's growing relationship with the United States has further shaped its legal system. This is evident in legal reforms, such as the shift from an inquisitorial to an adversarial adjudication process in 2002 and, more recently, the introduction of lay judges under the Citizen Judges Act in 2023 (Wilkinson 2023).

As a civil law jurisdiction, the legal system prioritizes statutes and codes over precedence and case law. Taiwan's legal framework operates as a hierarchical structure, with legal norms ranked in importance: the ROC Constitution at the top, followed by statutes and legislation and, finally, codes and regulations (Chiu and Fa 1994, 4). Consequently, courts look first to what the Constitution states and then to statutes, codes, and ordinances. While judicial decisions are considered, the doctrine of stare decisis is not formally applied, and court rulings typically bind only the specific case at trial. Nevertheless, precedents hold de facto authority, given the need for legal certainty and predictability as well as judicial habits of mental economy and fear of reversal (Chiu and Fa 1994, 7–8).

Similar to other civil law traditions, Taiwan's conflict-of-laws rules emphasize selecting one rule over another, rather than adopting a synthesis-oriented approach used in common law systems (Colangelo 2016, 18n65). For example, the Taiwan judiciary frequently employed principles of statutory construction that guided judges to more specific laws, such as *lex specialis* (whereby more specific laws take precedence over general ones), rather than to principles focused on harmonizing laws, like *in pari materia* (whereby statutes that share a common purpose or that relate to the same subject are construed together as one law).

In the Taiwan legal system, all parties have an absolute right to appeal in criminal cases (Code of Criminal Procedure, Art. 344). The principle of double jeopardy does not prevent prosecutors from appealing a not-guilty verdict. This is justified by a belief that allowing such appeals enhances oversight by higher courts (Su 2017, 218–19). Appeals are conducted de novo, meaning that appeals courts review both factual and legal issues anew. For all intents and purposes, criminal appeals function as a new prosecution based on the same facts and issues. This procedure has drawn criticism from criminal defense lawyers. One lawyer observed:

> Prosecutors can appeal as a matter of right. They do not need to have a reason. There does not need to [be] new evidence. They just contact the appellate court and say they want to appeal. Many people complain about this process, because it makes the district court's importance very little, maybe none at all. Because anyone can just appeal any case.[34]

The impact of Taiwan's appeals procedure in criminal cases involving Indigenous defendants was evident in rates of reversal. Nationally, reversal rates for district court decisions were not low, averaging 27 percent between 2010 and 2015 (Su 2017, 219). During my fieldwork, I observed only a few cases that completed the full cycle of trial and appeal, a process that could take several years. In the cases that did reach completion, some of which I detail in later chapters, it was striking that appellate courts tended to limit or overturn district court decisions that favored Indigenous litigants.

For example, in one case, the Kaohsiung High Court rejected all claims for damages to homes and lands caused by flooding that the Bunun claimants had previously won in the Kaohsiung District Court. Several claimants remarked that the judge avoided looking at them when delivering the decision, which they interpreted as an expression of the judge's "shame." Reflecting on this case, one Indigenous activist opined, "District court judges are more free to come up with new arguments, but then on appeal, the Indigenous litigants lose, because [appellate] judges feel less free and must conform to what the Supreme Court says."[35] These experiences led to a general perception among Indigenous activists that the likelihood of success for Indigenous litigants diminished as cases, whether civil or criminal, progressed from the district court to the appellate level.

In 2002, Taiwan transitioned from an inquisitorial to an adversarial trial system (see Code of Criminal Procedure, Art. 163; see also Wang 2011, 10). Along with this shift, the judiciary adopted U.S.-style rules of evidence, which increased the involvement of parties' representatives and required judges to assume a more neutral role during trials. This change significantly increased the workload of both prosecutors and defense lawyers (Wang 2011, 11). To address these challenges, Taiwan introduced plea bargaining in 2004 through a "summary proceeding" (*jianyi chengxu* 簡易程序) procedure (Code of Criminal Procedure, Art. 455–2). Under this system, defendants accused of nonserious offenses carrying sentences of three years or less could acknowledge guilt in exchange for a reduced or suspended sentence (Kennedy 2003, 115–16). While this approach streamlined legal proceedings, lawyers noted that it often pressured Indigenous defendants to plead guilty in exchange for a reduced penalty. This pressure stemmed from the risks of relying on unclear legal protections and the judiciary's lack of substantive knowledge about Indigenous peoples' cultures.

For example, one case in the Hualien District Court involved a young Indigenous man who allegedly had been driving a motorcycle under the influence of alcohol. He collided with another motorcycle, injuring its driver, a middle-aged Han Taiwanese man. The young man's lawyer considered presenting a cultural argument highlighting the social significance of alcohol consumption in Indigenous communities as a mitigating defense. Ultimately, the lawyer advised his client to opt for a summary proceeding, explaining:

> Would you risk going to jail for years trying to prove a [Indigenous] customary tradition when the judge does not understand the idea of culture, when you can take a guilty plea and get a suspended jail sentence, maybe pay a little fine, and go on? ... Even when the law is clear, it is not so clear. This is our job. It is risky to fight for cultural rights. So, many lawyers advise their clients to accept a summary proceeding and get a reduced sentence. The stakes are much lower in that procedure than if they go to trial. At trial, who knows what will happen? You see this a lot.[36]

Some local lawyers viewed summary proceedings as a serious threat to Indigenous peoples' cultural rights claims. As a result, they actively urged other lawyers to avoid using this procedure in cases involving Indigenous defendants.

In summary, proceedings in the ad hoc chambers tended to replicate ordinary court processes in the Taiwan national court system. They included few special procedures to address the unique aspects of cases involving Indigenous peoples. Such matters were left to the discretion of individual judges, who handled them on an ad hoc basis. Furthermore, several features of Taiwan legal process posed significant challenges for Indigenous litigants. They were subject to conflict-of-laws rules that favored more restrictive rights, absolute rights of appeal that exposed them to multiple criminal trials, appellate processes that frequently overturned lower-court decisions favorable to Indigenous parties, and summary proceedings that incentivized Indigenous persons not to raise cultural defenses provided by law.

To address some of these issues, the ad hoc chambers worked in coordination with other initiatives aimed at supporting Indigenous litigants. These included the Legal Aid for Indigenous Peoples Program, which provided free legal representation to Indigenous persons. It also included the development of a nascent system of courtroom interpreters fluent in Indigenous languages, discussed further below.

ACCESS MATTERS

As discussed earlier, the lives of Indigenous peoples in Taiwan experienced rapid change following the country's transition to democracy in the 1990s. This period was marked by a large-scale migration from rural village communities to urban areas, where more than half of the Indigenous population today resides. The 1990s also witnessed the emergence of an Indigenous movement, accompanied by efforts to advocate the recognition of Indigenous peoples' cultures and lands in legislation and policymaking. Despite these developments, many Indigenous individuals still struggle to earn a living amid the daily realities of discrimination and prejudice (Simon and Awi Mona 2023, 189), and Indigenous peoples continue to lag behind Taiwan's Han Taiwanese society in areas of education, employment, income, health, and life expectancy.

The challenges confronting Indigenous peoples today were poignantly captured in the testimony of a Truku elder, Rakaw, who had been charged with unlawfully occupying land. In June 2018, he addressed the ad hoc Chamber of Indigenous Courts of the Hualien District Court:

> I have a junior high school education. I am a farmer and my economic situation is not good, and I need to support my son who is in second grade.... Please deliver a verdict of not guilty. The land in this case has been used by my ancestors since the time of Japanese occupation. From then until now, there was no need for us to apply to use it. I do not know why it was classified as river land by the River Management Office.... Please for the sake of us Indigenous people, we are not using the hunter's lodge to make money. We are a harmonious people. We have absolutely no intention of stealing land.

His remarks highlight how inequalities are manifest in the daily lives of Indigenous peoples and underscore the enduring significance of land and cultural practices in Indigenous communities.

Like other ROC citizens, Indigenous persons have a right to access national courts and legal actors. The realities of daily life, however, pose substantial hurdles to meaningful access to the regulatory state, legal representation, courtrooms, and justice, including the ad hoc Chambers of Indigenous Courts. Obstructions stem from inconsistencies in Indigenous legal protections and their interpretations, a lack of institutional understanding of Indigenous cultures and relationships to land, and legal processes that often disadvantage Indigenous litigants. But obstructions also arise in less visible forms, such as in the physical locations of courts and lawyers, in the financial costs making accessing courts prohibitive, and in linguistic preferences. Therefore, it is important to situate the ad hoc chambers within the broader spatial, economic, and linguistic realities of contemporary Indigenous life in Taiwan.

Spatial Matters

Lisa Pruitt (2013) emphasizes that spatiality is a critical factor in access to justice. One aspect of space is physical distance. While about half of the Indigenous population now resides in urban areas, the remainder continues to live in rural or remote regions, often far from lawyers' offices and courthouses. The scarcity of lawyers in rural communities and the surfeit of lawyers in urban spaces made accessing legal counsel challenging for many. Similarly, courthouses located in urban centers were often inaccessible to Indigenous persons living in remote areas. Some Indigenous persons, including those with whom I worked, lived in circumstances in which they had to borrow vehicles and travel for hours to attend hearings at the local courthouse. Furthermore, trials were spread across time, such that a single case could be divided into multiple court sessions extending across months. This meant that Indigenous litigants had to make multiple trips to access courthouse spaces, month after month, imposing significant economic and time burdens on those who sought redress in the courts or were compelled to appear before them. As previously noted, physical space was important in another respect. Judicial reassignment procedures rotated judges from one court jurisdiction to another. In the process, judges took with them any knowledge they may have gained about Indigenous peoples in one region when they were reassigned to a court in a different Indigenous context.

Space is not only a material phenomenon; it is also a social one (Sack 1993, 326). As with other rural populations (Albrecht and Albrecht 2004, 435), the sparseness of eastern Taiwan, where many rural and remote Indigenous communities reside, cultivated close-knit communities, often with high levels of consensus on central values and morals. These bonds of connectedness and consensus were amplified by ongoing and intentional efforts to preserve historical ways of life and reclaim ancestral territories. This sense of community was evident in the Bunun and Truku communities with whom I worked. Community members often traveled together to court proceedings to provide support to litigants and demonstrate solidarity before the judge, particularly in cases impacting their community's lifeways or lands. For example, in one civil case, members of a Bunun village mobilized themselves for each court session, with elders, adults, children, and even babies piling into a van for the two-hour journey to the courthouse. Those unable to attend the proceedings stayed informed about the case's progress through close networks of kith and kin.

Centuries of subjugation, coupled with ongoing efforts to preserve local practices, have instilled in some rural and remote Indigenous communities a general ethic of state avoidance and a reliance on legal pluralism as people engaged with both state law and local Indigenous law in their daily lives. One Seediq man expressed this sentiment as follows: "The state legal system is not our system. We are forced to participate in the legal system. We must show up and participate in their foreign and expensive legal system. It is imposed on us."[37] As a result, self-identifying a legal need could itself be a hurdle, because communities did not contemplate a state law solution to the problems they faced.

Indigenous social structures also shaped the ways in which lawyers interacted with their clients. Given the strong community networks and a shared commitment to protecting cultural practices and territories, lawyers representing Indigenous clients sometimes found themselves engaging with an entire community, rather than just the individual client. For instance, one lawyer represented an Indigenous client accused of illegal hunting. Recognizing the case's potential implications for the entire community, other villagers actively sought to influence how it was handled. What initially appeared to be a simple, low-level criminal matter quickly became something resembling a class action lawsuit, with numerous individuals involved as interested, albeit unofficial, "parties." To navigate this complexity, the lawyer formed a working group of community members who served as intermediaries between him and the broader group.

Just as space and sociality are related, so too are space and power. This dynamic was evident in the litigants' and the judiciary's varying mobilities. Indigenous individuals living in rural and remote areas were forced to travel long distances to urban courthouses and legal professionals, often with limited resources and at great expense. It was not that courts were immobile. As described in later chapters, judges occasionally conducted site visits to Indigenous villages and lands. The judiciary, however, maintained firm control over decisions regarding the location of proceedings and travel requirements. In recent years, efforts have been made to address the inequalities produced by the relationship between space and power. Training programs at the Judicial Yuan now encourage judges to conduct site visits, and judicial education programs include visits to Indigenous villages (Judicial Yuan 2018a, 17–22). In 2017, the Judicial Yuan began discussions about creating a circuit court system, which would allow judges to conduct hearings physically in Indigenous communities (Judicial Yuan 2017, 36). As mentioned earlier, legal aid lawyers and staff also began traveling to Indigenous villages to share information about recent legal developments and to meet with community members about legal problems.

Spatiality thus played an important role in shaping Indigenous peoples' access to the ad hoc chambers. Those living in rural and remote areas sometimes had to overcome significant socio-spatial obstacles to engage meaningfully with the ROC legal system. Lawyers were few and far away, and courts were located in distant urban centers. Judges were transferred to other jurisdictions, taking their knowledge of local Indigenous groups with them. Indigenous communities could develop a sense of state avoidance, not viewing national courts as viable settings for resolving local problems and relying instead on local laws and justice practices. Compounding matters, persistently high poverty rates and social marginalization aggravated these challenges, making spatial access to the ad hoc chambers difficult.

Economic Matters

Economic costs precede and accrue during court cases in Taiwan. For instance, civil litigants are required to pay a court fee to bring a lawsuit, with the amount determined by whether the case involves proprietary or nonproprietary rights.[38] Additional litigation-related costs can include charges for photocopies, video recording, transcripts, translation services, publication in official gazettes and newspapers, daily fees, travel expenses for witnesses, and compensation for expert witnesses.[39] Furthermore, losing parties are typically responsible for covering the fees incurred during both the civil trial and the appeals process. Litigants who choose to hire legal counsel outside the legal aid system must also pay attorney fees.[40]

Being in an economically disadvantaged position, some Indigenous individuals were unable to pay the costs associated with court fees, litigation expenses, and lawyer fees. As a result, their access to the civil court system was more restricted than that of the Han Taiwanese population. These cumulative expenses had a reverberating effect on Indigenous peoples' engagements with the ad hoc Chambers of Indigenous Courts. A high court judge explained: "The Indigenous courts are officially in both the criminal and civil courts, both courts, but in reality, they are really mostly in the criminal because Indigenous people cannot afford the fee, so they typically do not go before the civil courts."[41]

The costs associated with litigation, therefore, shaped Indigenous peoples' access to the ad hoc chambers. They rendered the civil courts effectively inaccessible for some individuals seeking recourse through the Taiwan court system. Securing Indigenous peoples' access to the specialized units required more than simply permitting Indigenous persons and communities to file lawsuits. It also necessitated addressing the costs that placed courts out of reach due to Indigenous peoples' disadvantaged socioeconomic positions.

Linguistic Matters

Taiwan's Indigenous peoples speak forty-two distinct dialects of Austronesian languages, reflecting a rich linguistic diversity. At least one dialect is severely endangered, four are critically endangered, and eight more are classified as vulnerable (*Taiwan Today* 2017). Assimilationist laws and policies prohibiting the use of Indigenous languages, such as the introduction of compulsory education in Mandarin Chinese up to junior high school in 1968 (expanded to a twelve-year program in 2014), has significantly impacted language preservation. As a result, many Indigenous persons under the age of fifty cannot communicate fluently, or at all, in their mother languages (Sterk 2020a, 69).

In recent decades, the ROC government has taken steps to protect Indigenous languages. In 1998, the Ministry of Education introduced policies allowing elective mother-tongue courses for one to two hours per week, starting from third grade in elementary schools. In 2001, instruction in the "mother tongue" became mandatory for one hour per week for first through sixth grades in elementary schools and for junior high students. The outcomes of these initiatives, however, have been mixed. For example, Greg Huteson's (2003, 30) survey of the Rukai in Maolin Township, located in south-central Taiwan, revealed that younger Rukai were still not fluent in their local dialects, suggesting the limited effectiveness of these policies.

In 2017, the CIP drafted the Indigenous Languages Development Act, which designates Indigenous languages as national languages and aims to preserve their use and heritage. While Article 97 of the Court Organization Act mandates Mandarin Chinese as the official language of Taiwan courts, Article 13 of the Indigenous Languages Development Act allows Indigenous individuals to use their own languages in court proceedings and states that courts should provide interpreter services as needed. Article 14 further stipulates that official documents from government agencies, schools, and public enterprises in Indigenous regions must be written in Indigenous languages. Some government agencies have begun publishing official documents in Indigenous languages (Lee 2021). Similarly, in 2019, the Ministry of Culture introduced the Development of National Languages Act, which, under Article 11, grants citizens the right to select the national language they wish to use in judicial proceedings. While these legal developments have helped strengthen protections for Indigenous languages, promoting linguistic diversity is also closely tied to Taiwan's democratization and independence efforts, serving as an important element used to distinguish Taiwan from the PRC.

As part of these efforts, the Judicial Yuan created a special interpreter program to provide courts with interpreters proficient in Indigenous languages. By the end of 2019, the CIP had compiled a list of fifteen interpreters proficient in nine Indigenous languages to assist Indigenous litigants in courtrooms across Taiwan (Judicial Yuan 2018a, 29; Legal Aid Foundation 2019, 26). Lawyers and Indigenous activists were quick to identify deficiencies in this program. One issue was that interpreters were proficient in only a small number of Indigenous languages and dialects, leaving many unrepresented (see also Tsai 2015, 303–4). Another concern involved the quality of the interpreter services, in that interpreters often summarized testimony rather than providing verbatim interpretations. One lawyer recounted a case in which his Bunun clients testified in their mother language.[42] The court-appointed interpreter provided only brief summaries of the main points of their testimony and did not attempt to capture the emotions they tried to convey to the judge. This frustrated the lawyer's clients, who felt they were misunderstood and that their voices were not adequately represented in the court proceedings.

The interpreter program has also seen limited use in Taiwan courts. An internal review by the Judicial Yuan found that, across all levels of the court system, there were only twenty-four instances of using Indigenous-language interpreters in 2014, twenty-six in 2015, and twelve in 2016 (Judicial Yuan 2018a, 29–30). On the basis of these findings, the Judicial Yuan concluded that "regarding the actual use of special interpreters in recent years, currently the use of interpreters is still not a widespread state of affairs" (2018a, 30). One judge from the Hualien District Court noted that, although he believed that the interpreter program was critically important to the effective administration of Indigenous cases, he could not recall a single instance in which he had called for an interpreter.[43] Recognizing the infrequent use of Indigenous-language interpreters in courtrooms, during my fieldwork the Judicial Yuan was taking steps to strengthen the program. These efforts included developing a special handbook aimed at streamlining and standardizing the use of interpreters across the judicial system.[44]

Certain cases underscored the need for Indigenous-language interpreters. For example, cases involving cultural practices and territories tended to draw more senior members of Indigenous communities, who appeared in the courtrooms as litigants, witnesses, or observers. Taiwan legal procedures require witnesses to read aloud and sign an affidavit or oath, written in Mandarin Chinese, affirming that they will tell the truth.[45] In one case, senior members of a Truku community were called to testify at trial but were unable to read the Mandarin Chinese witness affidavits. Pursuant to court procedure, the court clerk stood over the witnesses' shoulders and read the text aloud in Mandarin Chinese, which the witnesses repeated. They then signed the affidavit, one of them marking it with an *X*, and returned it to the clerk. This process repeated itself in several civil and criminal cases involving Indigenous persons. Given their unfamiliarity with state legal procedures, coupled with these language issues, one was left to wonder whether these witnesses understood what they were affirming through their statements and signatures. This raised significant questions about their full and informed participation in the proceedings.

As mentioned earlier, Article 14 of the Indigenous Languages Development Act provides for the translation of official government documents into Indigenous languages. The act does not define what constitutes "official documents" (*gong wenshu* 公文書). In the context of the Judicial Yuan, it is reasonable to interpret official documents as including the public documents issued and utilized by the Judicial Yuan and the courts that it oversees. Given that witness affidavits are required by law, they could reasonably be considered official documents in the judicial system. Presently, these affidavits are not provided in Indigenous languages. This lack of linguistic inclusion is particularly significant because legal processes are textually mediated at nearly every point of institutional action (Pence 1997). Ensuring linguistic access to the texts circulating in the legal process, just as with spoken communications in courtrooms, is crucial for meaningful participation in, and comprehension of, the judicial system.

During my fieldwork, Indigenous litigants, witnesses, and audience members also sometimes used language as a means of expressing and performing their identities as Indigenous persons. As discussed in greater detail later, these linguistic performances were intertwined with nationalist ethnoracial structures that located indigeneity in markers such as language and dress, but they also had the capacity to challenge essentialist notions of indigeneity and introduced alternative ways of understanding and framing Indigenous identity in the context of legal disputes.

The Taiwan judiciary has thus come to recognize the importance of accommodating Indigenous languages in courtrooms. Recent laws and procedures have made Indigenous-language interpreters available, but these interpreters are proficient in only a limited number of Indigenous languages, and the overall system is infrequently used. Additionally, the judiciary has been slow to address matters of language in the texts through which the legal process is mediated, thus creating yet another obstacle for Indigenous peoples engaging with the ad hoc chambers. More intriguingly, language has become a powerful tool for the expression of Indigenous identities in Taiwan courtrooms. Addressing language-related issues is therefore important both for practical and for symbolic reasons in supporting Indigenous peoples' access to and participation in the specialized units.

SPANNING BOUNDARIES AND POSSIBLE FUTURES

Positioned along the boundary of the ROC legal system and Indigenous peoples, the ad hoc Chambers of Indigenous Courts operated as specialized institutions working to bridge differing perspectives on culture, laws, and territory in legal cases and make the court system more accessible to Indigenous individuals and communities. The units aimed to achieve this through special training programs for judges and prosecutors who handle cases involving Indigenous persons and through adjacent procedures to guarantee free legal counsel and provision of interpreters. This training was designed to equip judges and prosecutors with a deeper understanding of Indigenous peoples' cultures and special legal rights, enabling them to resolve disputes in a more informed and culturally sensitive manner. Guarantees of legal counsel aimed to ensure that Indigenous litigants had adequate legal representation in Taiwan courts. Indigenous-language interpreters facilitated communication across linguistic divides in the courtroom.

As a new system, hastily implemented, procedures for accommodating Indigenous cultures and languages in the ad hoc chambers were still being developed. As one Judicial Yuan representative emphasized, "The [Indigenous] courts are only five years old. Really new. It is still developing."[46] This was an ongoing process of acquiring knowledge about Indigenous peoples' cultures and life circumstances, finding effective ways to integrate Indigenous views and voices into legal proceedings, understanding the special legal protections afforded to Indigenous peoples, addressing the systemic disadvantages Indigenous individuals faced in the legal system, creating processes that ensured consistency across the judiciary, and building a repository of case law to guide future judges.

In these ongoing processes, the ad hoc chambers remained ambiguous institutions, even for those working in them. Local Indigenous laws were not recognized as normative sources, and Indigenous representation in the units was minimal. Training for judges and prosecutors was limited, resulting in little substantive knowledge about Indigenous peoples' cultures and legal rights. Attitudes among judges toward Indigenous claims and the specialized units themselves varied widely, and some groups, such as prosecutors, exhibited signs of increasing hostility toward the inclusion of Indigenous perspectives in court proceedings. Court procedures in the ad hoc chambers closely replicated processes in the national courts, with little to distinguish them as distinct judicial bodies. Structures in the units, like broad jurisdictional scope, also distracted judges' attention away from ensuring respect for Indigenous peoples' cultures and relationships to land. Certain procedures, such as summary proceedings, discouraged Indigenous defendants from raising cultural defenses guaranteed to them by law. Socio-spatial obstacles, such as distances from courts and lawyers, judicial reassignment and rotation procedures, and practices of state avoidance, hindered Indigenous peoples' meaningful access to the units. Economic pressures, like costs of litigation, placed civil courts out of reach, and professional incentives discouraged legal practitioners from acquiring substantive knowledge about Indigenous peoples' cultures and rights. Language obstacles emerged through the limited number of Indigenous languages spoken by court interpreters, the infrequent use of interpreters in proceedings, and inattention to the texts through which the legal process was mediated. Finally, as discussed in the previous chapter, the specialized units applied state laws designed to protect Indigenous peoples but were unsettled and inconsistent.

The ad hoc chambers, despite their aspirational efforts to mediate boundaries between Han Taiwanese and Indigenous social worlds, in many ways reproduced ambiguity as a hegemonic form that has characterized the ROC government's engagements with Indigenous peoples. Recognizing some of these issues, the Judicial Yuan laid out several goals for the units' future development (see Judicial Yuan 2017b, 35–36). Short-term goals included strengthening judicial training, establishing a professional certification system for selecting judges, and revising the bar examination to include laws protecting Indigenous peoples. Mid-term goals included reviewing all cases handled by the units, creating a circuit court system, forming an Indigenous judicial advisory committee to assist judges, and addressing cultural challenges in courtrooms through legislation. Long-term goals included investigating the feasibility of incorporating local Indigenous laws into national legislation and establishing an autonomous Indigenous court. It remains to be seen whether these measures will be implemented or prove effective in achieving the stated goals of respecting Indigenous peoples' cultures and securing their judicial rights.

While the Judicial Yuan was exploring ways to improve the ad hoc chambers system, Indigenous activists continued to advocate the creation of autonomous Indigenous court institutions managed by Indigenous peoples and grounded in local Indigenous laws. Indigenous groups, like the Truku, continued to rely on local forms of justice and dispute resolution outside the framework of Taiwan's national court system. Lacking Indigenous representation and ignoring local notions of justice, the establishment of ad hoc chambers was seen in some Indigenous communities as a positive, but weak, step toward meaningful recognition of Indigenous cultures, issues, and conceptions of justice.

In short, Taiwan's nascent system of ad hoc Chambers of Indigenous Courts has made progress toward removing some of the remoteness of the Taiwan legal system from Indigenous communities, but more work remained to solidify its role as an institution spanning Han Taiwanese and Indigenous worlds. Yet despite its limitations, there were signs that the ad hoc chambers could become forums for new, potentially transformative forms of engagement. The prosecutor-general's extraordinary appeal against Tama Talum's conviction, for instance, signaled a growing recognition within the ROC state of the harm inflicted on Indigenous peoples through the legal system as the state works to provide them access to it. Subsequent chapters will explore how judges, lawyers, Indigenous persons, and intermediaries developed innovative practices and strategies to integrate Indigenous perspectives and voices. These efforts made room for critiques of state governance and performances of Indigenous identities that were largely unavailable in other institutional contexts. In this sense, the specialized units indeed appeared to be "courts of opportunity," as Deputy Director Wu suggested, but not because of a likelihood of encountering generous Han Taiwanese state actors. Instead, they were "courts of opportunity" because of the collective efforts of many actors, working in diverse ways, to transform the units into boundary-spanning spaces that, by degrees, confronted the enduring and ongoing processes of colonialism persisting in the structure and administration of Taiwan courts.

The next chapter examines the ad hoc chambers in action by focusing on two cases involving members of the Truku community of Dowmung. These cases showcase key dispute-types that arose during my fieldwork in the specialized units: land rights and resource rights. They offer a ground-level perspective on how the units operated at both the district and appellate levels. What emerges is an image of two very different ad hoc chambers, each reflecting different approaches and visions for bridging Han Taiwanese and Indigenous perspectives on culture, law, and territory through court processes.

FOUR

One Community, Two Controversies

TWO CASES IN THE HUALIEN ad hoc Chamber of Indigenous Courts had a particularly profound impact on social and cultural life in the Truku community of Dowmung during my field research. Several community members had been summoned to appear before the Hualien District Court and High Court as defendants in cases involving activities that they viewed as integral to their cultural life and that took place on lands they identified as their ancestral territories. While these individuals engaged with the courts as subjects of the ROC legal system, they were not the only community members who participated in the proceedings. Other members played pivotal roles as local experts, assisting Han Taiwanese judges and lawyers in understanding Truku cultural practices and the community's deep connections to the land. Some served as informal interpreters, bridging a linguistic divide introduced by the use of Mandarin Chinese in court proceedings. Others attended as supporters, traveling together to hearings to show solidarity, comfort the accused, and reinforce their collective commitment to addressing local concerns.

These cases stood out from the typical matters handled by the ad hoc chambers as they involved issues that most participants, although not all, agreed were related to Indigenous culture and territory. As mentioned earlier, the specialized units usually dealt with routine cases that were largely indistinguishable from those heard in the regular courts. By debating issues directly tied to Truku cultural practices and territorial claims, these cases highlighted the ad hoc chambers' role as institutions bridging Han Taiwanese and Indigenous understandings of culture, land, and law. In these kinds of cases, the boundary-spanning capacities, and incapacities, of the ad hoc chambers obtained a new visibility and salience.

They showcase key dispute-types that emerged during my field research: land rights and resource rights. Land and resource rights were particularly contentious in Taiwan because they directly challenged state control and jurisdiction in a manner that encroached upon fundamental state values and dominant narratives of national history. They also intersected with broader concerns over natural resource management and conservation. These kinds of disputes were mingled with other pressing issues affecting Indigenous peoples, notably hunting rights, which at the time were undergoing review in the case of Bunun hunter Tama Talum. During my fieldwork, prosecutions related to wildlife hunting that had been central to my preliminary research were mostly suspended. In their place, prosecutions over land and resources became the primary focus of state efforts to regulate and manage Indigenous culture and identity.

In this chapter, I examine these two cases in detail, drawing on my ethnographic research conducted in the Hualien courthouses. Adopting a phenomenologically oriented approach to courtroom ethnography, I aim to capture the powerful atmosphere of the courtroom, or the "whole of relationally entangled human and non-human bodies co-present in space" (Bens 2018, 337). I do not confine myself to the courtroom space, but instead follow the disputes, ideas about law, and courts themselves as they traversed the courtroom walls and entered other spheres of social and legal action, including judicial chambers, lawyers' offices, and the streets of Indigenous communities. This chapter engages in what I call a *mobile ethnography of justice* to explore the ways in which participants in boundary institutions navigated legal pluralism. This analysis carves a path across what Sally Merry (1988) referred to as "classic" and "new" legal pluralism by examining law and courts in contexts of colonial-Indigenous encounters, but also looking beyond formal court settings to examine how law operates in the shadows and out on the streets.

The case descriptions that follow show Han Taiwanese judges and other legal actors struggling to understand the complexities of Indigenous cultural practices as well as the concept of culture itself. They also highlight the struggles of Indigenous persons and communities to navigate Taiwan's national court system and use court venues to advance their own understandings of culture, identity, and territory. Additionally, these cases underscore the important role of intermediary actors—experts, interpreters, and supporters—who were instrumental in resolving cases. Finally, they provide insights into how specialized units at different levels of the national court system operated, demonstrating how different judicial approaches shaped courtroom interactions and outcomes for Indigenous persons.

THE DOWMUNG BAMBOO HOUSE CASE

On October 18, 2017, a dilapidated van whizzed past me as I walked to the Hualien District Court. A hand waved out the window as the van screeched to a halt farther up the road. Ten people tumbled out, among them my friend Rakaw, the defendant in the criminal trial I was there to observe. He and the other passengers, five men and four women, all members of the Dowmung community, had made the thirty-minute journey from their village to the District Court in Hualien City in a borrowed van. They were dressed in matching white rattan vests, each adorned with the distinctive Truku "eye" motif embroidered in red. After exchanging greetings, we walked together toward the courthouse. Rakaw, a village elder, was due to stand trial, charged with unlawfully occupying land under Article 320, Item 2, of the Criminal Code of the Republic of China (Criminal Code). The charge stemmed from his role in coordinating the construction of a bamboo house that the community intended to use as a cultural center. He and other members of the community envisioned the structure as a space to preserve and transmit Truku language and law to the next generation. Rakaw explained the critical importance of the project in this way: "Our children do not know our language or Gaya. They do not know about Gaya. We need this center to teach them about Truku culture and language. If we do not, they will be lost."[1]

A few weeks earlier, I had met with Rakaw to discuss his upcoming case in the ad hoc Chamber of Indigenous Courts. He mentioned hearing about these specialized court units, which he described as "supposed to be for Indigenous peoples," but expressed deep skepticism.[2] Rakaw observed that the ROC government's promises to respect Indigenous lifeways always seemed to be accompanied by new justifications for denying them. His comments reminded me of a passage from Franz Kafka's 1925 novel *The Trial*, in which a man from the countryside seeks admittance to the Law, only to be endlessly denied by the doorkeeper. At the moment of his death, the man learns that the entrance to the Law was meant only for him. I shared this story with Rakaw, and we discussed its possible interpretations. Rakaw concluded that the tale mirrored Indigenous peoples' experiences with the Taiwan court system: Accepting the power of ROC state court institutions,

FIGURE 12. Dowmung cultural center and police presence during the court site visit, 2018.

including the ad hoc Chambers of Indigenous Courts, meant also accepting Indigenous peoples' exclusion. In other words, the promises of the ROC legal system were a ruse to placate, discipline, and ultimately erase Indigenous identities.

Closing the Door: The Dowmung Bamboo House

Local lawyers informally referred to Rakaw's case as the "Dowmung Bamboo House Case" (*tongmen zhuwu an* 銅門竹屋案). The bamboo house at the center of the case was inspired by the lodges that Truku hunters used to rest and process animals while in the mountains (figure 12). Compared to the imposing, government-built Hualien District Courthouse where Rakaw's trial would later take place, the bamboo house was a modest structure. It consisted of a medium-sized, single-room rectangular building constructed of bamboo, with internal steel scaffolding set on a bare concrete foundation. The house was perched near the edge of a bank that sloped downward toward the Mugua River far below. Sticks propped open bamboo window shades, allowing for air circulation and natural light. On either side of the building, small gardens of taro and sweet potatoes were carefully tended by the community. The road leading back to the village was lined with scattered home settlements. A dilapidated police station, abandoned several years earlier, stood nearby.

Many members of the community had contributed to building the bamboo house. When police arrived to investigate, however, they arrested only Rakaw, reasoning that he had organized and overseen the construction effort. The Hualien District Prosecutor's Office contended that the land beneath the house had been nationalized by the ROC government. The community was made aware of this, they argued, by the presence of physical signs near the structure indicating that the land was state owned, as well as by plat maps shared with the community before the house's construction. Because community members had not secured the necessary authorization to build on the land, prosecutors argued that Rakaw had violated the Criminal Code. Additionally, they noted that the land had been condemned due to the risk of flooding from the nearby Mugua River, which became a torrent of rapids during typhoon season and threatened to erode the bank beneath the structure. From the perspective of the Prosecutor's Office, the bamboo house was both built illegally and unfit for use.

Rakaw and the community countered that the land beneath the house was part of their ancestral territory. They provided evidence of continuous use over generations, including cultivation and hunting activities. To support their claim, they pointed to their own markers of ownership, such as logs and stones used to demarcate parcels for gardening and agriculture. The community also challenged the county's claim that the area was unsafe, noting that the government had previously invested in building the nearby police station, which suggested the land was not considered unsafe. Furthermore, they contended that since many community members had participated in constructing the house, the police should not have singled out Rakaw for arrest. If the construction was deemed unlawful, they argued, all participants should have been held equally accountable.

Despite these differing perspectives, the community was barred from accessing or using the bamboo house in the lead-up to Rakaw's trial. It stood dormant, empty, closed.

Waiting for the Doorkeeper: At the Courthouse

We met Rakaw's two defense lawyers in front of the courthouse. Both were Han Taiwanese lawyers actively involved in representing Indigenous individuals and communities across Taiwan. They were part of the Legal Aid for Indigenous Peoples Program, which provided free legal services to Indigenous persons. One of the lawyers, Lawyer Xu, was particularly well known for her staunch advocacy for Indigenous cultural and land rights. Her approach was sophisticated and multidimensional, and she frequently appeared on Taiwan television news programs to voice support for Indigenous causes. Being an outspoken Han Taiwanese woman in the public spotlight and on the forefront of progressive Indigenous claims also came with challenges. She faced criticism from some Indigenous activists, who accused her of turning cases into public spectacles. Others expressed concern that she maneuvered publicity surrounding certain Indigenous cases toward support for the DDP party, while many Indigenous persons supported the rival KMT. For his part, Rakaw told me that he felt fortunate to have her as his legal counsel.

Together, we entered the Hualien District Courthouse. Security officers sat at the entrance, registering legal parties and their lawyers. Rakaw and his lawyers checked in at the front desk, presenting their ROC-issued national identification cards. Rakaw's card included both his Chinese name and his Truku name in Romanized script, a feature that was not permitted on official Taiwan documents until 1995 (Gao 2015). The public entrance opened into a spacious indoor courtyard filled with potted plants and illuminated by skylights. A narrow concrete walkway and wall separated the courtyard from the courtroom doors that lined its perimeter, giving the courthouse interior a layout reminiscent of a motel. Visitors could choose to sit in the courtyard or wait in a designated area set apart by sliding glass doors. This waiting area offered air conditioning, comfortable seating, and a television set playing soap operas.

Everyone gathered in the waiting room. As we waited, people passed around betel nut to chew, ignoring the signs on the wall prohibiting its use. As the time for Rakaw's trial drew near, the group stood together, forming a circle and holding hands. Rakaw led a passionate Christian prayer spoken in Truku, his voice loud and intense, evoking the fervor of Pentecostal worship. Other community members joined in, murmuring their own prayers, creating a cacophony of voices that filled the small waiting room. It was a conspicuous display of Indigenous alterity and solidarity in a space otherwise dominated by Han Taiwanese ethnicity, Mandarin Chinese language, and Buddhist and Taoist ideas about spirituality. While such "hot and noisy" displays were not uncommon in Taiwan society, I could not help wondering to myself what the courthouse staff thought as they listened to these spirited Christian prayers spoken in Truku echoing through the building.

At the conclusion of the prayer, we sat back down and continued to wait. Some people flipped through a large Bible, while others nervously checked their smartphones. Rakaw spoke quietly with his lawyers in a corner. Above the door, an electric banner blinked on, displaying his case number (using "xxx" here as a placeholder for the number): 106年度原易字第xxx號. The structure of this case number carried institutional significance. It included the national year (106年度, corresponding to 2017), a marker of Rakaw's Indigenous status (原, referencing the term *Indigenous*), the case type (易字, indicating it was a simple criminal case), and the case's sequential number (第xxx號). Notably, the sole visible indicator marking the presence of the ad hoc Chambers of Indigenous Courts was an ethnoracial marker (原 for *Indigenous*), wedged between markers of state temporality (the ROC national year) and state normativity (case type and number). All these identifiers were expressed in the language and format of Taiwan's Han Taiwanese society and legal system (Judicial Yuan 2018b).

The banner finally signaled for Rakaw to proceed to Courtroom 4. We left the waiting room and entered the courtroom through its rear doors. Rakaw and Lawyer Xu passed through the wooden gate that separated the gallery from the tables designated for the parties and their legal counsel. The rest of us took seats in the gallery. The prosecutor was already seated at one table and did not look up as Rakaw and his lawyers walked past. After a few moments, the bailiff called for everyone to stand as the judge entered.

Before the Doorkeeper: The Trial

The judge presiding over Rakaw's case was Judge Li, a Han Taiwanese man in his mid-thirties who had received his legal education at the prestigious College of Law at National Taiwan University. Lawyer Xu regarded Judge Li as an intelligent and capable judge who brought urban sophistication to Hualien's more rural issues. Sitting in Judge Li's chambers the day before Rakaw's trial, he shared with me that he had volunteered to join the ad hoc chambers because it aligned with his intellectual interests in the complexities of Indigenous legal issues. He also noted that he had little direct experience with Indigenous persons prior to his appointment to the specialized unit.

Judge Li and his colleagues at the Hualien District Court shared a particular understanding of the ad hoc chambers' role in the national court system. During an interview in the courthouse library, I spoke with four of the nine judges assigned to the ad hoc chambers, including Judge Li. One of the judges described the purpose of the specialized units as follows:

The court applies Taiwan's law to Indigenous people, so they [judges] know about the context that they live in. For example, in drunk driving cases, unlike other places where there is public transportation, Indigenous people have to drive home after drinking alcohol, sometimes a long distance, so there are more arrests for drunk driving here [in Hualien County]. Also, unlike Indigenous people or others living in cities with good jobs who can pay a fine instead of going to jail, Indigenous people here do not have good jobs and therefore cannot pay a fine, so they go to jail.[3]

These remarks suggested that, from the perspective of some judges, fulfilling the Judicial Yuan's objectives for the specialized units primarily involved a judicial attunement to Indigenous peoples' disadvantaged socioeconomic circumstances, rather than a deeper respect for their cultures. When I asked how this attunement shaped their approach to Indigenous cases, two of the judges shrugged, stating that they applied the law in the same way as they did in non-Indigenous cases, with little or no difference. Another judge explained, "It depends upon the judge how Indigenous peoples' issues will be handled."[4] This refrain of "it depends upon" (*yaokan* 要看 or *deikan* 得看) became a recurring theme in my conversations with judges, lawyers, and activists about how Indigenous cases were managed in the ad hoc chambers.

Once everyone had taken their seats and settled in, Judge Li invited Lawyer Xu to make a statement. Speaking confidently, Lawyer Xu outlined Rakaw's three-part defense to the charges brought by the Prosecutor's Office. She argued forcefully that the community had maintained a deep relationship to the land where the bamboo house stood, spanning many generations; that the government had failed to provide adequate notice regarding its designation as national land; and that the construction of the community center had involved many members of the community, not just Rakaw. She concluded her statement by suggesting that the court visit the site to see the bamboo house firsthand. Judge Li acknowledged her request and stated he would take it under advisement.

Rakaw's trial was divided into multiple hearings across several months. Two months after the initial hearing, the trial resumed, and the parties called their witnesses. The prosecution called a single witness, a government employee from the River Management Office, who was expected to testify that the plat map provided to the community clearly indicated that the land was designated as national property. When the witness took the stand and examined the map, however, he could not read it. The map was illegible, covered in indecipherable text and obscure markings. The witness admitted to

Judge Li that he could not decipher the map and suggested that someone else needed to be brought in to explain it. With that, he stepped off the stand.

The defense team called four witnesses, including several elders from the community, who provided compelling testimony on various topics. They spoke about land deeds that demonstrated the community's ownership of the land where the bamboo house was built. They described an older structure that once served as a language center but had since fallen into disrepair. They detailed the use of customary markers, made of wood and rocks, to demarcate plots within their territory. Additionally, they expressed frustration over the illegible materials provided to them by the county government. While Judge Li asked only a few questions of the River Management Office worker, he engaged extensively with the community's witnesses. His questions indicated an interest in the community's ties to the land, the land deeds, the history of the older building, and the nature of the documents provided by the government.

Six months later, Rakaw appeared in court to deliver his testimony. Lawyer Xu opened the hearing by revisiting the defense's arguments against the criminal charges. During her remarks, she directly referenced the ad hoc Chambers of Indigenous Courts, stating, "Article 30 of the Indigenous Peoples Basic Law created the special Indigenous courts, which are designed to be respectful of Indigenous cultures and to secure Indigenous peoples' rights. This case is about these things. It is about Indigenous land, which is integral to their culture." Her statement served as a powerful reminder about the profound connection between Truku culture and land. It was also one of only a few instances, during my fieldwork, in which a legal actor explicitly mentioned the ad hoc chambers during a proceeding. Most often, no mention was made of the units.

Rakaw stood at the table to deliver his testimony. Although I recounted his statements earlier, their importance warrants repeating here:

> I have a junior high school education. I am a farmer and my economic situation is not good, and I need to support my son who is in second grade.... Please deliver a verdict of not guilty. The land in this case has been used by my ancestors since the time of Japanese occupation. From then until now, there was no need for us to apply to use it. I do not know why it was classified as river land by the River Management Office.... Please for the sake of us Indigenous people, we are not using the hunter's lodge to make money. We are a harmonious people. We have absolutely no intention of stealing land.

His statements powerfully conveyed the deep significance of the land to the community. They provided a vivid picture of the challenges of life as an Indigenous person in Taiwan. They also addressed a point that was never directly stated but that lurked in the background of his case: that the community somehow stood to gain financially from the bamboo house.

Beyond the Door: The Site Visit

Judge Li agreed to visit the bamboo house. When I arrived in Dowmung on the scheduled day, forty-seven members of the community, mostly older women and men, had made the fifteen-minute journey from the village to the site on scooters. They waited anxiously, eager to witness what would unfold for Rakaw and their cultural center.

As I approached the bamboo house, I saw Rakaw standing alone beside a fire, performing a Truku ceremony. Using smoke, rice wine, and verbal incantations, he called upon the spirits of the ancestors, asking them to assist the community during Judge Li's site visit. With his back to the gathering crowd, Rakaw gazed over the Mugua River Valley. Stretching his arms wide to encompass the sky and the valley, he called to the ancestral spirits. Later, I asked him about this display of Truku spirituality and how it related to the earlier Christian prayer offered in the courthouse. He explained it as a spiritual division of labor, saying, "Here, ancestors are responsible for the land and the people. Out there, God is responsible for everything. So, it makes sense." Vernacularization of globalized religion into local forms of spirituality was thus not merely a matter of top-down translations of norms and precepts into local order. It could also be jurisdictional, with some global precepts not viewed as being within the purview of local matters (see also Simon 2023b).

Judge Li and his entourage arrived promptly in a black government SUV, its doors bearing the insignia of the Hualien District Court, accompanied by another six sleek, black government vehicles. Stepping out of the car, Judge Li wore a dark formal suit, his judicial assistant by his side. A contingent of uniformed police officers, their vests and shoulders adorned with the ROC flag, gathered around him. The officers moved efficiently, taking up strategic positions around the site. Some set up a video camera to record the events, while others took photographs of the area. A few measured the bamboo house and the adjacent roadway. Some milled about, taking notes on pads of paper. The scene was a flurry of activity. Meanwhile, I sat with several community members on red plastic stools, chatting and sharing sweetened roselle as we watched the police officers go methodically about their work.

The site visit featured far more state actors than were typically seen in the Hualien District Court, and they were of a different kind. Instead of bailiffs, the area was swarming with uniformed police officers, giving the scene the feeling of a high-stakes criminal investigation. If the overwhelming police presence was meant to project state authority, however, it seemed to fall flat. The community members around me responded with quiet amusement at the sheer number of officers. As we watched yet another group of police officers climb out of a vehicle, someone joked, "Any more in there?" Community members also roamed around the site freely, often stepping in front of officers taking pictures or measurements. Rather than expressing anxiety about the police, members of the community appeared to be at ease, even bemused. Any anxiety seemed to be on the part of the state, as it overcompensated with the numbers of police officers present.

The presence of state agents and their language, symbols, and technologies stood out in this space. Ubiquitous displays of Truku culture and life surrounded and enveloped these representations and enactments of ROC authority. Huge murals of Truku hunters and painted concrete sculptures of their special hunting knives lined the roadway leading to the bamboo house. The community members who had gathered to observe the police investigation spoke loudly in Truku and Taiwanese Hokkien, their voices drowning out the police officers' conversations in Mandarin Chinese. The bamboo house and the lush greenery of the mountain forest stood in sharp contrast to the gray, cracked concrete of the Hualien District Courthouse. What likely went unnoticed by most judicial actors and police officers was the deliberate and carefully cultivated nature of this greenery, reflecting many generations of Truku agroforestry practices. I must admit, I too failed to see this at first. Months into my visits to the community, a Truku friend politely pointed out to me that I had sat on a plant that was one of many ground crops among the trees.

Perhaps even more revealing was the dilapidated police station near the bamboo house. Years earlier, the Hualien police had constructed the small station to monitor and regulate access to the mountain road, citing environmental protection and public safety as their primary concerns. Travelers were required to show identification cards and complete an entry form before being allowed to use the road, which led to Dowmung ancestral territories. Police actions, however, soon revealed a different priority: issuing numerous mountain entry permits to tourism operators. Influxes of buses and tourists created intense traffic in the village and pollution in the mountains. In 2015, Dowmung leaders organized a protest, blocking the road and firing hunting guns into the air to reclaim their ancestral lands. This history of protest involving the community, and the fact that it took place near the disputed bamboo house, likely figured into the police's overcompensated performance of state authority during the site visit.

The Hualien police had since abandoned the station, leaving it to decay. Weeds now grew on the roof, and deep cracks ran through the concrete walls. The station's closure had effects that extended beyond reopening access to the mountain. Without the police presence, Dowmung hunters no longer felt compelled to register their hunting firearms or submit hunting applications, as required by ROC law. These activities suggested that the community felt it had greater freedom to engage in cultural activities without government oversight. One community member noted, however, that registering firearms and filing hunting applications had never been particularly high priorities for the community, even when the station was operational.

One police official took it upon himself to guide Judge Li around the site, a move that proved too much for Rakaw and other community members to tolerate. They followed the official closely, voicing their objections at every step. At one point, the official gestured toward a painted line on the roadway, explaining to Judge Li that it marked the boundary of national property. Rakaw, unable to hold back his frustration, shouted angrily in Mandarin Chinese into the official's ear, saying, "You say this line marks ROC land. This is our land! You came here, and you took our territory without asking!" Moments later, the official pointed to a faded metal sign beside the road, claiming that it designated the area as national land. Once again, Rakaw yelled forcefully, "You say this sign says this is ROC land. This is our land! You put your sign here on our land without telling us. Now you claim the land!"

These heated exchanges continued for thirty minutes. Rakaw was unrelenting and defiant throughout, his tone and words leaving no room for doubt about his stance. Meanwhile, the official conspicuously pretended not to hear the man shouting into his ear. Rakaw's statements and actions were not just expressions of anger; they were a refusal, to use Audra Simpson's (2016) term, to acquiesce to colonial claims over history and territory. For him, this space was unequivocally Truku land, not ROC land, and it was governed by local norms of Gaya.

Judge Li was an engaged observer, carefully listening both to the police official and to Rakaw. After the police official concluded the tour, Rakaw took the opportunity to lead one of his own. He first brought Judge Li to the fire, where he had called upon the ancestral spirits. Standing there, Rakaw explained the significance of this place to him and the community. Next, he guided the judge to the bamboo house, describing its purpose and the rationale behind its design. Rakaw shared that the structure was modeled on Truku hunters' lodges and was intended to serve as a cultural center to educate the younger generation. Speaking earnestly to Judge Li, he said, "Our children do not know about Truku culture, language, or customs. We need a place where we can teach them these things, about our traditional culture, Gaya."

Off the Hinges: Making Justice Mobile

In general, courts stay put; they are immobile and do not travel. In this case, circumstances were such that Judge Li recognized that visiting the bamboo house could provide valuable insights. Site visits lend themselves to certain kinds of disputes, such as territorial disputes or property damage, as they allow judges to gain a firsthand understanding of the situation. In Taiwan, however, judges frequently deny such inspection requests for various reasons. These include seeing courts as concerned with resolving disputes under law rather than investigating facts, concerns about safety at the site, and the logistical challenges and expenses involved in organizing such visits.

The Judicial Yuan has increasingly come to recognize the intimate relationship between Indigenous peoples and the land. As part of this shift, judges in the ad hoc chambers are now encouraged to conduct site visits to gain a better understanding of local circumstances, and some have taken this encouragement to heart. Around the time of Rakaw's site visit, for example, a judge in the Pingtung District Court conducted a similar site visit to a Paiwan cemetery that the village claimed had been improperly destroyed by developers. These initiatives, along with other exploratory concepts, like the idea of a court that would "ride circuit" into Indigenous communities, suggested that the mobility of justice was increasingly becoming part of the conversation of Indigenous justice in Taiwan.

In Rakaw's case, making justice mobile revealed new assemblages and dimensions of power. By stepping outside the courtroom and into Indigenous territory, state assumptions about history, language, normativity, and power were unsettled. While members of the Dowmung community undeniably felt the presence of the ROC government during the state visit, mobility threw into relief questions about the extent of its power. Rakaw's ceremonial invocation of the ancestral spirits asserted an Indigenous claim to the land. His confrontations with the police official, along with the casual defiance of community members walking in front of or ignoring the police, displayed a boldness not seen in the courtroom. The colorful artwork, sculptures, and lively din of Truku and Taiwanese Hokkien languages underscored the perception that the ROC state was the outsider here, not Indigenous persons. Rakaw's complaint about the state unjustly taking Indigenous land reframed the discussion by embedding the land in its historical and cultural context, something that had not occurred in the courtroom. The abandoned police station also suggested a retreat of state authority from Indigenous lands, while the conspicuous and excessive police presence during the visit signaled a deep-seated anxiety about losing control. This overcompensated display of state power, at times almost comical, highlighted the tenuousness of the state's hold in this contested space.

Making justice mobile also aligned the ad hoc chambers with the expectations held by some of its Indigenous subjects. During the site visit, an elder grabbed my elbow. Gesturing toward Judge Li and Rakaw, he remarked, "This is the important part [of the ad hoc Chamber of Indigenous Courts]. That it includes our knowledge. The judges know nothing. We must take our customs to the court, or it must come to us."[5] His comments echoed points raised by Paelabang Danapan (1991), a Pinuyumayan scholar, about the need to take Indigenous peoples' knowledges and oral traditions seriously.

The ambiguities surrounding state power lingered as the site visit came to an end. After concluding their inspection, Judge Li and his entourage climbed back into their government vehicles and departed, leaving behind a solitary police officer with an unenviable task: securing the signature of someone, anyone, to serve as a documented witness to the site visit. His efforts were met with quiet but firm resistance. Community members would glance at the form written in Mandarin Chinese and silently walk away. At one point, a man snatched the form from the officer's hand, huffed loudly, and threw it on the ground. The officer picked up the crumpled form, brushed it off on his pants leg, and moved on to seek a signature from someone else. From what I could see, he never got one.

As the police officer drove away, people started talking about Judge Li's visit. They lingered, chewing betel and sipping rice wine, exchanging their thoughts. The discussion initially focused on the misguided police official and the overwhelming number of officers present at the site. Gradually, the topic shifted to the bamboo house, with people admiring its craftsmanship and speculating about its future. After a few minutes, someone suggested taking a group photo. We gathered beside the bamboo house, with the Mugua River Valley stretching out behind us. Everyone smiled as the picture was taken. In that moment, it felt as though the community was documenting a small but meaningful victory.

The Door Ajar: The Decision

Rakaw and other members of the Dowmung community later returned to the Hualien District Court to hear Judge Li's decision. It had been approximately 481 days since the police began investigating the bamboo house and 204 days since the first court hearing. The tension was palpable. In the waiting room, Lawyer Zhou, the other legal aid lawyer representing Rakaw, paced nervously. While he reassured Rakaw and the other community members, Lawyer Zhou privately confided to me that he had no idea how Judge Li would rule. The stakes were high. Rakaw might leave the courtroom acquitted and vindicated in his dedication to preserving this community's culture, language, and lands. But it was also possible that he would be convicted and issued a fine, or worse, several years of imprisonment. Before entering the courtroom, Rakaw and the others held another Christian prayer. Compared to the prayer several months earlier, this one was much more somber and reflective.

When we finally entered Courtroom 4, everyone settled into the seats they had become accustomed to taking during the trial, except for Rakaw and Lawyer Zhou, who now found seats in the audience section. There was no ceremony. Judge Li was already seated at his bench. In a formal tone, he delivered the verdict: "Because the community did not know and were not sufficiently notified that the cultural center was on national land, the defendant is found not guilty of the allegations."

As Judge Li announced the verdict, Lawyer Zhou buried his face in his hands, his shoulders trembling with emotion. Those nearby reached out to comfort him, patting him gently on his back. As we walked out of Courtroom 4, nearly everyone was in tears. We exchanged hugs and passed around tissues. The decision had decided the fate of their family member and friend, even if it did not affirm a particularly strong claim to their lands. Still, there was a shared sense that Judge Li's decision was an outcome that favored the community, cast in a legal technicality. Amid the outpouring of emotion, Rakaw stood apart. He was one of the few people not crying. Instead, he approached Lawyer Zhou, gave him a half smile, and slapped him hard on the shoulder. Without a word, he turned and walked out the courthouse doors.

The Hualien District Prosecutor's Office later filed an appeal, seeking to overturn Rakaw's acquittal. In an unexpected turn, the Hualien High Court dismissed the case, fully acquitting Rakaw. Happy endings in the ad hoc chambers, although hard fought, were possible. Yet such outcomes were never guaranteed, as five other Dowmung defendants discovered when they faced the ad hoc chambers under different circumstances.

THE DOWMUNG ROSE STONE CASE

In June 2016, as the community began constructing the bamboo house, five Dowmung men traveled to an area along the Mugua River where the community had gathered minerals and hunted for generations. Situated a half-day's walk from their village, the men spent two days in the mountains searching for stone ores. Using iron mallets and chisels, they extracted fourteen rhodonite ("rose stone") ores, a regulated semiprecious stone, totaling 220 kilograms. The group carried their haul down the mountain using special backpacks and left the ores by the roadside. One man returned to the village to retrieve a vehicle. On their way home, they encountered Forestry Bureau police officers on patrol. Believing that the officers were targeting illegal loggers, the men explained that they were collecting stones, not wood, and so had done nothing wrong. Interpreting this as an admission of a potential crime, the police detained the men and took them to the local police station.

A few days later, one of the men agreed to guide a police officer to the site where the ores had been collected. According to court records, the officer noted that they followed a special path used by Truku people, one rarely accessed by outsiders. During the walk, the man reportedly told the officer that he knew that the land was state-owned and that mining was illegal. The officer claimed the man said, "We, Indigenous people, have been caught before. It does not matter if you get caught. I know it is illegal." After confirming that the collection site fell within Forestry Bureau jurisdiction, the police arrested the men and confiscated the ores.

As the name suggests, rose stone is characterized by striking rose-red hues, a product of its high manganese content. These semiprecious stones are classified as "Gem & Jade" stones under Taiwan's Mining Act and are subject to strict regulation. The Dowmung men claimed that they intended to use the stones in home construction, following a Truku cultural practice that predated the period of Japanese colonization. Rose stones are, however, also highly valued on the black market. Middlemen sometimes recruit Indigenous persons to source valuable stones like these for illicit trade. It remains a common perception among the Han Taiwanese that Indigenous persons frequently engage in such quick-profit activities. The approximate market value of the stones collected by the men was NTD 200,000, equivalent to several months' wages.

The Hualien District Prosecutor's Office charged the men with violating Article 69 of the Mining Act and Article 320 of the Criminal Code. Prosecutors argued that the men had unlawfully collected the regulated minerals from an area not designated as Indigenous reserve land and that the men had committed larceny against the ROC government by taking the ores without authorization. In their defense, the men contended that they had gathered the stones on Truku territory, even if it was not officially recognized as such. They emphasized that collecting these stones was a long-standing Truku cultural practice and integral to their identities as Truku persons. The men insisted that they had no intention to sell the stones for profit but planned to use them for the same decorative purposes the community had used such stones for over generations.

The men's case progressed through two levels of Taiwan's national court system: the Hualien District Court and Hualien High Court. While the men obtained an acquittal in the District Court, the High Court overturned the verdict and convicted them after a second trial. I summarize the lower-court case but focus primarily on the appeal to explore why two different outcomes occurred, based on the same facts and law, and how the dispute and Indigenous rights obtained a different character in the High Court appeal.

A Promising Beginning

A Han Taiwanese lawyer, Lawyer Yang, represented the five men during their trial in the ad hoc Chamber of Indigenous Courts of the Hualien District Court. In his mid-thirties, Lawyer Yang had taken the case pro bono. He worked at a small law firm in downtown Hualien City, and he specialized in general litigation rather than Indigenous cases. His law partner, who had experience handling Indigenous legal matters, persuaded him to take the case. Personable and humorous, Lawyer Yang was intrigued by the complexities of cases involving Indigenous issues, and we quickly formed a friendship.

During the trial, Lawyer Yang called a community elder as an expert witness. Like other cases described earlier, the elder was unable to read the witness affidavit. The court clerk stood beside him and read the document to him. He repeated the clerk's words and then scribbled a signature. The elder spoke in Truku as he testified. Other members of the community had traveled with him and served as his interpreters, speaking from the audience section. Through them, he recounted how their ancestors had once lived higher in the mountains, where they quarried stones and stacked them to build retaining walls around their homes. These walls protected their houses from earth and rock flows caused by the steep terrain. He explained that the ancestors regarded rose stone as an ordinary stone used for practical purposes, not decoration. More recently, however, the community had begun using rose stones and other semiprecious stones for decorative purposes, appreciating their aesthetic qualities. The elder testified that he did not know if the five accused men had ever sold ore, but he had seen them, and others in the community, use rose stones and other semiprecious stones to adorn their homes and as gifts to others.

Debates during the trial revolved around the ROC Constitution, the Mining Act, and the Criminal Code. Lawyer Yang argued that the defendants' actions were protected by Article 19 of the Indigenous Peoples Basic Law, which permits Indigenous persons to "collect[ ] minerals, rocks and soils ... for traditional culture, ritual or self-consumption." He explained that the men were gathering the rose stone ores in accordance with Truku cultural practice and emphasized that their purpose was self-use, not profit. Lawyer Yang pointed out that the Legislature had not yet amended the Mining Act to make it align with the Basic Law by exempting Indigenous mineral-gathering activities. He argued that the Basic Law should govern the case and that the men should not be penalized for the Legislature's inaction.

The judge agreed and acquitted the five men. In the ruling, the judge concluded that the location where the men had collected the ores was part of Truku ancestral territory, even though it was not formally designated as Indigenous reserve land. The judge also concluded that the men were acting in accordance with Truku cultural practice. In a sharp critique of the Legislature, the judge condemned its "legislative laziness" (*lifa daiduo* 立法怠惰) in failing to amend the Mining Act to align with the Basic Law. The judge emphasized that the burden of inconsistencies and gaps in the system of Indigenous rights should not be borne by Indigenous persons (Xu 2017).

The District Court's ruling was the first of its kind concerning Indigenous mineral-gathering practices. Lawyer Yang expressed surprise at the outcome, saying, "No one has ever won this kind of case before."[6] The decision was seen as a step toward greater recognition of Indigenous peoples' claims to ancestral lands and rights to control the natural resources found there. In Dowmung and other Indigenous communities in Hualien, the ruling was celebrated as heralding the beginning of restorative justice. The decision also clarified the role of the Basic Law in safeguarding Indigenous cultural practices and territories. The chief prosecutor noted the particular impact of the Basic Law on the outcome, stating, "Because of the provisions of the Indigenous Peoples Basic Law, the acquittal was given for lack of illegality" (Wen 2017). This progress, however, soon met a significant obstacle. The Hualien District Prosecutor's Office exercised its absolute right to appeal, and the men found themselves the subjects of a new prosecution in the ad hoc chamber of the Hualien High Court.

Leveling Up

In October 2017, I joined the five men at the Hualien High Court, coinciding with the start of Rakaw's prosecution in the District Court. It was a rainy day, and we gathered under the building's awning. The men were alone. No community members had traveled to the High Court to show support for them. They stood in wet jackets, rumpled t-shirts, and jeans, chewing betel nut and smoking cigarettes. Frustration and anxiety were etched on their faces as they spoke about what they saw as an ongoing injustice. They were worried about whether the High Court would acknowledge and respect their culture and identities as Indigenous persons. One of the men voiced his frustration, asking defiantly, "Why are we here at a court again? We already won our case. The courts do not like us. They do not know anything about our culture."[7] As the rain continued to fall, everyone stood silently, the mood heavy with tension.

The appeal was assigned to Judge Chen, a Han Taiwanese jurist with an impressive background. He had earned a graduate degree from a prestigious U.S. law school and possessed extensive expertise in Indigenous peoples' rights and related legal issues. His scholarly contributions included published journal articles on these topics. By all accounts, and certainly compared to many other judges in Taiwan, Judge Chen was exceptionally well qualified to preside in the ad hoc Chamber of Indigenous Courts.

At the first hearing, Judge Chen led the questioning of the five men. From my outsider perspective, his approach felt more like that of a prosecutor than an impartial decision-maker, with his rapid-fire, aggressive inquiries. He pressed them on the location of the stone ores, their understanding of the ores' value, and their intended use for the ores. The men avoided eye contact with Judge Chen, sitting slumped in their chairs and staring at the floor or at the opposite wall. They seemed disengaged, offering murmured, incomplete answers that trailed off into silence. Their body language conveyed anything but submission to the court's authority; it radiated profound apathy toward the entire process.

In one of the rare moments of engagement, one of the men attempted to explain Truku practices related to the collecting of ores. Judge Chen, however, dismissed his explanation, stating, "There is nothing in your culture about collecting minerals." He followed up with a pointed question, "Do you really expect me to believe that you are not going to sell them? That was a large amount of rocks." Unlike in the District Court trial, where Truku culture was considered relevant, Judge Chen appeared unwilling to consider it in this case, saying,

> All cultures would take the rocks for some sort of benefit, like an economic benefit, not just for decoration or self-use. There is no culture that would do that. So, it is not a Han Chinese versus Indigenous cultural difference. These men were going to try to get some benefit from it, but there is no evidence that they did, so they may not be guilty under the Mining Act, but they could still be guilty of stealing from the government.

On the basis of this reasoning, Judge Chen denied the men's request for expert testimony on Truku cultural practices, an element that had been pivotal to their acquittal in the District Court.[8]

Doubling Down on a Triple Threat

As in the District Court, Lawyer Yang argued that the men's actions were protected under the Basic Law and that the case represented a conflict between the Basic Law and the Mining Act. Judge Chen rejected the notion of such a conflict. Applying the principle of *lex specialis*, he characterized the

Basic Law as a general law encompassing broad rules, whereas the Mining Act was a narrower law that specifically addressed the conduct in question. Accordingly, Judge Chen determined that the Mining Act was the controlling law in the case.

From Judge Chen's perspective, the issue was not merely that the Basic Law was less applicable as a general law. He viewed it as potentially conflicting with the ROC Constitution and with Taiwan's human rights obligations, while also posing a threat to the state's sovereign control over land and natural resources. In multiple hearings, Judge Chen described the Basic Law as "dangerous" (*henweixian* 很危險), particularly in its provisions protecting self-consumption practices. He summarized his concerns as follows:

> This is not a conflict of laws, but a higher-level issue, that is, whether the Basic Law is unconstitutional or not.... The "self-consumption" part seems to be infinitely expanded, which is inconsistent with constitutional amendments and the two covenants [the International Covenant on Civil and Political Rights and the International Covenant on Economic, Social and Cultural Rights].... Does this not create another kind of inequality? ... As long as the area is an Indigenous area, any behavior related to plants, minerals, and wild animals in the area by Indigenous people of any group would be legal.... In what you say, the capture, breeding, etc., of endangered animals by Indigenous people in designated areas will exonerate them. And are not Taiwan's endangered fauna, flora, and minerals mostly found in Indigenous areas? ... For resources protected by special laws, like the Forestry Act, many are irreversible once they dry up.

Instead of interrogating the conflicts between the Basic Law and other domestic laws in Taiwan, Judge Chen reframed the issue as a "higher-level" conflict between the Basic Law and the ROC Constitution, specifically the constitutional principle of equality, as well as Taiwan's human rights obligations. He also presented the Basic Law as a potential threat to state control, arguing that it allowed Indigenous persons to extract natural resources without regard to any system of order—not considering the Truku law of Gaya, which governs such activities. In this view, the Basic Law posed a triple threat to constitutional equality, human rights, and state sovereignty. Lawyer Yang summed up Judge Chen's stance more bluntly: "The judge thinks the Basic Law is ridiculous."[9]

In personal conversations, Judge Chen reiterated his view that the Basic Law was "dangerous" and "too big" (*tai da* 太大) because it granted Indigenous peoples significant freedoms. Sitting in his judicial chambers over tea, he elaborated: "[The Basic Law] can open up to everything, which is dangerous. It is too big. Anybody can claim to go hunting. They can just go hunting and kill all the animals."[10] Further, the Legislature's slow implementation of the Basic Law had undermined its legitimacy.

Lawyer Yang also invoked Taiwan's human rights obligations to defend the men's actions. He argued that the International Covenant on Civil and Political Rights and the International Covenant on Economic, Social and Cultural Rights, which had been incorporated into ROC law through the Two Covenants Act, explicitly protected Indigenous cultural practices, including mining activities. As fundamental human rights, he contended, these protections superseded ROC statutes and codes. Again, Judge Chen disagreed. He explained that the Legislature had incorporated the two covenants as ordinary statutes, granting them no superior status in the ROC legal system. In his view, they held the same weight as any other statute or code. Moreover, he dismissed their relevance, stating that the covenants were "too general to be useful in Taiwan."

The prosecutor assigned to the case extended Judge Chen's position even further. During one hearing, she argued, "Maybe if we give them [Indigenous peoples] more rights, it will be bad for them." Her statement suggested that legal protections for Indigenous peoples posed threats not only to equality, human rights, and sovereignty, but also to the purity of indigeneity. She implied that granting such rights might encourage Indigenous groups to abandon their lifeways and become modern. Her position reflected a striking paternalism in regard to Indigenous peoples. It also articulated an image of Indigenous peoples as guided solely by knowledge systems that reinforce the past, not engaging with the present or looking toward the future.

Professional Vision and Revision

Charles Goodwin (1994) describes discursive practices of coding, highlighting, and graphic representation, which use particular techniques of inscription to create what he terms a "professional vision." These practices played a particularly influential role in shaping the Dowmung men's appeal in the Hualien High Court.

Coding generally refers to the process of transforming observations into objects of knowledge. Goodwin illustrates this with examples from the Rodney King trial, in which defense lawyers coded police batons, violent kicks, and stomps as "tools" for controlling situations. In the men's appeal hearing, similar coding practices were used to frame their actions as potentially violent. The five men had used iron mallets and chisels to extract the rose stone ores. During the appeal, however, their mallets and chisels were described not as instruments or tools but as "lethal weapons" (*xiongqi* 兇器) intended for criminal purposes. Further, the men were portrayed not as a group of individuals but as a "gang" (*jiehuo* 結夥) of three or more people. This framing depicted them not as participants in a Truku cultural practice but as a dangerous posse, roaming the mountains armed with weapons. Ordinary tools were recast as implements of violence, and collective activity was transformed into organized criminal behavior. This shift in framing also significantly raised the stakes. What had initially been presented as a case of common theft against the ROC state was redefined as an aggravated offense under Article 321, paragraphs 3 and 4 of the Criminal Code, carrying mandatory prison sentences.

Another discursive practice was highlighting, which involves emphasizing specific phenomena within a broader perceptual field. Goodwin illustrates this with examples of defense lawyers highlighting still images from the videotape of police attacking Rodney King and archaeologists tracing features in the soil. In the men's appeal, the court highlighted text rather than images. Judge Chen framed the legislative intent behind the Basic Law as an effort to promote respect "within a reasonable scope" (*zai heli zhi fanwei* 在合理之範圍) for Indigenous cultures, particularly in the domain of territorial rights. By interpreting the Basic Law through this lens, Judge Chen highlighted its limiting language. He pointed out that the norms in Articles 4, 7, 9, 12, 13, 17, and 20 of the Basic Law would be "stipulated by laws" (*ling yi falü dingzhi* 另以法律定之) and that Articles 2–1, 15, 21, and 24 refer to "measures" (*banfa* 辦法) that would be "separately prescribed" (*ling dingzhi* 另定之) by competent authorities. Additionally, he drew attention to Article 34, which stated, "The relevant authority shall amend, make, or repeal relevant regulations in accordance with the principles of this law within three years from its effectiveness." By highlighting these textual elements, Judge Chen emphasized the constraints embedded in the Basic Law rather than its potential for expansive protections.

Drawing on this interpretation, Judge Chen concluded that each right outlined in the Basic Law required separate enactment to have legal and practical effect. This approach fragmented the text into discrete units, transforming the Basic Law from a cohesive framework into a collection of isolated paragraphs, each requiring individual implementation. The division extended even further: The content of each paragraph was similarly broken down into separate components, each necessitating its own legislative action. Focusing on Article 19, Judge Chen noted that the activities mentioned—hunting, plant gathering, mineral collection, and water resource use—corresponded to distinct sets of resources, penalties, interests, values, and rights. In his view, Article 19 could not be treated as a unified provision; instead, each activity required separate legal implementation. While the Legislature had addressed Indigenous hunting and forest product-gathering practices in other statutes, it had not extended similar recognition to mineral-gathering activities. As a result, Judge Chen concluded that the accused men's conduct fell outside the scope of protection and was therefore subject to criminal sanction.

This interpretation of the Basic Law effectively reduced it, as the court's decision phrased it, to "nothing more than a prescriptive norm or what scholars refer to as a duty-of-effort norm." In other words, the Basic Law constituted a set of aspirational, abstract principles and guidelines, not "real" law, and therefore could not serve as the basis for a criminal defense. As Judge Chen put it, the Basic Law was "a law, but not a law in practice."[11] Other judges with whom I spoke shared similar views. One district court judge noted, "The Legislature's lack of changing laws indicates their desire that 'in accordance with law' means the present laws should trump the Basic Law. In a conflict-of-law situation, the present laws should be higher in the hierarchy than the Basic Law."[12] Through a deft reframing, Judge Chen and these other judges had effectively neutralized the Basic Law's "dangerous" qualities, reducing it to a guiding but largely irrelevant text.

The Indigenous activists with whom I worked had a different perspective on the Basic Law. To them, it was a cohesive framework organized around a principle of protecting the fundamental rights of Indigenous peoples. While Judge Chen focused on the letter of the law, they invoked its spirit. For these activists, the activities in Article 19 were inseparable, each equally deserving of protection. They, too, highlighted text, crafting their own narrative of the Basic Law. Like Judge Chen, they quoted its provisions, pointing to Article 34, which mandates that the Legislature "shall" (*ying* 應) amend all "relevant laws and regulations" (*xiangguan faling* 相關法令) to align with the Basic Law "within three years" (*san nian nei* 三年內). Now, with the three-year deadline long past and minimal legislative progress to show for it, they questioned whether the Basic Law was anything more than a fraud perpetrated on Indigenous peoples. Some judges seemed to agree. One high court judge candidly remarked, "Yes, [the Basic Law] is a false promise for political purposes. My theory is that the law was created to appease Indigenous people and get their votes."[13] From this perspective, the Basic Law was little more than realpolitik: a symbolic gesture by politicians seeking to appear supportive of Indigenous peoples' rights without committing to substantive action.

To some judges, the system of ad hoc Chambers of Indigenous Courts represented yet another empty promise to Indigenous peoples. Sitting in his chambers, Judge Chen shared his perspective on the specialized units, stating,

> It is just designed to be friendly to Indigenous people, to help them understand Taiwan law, not to help them or protect Indigenous culture, whatever culture means, or fill in gaps [in law].... The court is the same court as the other ones, it is just more friendly, get to know one another more but not to fill in the gaps left by the Basic Law.... There is really not much that we can do. Our hands are tied.[14]

His statements reflected a narrow interpretation of the purpose and capabilities of the units. To Judge Chen, they served as "friendly" spaces designed to fulfill the Judicial Yuan's objectives by helping Indigenous persons and communities better understand ROC law. They were not, as the District Court judges quoted above believed, spaces for addressing the socioeconomic disadvantages faced by Indigenous peoples. Nor were they, as suggested in the Judicial Yuan's press releases, spaces for accommodating Indigenous peoples' cultural differences. While Judge Chen's perspective was not widely shared among other judges I encountered, it highlighted the range of forms the units could take at different levels of the national court system.

Appeals to Culture

Judge Chen's remark, "Indigenous culture, whatever culture means," conveyed an ambivalence, perhaps even skepticism, toward social scientific concepts like culture, which were integral to Indigenous peoples' cases involving cultural practices and territories. In Taiwan's Indigenous rights discourse, the term *culture* (*wenhua* 文化) is nearly everywhere invoked and virtually nowhere explained. It appears in the ROC Constitution, national statutes and regulations, government reports, museum exhibitions, tourism materials, and cultural parks.[15] It also appeared in debates in the ad hoc chambers. In one hearing I attended, participants used the term *culture* fifty-six times in the course of a forty-five-minute-long proceeding.¹⁶ These references ranged from broad descriptions of "Indigenous peoples' cultures" (*yuanzhuminzu wenhua* 原住民族文化) to more specific mentions of "Paiwan culture" (*paiwanzu de wenhua* 排灣族的文化) and "Paiwan funerary culture" (*paiwanzu de binzang wenhua* 排灣族的殯葬文化), which was central to the dispute over lands and burial practices.

While many ROC legal texts and actors frequently referred to "culture" and its associated concepts of "tradition" (*chuantong* 傳統) and "ritual" (*jiyi* 祭儀), they rarely provided clear definitions of these terms. State documents, however, offered some insight into their interpretation. For instance, Article 2.1 of the Wildlife Management Measures defines *traditional culture* as "the general term for the values, norms, religions, art, ethics, institutions, languages, symbols and all other aspects of life that have existed in the Indigenous society for a long time and passed on from generation to generation." Similarly, Article 2.2 defines *ritual* as "ritual activities and ritual acts of the traditional culture of the Indigenous people, which are repeated according to their religion, beliefs or habits and passed down from generation to generation." These definitions reflected a Tylorian (Tylor 1871) approach to culture with a commitment to an ideological frame of evolutionism that cultural phenomena are those that survive the set of conditions under which they developed. They inscribed an understanding of culture that was inconsistent with contemporary anthropological perspectives emphasizing its contested, dynamic, and fluid features.

Working in an institutional space that often demands singularity and clearly defined categories (Weinauer 1996, 43), judges in the ad hoc chambers sometimes grappled with the complexities of "culture." Judge Chen wrestled with the concept and its implications in the Dowmung men's case. During one hearing, he engaged in a debate with Lawyer Yang about the concept of culture:

> The traditional culture of Taiwan's Indigenous peoples is actually not unified, solely a single ethnic group. The traditional cultures of mountain ethnic groups, plains ethnic groups, even seaside ethnic groups and so on, may not be the same, not to mention the different ethnic groups. How do you define it in this situation? It is also a question of which generation to demarcate, for example, from the Qing to the Japanese to the ROC government.... The same thing, maybe the same people in different times and different regions are not the same. What point should mark the beginning of culture? And if a certain ethnic group has migrated many times over the years, is it true that

the lands that they have inhabited from north to south are all traditional territories? And the competent authorities have not set out their view on this content and it has become an uncertain legal concept?

His remarks reflected an effort to translate "culture" into a legally legible concept, probing its contours, temporal dimensions, and connection to land. Finding many questions but few answers, he concluded that the concept was fraught with complexities that militated against its use as a reliable tool in the courtroom. In a later conversation with me, he elaborated:

> Culture is very hard to understand. The term is used all over the place, but it is unclear. There are no writings, so I get elders so I can hear about the old times or stories they heard. But when I ask elders in the village to tell me about their culture, one tells me one thing and another tells me something somewhat different. I have to figure out the real story. It is very hard.[17]

Other judges encountered similar difficulties when attempting to apply the concept of culture to cases involving Indigenous persons and communities. As one district court judge remarked,

> I sometimes need elders to come into court as experts to testify about hunting practices in that community. I asked the elder, "Does everyone in the community come and ask the elders for permission to go hunting before they go to receive a blessing or do they just go without asking?" The elder said, "About 80 percent." Well, did that make it a traditional practice or not? What was I supposed to do?[18]

"Culture" had an uneasy fit in the one space in the Taiwan court system where it arguably mattered most. Despite frequent references to "culture" in disputes and the laws protecting Indigenous peoples, few judges in the ad hoc chambers considered what the concept meant in the context of Indigenous cases. Ultimately, these concerns were rendered moot in the Dowmung men's case as Judge Chen excised Truku "culture" from the case altogether.

Delaying Justice Denied

After a year of proceedings in the Hualien High Court, the five Truku men exited the courthouse for the final time in October 2018. As I walked with them, they expressed deep frustrations with the legal process and the ad hoc chambers. "We just give up. Why bother? It is our culture. I don't even look at him [the judge]. He thinks he knows everything, but he will just decide.

We will be guilty," one of the men said.[19] They spoke of Lawyer Yang with a mixture of gratitude and resignation, saying, "He is a good person. He works hard for us. But he cannot help us win. The courts do not understand our culture. They do not like us, so we will lose."[20]

Later that day, I met with Lawyer Yang to discuss the case. He described the men as having all but given up, stating, "They said they would just sleep. They do not care. Just do not care. I think they just give up. No point in fighting. Just pay the fine or go to jail for a little while. They just give up. They do not want to fight."[21] Lawyer Yang believed that this resignation explained their demeanor during the proceedings, speculating, "They knew they would get caught. They do not care. They use it to get angrier."[22] The anger to which he referred stemmed from the men's deep resentment at being repeatedly arrested and prosecuted for practicing their culture on their ancestral territories.

Lawyer Yang's appeal strategy centered on a single, crucial tactic: delay. Three key aspects of the case made this approach particularly advantageous. First, Judge Chen had hinted at his intention to rule against the men. His comments on the lower court's decision and his narrow interpretation of the Basic Law and human rights left little doubt about the likely outcome. Second, a recent amendment to the Criminal Code introduced a significant procedural change. Previously, simple criminal cases could be appealed only to the High Court, not to the Supreme Court. Under the new procedural change, if a lower court acquitted a defendant and an appellate court found them guilty, the defendant could appeal directly to the Supreme Court. The amendment had not yet taken effect, and delaying the case could ensure that the new procedure would apply. Third, a proposed revision to the Mining Act was working its way through the Legislature. The draft included a potential exception for Indigenous mining activities. Together, these factors made delay the most promising strategy for the accused men.

Judge Chen agreed to suspend the proceedings while the Constitutional Court reviewed Tama Talum's hunting case. The outcome of Mr. Talum's case had the potential to clarify the role of the Basic Law in the ROC legal system, including its relevance in the men's case. Nearly three years later, the Constitutional Court issued its interpretation, upholding Mr. Talum's conviction. As previously noted, its decision did not address the Basic Law. Shortly thereafter, Judge Chen issued a ruling overturning the District Court's acquittal. He found the men guilty of aggravated larceny against the ROC government and sentenced each to four to five months in prison. With the new criminal procedure in effect, the men appealed their convictions, and their case is currently pending before the Supreme Court.

CONCLUSION

This chapter examined two cases involving the Truku community of Dowmung heard in the ad hoc Chambers of Indigenous Courts in Hualien. These cases stood out for their direct engagement with Indigenous cultural practices and relationships to land. In these cases, the boundary-spanning operations of the specialized units became visible as local actors navigated and negotiated Han Taiwanese and Indigenous understandings of culture, land, and law, both within the courtroom and beyond. While the Judicial Yuan envisioned that the specialized units would promote respect for Indigenous cultural differences and improve court accessibility for Indigenous individuals and communities, these cases highlight the complexities of achieving those goals in practice. Efforts to understand Indigenous cultures, include Indigenous voices, safeguard their legal rights, and address inequalities in the legal system were shaped by numerous factors. These included court procedures dictated by ROC law, varying attitudes of judicial actors toward Indigenous claims, and broader dynamics extending beyond the immediate dispute and courtroom context.

As is evident in the discussion above, Taiwan judges held different views on the role of the ad hoc chambers. Some interpreted the units' mandate broadly, emphasizing the integration of Indigenous voices and cultural perspectives into judicial processes. Others adopted a narrower view, seeing the units' purpose as limited to recognizing Indigenous peoples' disadvantaged socioeconomic circumstances or as a space for educating Indigenous peoples about ROC state law. Judges also held different views about the relevance of Indigenous cultures, the scope of their rights, and the motivations behind their claims. While some judges treated Indigenous assertions of cultural and territorial rights seriously, others were skeptical, perceiving such claims as ploys to mask illicit intentions or as challenges to state authority. Similarly, judges' views on human rights varied significantly. For some judges, these rights were important normative resources, while others dismissed them as irrelevant or even as limiting Indigenous peoples' rights.

Indigenous peoples engaged with the ad hoc chambers in varied and complex ways. Some individuals and communities actively participated in legal processes administered by the specialized units. They traveled to courthouses as groups, offered testimony as expert witnesses, and served as informal interpreters in courtroom proceedings. At other times, especially when the units seemed to close themselves to Indigenous claims or when prosecutions and litigations became repetitive, they grew more withdrawn. Their disengagement reflected skepticism about whether the units had their interests in mind or, more broadly, could meaningfully advance Indigenous justice and reconciliation.

Processes beyond formal legal procedures also shaped the proceedings in the ad hoc chambers. As the specialized units ventured beyond the courthouse and into Indigenous communities, new configurations and dynamics of power emerged where Han Taiwanese actors and the ROC state became the "other." Discursive framings shaped perceptions of Indigenous persons and their activities: Mallets and chisels were recast as lethal weapons, and semi-organized small-group activities were reframed as violent gang behavior. Legal logics struggled to integrate social scientific concepts, such as culture, despite their inclusion in ROC laws and regulations and their centrality to certain disputes handled by the units. Lawyers adjusted their litigation strategies to the particularities of individual judges, sometimes delaying cases in hopes of favorable changes in law and procedure.

In short, the boundary-spanning operations of Taiwan's ad hoc Chambers of Indigenous Courts were multifaceted and varied between chambers. Mediating the differing understandings of culture, land, and law between Han Taiwanese and Indigenous social worlds in court cases involved interactions across many kinds of actors—judges, lawyers, litigants, and community members. Among these, judges held particular sway in the units; however, the contributions of Indigenous actors in influencing proceedings could not be ignored. Indigenous persons and communities asserted their claims to cultural practices and territories. Elders served as expert witnesses, educating judges and lawyers about their cultures and relationships to the land. Community members bridged language divides by serving as interpreters and traveled together to demonstrate solidarity and share concerns about issues. Yet these engagements with the units were not without challenges. Indigenous participants sometimes grew disillusioned, frustrated by protracted legal processes and interpretations of law that reinforced their marginalized position in the national court system.

Making justice mobile proved to be a productive step toward bringing the ad hoc chambers closer to their intended goal of promoting respect for

Indigenous cultural differences. Dislocating state laws and court proceedings from their familiar settings and resituating them in Indigenous spaces rendered them "out of order," so to speak. This created new opportunities for dialogue about Indigenous cultural differences, understandings of land and territory, and community needs. Making justice mobile offered an opportunity to strengthen the boundary-spanning work of the units, but other changes were also needed. The judiciary had to confront the discursive framings that mischaracterized Indigenous practices, address the limitations of legal logics in engaging with social-scientific concepts related to Indigenous issues, and attend to the shifting terrain of Indigenous rights, which judges interpreted in varied and sometimes contradictory ways.

The next chapter explores the practices that judges and Indigenous parties developed, in collaboration with intermediaries—including lawyers, experts, and Indigenous elders and community members—to push the ad hoc chambers toward the Judicial Yuan's goal of promoting respect for Indigenous peoples and their cultures. While some of these practices showed promise for strengthening the boundary-spanning capacities of the ad hoc chambers, they frequently fell short. As a new system of courts, the units were in a process of becoming, and some of the most effective strategies for bringing them to life stemmed not from the establishment of new formal procedures, which were generally lacking, but from improvisational and strategic efforts of many kinds of actors who worked to make the specialized units meaningful, relevant, and concrete realities in the Taiwan national court system.

FIVE

Hybrid Practices and Legal Indigeneities

IN AUGUST 2018, STAFF at the Legal Aid Foundation's Legal Center of Indigenous Peoples in Hualien mentioned a criminal case being handled by the Hualien District Court that might interest me. It involved a Bunun man, but they provided few other details. Since I was already planning to visit the courthouse that day, I decided to attend the hearing. As I entered the courtroom, the man was in the middle of testifying. What stood out immediately was that he was speaking in Bunun. He served as his own interpreter and translated his testimony into Mandarin Chinese for the judge and lawyers. After the hearing, I met the man in the courtyard outside the courtroom. Curious, I asked why he had chosen to testify in Bunun when knowing that everyone in the courtroom spoke only Mandarin. He responded, saying, "I wanted the judge to understand that a different culture was in the courtroom; that he should be sensitive to my culture. That they have to use my language to talk about it."[1]

A few weeks later, I returned to the Hualien District Court for a meeting with Judge Zhang, an experienced judge who was well versed in Indigenous peoples' legal issues and a passionate advocate for addressing their unequal position in the Taiwan court system. Over the course of my field research, we had developed a friendship. One day, he invited me to join him on a visit to a Truku community in Taroko National Park in eastern Taiwan, named for the Truku people. We drove together to Xincheng Township, where we met several Truku men working in a warehouse. Sitting on large bags of rice in the sweltering heat, we chewed betel nut and talked. Judge Zhang shared updates on recent developments in Indigenous legal cases, including experimental efforts in the ad hoc Chambers of Indigenous Courts to address cultural differences in judicial decision-making. He offered an example:

Judges in criminal divisions were attempting to integrate Indigenous worldviews into their interpretations of criminal intent, or mens rea. Prohibited from recognizing local Indigenous laws as authoritative, some judges were exploring creative workarounds. In this case, the judges were working to incorporate Indigenous cultural understandings of the world—or, at least, their perceptions of these understandings—into their analyses of intent in criminal statutes.

This chapter examines the productive practices that local actors developed to push the ad hoc Chambers of Indigenous Courts toward achieving the Judicial Yuan's goal of promoting respect for Indigenous cultures and bridging state-Indigenous divides in the national court system. Having few formal procedures beyond specialized training for judges and prosecutors, the specialized units were marked by significant ambiguities and ambivalences as institutions intended to span Han Taiwanese and Indigenous social worlds. In many ways, it was up to local actors to maneuver and improvise to make the units realities in the Taiwan court system.

To appreciate the impact of these activities on court proceedings involving Indigenous persons and communities, it may be helpful to recall some of the ambiguities that characterized the ad hoc chambers. The units generally applied ROC state laws rather than local Indigenous laws or justice practices. They were predominantly staffed and administered by Han Taiwanese judges and legal actors, with little or no Indigenous representation. Special training for judges and prosecutors was limited, resulting in a lack of in-depth knowledge about Indigenous cultures, issues, and rights. The language of law was Mandarin Chinese, while Indigenous languages and dialects were secondary and accommodated through a special, but rarely used, interpreter program. Judges often held varying, and sometimes contradictory, views on Indigenous rights claims and the overall purpose of the units. The units had a broad jurisdictional scope, which meant they infrequently dealt with cases directly involving Indigenous cultural practices or territories. Routinized activities generally replicated ordinary court procedures, and certain processes, such as summary proceedings, disincentivized Indigenous parties from raising legal defenses provided to them by law. The presence of the units was rarely invoked or discussed during court proceedings. Cases involving Indigenous persons were not always assigned to the units, because other specialized units had priority over certain matters. Courthouses generally lacked any representations of Indigenous peoples' cultures or identities. During my field research, none of the courthouses I visited had a public display acknowledging that they were located on Indigenous territories.

The ad hoc chambers had a shadowy presence in Taiwan courthouses. According to the Judicial Yuan, they were present and actively working to promote respect for Indigenous cultures, but standing in courtrooms and observing interactions and cases as they unfolded, things appeared much less certain. During my fieldwork, the specialized units found their strongest case as institutions working to bridge state-Indigenous divides through strategic and innovative practices developed by local actors. Here, I concentrate on the practices developed by Han Taiwanese judges and Indigenous parties as they worked with intermediaries, like lawyers, experts, and Indigenous elders and community members, to navigate the units' many ambiguities and address issues of Indigenous cultural and linguistic difference in specific cases.

I begin with judges and the practices they developed to integrate Indigenous cultural ideas and practices into legal process and decision-making. I highlight four key practices. These include integrating Indigenous worldviews into applications of criminal statutes, applying balancing review frameworks, reconfiguring the hierarchy of ROC law, and engaging with notions of justice and human dignity derived from natural law. Next, I turn to Indigenous litigants and the performances of indigeneity they used to push the units to recognize, and sometimes trouble, Indigenous cultural and linguistic differences in the courtroom. I consider three such encounters. These include assertions of Bunun identity in a flooding case, linguistic performances in the prosecution of a Tayan hunter, and the creation of an Indigenous legal center to manage the failures of ROC governance. Throughout these discussions, I emphasize the critical role of intermediary actors—lawyers, witnesses, experts, interpreters, and audience members— who facilitated engagements between judges and Indigenous litigants to bridge cultural and linguistic divides in the courtroom.

These strategic and innovative practices were dynamic, experimental, and held transformative potential. They had the capacity to empower Indigenous persons and communities, generate knowledge about Indigenous peoples' cultures and laws, and change the attitudes of the actors involved. Success, however, was never guaranteed. Just as these practices could benefit Indigenous parties, they could also work against them. Yet these practices demonstrated the efforts of local actors to bring the ad hoc chambers to life as institutions working to bridge Indigenous and non-Indigenous divides in the courtroom.

Judges held different views about Indigenous rights claims and the purpose of the ad hoc chambers. This had the effect of generating a multitude of specialized units, each with its own character and approach to addressing Indigenous peoples' legal issues. To some extent, this was to be expected, given that part of the purpose of the units was to explore new strategies and techniques for addressing difficult situations at the unwieldy intersections of Indigenous cultures and state law. These insights could then be integrated by the Judicial Yuan into broader court reforms and training programs related to the units.

Some judges, particularly those with more conservative leanings, believed there was little room for reconfiguring legal practices to give practical effect to the ad hoc chambers. In their view, the units functioned merely as an Indigenous docket, a space primarily intended to educate Indigenous persons and communities about ROC law, rather than addressing their cultural differences or unequal position in the court system. Other judges, however, saw things differently. As previously mentioned, they emphasized the importance of adopting "a new view of the law" and "a different starting place" to address Indigenous peoples' unique social and legal issues and needs. Committed to fulfilling the units' mandate to "respect" Indigenous peoples' cultural and linguistic differences, but with limited tools at their disposal, these judges turned to creative practices to integrate Indigenous perspectives and cultural concepts into established courtroom practices.

These practices embodied forms of hybrid practice. *Hybrid practice*, as I intend the term, refers to new ways of working from the specific functioning of new objects and the need to simultaneously meet the requirements of different domains of knowledge, disciplines, specializations, and worlds (Gustafsson and Lidskog 2013; Lindberg, Walter, and Raviola 2017; C. Miller 2001; cf. Latour 1993). Judges in the ad hoc chambers faced the challenge of applying new and often ambiguous laws to disputes involving Indigenous cultural practices and territories. In doing so, they had to navigate the expectations of the Judicial Yuan, the constraints of Taiwan's civil law tradition, and Indigenous peoples' desires for recognition and respect. The hybrid practices that emerged reflected how judges brought these different domains together in particular cases. These activities facilitated communication and engagement across cultural and legal divides separating Han Taiwanese and Indigenous social worlds. While such practices could improve recognition for Indigenous cultures and identities in the courtroom, at times they could also end up diminishing Indigenous perspectives and practices.

Integrating Indigenous Worldviews

As Judge Zhang highlighted in the anecdote above, one judicial practice involved integrating Indigenous cultural perspectives into interpretations of criminal intent, particularly in cases related to Indigenous cultural practices and territories. While court protocols prohibited judges from treating Indigenous laws as authoritative, some judges circumvented this restriction by weaving Indigenous norms and worldviews into their applications of criminal statutes. In fact, the Judicial Yuan division overseeing the ad hoc chambers encouraged this blending of legal norms when interpreting criminal intent.[2] Such an approach, however, presumed an informed understanding of Indigenous peoples' norms and worldviews, an area the judiciary had struggled to address in its training programs for judges and its procedures for admitting Indigenous expert witnesses.

Judges explained that this practice allowed them to incorporate elements of Indigenous norms into the application of criminal statutes while remaining consistent with Taiwan judicial practice. By attempting to read an Indigenous individual's mindset into applications of criminal intent, this approach was seen as an opportunity to enhance the boundary-spanning work of the ad hoc chambers. While it opened new possibilities, it also risked oversimplifying and distorting Indigenous worldviews in significant ways.

In July 2015, I met with a judge from the Taichung District Court to discuss legal developments related to Indigenous cultural practices.[3] The judge recounted a recent case involving the prosecution of an Indigenous hunter who had a heated argument with his Han Taiwanese neighbor. After the argument, the man returned home and retrieved his hunting rifle, prompting his frightened neighbor to call the police. The police arrested the man, and prosecutors charged him with assault. During the trial, the defendant testified that he had intended to go hunting, a practice deeply rooted in his cultural tradition, and was unaware that the presence of a firearm would alarm his neighbor. The judge explained that, under ordinary circumstances, the defendant would likely have been convicted of assault. Recognizing the cultural context of the case, however, the judge attempted to integrate the defendant's Indigenous worldview into the interpretation of criminal intent. Considering the cultural significance of hunting for many Indigenous groups on the island, the judge reasoned that the defendant was engaged in a long-standing cultural tradition and did not know that the firearm would cause his neighbor distress. As a result, the judge dismissed the charge.

During our conversation with the Truku men, Judge Zhang cited this case as an example of recent efforts to accommodate Indigenous cultural differences in court proceedings. Later, as we drove home, he shared his thoughts on the challenges of integrating Indigenous perspectives into the legal process. He pointed out that some Indigenous groups lacked certain legal concepts found in ROC law. For instance, he noted that the Truku law of Gaya does not include the concept of unjust enrichment (benefiting unfairly from another person). This perceived absence, in his view, made it challenging to explain certain legal principles to Indigenous persons or to incorporate their perspectives in cases involving claims of unjust enrichment.

A district court judge in Taipei shared a case involving the prosecution of an Indigenous man charged with theft under the Criminal Code.[4] In evaluating the man's conduct, the judge focused on the intent element of larceny. Under Article 320 of the Criminal Code, larceny requires the intent to unlawfully control another's property. The judge reasoned that certain Indigenous groups maintain community property governance systems, such as shared access to water resources, and may therefore lack a strong conception of personal property. On this basis, the judge concluded that the defendant had not committed theft because he had not formed—and, indeed, could not have formed, according to the judge—the requisite mental state to be guilty of unlawfully controlling someone else's property, an impossibility due to his lack of a robust concept of private ownership. Although a problematic presupposition, the judge explained that his belief that the Indigenous man "could not" have formed the necessary intent compelled him to acquit.

The practice of incorporating Indigenous perspectives into interpretations of criminal intent surfaced in other cases as well, including the 2007 Taiwan High Court decision acquitting three Smangus men, discussed earlier. Briefly, prosecutors had charged three Smangus men with theft of forestry products under the Forestry Act. When the Supreme Court remanded the case to the Taiwan High Court, the latter worked to integrate Tayan ontologies and relations to land into its legal analysis. To better understand Tayan law, Gaga, and local attitudes toward forests, animals, and natural resources on ancestral territories, the court relied on the testimony of anthropologists and other academics serving as expert witnesses. On the basis of this testimony, the court concluded that the Smangus men lacked the requisite intent to commit larceny. The men did not intend to take the wood away from others; instead, they sought to share in the natural resources provided by the land, which were considered communal and accessible to all. As the court stated, "From traditional Tayan use of mountain forest resources, it may be seen that wild plants are not owned by any individual and can be used by everyone. This is a kind of concept of sharing."[5]

Expert witnesses played a pivotal role in integrating Indigenous worldviews into applications of criminal statutes. These witnesses included academic specialists, Indigenous elders, and community members who offered valuable testimony on a range of topics, from the Indigenous experience under Japanese colonial rule to cultural and ritual practices and the contemporary challenges of Indigenous life. Some judges, however, reported facing pressure from bureaucrats to avoid calling local elders as witnesses, due to administrative complications and expenses.[6] Additionally, some judges preferred not to involve elders, whose testimonies often introduced ambiguities about Indigenous cultures that, while part of daily life, were unhelpful to judges seeking clear-cut categories. Others, like Judge Chen in the Rose Stone Case, chose not to involve experts because they regarded cultural issues as irrelevant.

Efforts to integrate Indigenous norms and worldviews into state laws through interpretations of criminal intent could sometimes benefit Indigenous defendants. But these activities required a deep understanding of Indigenous norms and worldviews, knowledge often lacking among Han Taiwanese judges overseeing the ad hoc chambers. Judges' ability to rely on local Indigenous experts for guidance was also hindered by administrative challenges and conceptual barriers. Furthermore, the practice of attempting to read an Indigenous mindset into criminal intent risked reinforcing hierarchical views by placing Han Taiwanese society over "other" Indigenous peoples who "could not," as the judge above assumed, imagine possibilities beyond their own cultural frameworks.

Balancing State-Indigenous Interests

The concept of balance frequently arose in conversations with judges working in the ad hoc chambers. When asked about the greatest challenge in handling cases involving Indigenous cultures or territories, one high court judge replied, "Making the balance between respecting tradition [of Indigenous peoples] while still maintaining the status of the law."[7] The Judicial Yuan also framed the work of the ad hoc chambers as an effort to achieve such a balance. In a 2012 promotional video introducing the units, it stated: "It is a matter of finding a balance between traditional hunting culture and legal norms. In fact, apart from traditional courts, there are now ad hoc Chambers of Indigenous Courts to listen to Indigenous peoples' voices" (Judicial Yuan 2012a).

To achieve such a balance, some judges moved away from rigid, mechanical applications of the law and instead adopted a review framework that integrated Indigenous cultures and values into their legal analysis, particularly in cases where Indigenous interests clashed with those of Taiwan's Han Taiwanese society. These judges believed that a balancing approach allowed for deeper consideration of the cultural issues underlying these disputes than a strict application of the law could provide. In cases ranging from wildlife hunting to territorial access, these judges sought to balance the interests of Indigenous peoples with the competing interests of Han Taiwanese society by weighing the respective costs and benefits to arrive at a just outcome. This approach required them to take a broader view, considering the cultural, economic, and social dimensions at stake in the dispute. By doing so, they departed from the constraints of formal rule-based reasoning to address the cultural differences and competing interests between Han Taiwanese and Indigenous societies directly.

In April 2018, I attended a criminal hearing at the Hualien District Court involving a Truku hunter. After the hearing, I had the opportunity to sit down with the judge to discuss his approach to cases involving Indigenous cultural practices, including hunting.[8] Our conversation turned to the Wildlife Conservation Act and the regulations surrounding Indigenous peoples' right to hunt animals for cultural or ritual purposes. The judge explained that he applied a balancing framework when handling prosecutions of Indigenous hunters. He distinguished between "smaller and larger" violations of the Wildlife Conservation Act, aiming to create room for Indigenous cultural expression in cases where strict application of the law might otherwise lead to conviction. In situations where an Indigenous hunter violated hunting protocols by killing a single, or a small number of, non-protected animal species, the judge searched for ways to dismiss the charges or issue a small fine. He reasoned that in such instances, the cultural significance of Indigenous hunting practices outweighed a broader public interest in wildlife conservation, given the small number and non-threatened status of the species involved. Violations involving protected animal species or a larger number of non-protected animals, however, were a different matter. Such cases, he explained, began to infringe upon the public interest in conserving wildlife. In these cases, he was less inclined to accommodate Indigenous hunting practices and would strictly apply the law.[9]

Two years earlier, in July 2016, I met with a judge at the Taichung High Court to discuss legal developments concerning Indigenous peoples' land rights.[10] As we walked through the courthouse, he described a civil case involving a Thao community's efforts to reclaim part of their ancestral territory. The land in question was covered by water from a reservoir dam built eighty years earlier by Japanese colonial authorities. The dam, constructed to generate hydroelectricity, played a pivotal role in powering the resource-intensive industries that later fueled Taiwan's remarkable economic growth in the latter half of the twentieth century. As Scott Simon (2002) observes, the costs of this "Taiwanese miracle" were disproportionately borne by Indigenous peoples like the Thao. The rising waters of the reservoir flooded the community's settlement and lands, forcing their relocation to a nearby village where each person was allotted just 0.2 hectares of land. This displacement contributed to the community's gradual population decline. The judge had studied similar legal cases in Japan and examined international human rights instruments, including the ICCPR. He determined that the community's rights had indeed been violated under domestic and international law, but because the dam was already in place and served critical public interests by providing hydroelectric power and clean drinking water, he concluded that these broader public interests outweighed the community's claim to their ancestral territory. On this basis, he decided that the reservoir and dam should remain.

In these cases, the law prescribed specific outcomes under a rule-based analysis: conviction for the hunter and land restitution for the community. These judges, however, went beyond rigidly applying the law, weighing the competing interests to determine what, in their view, would be equitable under the circumstances. This process involved identifying the relevant elements to be balanced and assessing the legal effect of the outcome. The judges' approach was oriented toward result and outcome, prioritizing the broader consequences of their decisions, rather than focusing strictly on evidence or rules. In certain situations, this balancing procedure worked in favor of Indigenous persons, as it did in cases of "small" violations by Indigenous hunters. More often, however, the balance tipped toward the interests of Taiwan's Han Taiwanese society, who deemed wildlife conservation and economic development more pressing concerns than Indigenous rights to cultural practices or ancestral territories. While balancing approaches are sometimes characterized as an enfant terrible of judicial reasoning (McFadden 1988, 586), some judges in the ad hoc chambers used this strategy as a way to incorporate Indigenous cultures and values into their decision-making when they were not explicitly protected by ROC law. Yet this same approach could also lead to decisions that dismissed and diminished Indigenous peoples' claims and interests.

Hierarchies of Law

As we have seen, Taiwan operates under a hierarchical system of law that ranks legal norms by their level of authority, with the ROC Constitution at the top, followed first by statutes and legislation and then by regulations. Courts in Taiwan, including the ad hoc Chambers of Indigenous Courts, adhere to this hierarchy by first consulting the Constitution before turning to national statutes, codes, and ordinances. This respect for the legal hierarchy is a cornerstone of the rule of law, ensuring clarity and consistency in how different levels of law are applied in practice.

The Legislative Yuan has been slow to implement the provisions of the 2005 Indigenous Peoples Basic Law by amending or repealing outdated laws. As previously mentioned, this legislative inactivity did not mean that the Basic Law was idle. Nonetheless, from the perspective of some judges, this inactivity left the Basic Law in an ambiguous position in the ROC legal system. As one high court judge described it, "The Basic Law falls into a gray zone."[11] Judges expressed different views about the status of the Basic Law in Taiwan's legal system. One district court judge stated, "The Basic Law is on the same level as the Constitution."[12] Another district court judge maintained, "The [Basic] Law is between the Constitution and all other laws."[13] Still another believed, "The Indigenous Basic Law is at the level of statutes."[14] One high court judge told me that the Basic Law was "below statutes."[15] And some judges, like Judge Chen, regarded the Basic Law as "dangerous" and incompatible with fundamental principles in the Constitution and in Taiwan's human rights obligations. As noted earlier, the status of human rights instruments' (e.g., ICCPR and ICESCR) incorporation into ROC law faced a similar degree of uncertainty.

Some judges leveraged the ambiguity surrounding the Basic Law to reimagine Taiwan's legal hierarchy as a strategy to secure Indigenous peoples' domestic and human rights. In August 2015, I met with a judge from the Taipei District Court to discuss the ROC legal system and the status of the Basic Law. Seated in his chambers, he explained that treating the Basic Law as equivalent to an ordinary statute created significant problems for securing Indigenous rights. Principles of statutory construction used in civil law traditions, like *lex specialis*, directed attention away from the Basic Law to other, more specific laws that provided far narrower protections for Indigenous peoples. To address this issue, the judge adopted a novel approach: He reimagined the hierarchy of ROC law, positioning the Basic Law on an intermediate level between the Constitution and national statutes. He stated,

> Judges in the Indigenous courts must reconsider the structure of Taiwan law if they want to recognize Indigenous rights. We must shift towards seeing the Basic Law as above other statutes, where legal analysis starts with the Constitution, then the Basic Law, and then other statutes; otherwise, the Basic Law loses its content.[16]

He believed that this approach would help ensure that conflicts of law were resolved in favor of the Basic Law, which, in his interpretation, would take precedence over statutes and regulations. He also noted that this perspective was gradually gaining support among judges, particularly those serving in the district courts.

Navigating these same ambiguities led other judges, however, to interpretations that excluded Indigenous peoples' rights. A high court judge in Taichung pointed to the Basic Law's provision requiring the ROC government to amend or repeal existing statutes and regulations "in accordance with the principles of this law." Like Judge Chen in the Rose Stone Case, this judge argued that the Legislature's refusal to amend the laws indicated that those statutes and regulations superseded the Basic Law. He explained, "The Legislature's lack of changing laws indicates their desire that 'in accordance with law' means the current laws are above the Basic Law. So, in a situation of conflict of laws, the present laws should be higher in the hierarchy than the Basic Law."[17] He ultimately concluded that the Basic Law represented a "false promise" to Taiwan's Indigenous peoples, a view he also extended to the ad hoc Chambers of Indigenous Courts.

These examples demonstrate how judges worked to create room for Indigenous norms and practices within the legal system, not by directly incorporating them, but by attending to factors for their effective integration into the legal hierarchy. These exploratory reconfigurations of law attempted to advance the objectives of the ad hoc chambers by addressing the ambiguous terrain of Indigenous rights protections. As with other judicial practices, rethinking the hierarchy of ROC law sometimes worked in favor of Indigenous litigants, while at other times it worked against them.

Natural Law and Human Dignity

Recognizing the shortcomings and inconsistencies in ROC law regarding Indigenous peoples' rights, some judges turned to Kantian ideas of human dignity as an alternative normative foundation for securing their rights. In May 2018, I traveled to Tainan, the historic capital of Taiwan, to meet with a judge at the Tainan High Court. We met in his judicial chambers to discuss Indigenous rights and their place in the ROC legal system. During our conversation, he explained that the Basic Law "is not a direct law" because it lacks enforceable penalties or punishments. Instead, he saw the Basic Law as a source of law grounded in principles of natural law, which, in his view, "required Kant's understanding of human dignity."[18] Immanuel Kant (1785) is often regarded as a foundational thinker in the development of modern conceptions of human dignity. The judge explained,

> The Basic Law relates to natural law, which is higher than the Constitution or human rights. Human rights relate to state law. Human dignity, which is what the Basic Law is about, is higher than human rights and the Constitution. Only human dignity can solve the problem of respecting Indigenous peoples' cultures.

He said that he actively applied this approach in his review of cases involving Indigenous persons and advocated for it through presentations at the Judicial Yuan.

The judge referenced a case from the Taipei District Court, which he interpreted as engaging with Kantian principles of human dignity. In this case, the court acknowledged the profound influence of the "cultural essence" (*wenhua jingsui* 文化精髓) of Indigenous peoples on their worldviews and behaviors.[19] A Tayan man had been charged with violating the Forestry Act and Criminal Code for burying his mother according to Tayan practice in a regulated forest area. The court acquitted the man, ruling that treating this act as a legal violation would strip him of his dignity and destroy his culture. In its decision, the court stated, "If traditional culture is eroded, it will mean that the community will lose itself and gradually perish. They will no longer be Indigenous." The ruling identified an inseparable connection between cultural practices and Indigenous identity, suggesting that any disruption to this bond threatened both the individual and the survival of the community.

A few months later, the same judge and I traveled to central Taiwan to visit Tsou leaders in Dabang village and nearby communities. The judge had recently presided over an appeal involving a Tsou hunter and had worked with leaders from these communities. The issue before the Tainan High Court was whether the Tsou hunter's use of firearms in the mountains qualified as "living tools" (i.e., instruments used in daily living) as required by Article 20 of the Firearms, Ammunition, and Knives Control Act. The judge had voluntarily participated in training about Tsou culture as part of his appointment to the ad hoc chamber, but he recognized that he and other members of the panel still lacked a deep understanding of Tsou hunting culture. To address this, he sought expert testimony on Tsou hunting practices and *hupa* (hunting territory). He explained, "There are so many complexities with Indigenous cases. The training is helpful, but to understand and be respectful of their customs, I must either seek an expert professor or seek a more respectful approach and ask the Kuba Committee for suggestions about Tsou hunting."[20] The judge ultimately decided to consult the Kuba Committee for recommendations on a local expert, believing that this approach conveyed the respect and dignity that courts should extend to Indigenous communities.

The Kuba Committee recommended two experts: a professor from Pingtung and a Tsou elder. The court invited them both to testify at the trial. The judge explained, however, that the prosecutor and the Tsou hunter's lawyer asked the experts only a few questions. They simply did not know what to ask. When the judges on the panel attempted to question the experts, the experts struggled to articulate Tsou cultural practices related to hunting. This posed a challenge for the court. The expert testimony was weak and failed to establish the "fact" that hunting was a Tsou cultural practice.

The panel turned to the work of Professor Wang Tay-sheng, a renowned legal historian in Taiwan. In his research, Professor Wang (2015) distinguished among three levels of custom, ascending in importance: "habit," "customary law," and most importantly, "customary legislation."[21] The panel determined that respect for the dignity of Indigenous peoples required that Indigenous customary legislation be granted the same legal standing as ROC state law. Building on this reasoning, the panel concluded that if hunting was a matter of customary legislation, it could be understood as involving a "living tool" within the meaning of Article 20 of the Firearms Act, even if the specific facts surrounding Tsou hunting remained ambiguous. The panel concluded that Tsou hunting did, in fact, rise to the level of customary legislation and not merely a habit or a customary law. As a result, the defendant's hunting activities met the legal definition of "living tools" and the panel found him innocent.[22]

Other judges, however, invoked the concept of human dignity to restrict the legal protections for Indigenous peoples. For instance, in a 2016 case involving Truku defendants accused of illegally collecting forest products under the Forestry Act, the Hualien District Court stated:

> At this time, the state should give the highest respect to Indigenous peoples' land and use of natural resources. Unless Indigenous peoples' traditional culture and use of ceremonies have caused serious irreversible damage to land and natural resources (for example, using excavators or other equipment to cut down trees) or *infringe upon the human dignity of others* (for example, stealing or robbing others of legally collected forest products) otherwise the state must not arbitrarily restrict it.[23]

The human dignity under concern in this statement appears to be that of Han Taiwanese persons who may suffer from Indigenous peoples' misconduct. Similarly, the Constitutional Court's Interpretation no. 803, discussed earlier, invoked the notion of Indigenous "human dignity" while simultaneously upholding restrictions on Indigenous hunting practices.

While Kantian notions of human dignity could serve as an alternative foundation for securing Indigenous peoples' rights, other interpretations of human dignity could be used to restrict them. Judges' explorations of alternative normative foundations for Indigenous rights thus had the capacity to create new opportunities for recognition and cultural expression in certain circumstances; in other circumstances, though, they closed them off.

ASSERTIONS OF INDIGENOUS IDENTITY AND MEANING

Just as Han Taiwanese judges experimented with hybrid practices, Indigenous individuals and communities actively sought to push the ad hoc Chambers of Indigenous Courts to function as boundary-spanning institutions. The units presented spaces where Indigenous peoples' legal and cultural identities intersected directly. Indigenous litigants, defendants, witnesses, and communities used performances of indigeneity to advance their own understandings of culture, knowledge, and experience in legal proceedings. These displays of Indigenous identity were multivalent, in that they carried with them constraints and assumptions that were oppressive as well as emancipating, and they involved a repertoire of creative activities shaped by context, goals, imagination, and rights (Graham and Penny 2014).

Performances of Indigenous identity reveal the contextual, emergent, and processual nature of indigeneity, as individuals and groups fashion their identities through action and speech. For both individuals and communities, these performances are often "deeply contextualized and historically contingent creative acts" (Graham and Penny 2014, 2). They function as "sites of persuasion" as Indigenous individuals work to get their versions of history and regimes of value recognized and shared with wider audiences (Morphy 2006, 471–72). Through this dialogic process, Indigenous actors draw on histories and cultural practices to "make" (Butler 1990, 1993) themselves and engage with wider publics through acts of performance. In so doing, they structure the possibilities for destabilizing power (Rai 2010, 288). As such, Indigenous performance serves as a potent means of asserting, constituting, and expressing Indigenous identity in a historical context in which the stakes of being identified and recognized as "Indigenous" have reached new heights with the emergence of a global discourse on indigeneity and the rise of an Indigenous movement in Taiwan.

Performances of indigeneity in the ad hoc chambers took many forms. At times, they were dramatic displays of Indigenous identity akin to what Bernard Perley (2011) calls "charismatic indigeneity." These self-conscious, amplified performances evoked popular imaginings of Indigenous peoples through dress, including headdresses and ornamentation, as well as through language, to ensure that non-Indigenous actors recognized their cultural distinctiveness (Conklin and Graham 1995). A striking example of charismatic indigeneity appears in the anecdote that opens this book, when Pinuyumayan claimants donned sashes, vests, chaps, floral headpieces, and other formal attire while performing a ceremony on the steps of the Kaohsiung High Administrative Courthouse. At other times, performances of Indigenous identity involved low-key performances, what Greg Johnson (2014) describes as "bone-deep indigeneity." These were less visible, more mundane displays that worked to promote Indigenous peoples' interests and rights through such activities as establishing a legal aid center for Indigenous peoples. Equally important were the relational and reciprocal processes of identity construction embedded in everyday life, such as chewing betel nut and speaking Indigenous languages.

I examine three encounters in the ad hoc chambers that illustrate how performances of Indigenous identities shaped court proceedings and influenced dispute resolution. The first involves the complex expressions of Bunun identity in a civil case over a flood that devastated homes and fields of the Fuxing community in Kaohsiung City. The second is focused on linguistic performances in the prosecution of a Tayan hunter in Taipei City and similar cases. The third describes the creation of an Indigenous legal center designed to address the failures of Taiwan's governance of Indigenous peoples. These performances of Indigenous identities accomplished many kinds of objectives in the specialized units. They disrupted the essentialist and static conceptions of indigeneity that dominated the imaginations of Taiwan's Han Taiwanese society. They introduced alternative ontological frameworks into debates over Indigenous cultural and land rights. And they assumed governance responsibilities that the state had neglected.

These activities pushed the ad hoc chambers to recognize Indigenous peoples' cultural and linguistic differences, and, in the process, worked to move them toward functioning as boundary institutions. Like judges' hybrid practices, the benefits of this labor for Indigenous litigants were never guaranteed. These performances, however, demonstrated how Indigenous individuals and communities played a role in shaping the character of the units and making them serve their interests, even as they were compelled to engage with the courts as subjects of the ROC legal system.

Disjunctions and Discontinuities of Indigeneity

Elizabeth Povinelli (2002) argues that the recognition of Indigenous identities within liberal multicultural discourses is fraught with contradictions and deeply embedded in power relations. Building on the Lacanian concept of "meconnaissance," she shows that multiculturalism aspires to welcome and solicit a plurality of ways of life while reserving a power to refuse behaviors and ideas that are offensive to it, a dynamic present in many cultures, including Indigenous cultures (see Sterk 2020b). For Povinelli, "law is one of the primary sites through which liberal forms of recognition develop their disciplinary sides as they work with the hopes, pride, optimism and shame of

Indigenous and other minority subjects" (2002, 184). To be recognized, Indigenous peoples must "transport to the present ancient pre-national meanings and practices in whatever language and moral framework prevails at the time of enunciation" (2002, 6). Performance, therefore, becomes a crucial arena where Indigenous persons "struggle to inhabit the tensions and torsions of competing incitements to be and identify differentially" (2002, 13).[24]

Indigenous individuals and communities entering the ad hoc Chambers of Indigenous Courts encountered similar contradictions of acceptance and expectations. Their engagements with these tensions were situational and strategic as they worked to get their histories and values systems recognized in the courtroom through performances of Indigenous identities. This was evident in the multifaceted displays of indigeneity in a civil case brought by the Bunun community of Fuxing against the Kaohsiung City government and other local agencies for failing to maintain a riverbed adjacent to their village.

On June 11, 2012, heavy rainfall caused severe flooding along the banks of the Lacus Creek in Kaohsiung, damaging homes and fields belonging to members of the Fuxing community. A year later, in 2013, the community filed a civil lawsuit in the Kaohsiung District Court, seeking compensation from the city government and other agencies for property damage and mental distress.[25] Three years into the litigation, when I began working with lawyers representing the community, the case was reassigned to a new judge. As mentioned earlier, rotations of judges in and out of the ad hoc chambers were common. Members of the community expressed concerns about this change, believing that the original judge had been sympathetic to their claims. Knowing little about the new judge, they feared how this change might impact their case.

Throughout the litigation, community members coordinated their dress when attending hearings at the Kaohsiung courthouse. Their goal was to remind the new judge of their cultural distinctiveness while also avoiding having their identity essentialized as backwards or inferior. Earlier discussions had centered on whether to wear formal Bunun attire to the courthouse or to incorporate elements of cultural aesthetics, such as color, but not necessarily wear formal dress. Ultimately, community organizers reached a decision: "Not traditional clothes. That makes us look ancient. We should wear something that shows we are all together, in unity, that we are here but not like we are in history."[26]

At a July 2016 hearing, twenty-two members of the Fuxing community traveled two hours from their village to the Kaohsiung District Courthouse. They arrived wearing black t-shirts and polo shirts, black being a color used in Bunun formal dress. Organizers had created special black shirts for the case embroidered with the words "Self-Help Association of Fuxingli" (*fuxingli zijiuhui* 復興里自救會) in Mandarin Chinese characters. Some individuals also incorporated additional elements of formal Bunun attire, such as embroidered jackets and gathered skirts. Wearing these black shirts, community members attended the court hearings.

This was a powerful demonstration of community solidarity, both in the number of participants and in their coordinated dress. It also reflected a keen awareness of the risks and benefits of presenting themselves as "Indigenous" in Taiwan courts. As Ronald Niezen (2003a, 8) notes, courts of law tend to frame Indigenous cultures as static and "frozen in time," dismissing innovations that occur after the arrival of settlers as not being integral to Indigenous tradition. Addressing a similar concern, Fuxing community members chose a version of dress that highlighted their cultural distinctiveness while also resisting such a limited interpretation of their culture. This strategic use of dress was also not unique to the Fuxing community. As previously mentioned, members of Dowmung also coordinated their attire for court appearances, wearing matching white vests adorned with the Truku "eye" motif to the Hualien District Courthouse. Some members of the Fuxing community, however, took a different approach, incorporating elements of formal wear. This variation reflected different perspectives on what was necessary in their performances of indigeneity before the new judge.

Beyond strategic decisions in dress, the Fuxing community also took a meticulous approach to organizing their legal materials. Over the course of the lawsuit, they compiled and bound materials related to the case into a single volume. This resource was made possible by one plaintiff, a former politician, who knew how to access information relevant to their claims. This well-used volume contained diagrams, legal filings, maps, court orders, photographs, and transcripts, all densely marked with sticky notes, handwritten comments, highlighting, and annotations. But the volume was more than just a repository of information; it was active. During hearings, community members in the audience passed it around as different individuals requested to see information. It bounced from hand to hand, sometimes high in the air. When it reached its destination, the recipient would ruffle through the pages, point to a text, and mumble audibly to their neighbors. This was such a conspicuous display that, at one point, the lawyers in the courtroom turned their attention away from the proceedings to watch the action in the audience.

The volume was thus an important tool for the community, not just for recordkeeping but also for identity construction. During one hearing, the defendants' lawyer presented technical details about the river to argue that the county had properly maintained the riverbed. This was too much for one Fuxing litigant to bear. Seated in the gallery, the man abruptly sat upright, raised the volume high in the air, which he had opened to a hearing transcript, and declared loudly, "But you just said the opposite the last time. Look here!" his finger jabbing at the page. The bailiff took a cautioning step toward the gallery, prompting the man to sit back in his chair, muttering to his neighbors. This interjection was not an isolated incident. Throughout the hearing, and in others, members of the community repeatedly drew attention to the bound volume and to themselves through well-timed gestures, murmured remarks, and answering the judge's questions before the lawyers had an opportunity to respond.

If there was a subtext to these displays, it was "We know this game of law, too." This was a performance demonstrating the Fuxing community's investment in and knowledge about the case. It projected an image of their community as organized and sophisticated legal actors. Like the lawyers, they arrived at proceedings carrying this bound volume of materials. Its well-used pages, dense with notes and highlighting, and their quick work in finding relevant texts and images, testified to their careful study of the materials outside the courtroom. In some ways, their conduct suggested they were *more* capable as legal actors than the legal professionals in the courtroom, indicated by moments when they corrected lawyers and answered questions for them. In these instances, performances of legal aptitude and, more generally, modernity, were interwoven with Bunun cultural distinctiveness.

Amid strategic decisions about attire and passing around documents, members of the Fuxing community spoke to one another in Bunun and Taiwanese Hokkien in the courtroom. As previously mentioned, assimilationist ROC laws and policies had long prohibited the use of Indigenous languages, with Mandarin Chinese becoming the compulsory language of education in 1968. The low din of Bunun and Taiwanese Hokkien in the gallery gave the courtroom the feeling of a meeting in the village cultural center. And just like at those meetings, the potent, distinctive smell of betel nut filled the air as community members chewed the nut while they watched the courtroom drama unfold. In the empty space of formal pauses in the turn-taking format of legal proceedings, the sounds of chewing and sucking punctuated the silence, as both women and men in the audience worked betel nuts in their mouths. In Taiwan, betel nut consumption is strongly associated with Indigenous peoples (Ma et al. 2017), although it is also commonly used by Han Taiwanese men as a stimulant. Here, in the courtroom, the use of Bunun language and scent of betel nut were more than sensory details: They were aural and olfactory markers of an Indigenous presence in the courtroom.

Few community members seemed to pay much attention to their own linguistic and consumption practices. These acts were largely unconscious expressions of Bunun identity, embedded in habit rather than deliberate assertion. Erving Goffman (1959, 208) refers to this as "impression management," a mix of conscious and unconscious behaviors that shape the image of ourselves we project to the world. In the village, speaking Bunun and chewing betel were unremarkable, everyday practices. But in a national courtroom—where, as Mary Douglas (1966, 44) might describe, they were "matter out of place"—these same acts took on a charged symbolic significance. Many in number, speaking an Indigenous language, and engaging in behaviors associated with Indigenous identity, the community subtly but powerfully "occupied" this space. No signage permitted these acts; in fact, signs explicitly forbade talking during proceedings and chewing betel nut. Yet, through these small, routine gestures, normally reserved for village life, the courtroom gallery, if only briefly, became an Indigenous space, claimed through the quiet persistence of everyday practices.

"Being" Bunun in the courtroom was a complex, multi-coded affair reflecting different degrees of amplifying cultural difference and varying levels of awareness about identity performance. The way Indigenous peoples relate to the state and their own place is not necessarily through identifying with a tribal slot or global Indigenous identity, but through positioning within broader fields of power (Simon 2010, 726). Here, some performances aimed to remind the court about Bunun difference while adapting it to address discriminatory attitudes toward Indigenous peoples. Others eschewed cultural difference for a form of practice that presented the community as knowledgeable and experienced actors. Still other displays unconsciously rehearsed everyday behaviors ordinarily reserved for the village. Individuals further complicated matters by approaching the issue of identity construction in different ways. The range of these fluid and varied expressions of Bunun identity unsettled static and essentialized notions of Bunun identity, revealing the disjunctions and discontinuities of what it meant to "be" Bunun in the ad hoc chambers.

These performances of Bunun identity also appeared to have a tangible impact on the trial. In a remarkable move, the only such instance I observed during my field research, the new judge announced at the end of the hearing that, at the next hearing, each Fuxing litigant would be given five minutes to speak directly to him about how the flooding had affected their lives and community. Ultimately, the judge ruled in favor of the community, awarding damages for property loss caused by the flooding but denying compensation for mental distress. On appeal, the Kaohsiung High Court overturned the lower court's property damage award.[27] The Fuxing community later prevailed in the Taiwan Supreme Court,[28] and their lawsuit continues today.

Language Games in the Courtroom

In August 2018, I attended a hearing at the Taiwan High Court in Taipei, where a Tayan man was appealing his criminal conviction for possessing illegal firearms.[29] Like many Indigenous groups in Taiwan, the Tayan continue the hunting and gathering practices of their ancestors, including the use of firearms for hunting, a practice regulated by local Tayan law, Gaga. As previously noted, ROC law generally prohibits possessing firearms or hunting wildlife, except in limited circumstances in which Indigenous persons are allowed to hunt for cultural or ritual purposes or for self-use. The central issue before the court was whether the man's firearms fell within this exception.

The Taiwan High Court assigned the man's case to the ad hoc Chamber of Indigenous Courts. As the hearing time approached, the lawyer representing him mingled with community members who had traveled to the courthouse to show support. While they waited, the group sat on the benches lining the hallway outside the courtroom, quietly conversing in Mandarin Chinese to ease the tension.

Once the hearing began, the judicial panel called a female relative of the man to testify about his use of firearms and participation in cultural hunting activities. Although she had been speaking Mandarin Chinese outside the courtroom, she did not respond to the questions in Mandarin. Instead, she remained silent, waiting for community members seated behind her to interpret the judges' questions into Tayan. She then patiently answered in Tayan, with some Mandarin Chinese interspersed, while the other community members interpreted her words into Chinese. For twenty minutes, the exchange between the judges and witness continued in this manner, with the lawyer occasionally interjecting to clarify and expand on her responses. In the end, the panel accepted her testimony and ruled that the man had been using his firearms for cultural purposes within the meaning of the legal exception.

After the hearing, I asked the lawyer about the courtroom exchange and why the witness responded in Tayan. The lawyer explained,

> We needed a witness to tell the judges that the guns were used for traditional hunting purposes. But if you just say that the judges may not believe you. So, they talked about using their mother tongue. They had heard that other people do this, so they used their mother tongue to make the court see their culture is different.[30]

Language was an important tool in the ad hoc chambers. The Tayan community had strategically decided that the most effective way to ensure that the judges took their explanation of hunting practices seriously was to engage in a linguistic performance that underscored their cultural distinctiveness. While such linguistic performances can reinforce nationalist ethnoracial frameworks that authenticate indigeneity through language and dress (Boj Lopez 2017, 205), they also serve disruptive and meta-communicative functions that invoke Indigenous peoples' power and sovereignty.

In certain disputes, particularly those involving cultural practices and ancestral territories, litigants, witnesses, and audience members used language as a means of performing identities as Indigenous persons. Sometimes this was a personal decision; other times, it was a strategy guided by legal counsel. These performances included testifying in their mother language, but they also extended to code-switching between Mandarin Chinese, Taiwanese Hokkien, and Indigenous languages. The performative dimensions of language emerged clearly in an anecdote shared by one lawyer.[31] During a criminal hearing, the lawyer advised his Paiwan client to testify in his mother language rather than in Mandarin Chinese. His client, however, could not speak Paiwan very well. As a result, his testimony became an extended soliloquy of Paiwan-sounding but largely unintelligible words. The lawyer used this performance to request an interpreter, both as a tactic to highlight the case's cultural dimensions and as a strategic move to delay the proceedings.

Indigenous actors and their advocates used linguistic performances for multiple purposes. They used language to emphasize cultural difference, as seen with the Tayan witness above. They also used language to delay proceedings, echoing earlier observations on lawyers' strategies of procedural delay, by compelling courts to arrange for interpreters or take time in the courtroom to discuss language issues. These disruptions resembled what James Scott (1985) describes as "weapons of the weak," but they were more than mere acts of resistance. Through language, Indigenous actors actively worked to control discourse about indigeneity in the courtroom.

The Bunun defendant in the Hualien District Court, mentioned earlier, wanted the court to recognize that "they have to use my language to talk about it." His insistence on conducting the discussion of Bunun culture in "my language" was not just a linguistic preference but a fundamental assertion of Indigenous existence not preconditioned by colonial categories or norms. Like Rakaw's earlier declaration that the land beneath the bamboo house was unequivocally Truku territory, the Bunun defendant's demand to use "my language" was a refusal, to use Audra Simpson's (2014) term, to play the colonial game. It was a claim to Indigenous ontological parameters by refusing to allow the ROC state to determine how Bunun culture was represented and framed through language in the courtroom. Strategic language use and code-switching, therefore, functioned as discursive shifters, transforming not only the linguistic landscape of the courtroom but also its power hierarchies. Even if the long-term impact of these acts was uncertain, they momentarily reconfigured the terms of engagement by asserting Indigenous agency in a space designed to regulate it.

Ludwig Wittgenstein's (1953) concept of "language games" provides a useful framework for understanding how linguistic performances in the courtroom functioned both disruptively and meta-communicatively. In his later work, Wittgenstein argued that every word we speak is part of a "language game," meaning that speaking is fundamentally "part of an activity, or of a life-form" (1953, 23). Language games are the conceptual parameters we share that make it possible to identify and produce signs and create relations of signification and representation. They also operate at different levels of abstraction. Wittgenstein identifies "families" of language games (1953, 65–71). For example, mastering a field such as law requires learning the associated language games of interpreting legislation, courtroom procedure, drafting complaints, witness interrogation, and so on (Gozzi 1998, 190). These language games may be considered part of a larger family group of language games one might identify as "the justice system."

In the ad hoc chambers, judicial actors and Indigenous persons engaged in multiple language games. Judges adhered to the language game of Taiwan courtroom procedure, which belonged to the broader family of "justice system" language games in Mandarin Chinese. Indigenous participants, at times, strategically played a different set of language games. For instance, the Tayan witness deliberately played the "wrong" language game by speaking Tayan in court, disrupting linguistic expectations to emphasize Indigenous cultural distinctiveness. Meanwhile, the Bunun defendant used his linguistic performance not only to highlight cultural difference but also to reject the state's imposed language game. He insisted that discussions about Indigenous cultures should be conducted in Indigenous languages rather than the language of the state. This was a "meta" language game; Indigenous actors, like the Bunun defendant, staked a claim about the language game that *ought* to be played in the courtroom. What appeared from one perspective to constitute the "wrong" language game was, from another perspective, a language game of a higher order, one that conveyed a metapragmatic instruction to judges that they should be reflexively aware of language use in the courtroom and of the role of language in colonial erasures and displacements of Indigenous peoples and identities.

For this communicative operation to be effective, judges had to share in the rules of the "meta" language game. The structure of the ad hoc chambers facilitated this sharing of rules about communication. Mandated to respect Indigenous peoples' cultural differences and secure their judicial rights, although judges interpreted this mandate differently, the ad hoc chambers provided forums for critical commentaries to emerge, here through dislocations of language. Judges working in the units were aware of these linguistic strategies. As one judge noted,

> Have you seen when Indigenous people use their language in court? Sometimes they will do this even when they can speak Mandarin Chinese. But I know why. They are not trying to make trouble, I do not think. They want me to know that they have a different culture, that they are not Han Chinese. I know this.[32]

The ad hoc chambers provided a space within the ROC legal system for reflexive thinking about language and state power. They were forums where performances of Indigenous identity had an opportunity to be "heard" (cf. Torres and Milun 1990, 649), although that was not always the case and sometimes they were heard imperfectly. Indigenous actors leveraged this discursive space, using it not only to emphasize their cultural distinctiveness but also to create disruptions and insist on their own ontological parameters.

These dynamics suggested that while performances of Indigenous languages in Taiwan courts sometimes reflected the tensions in dichotomous notions of authentic versus inauthentic Indigenous cultures and identities, they also appeared to move beyond these constraints. They became exercises of Indigenous power by pushing the state to recognize their cultural differences, adjust its practices, and accept Indigenous ontologies and ways of knowing.

Managing a Broken System

In October 2017, I attended a preliminary meeting for a new law center created to serve Indigenous peoples in eastern Taiwan. Before my arrival, the center had faced significant challenges. The previous year, a skilled Han Taiwanese legal aid lawyer had secured government funding to establish the center, envisioning that it would concentrate on cases involving Indigenous cultural practices and territories. The lawyer encountered resistance, however, from Indigenous legislators who insisted that only Indigenous staff be hired (Gerber 2017). This led to months of delays, and ultimately, the director position was eliminated because of a lack of suitable candidates. Indigenous legislators were not the only ones skeptical of the new law center. The Hualien County Bar Association also opposed it, fearing that it would disrupt the local legal market by diverting cases and income from local lawyers. According to one lawyer, the bar association eventually dropped its objections after receiving assurances that the center's activities would remain limited in scope.[33]

A well-respected Seediq legal scholar, Professor Awi Mona, ultimately took the helm of the center, leading to the establishment of the Legal Aid Foundation's Legal Center of Indigenous Peoples (LCIP) in 2018, as mentioned earlier. As an extension of the Taiwan Legal Aid Foundation, the LCIP specialized in complex legal issues related to Indigenous peoples' land rights and cultural practices, including hunting, fishing, and gathering forest products and minerals. It provided free legal services to Indigenous persons and communities in the region (Legal Aid Foundation 2018a). Lawyers at the LCIP highlighted the urgent need for such a center, stating, "There is a significant lack of knowledge about Indigenous peoples' cultures and rights among Taiwan judges and lawyers. This center will be one of the ways to fill that space."[34] Similarly, at the center's official opening ceremony on March 12, 2018 (see Legal Aid Foundation 2018c), a speaker emphasized the importance of the LCIP's mission. He stated, "Taiwan has many protections for

Indigenous peoples, including the Indigenous Peoples Basic Law, but we have a long way to go. We have many protections for Indigenous peoples, but they are not recognized or not used effectively. This center is important for securing recognition of Taiwan's Indigenous peoples." The LCIP's primary role was thus to serve as a "lubricant" to help Indigenous individuals and communities navigate the legal system and secure the best outcomes possible given the ambiguities surrounding domestic legal protections for Indigenous cultural practices and lands (Gerber 2017).

The LCIP was ultimately composed of four Han Taiwanese staff attorneys and several support staff members of Indigenous descent. The team possessed specialized expertise in Indigenous peoples' rights and had strong personal connections with many Indigenous communities. They were deeply committed to advocating for Indigenous persons and communities in the ad hoc chambers. The LCIP also collaborated with a special committee of Indigenous representatives from Hualien's six officially recognized groups: the Bunun, Kavalan, Pangcah, Sakizaya, Seediq, and Truku. By combining their legal expertise with the committee's cultural knowledge, the LCIP staff and committee worked together to evaluate cases, determine which ones to take, and develop legal strategies that best served the interests of Indigenous peoples in Taiwan courts.

Since its establishment in 2018, the LCIP has served as a vital bridge between Taiwan's legal system and Indigenous peoples. Advocating on behalf of Indigenous individuals and communities, the LCIP provided essential knowledge about Indigenous cultures and legal rights, knowledge that has been largely absent in the judiciary and legal profession, including in the ad hoc Chambers of Indigenous Courts. Legal representation was, however, only one facet of the LCIP's work. The center also played a crucial role in legal education and community outreach. It organized annual seminars on developments in domestic Indigenous rights and provided free workshops for local lawyers, equipping them with the knowledge and skills needed to litigate cases involving Indigenous cultural practices and lands. Additionally, the LCIP traveled to Indigenous villages, hosting presentations on legal developments, advising community members about their rights, and assisting individuals with legal paperwork (figure 13). In court, LCIP lawyers actively challenged judicial structures that worked against Indigenous peoples, such as the overuse of "summary proceedings." The center also took on high-profile cases, including the representation of Bunun hunter Tama Talum,

FIGURE 13. LCIP lawyer working under a tent in the Dajili community in eastern Taiwan, 2018. Courtesy of the Legal Center of Indigenous Peoples, 2018.

mentioned earlier, whose fight for hunting rights was seen by many activists as part of a broader struggle for Indigenous rights and self-determination.

In effect, the LCIP took responsibility for managing, in part, Taiwan's broken system of legal protections for Indigenous peoples. As indicated throughout this discussion, performances of Indigenous identity in and around the ad hoc chambers took many forms, not all of them dramatic displays. Neither could these performances be characterized as inevitably embracing counter-hegemonic positions against the colonizing society or state (Graham and Penny 2014, 17). At times, Indigenous actors assumed the responsibility of managing the failed or broken systems of governance. Greg Johnson's (2014) work on legal battles in Hawai'i highlights the ways in which indigeneity is dynamically performed at the visible and invisible ends of the spectrum to manage the broken system of law in Hawai'i. He argues that these practical performances of indigeneity, through state administrative law, are underappreciated assertions of Indigenous authority and identity that warrant greater attention. As Johnson notes, the "mundane but intense efforts that are propelling Indigenous interests vis-à-vis various manifestations and failures of governance" can also be "significant religious and cultural happenings" (2014, 248, 265).

The LCIP exemplified this mundane but intense performance of Indigenous authority and identity. A low-key and relatively unmarked institution, the LCIP worked every day to manage deficiencies in the ROC legal system, operating as a key translator in legal matters between Taiwan's Han

Taiwanese and Indigenous societies. It would likely be an overstatement to suggest that the LCIP viewed Taiwan's national court system or the ROC state as an ally in this endeavor, even as it received funding from the Judicial Yuan and the Legal Aid Foundation. Its work indicated, however, that the state was not the only problem facing Indigenous peoples. Rather, state apparatuses like the ad hoc chambers could, if properly educated and managed, be mobilized to serve Indigenous interests. The LCIP undertook such a project, working within the court system to secure Indigenous peoples' rights, and with some success. Like other performances of indigeneity, the LCIP's low-key activities were contested and entangled in competing narratives and representations of Indigenous identity that shaped the kinds of expressions and assertions that were possible in Taiwan's court system.

CONCLUSION

The development of judicial hybrid practices and performances of indigeneity by Indigenous persons were among the innovative and improvisational strategies used in the ad hoc Chambers of Indigenous Courts to bridge state-Indigenous divides in the courtroom. While many aspects of the specialized units mirrored standard court procedures and reinforced Han Taiwanese cultural assumptions about law and social order, local actors developed exploratory practices to unsettle these procedures and assumptions. In the process, they brought the specialized units to life as boundary institutions.

As judges in the ad hoc chambers applied new and ambiguous laws related to Indigenous peoples' rights, they had to navigate a complex legal landscape that required them to balance the Judicial Yuan's expectations, the constraints of Taiwan's civil law tradition, and Indigenous peoples' demands for recognition and respect. To do so, they developed a range of exploratory practices that included integrating Indigenous worldviews into applications of criminal intent, shifting away from mechanical applications of law toward review frameworks aimed at balancing interests, reimagining the hierarchy of state law, and engaging with principles of natural law and human dignity. A common thread running through these efforts was a willingness to think reflexively about how Han Taiwanese ideas about law, culture, and lived experience entered courtroom procedure and legal interpretation. This shift was exemplified by a growing recognition that a "different starting place" was needed to acknowledge and accommodate Indigenous identities and cultural frameworks in the judicial process.

Performances of indigeneity by Indigenous individuals and communities similarly pushed the ad hoc chambers in new directions. Expressions of Indigenous identity in the units drew from a diverse repertoire of creative practices encompassing language, dress, consumption, documents, and institutions. At times, these performances involved overt and dramatic assertions of Indigenous identity. At other times, they were more mundane and less visible. At still other times, they were relatively unconscious acts ordinarily reserved for the village. These acts had the capacity to destabilize essentialist notions of indigeneity, introduce alternative ontological frameworks, and assume governance responsibilities that the state failed to perform.

These practices often relied on intermediary actors—lawyers, witnesses, experts, interpreters, and audience members—who played crucial roles in facilitating these exploratory and strategic practices. Lawyers introduced new legal arguments, advised Indigenous clients on performances of cultural and linguistic difference, and strategized to secure just outcomes for Indigenous litigants and communities. At times, they embodied acts of boundary spanning, such as shaking betel nuts in their hands during oral arguments. Community elders and academics, including anthropologists, served as expert witnesses, providing judges with crucial insights into Indigenous cultural practices and relationships to ancestral territories. Interpreters, especially informal interpreters who traveled from Indigenous communities, bridged linguistic divides and facilitated performances of Indigenous languages intended to emphasize cultural difference. Audience members, too, played an active role. They coordinated their attire and arrived in large numbers to hearings to demonstrate solidarity before the court. They collected volumes of legal materials and answered judges' questions before lawyers had an opportunity to respond, blending cultural distinctiveness with legal aptitude. And they unsettled power dynamics by "occupying" the courtroom through everyday acts of indigeneity.

These improvisational and strategic activities had transformational potential. They empowered Indigenous individuals, communities, and peoples in asserting their claims to cultural practices and lands. They generated critical knowledge about Indigenous peoples' cultures, languages, and laws, filling gaps in the understanding of judges and legal practitioners in the ad hoc chambers. Beyond knowledge production, these activities also had the capacity to reshape Taiwan law by reconfiguring the legal framework and drawing upon alternative normative foundations. Perhaps most importantly, they had the power to shift the perspectives and attitudes of those involved, influencing how Indigenous rights were recognized and adjudicated. Their success, however, was never guaranteed. The ad hoc chambers were new judicial bodies, and laws were changing rapidly. Local actors were still figuring out how to make the units concrete realities. The practices they developed could serve Indigenous peoples' claims and interests, but they could also produce outcomes that were unhelpful to Indigenous litigants and that reinforced Indigenous peoples' unequal position in the court system.

Through these practices, the ad hoc chambers emerged as dynamic and experimental spaces, breaking from the ordinariness of their typical operation. Their presences in Taiwan courts were tied less to formal procedures than to a range of creative and exploratory practices developed by local actors aimed at finding ways to recognize and respect Indigenous cultures and relationships to land. While these practices did not guarantee that Indigenous identities would be recognized in the courtroom or that courts would transcend their colonial structures or processes, they revealed the ways local actors were actively shaping the units into boundary institutions, doing the work of managing and spanning Han Taiwanese and Indigenous divides in the courtroom.

In certain respects, these practices reconfigured the character of the specialized units. When judges developed hybrid practices and Indigenous litigants performed identities as Indigenous persons, the units transformed into something more than courts of law. They were forums for debate, not just in terms of the adversarial nature of legal proceedings, but in negotiating ontologies of indigeneity and the state. In aspiration, the ad hoc chambers were intended to facilitate communication between Han Taiwanese legal actors and Indigenous persons in courtroom disputes while addressing the systemic disadvantages Indigenous peoples faced in the national court system. Evaluating the dynamic practices that constitute the units suggests that we are not left with either the optimism of inevitable reconciliation of Indigenous peoples and the state or the pessimism of an inescapable derangement of Indigenous cultures. Instead, middle spaces predicated on agonism,[35] on debate and contest, like the ad hoc chambers, may also play a meaningful role in advancing Indigenous recognition and shaping state-Indigenous relations.

SIX

Boundary Institutions and Beyond

THIS BOOK HAS TRACED the development of a new set of court institutions in Taiwan designed to bridge cultural, linguistic, and legal divides separating the ROC state (and its dominant Han Taiwanese society) and Indigenous peoples through the administration of court cases. My aim has been to understand how the ad hoc Chambers of Indigenous Courts navigated questions of indigeneity and the nature of Indigenous peoples' rights in court proceedings, particularly in moments of encountering Indigenous difference in disputes over Indigenous cultural practices and territories. What I found was a system of specialized court units formed not only as a concession to Indigenous communities in a moment when the state found it advantageous to do so, but also as another instrument through which the state extended and secured its control over Indigenous peoples. The units were part of the variety of ways in which colonial structures and processes maintain their stability and permanency through changing form or the establishment of new institutions. But more importantly, they revealed how Indigenous communities have responded to this shifting terrain of institutions and law and the activities of many kinds of actors in shaping the units to serve the ends of decolonization and reconciliation. I have argued that it was through creative and improvised practices to bridge Han Taiwanese and Indigenous divides, rather than routinized procedures, that the ad hoc chambers emerged as distinct and meaningful institutions in Taiwan courtrooms.

At first, I assumed that examining the structure of the specialized units would reveal their boundary-spanning dimensions and capacities. I soon learned that this was not the case. Structurally, the units bore little distinction from ordinary courts. In fact, the units' special features were so few that even those working within them sometimes disagreed about their presence in Taiwan courtrooms. While representatives of the Judicial Yuan firmly maintained that the units were present and active in promoting respect for Indigenous peoples in the national courts, others, like Indigenous defendants and litigants, their lawyers, and some judges, were less convinced that anything new or different was taking place. I began to wonder how to make sense of things.

One avenue, adopted here, has been boundary work theory, which views boundaries as constructed entities that shift or are sustained through discourses and practices. Constructions of what it meant to be Indigenous following centuries of multiple colonialisms and disputes over Indigenous cultural practices and territories were productive places, although not the only places, to start. This required integrating boundary work theory with Taiwan's multicultural politics and ongoing constructions of rules and norms in Taiwan courtrooms and beyond.

Bringing these perspectives together has been critical for understanding how the ad hoc chambers operate as boundary institutions. It highlighted key features of these specialized units, in particular their elements of hybridity, process, practice, and power. The units emerged as hybrid spaces where cultural identities, languages, and normative orders intermingled and sometimes merged. They were generative spaces in the court system, redirecting the levels of engagement and transforming over time with new developments. Participants in the units explored new ways of working and adapted old ways to navigate the tensions of spanning state-Indigenous divides, oftentimes facilitated by intermediaries, like lawyers, witnesses, experts, interpreters, and audience members. All these activities were embedded in relations of power that privileged ROC state interests and Han Taiwanese perspectives but that could also be disrupted by Indigenous actors and their supporters.

Disputes over Indigenous cultural practices, territories, and laws in the ad hoc chambers were never just about the specifics of individual cases, although they were that too. These cases were entangled in broader transformations shaping Taiwan, including shifts in international order, regional political tensions, struggles for sovereignty and recognition, efforts toward decolonization and reconciliation, and contested visions for a future Taiwan. The entanglements of indigeneity and state sovereignty were apparent as I walked through the Taiwan Taoyuan International Airport to begin my research in 2015. Making my way through the airport, I was struck by how much had changed since I had lived in Taiwan as a youth. At that time, derogatory references to Indigenous peoples were common, and it was rare to see Indigenous persons wearing their customary attire in public or openly discussing their Indigenous heritage. The airport was called Chiang Kai-shek International Airport, named after the authoritarian ROC leader who had imposed martial law and suppressed both native Taiwanese and Indigenous peoples. Now, twenty-five years later, the first thing I noticed in the airport was the presence of Indigenous art adorning the walls of the terminal. Created by an Amis artist, the artwork featured flying fish, dense forests, towering mountains, and vibrant geometric designs, expressions of the rich cultural and artistic traditions of the Amis people. Trendy shops in the terminal catered to international travelers by selling magnets, bags, and other goods produced by "Formosan aborigines."

After leaving the airport, I took a taxi to my apartment near the Presidential Office Building. The road leading to the building had once been called Chie-shou Road, short for "Long Live Chiang Kai-shek" Road. In 1996, it was renamed Ketagalan Boulevard to honor the Indigenous group that originally inhabited the region making up present-day Taipei. A few days later, I boarded the Puyuma Express, a high-speed train bound for southern Taiwan. *Puyuma* means "united" or "together" in the language of the Pinuyumayan people (Shan 2012). When I arrived in Taitung, the tunnel leading out of the railway station was lined with photographs of Indigenous women and men smiling and inviting tourists to visit the mountains. Later, settling into the home I rented in Hualien, I turned on the television set and found Taiwan Indigenous Television, a station dedicated to Indigenous peoples' cultures and issues. And when my fieldwork came to an end, I walked once again through the Taiwan Taoyuan International Airport. Each departure gate in the terminal featured a display dedicated to a different Indigenous group in Taiwan, such as the Tsou (figure 14).

These changes over the past twenty-five years reflected a profound political and social shift in Taiwan toward Indigenous peoples, from erasing and demeaning Indigenous identities to recognizing and celebrating their arts, crafts, languages, and cultures. This transformation was part of a broader reckoning with Taiwan's colonial past and an ongoing movement toward constitutional multiculturalism and independence. Indigenous identities, previously hidden, were now on display, even promoted in certain arenas of public life, and they had become integral to Taiwan's self-presentation to the

FIGURE 14. Display on Tsou culture at Taiwan Taoyuan International Airport, 2022.

world. Indigenous cultures, languages, and identities were being mobilized by many kinds of actors toward many kinds of aims.

This concluding chapter steps back to consider again the connections between indigeneity and sovereignty in Taiwan and the possibilities and challenges of securing Indigenous recognition in a context of multiple colonialisms and contested sovereignty. I begin by examining how colonial authorities historically regarded the sovereignty of Taiwan's Indigenous peoples. I then consider the tactical, creative, and spontaneous everyday acts of self-governing through which Indigenous sovereignty is asserted, in addition to more formal avenues of advocacy surrounding reforms in law and policymaking. I suggest that these everyday enactments of self-governance reflect a form of "as-if sovereignty," a concept that captures a particular mode of exercising Indigenous sovereignty in constrained circumstances that also describes certain sovereignty-making practices of the ROC state. I conclude by reflecting on the implications of as-if sovereignty for the operations of the ad hoc Chambers of Indigenous Courts, particularly in their role in promoting respect for and securing the judicial rights of Indigenous peoples in Taiwan's national court system.

SOVEREIGN MATTERS

As Indigenous peoples in many different contexts have learned, there are important distinctions between de recto, de jure, and de facto sovereignty (Kalt and Singer 2004, 6). De recto sovereignty refers to sovereignty by moral principle or right. De jure sovereignty concerns sovereignty conferred by legal decree or legislative act. De facto sovereignty means sovereignty by practice. Indigenous peoples and their supporters can often articulate a compelling claim to de recto sovereignty and petition for de jure sovereignty, but what ultimately matters is the ability to assert self-governance in daily life, or de facto sovereignty. Considering these forms of sovereignty in the context of Taiwan highlights how Indigenous persons and communities have, in recent years, actively worked to reclaim control over their futures, not just through legal and political avenues but also through lived practice and assertions of their cultural identities and relationships to land.

Over the past four centuries, colonial authorities in Taiwan have granted Indigenous peoples varying degrees of de jure rights to manage their people, property, and resources. As previously mentioned, Dutch administrators in the mid-seventeenth century negotiated treaties with Indigenous villages, stipulating that they recognize the States General of the Netherlands as their governing authority. While these arrangements positioned Indigenous peoples as vassals of the Dutch East India Company, they nonetheless preserved, in principle, aspects of Indigenous sovereignty. For example, Indigenous villages retained their rights to land, and their territories could not be alienated without the community's consent. These treaty-based rights expired with the Dutch expulsion in 1662.

Several centuries later, during Taiwan's 1999 presidential election, DPP candidate Chen Shui-bian signed the "New Partnership Between Indigenous Peoples and the Taiwan Government." This agreement recognized the inherent sovereignty of Indigenous peoples and committed the ROC government to promoting Indigenous autonomy. Chen agreed with Indigenous representatives that this new partnership was equivalent to a nation-to-nation treaty (Simon and Awi Mona 2013, 102). In 2000, the DPP formalized the agreement into a "White Paper on Aboriginal Policy," which pledged to recognize Indigenous sovereignty and support Indigenous self-government. These two documents laid the foundation for the 2005 Indigenous Peoples Basic Law, which enshrined key legal rights for Taiwan's Indigenous peoples, including the right to establish autonomous zones, manage natural resources, and approve or reject development projects on Indigenous reserve land (Awi Mona and Simon 2011, 55).

In 2014, the Legislative Yuan restored the rights of five Indigenous towns to elect their own representatives, correcting an earlier error that had stripped them of their political status when cities and counties were amalgamated. The following year, the Legislature amended the Basic Law to restore certain self-governance powers by allowing Indigenous groups to incorporate as "tribal public corporations." In 2016, the CIP enacted regulations aimed at empowering Indigenous groups to be more involved in the process of planning discussions, land-use policies, research, and regulatory frameworks. That same year, President Tsai Ing-wen issued her formal apology to Taiwan's Indigenous peoples, pledging her administration's commitment "to implement the Indigenous Peoples Basic Law, to serve Indigenous historical justice, and to lay the foundation for Indigenous self-government" (Tsai 2016). In 2017, the CIP took another step by issuing regulations that designated an estimated 800,000 to 1.8 million hectares of land as Indigenous territories but, controversially, excluded private lands.

More recently, Indigenous peoples in Taiwan have pursued sovereign recognition through their hunting rights, which is fundamentally a matter of self-management over wildlife resources on ancestral lands. In 2017, Taiwan's Forestry Bureau began working with Indigenous groups to develop pilot programs that would allow Indigenous communities to oversee and manage hunting activities on their territories (Chang 2023). These small-scale, decentralized, and quasi-independent models of wildlife management were designed to empower Indigenous communities, providing them an opportunity to assert their autonomy and exercise self-governance over their lands through hunting practices.

TAKING MATTERS INTO THEIR OWN LANDS

The developments outlined above reflect activities to secure Indigenous recognition and sovereignty through formal avenues of state law and policymaking. These efforts have worked to carve out special, although often limited, spaces for Indigenous self-governance. Efforts oriented toward de jure sovereignty are, however, only one way Indigenous peoples pursue sovereign power. Indigenous persons and communities may also exercise sovereignty through de facto practices of self-rule and management. These are strategic, creative, and sometimes spontaneous everyday governance practices to pursue sovereignty in the absence of formal recognition of a power to do so, something Kalt and Singer (2003, 6) describe as "just do it" sovereignty, like the Nike slogan. Given the ROC state's slow implementation of legislation supporting Indigenous self-governance, Indigenous groups have taken matters into their own hands and own lands.

Activities in Truku communities illustrate these kinds of de facto sovereignty practices. When I arrived in 2017, members of Dowmung were still grappling with the impacts of uncontrolled tourism on their territories. Han Taiwanese tourists were leaving garbage, pollution, and even human waste in the mountains, while busloads of visitors clogged the village streets, creating disorder. The previous year, a tourist had also drowned in the nearby Mugua River. Despite local regulations capping daily visitors at six hundred, by 2014 as many as three thousand tourists were visiting the mountain in a day (*The News Lens* 2015). In response, community leaders invited Hualien government officials to witness firsthand the environmental damage caused by this unchecked tourism. They urged the government to suspend tourism permits for one year to allow the mountain forest to recover. After receiving no meaningful response, the community took action. In 2014, they closed the road leading to their lands, putting up obstacles to block the influx of tourist buses but still allowing visitors to enter the mountains on foot.

Gathering at a memorial for the victims of the Typhoon Ophelia landslide in 1990, which had claimed the lives of twenty-six residents, community leaders performed a ritual of smoke, rice wine, and duck blood to communicate with the ancestors. As part of the ceremony, they fired shots into the air using their hunting firearms. Shortly afterward, nine members were charged with intimidation, obstruction of freedom, public endangerment, and firearms violations under ROC law. Lawyers from the Legal Aid Foundation intervened and explained to the Hualien District Prosecutor's Office the cultural significance of the community's actions in response to the intrusions on their land. In the end, prosecutors declined to prosecute the men on the grounds of "understanding the situation of Indigenous peoples and respecting their traditional culture" (*The News Lens* 2015).

In the absence of government action, the community took matters into their hands. They closed the public road leading to their territory and asserted a Truku claim to the land through ritual practice. Other Indigenous communities in the region engaged in similar practices of sovereignty making through establishing self-governance structures, managing their lands, and leading biodiversity and ecological conservation initiatives outside the state system.

In 2017, the Amis community of A-tolan in Dulan, Taitung, unilaterally declared their territorial boundaries, extending three nautical miles into the Pacific Ocean (Zhang 2017). Despite the ROC government's promises to help Indigenous groups establish their ancestral territories, repeated delays had left the community frustrated. A group of A-tolan leaders gathered at A-toalanpi, the site where their Amis ancestors had first arrived. Using smoke signals, they proclaimed both the land and surrounding waters to be A-tolan ancestral territory. As a symbolic act of sovereignty, elders in the community dug into the soil with hoes, signifying their claim to the land for the benefit of future generations.

The Amis in Dulan also established a self-government system rooted in their social organization of age-groups (Bekhoven 2018, 193). Following Amis cultural practice, they elected a chief every five years. While the chief held no formal political power, he played a crucial role in the community's social structure. Through this leadership structure, the Amis planned to manage their public affairs as much as possible outside the state political system.

The Truku in Hualien developed an ambitious self-governance plan, drawing inspiration from First Nations in Canada. Under this plan, the "Truku Nation" would govern an autonomous region encompassing their ancestral territory. Local leaders drafted a self-government law that outlined the establishment of their own court, police force, and other governing institutions. Over time, the Truku shifted their focus from self-governance to comanagement over Taroko National Park. The revised plan emphasized self-governance over natural resources and the creation of a tribal council to oversee community affairs. As Scott Simon (2012b, 195) notes, Truku elites were the main drivers of this self-government project, and it did not receive substantial support in local villages.

During my fieldwork, Truku hunters were actively working to self-manage hunting activities and wildlife resources on their territories. Members of the hunters' association had drafted a hunting convention, codifying the Truku law of Gaya and carving out exceptions in state law for local hunters. Under this convention, the association held the authority to issue hunting identification cards and enforce penalties for violations of Gaya. The association hoped that the convention would shield hunters from prosecution in Taiwan courts and encourage greater adherence to Gaya at a time when ROC laws presented a competing normative framework.

Indigenous communities also pursued sovereignty through daily activities of maintaining cultural practices and creating institutions to transmit their knowledges and languages. For example, research with Paiwan communities has shown that Paiwan villages rely on local methods of dispute resolution rather than appealing to state courts (Tsai 2015, 338–42). Truku community members in Dowmung constructed a cultural center to transmit Truku culture and language to future generations. Bunun men prioritized their ancestral law of Samu over state regulations when hunting and used hunting activities to transmit Bunun cultural knowledge to their children and grandchildren.

Other activities indirectly supported these emergent forms of sovereignty-making practice. Indigenous activists and politicians established the Legal Center of Indigenous Peoples to educate courts about Indigenous peoples' cultures and rights, while lawyers worked to secure favorable outcomes for Indigenous defendants facing prosecution for engaging in cultural practices. The launch of Taiwan Indigenous Television, reportedly the first publicly funded Indigenous television channel in Asia, aimed to preserve Indigenous languages and increase public awareness about Indigenous issues (Smith 2014). The i-Tribe program addressed disparities in broadband access by providing free Wi-Fi to rural Indigenous communities, enabling them to access educational resources, share information, and promote their cultural identities to wider audiences (Ruckus 2018).

Assertions of Indigenous identities and claims have also emerged in local politics. On December 25, 2018, Ingay Tali, an Amis politician, took the oath of office as a Tainan City councilor in Amis language while wearing formal Amis attire. As he delivered his oath, he turned his back to the portrait of Sun Yat-sen, the founder of the ROC government and former leader of the KMT, hanging in the legislative chamber (Hioe 2018). Mr. Ingay later explained that his actions were meant to draw attention to the fact that Indigenous peoples had been forced to assimilate into Chinese society, offering a broad critique of the ROC government. While Indigenous activists celebrated his courage, his actions provoked outrage from local officials. The city initially declared his oath invalid on the grounds that it was conducted in Amis. Coincidentally, on the same day, the Legislative Yuan passed the Development of National Languages Act, which affirmed that all languages spoken in Taiwan would be treated equally, without limitations placed on their usage. Despite Taiwan's aspirations to foster a multicultural society, certain spaces remained resistant to change. The city government viewed

Mr. Ingay's use of Amis in his oath as offensive and subversive. On January 8, 2019, however, officials reversed their stance and recognized Mr. Ingay's oath in Amis (Tali 2019).

Assertions of Indigenous identities and claims have likewise entered cross–Taiwan Strait relations. On January 8, 2019, representatives in the Indigenous Historical Justice and Transitional Justice Committee issued a joint declaration affirming Indigenous peoples' sovereignty in response to China's territorial claims to Taiwan. This declaration came just days after a speech delivered by Chinese President Xi Jinping on January 2, 2019, in which he threatened the use of force if Taiwan continued to resist reunification and urged acceptance of the "One Country, Two Systems" framework (Hwai 2019). In the joint declaration, the committee asserted a strong de recto claim to territorial sovereignty, stating, "We, Taiwan's Indigenous peoples, are determined to remain steadfast in guarding and preserving our Motherland. We have persevered for thousands of years, and we will continue doing this" (IHJTJ Committee 2019). While criticizing the ROC government for only recently addressing issues of historical and transitional justice, the declaration stressed the importance of nation building as a collaborative effort. It stated, "Taiwan is a nation that we are all still striving to build together, along with other people who recognize this land for what it actually is." The declaration framed sovereignty in terms of stewardship and collaboration, emphasizing the need to work across differences to shape the nation's future.

SOVEREIGNTY IN THE "AS-IF"

In many places one looks in Taiwan, Indigenous individuals and communities have engaged in everyday practices of de facto sovereignty, alongside pursuing recognition through formal avenues of state law reforms and policymaking. They seize opportunities to assert their identities, reclaim ancestral territories, establish self-government systems, issue official documents, revitalize cultural practices, develop infrastructures, and foster pragmatic coexistence with the ROC government.

I use the concept of "as-if sovereignty" to explain these practices. As-if sovereignty refers to everyday enactments of sovereignty that, while not being totalistic, are meaningful and powerful in their own right in shaping control over lifeways, lands, and futures. The term draws from Jacques deLisle's notion of "as-if participation," which describes how states in situations of contested sovereignty, Taiwan being a key example, commit themselves "unilaterally but publicly and solemnly to acting as if it is (or as if it were) a member of an international organization or regime, pledging to live up to all relevant standards" (deLisle 2011; see also deLisle 2019). This is a performance of sovereignty by walking, talking, and acting like a recognized state alongside other strategies. I build on this idea by emphasizing that such performances have multiple audiences. While the state and international community are often seen as the primary observers of sovereignty claims, Indigenous individuals and communities, other Indigenous groups, and the colonizing society are also critical audiences. What counts as acts of sovereignty making, and how its effects are understood, may vary across these different constituencies.

The concept of as-if sovereignty aligns with recent anthropological and socio-legal approaches to sovereignty and legal power that move beyond unitary, totalizing frameworks. Aihwa Ong (2006) describes "graduated sovereignty" to capture how governments flexibly manage sovereignty, adjusting political spaces to accommodate global capital and giving corporations indirect power over citizens in key economic zones. Sara Friedman (2021) offers "aspirational sovereignty" to explore the political logics and everyday governing practices generating recognizable and recognized sovereignty. In a related move, Amy Cohen and Bronwen Morgan (2023) identify practices of "prefigurative legality" to describe how people use existing forms of legality to construct alternative possible futures through temporary, playful experiments outside of dominant statist and capitalist rationalities.

Scholars have also explored expanded understandings of sovereignty in Indigenous settings and their entanglements with colonial institutions. Jessica Cattelino (2008) conceptualizes Indigenous sovereignty through the lens of "economic nationalism," illustrating how Seminole sovereignty in the United States is shaped through interdependent relations among tribal, state, and federal institutions. Justin Richland (2021) refers to practices of Indigenous "insistence" as communities creatively navigate the contradictions of insisting on their sovereignty while also engaging in the daily work of self-governance under ongoing processes of colonialism. In the Taiwan context, DJ Hatfield (2020) describes forms of "sovereign assertion" through which Indigenous peoples assert their continued existence as polities. What unites these alternative approaches to sovereignty in Indigenous settings and beyond is an interest in how actors engage in everyday acts to will themselves to have power, notwithstanding the absence of a formal recognition that they have such power. These activities are goal-oriented and imaginative deployments of logics of economic relations, political governance, and legal forms toward collective self-determination.

Some Indigenous scholars have warned against the uncritical adoption of sovereignty as a framework for conceptualizing Indigenous politics. Taiaiake Alfred (1999) critiques the applicability of Western, state-centric notions of sovereignty in Indigenous contexts, arguing that such frameworks risk reproducing colonial structures and undermining Indigenous self-determination by imposing foreign models of governance. Glen Coulthard (2014) similarly critiques recognition-based politics, contending that the forms of recognition offered by settler states often serve to reinforce colonial power relations. In place of sovereignty as conventionally understood, he advocates "grounded normativity," or ethical frameworks and political practices rooted in Indigenous relationships to land. Audra Simpson (2014) takes this further by critiquing the demand that Indigenous nations perform sovereignty in ways legible to the settler state. She introduces "refusal" as a mode of political life that resists recognition and the trap of proving sovereignty within settler frameworks.

The concept of "as-if," as I use it here, builds on the Kantian notion of the "consciously false." The idea refers to the fact that we can never really grasp the underlying structure of reality, so we construct systems of thought and act "as if" the world conforms to these models (see Vaihinger 1935). For instance, in the physical sciences, certain phenomena have never been observed, yet scientists operate "as if" they exist, using them to create new and better constructs (Hacking 1999). These are fictions that are accepted not because they are empirically proven, but because they offer nonrational solutions to problems that lack rational answers. Such fictional concepts are "not subject, like hypotheses, to proof or disconfirmation, only, if they come to lose their operational effectiveness, to neglect" (Kermode 2000, 40).

Rooted in anteriority, a being-before, sovereignty was not, from an Indigenous perspective in Taiwan, something subject to proof merely through laws or through moral claims. It was something to be enacted. Indigenous sovereignty was always there, subject only to its neglect. It was not that Indigenous persons or communities ignored or refused to acknowledge the existence of the ROC state. Rather, Indigenous sovereignty was a proposition that lay always latent in the background, ever present and waiting to surface. It surfaced opportunistically in spaces of ambiguous power, government inaction, or bald assertion. These were embodiments of a narrative about Indigenous organization and power on the Taiwan landscape. And through everyday opportunistic practices, Indigenous individuals and communities enacted and projected claims of sovereignty, asserting control over their lands, lifeways, and futures.

The fact that these everyday acts of sovereignty making were performative fictions, in the sense that they were not officially sanctioned, did not detract from their potency. Proof of their effectiveness lay in their pragmatic usefulness for securing Indigenous peoples' capacity to self-govern certain domains of life and territory beyond, and sometimes interwoven with, the state system. Equally significantly, these practices disrupted dominant narratives of sovereignty. When placed alongside Indigenous peoples' claims to territory and culture after experiencing multiple colonialisms, similar claims made by the ROC, as a recent colonial power having an ambiguous international status, appeared to be weak and vulnerable. From an Indigenous perspective, if there was any false performance of sovereignty, it belonged exclusively to the ROC state.

These everyday practices of Indigenous sovereignty making also revealed something else. They resembled the way the ROC government itself enacted sovereignty. A founding member of the United Nations and once the internationally recognized government of China, the ROC now exercises authority only over Taiwan and its associated islands. Since 1971, the PRC has largely supplanted the ROC in the global arena, leaving Taiwan isolated from many international organizations and regimes despite its emergence as an economic power. Taiwan exists as a de facto independent state, meeting many, but not necessarily all, of the commonly recognized criteria for sovereign status under international law (deLisle 2011; see also Clough 1993). Taiwan's unusual status has compelled it to adopt innovative and unconventional strategies to assert its position as an international actor. These efforts have included forging ties with international organizations, integrating global norms into domestic law, engaging in humanitarian initiatives, and exercising "warm power" through long-term collaborations with other states (Cain 2021). As Simon and Awi Mona (2015, 4) note, Taiwan must interact visibly with international orders to justify its existence as a sovereign state.

International law and human rights have been essential tools for Taiwan's performance of sovereignty. By adopting international norms and committing to uphold them, Taiwan has strengthened its status as a sovereign state. This strategy is explicitly outlined in the DPP's "White Paper on Foreign Policy for the 21st Century," which emphasized the importance of global legal and human rights standards as a means of bolstering Taiwan's international legitimacy, stating that "as an important member in the international community, Taiwan should commit itself, as a sovereign nation, to abide by the UN Charter and various international conventions, and to exercise its proper rights and obligations by contributing to world peace and development" (Democratic Progressive Party 1999). As noted earlier, Taiwan incorporated the ICCPR and ICESCR into its domestic law in 2009. In the years that followed, it added four additional UN human rights treaties, each with provisions for state reporting and international review: the Convention on the Elimination of All Forms of Discrimination Against Women, the Convention on the Rights of the Child, the Convention on the Rights of Persons with Disabilities, and the Convention Against Corruption.[1]

Beyond human rights, Taiwan has also committed itself to international standards in spaces where it does not hold official membership. It has made public pledges to abide by key security agreements, including the Nuclear Non-Proliferation Treaty, the Biological and Toxin Weapons Convention, the Chemical Weapons Convention, and the Missile Technology Control Regime (Cain 2021). Taiwan has further positioned itself as a regional leader in progressive social policies. It became the first country in Asia to legalize same-sex marriage in 2019 (Chau 2022) and ranks strongly for gender equality in the UN Gender Inequality Index (*Taiwan Today* 2023). Taiwan's efforts to walk and talk like a state have also included more mundane but significant everyday governing activities, like conducting border evaluations at ports of entry (Friedman 2015). By cultivating an image of Taiwan as a model of international order through adherence to global norms and rhetoric of equal rights and through everyday governance activities, Taiwan has strategically performed recognized sovereignty and emphasized crucial distinctions between itself and mainland China.

Indigenous peoples and their issues have figured prominently in efforts to enhance Taiwan's international standing. Since 1991, ROC state organs and civil society NGOs have represented Taiwan at UN meetings on Indigenous affairs (Palemeq 2012; Simon and Awi Mona 2015), despite strong opposition from the PRC (Horton 2018). Taiwan has also pursued bilateral cooperation on Indigenous issues. In 1998 and 2004, the CIP signed memoranda of understanding with Canada and New Zealand to establish intergovernmental cooperation in managing Indigenous affairs (Government of Canada 2018; Munsterhjelm 2014). Additionally, Taiwan Indigenous representatives have participated in cultural exchanges with Indigenous communities abroad, such as Austronesian communities in Oceania (Johnson 2019). Further solidifying its global Indigenous partnerships, Taiwan cofounded the Indigenous Peoples Economic and Trade Cooperation Arrangement in 2022, alongside Australia, Canada, and New Zealand (*Taiwan Today* 2022). These initiatives not only strengthened Taiwan's diplomatic ties, but also underscored its commitment to Indigenous issues as a fundamental aspect of its international legitimacy.

Addressing Indigenous peoples' rights and issues has arguably performed yet another function: creating a channel for engagement with Taiwan's powerful neighbor, the PRC. Some have identified a metapragmatic function at work in Taiwan's Indigenous rights framework, where the ROC government uses Indigenous rights and its management of Indigenous peoples to model for the PRC its preferred mode of relations. As one high court judge explained,

> Taiwan can get some moral capital by treating its Indigenous population with respect and dignity, and present this to China as how they should treat Taiwan. The relationship between Taiwan and Indigenous people is a quasi-national relationship. It is like the relationship between China and Taiwan. If we treat our [Indigenous] population with respect and autonomy, then China should do the same and treat Taiwan with respect and autonomy. I think this is why Taiwan has so many Indigenous laws since 2001. It was advantageous to the Taiwan government to model an appropriate relationship with Indigenous people.[2]

From this perspective, Indigenous rights offered a platform for the ROC government to signal to the PRC, by treating Indigenous peoples with respect and recognizing their autonomy, how China should engage with Taiwan. The extent to which ROC laws have not yet secured Indigenous peoples' autonomy likely undermines important elements of such a message.

SOVEREIGN FUTURES

Intertwined on the Taiwan landscape, practices of Indigenous sovereignty making and ROC strategies for asserting sovereignty share a common logic in that both rely on performative acts to assert legitimacy and sustain their claims in the face of contested political realities. These performances of sovereignty involve navigating available spaces to exercise everyday acts of governance, seizing and shaping opportunities to regulate activities and control their own affairs while also pursuing recognition through formal channels. Yet critical differences remain. Unlike Indigenous sovereignty, ROC sovereignty does not lie latent, waiting to be reasserted. The ROC cannot claim a direct line between a "past" ROC sovereignty and Taiwan's current de facto sovereignty. Instead, ROC sovereignty demands continual demonstration, being subject to proof in ways that Indigenous sovereignty is not.

The ROC government might reflect on this parallel with the situation of Indigenous peoples in Taiwan: Just as it has struggled for international recognition in the face of formidable pressure from the PRC, Taiwan's Indigenous peoples have long fought for recognition from imperial, colonial, and state powers. Acknowledging these coexisting sovereignty claims may open a space for mutual recognition, where the ROC could formally recognize Indigenous sovereignty as legitimate and enduring, not conditional or symbolic, alongside state sovereignty. It may consider how expanding institutional support for Indigenous self-governance through recognition of Indigenous political and legal structures could foster more equitable relations. Reflection on the burdens placed on Indigenous claims by state-defined standards of proof and authenticity could prompt a reassessment of bureaucratic and legal processes and a greater appreciation of Indigenous epistemologies and legal traditions. The government might also see value in engaging more consistently with international legal norms that affirm Indigenous rights to support Indigenous communities. Taiwan is uniquely positioned to think reflexively about commonalities in navigating contested legitimacy to open new pathways for engagement with Indigenous communities and expressions of Indigenous self-governance. Ultimately, this may mean decoupling Indigenous cultural, legal, linguistic, and political rights from the nationalist goals of the Han Taiwanese–dominated ROC government.

Sovereignty is an unfolding narrative, a story told about power and rule, enacted through institutions, mechanisms, organizations, and systems aimed at self-determination. Performances of sovereignty need not be totalistic to be meaningful and powerful, but they do rely on audiences that recognize them as such (Rutherford 2009). Appearing in many different forms, everyday acts of self-governance enable states and communities to pursue self-governance and secure control of their futures. A potential lesson on sovereignty comes from the Indigenous representatives mentioned earlier. In their letter to Chinese President Xi, they asserted that power and rule were about not exclusion but collaboration; that sovereignty, rather than being a bald assertion of authority, is rooted in engagement. The work of this committee has been contested in Indigenous communities, but from this perspective, sovereignty is not just about control; it is also about creating spaces for dialogue, bridging divides, and working through differences. The ad hoc Chambers of Indigenous Courts, in their role as boundary institutions, may potentially serve as such spaces for debate and negotiation. But as units embedded in the national court system and dominated by Han Taiwanese interpretations of indigeneity, language, and law, their potential to effect substantive change remains uncertain.

Tackling and transforming the power structures that sustain Indigenous marginalization is critical and difficult work. The ad hoc chambers reveal how deeply colonial logics penetrate state initiatives designed to help Indigenous peoples and underscore the need for empirical research on the everyday practices and processes through which institutions navigate the tensions between Indigenous and non-Indigenous discourses on culture, land, and law. Bunun poet Salizan Takisvilainan observes that more is needed than mere legal reforms and adaptations to legal institutions. Such measures, he warns, often perpetuate colonial inequalities rather than dismantle them, and they rarely lead to substantive change. In a tone reminiscent of Kafka, his poem, "The Indigenous Peoples Basic Law" (Takisvilainan 2013), captures the concerns of many Indigenous communities as he describes the unfulfilled promises of state legal reforms and creation of new institutions, like the ad hoc Chambers of Indigenous Courts, intended to uplift Indigenous peoples:

> At the gate of the community
> You made a sculpture
> Hunters shooting into the future
> Women weaving happiness
> Children running toward laughter
> The image at the entrance
>
> In the gale of improper development
> In the torrential rain of false autonomy
>
> In the sunshine of upgrading and annexing counties and cities
> In the rain of community relocation
>
> One by one they collapse
> One by one they erode
> One by one they weather
>
> In the end
> Nothing
> But the law remains

GLOSSARY OF TERMS IN ENGLISH, PINYIN, AND CHINESE CHARACTERS

Ad hoc Chamber(s) of Indigenous Courts	*yuanzhuminzu zhuanye fating*	原住民族專業法庭
Articles of the Dowmung Hunters Self-Governance and Self-Discipline Convention	*tongmen buluo lieren zizhu guanli zilü gongyue tiaowen*	銅門部落獵人自主管理自律公約條文
"Assessing the Feasibility of Setting Up a Special Indigenous Court"	*pinggu shezhi yuanzhuminzu zhuanye fating zhi kexingxing*	評估設置原住民族專業法庭之可行性
Born in the backwoods	*chushen qiongxiangpirang*	出身窮鄉僻壤
Bureau of Pacification and Reclamation	*fukenju*	撫墾局
Civilized society	*wenming shehui*	文明社會
Community (tribe, band)	*buluo*	部落
Constitutional Court	*xianfa fating*	憲法法庭
Control Yuan	*jianchayuan*	監察院
Cooked savages	*shoufan*	熟番
Cultural essence	*wenhua jingsui*	文化精髓
Culture	*wenhua*	文化
Customary legislation	*xiguan lifa*	習慣立法
Dangerous	*henweixian*	很危險
District court(s)	*difang fayuan*	地方法院
Dowmung Bamboo House Case	*tongmen zhuwu an*	銅門竹屋案
Dowmung people	*tongmenren*	銅門人

Dowmung village	*tongmencun*	銅門村
Earth-oxen trench	*tuniugou*	土牛溝
Examination Yuan	*kaoshiyuan*	考試院
Executive Yuan	*xingzhengyuan*	行政院
Gang	*jiehuo*	結夥
General Bureau of Camphor Affairs	*naowu zongju*	腦務總局
High court(s)	*gaodeng fayuan*	高等法院
Hunter	*lieren*	獵人
Hunters Self-Governance and Self-Discipline Convention	*lieren zizhu guanli zilü gongyue*	獵人自主管理自律公約
Hunting gun	*lieqiang*	獵槍
Indigenous people	*yuanzhumin*	原住民
Indigenous peoples	*yuanzhuminzu*	原住民族
Indigenous peoples' cultures	*yuanzhuminzu wenhua*	原住民族文化
Interpreters	*tongshi*	通事
It depends upon	*yaokan / deikan*	要看/得看
Judicial rights and interests	*sifa quanyi*	司法權益
Judicial Yuan	*sifa yuan*	司法院
Law	*fa*	法
Legal Aid for Indigenous Peoples Program	*yuanzhuminzu falü fuwu zhuanan*	原住民族法律服務專案
Legal Aid Foundation	*caituan faren falü fuzhu jijinhui*	財團法人法律扶助基金會
Legal Aid Foundation's Legal Center of Indigenous Peoples	*caituan faren falü fuzhu jijinhui yuanzhuminzu falü fuwu zhongxin*	財團法人法律扶助基金會原住民族法律服務中心
Legislative laziness	*lifa daiduo*	立法怠惰
Legislative Yuan	*lifayuan*	立法院
Lethal weapons	*xiongqi*	兇器
Mainlanders	*waishengren*	外省人
Measures	*banfa*	辦法

Mountain compatriots	*shandi tongbao*	山地同胞
Mountain Greenery (newspaper)	*gaoshanqing*	高山青
Mountain produce	*shanchan*	山產
Mountain reserves	*shandi baoliudi*	山地保留地
Musha Incident (Wushe Rebellion)	*wushe shijian*	霧社事件
Name rectification movement	*zhengming yundong*	正名運動
Nanzhuang Incident	*nanzhuang shijian*	南庄事件
Native Taiwanese	*benshengren*	本省人
Official documents	*gong wenshu*	公文書
Open the mountains, pacify the Indigenes	*kaishan fufan*	開山撫番
Paiwan Alili Incident	*paiwanzu alili shijian*	排灣族阿力力事件
Paiwan culture	*paiwanzu de wenhua*	排灣族的文化
Paiwan funerary culture	*paiwanzu de binzang wenhua*	排灣族的殯葬文化
Plains Indigenous peoples	*pingpuzuqun*	平埔族群
Presidential Office Indigenous Historical Justice and Transitional Justice Committee	*zongtongfu yuanzhuminzu lishi zhengyi yu zhuanxing zhengyi weiyuanhui*	總統府原住民族歷史正義與轉型正義委員會
Raw savages	*shengfan*	生番
Recovery Road	*guangfulu*	光復路
Relevant laws and regulations	*xiangguan faling*	相關法令
Reserve land	*banjin shoyôchi*	Japanese: 蕃人所要地
Respect	*zunzhong*	尊重
Ritual	*jiyi*	祭儀
Scorched-earth line	*aiyūsen*	Japanese: 隘勇線
Self-Help Association of Fuxingli	*fuxingli zijiuhui*	復興里自救會
Self-made	*zizhi*	自製
Self-use	*ziyong*	自用
Separately prescribed	*ling dingzhi*	另定之

Service center	*fuwuzhan*	服務站
Shall	*ying*	應
Smangus Beechwood Incident	*simakusi jumu shijian*	司馬庫斯櫸木事件
Specialized court(s)	*zhuanye fating*	專業法庭
Specialized district court(s)	*zhuanye difang fayuan*	專業地方法院
Stipulated by laws	*ling yi falü dingzhi*	另以法律定之
Summary proceeding	*jianyi chengxu*	簡易程序
Supreme Court	*zhonghua minguo zuigaofayuan*	中華民國最高法院
Taitung Bunun Youth Group	*dongbuqing*	東布青
Taiwan Hualien District Court	*taiwan hualian difang fayuan*	臺灣花蓮地方法院
Taiwan Hualien High Court	*taiwan gaodeng fayuan hualian fenyuan*	臺灣高等法院花蓮分院
Too big	*tai da*	太大
Tradition	*chuantong*	傳統
Traditional style	*chuantong fangshi*	傳統方式
Transformed savages	*huafan*	化番
Tribal public corporations	*buluo gongfaren zuzhi*	部落公法人組織
Truku Name Rectification Campaign	*tailugezu zhengming yundong*	太魯閣族正名運動
Truku War	*tailuge zhanzheng*	太魯閣戰爭
Tsou Leader Honey Incident	*zouzu toumu fengmi shijian*	鄒族頭目蜂蜜事件
Village	*cunluo*	村落
White Terror	*baise kongbu*	白色恐怖
Within a reasonable scope	*zai heli zhi fanwei*	在合理之範圍
Within three years	*san nian nei*	三年內
Xincheng Incident	*xincheng shijian*	新城事件

NOTES

INTRODUCTION: OF COURTS AND ANCESTRAL SPIRITS

1. The events described occurred in relation to Kaohsiung High Administrative Court 102 [2013] No. 109 and are based on accounts provided by advocates and litigants who participated in the proceedings.

2. This book follows scholarship that translates the term *yuanzhuminzu zhuanye fating* as "ad hoc Chamber of Indigenous Courts" (Awi Mona and Huang 2021; Tsai 2015). A variety of terms have been used to describe these court units, including "aboriginal courts" (Tang 2013), "Indigenous courts" (Hsu 2015), "special court of Indigenous peoples," "special unit of Indigenous peoples," and "special court (unit) of Indigenous peoples" (Executive Yuan 2016a). I adopt the formulation "ad hoc Chamber of Indigenous Courts" because it captures two key characteristics of these court bodies: They are ad hoc (that is, established for a specific purpose) and they are internal chambers within Taiwan's national court system, rather than independent, stand-alone courts.

3. In Taiwan, the Judicial Yuan, Executive Yuan (*xingzhengyuan* 行政院), Legislative Yuan (*lifayuan* 立法院), Examination Yuan (*kaoshiyuan* 考試院), and Control Yuan (*jianchayuan* 監察院) form the five branches of the ROC government. The Judicial Yuan is vested with the power of adjudication, discipline, interpretation, and judicial administration, and it oversees the national court system. Within the Taiwan national court system, there are twenty-two district courts (*difang fayuan* 地方法院), six high courts (*gaodeng fayuan* 高等法院), one Supreme Court (*zhonghua minguo zuigaofayuan* 中華民國最高法院), and one Constitutional Court (previously Council of Grand Justices) (*xianfa fating* 憲法法庭) (Chiu and Fa 1994). Taiwan's national courts oversee millions of individual cases a year, with over 3.1 million cases opened in the district courts in 2019 alone (Judicial Yuan 2020). These courts employ hundreds of judges and supporting staff, and expenses associated with maintaining Taiwan's national courts account for 1 percent of the national government budget per annum (W.-c. Chang 2018, 348).

4. The idea of "boundaries" has enjoyed renewed interest in the social sciences, including in anthropology, history, political science, and sociology. Rooted in traditions

of thought in Durkheim, Marx, Weber, and Foucault, recent explorations into boundaries have examined identity formation, social inequality, knowledge production, and nation building, among other topics (see Fassin 2011; Gustafsson and Lidskog 2018; Lamont and Molnár 2002).

5. Scholars have long highlighted the significance of place names (Basso 1990) and the politics surrounding their creation (Scott, Tehranian, and Mathias 2002). Examining the many names that have been applied to Hualien offers a window into the region's complicated history of colonialism, imperialism, and state control. As I heard repeatedly during my fieldwork, the region was originally called Kilai, named for the Sakizaya people and their settlement in the area. In 1622, when Spanish mariners arrived to mine for gold, they listened to the local language and called the area Turumoan. Under Qing rule, Hualien remained one of the last places to be settled by Chinese immigrants, largely due to its isolated location. During this period, the area was officially renamed Huilan, referencing the whirling effect caused by rivers flowing into the ocean. When Japanese authorities took control of Taiwan, they chose not to transliterate the name as Kilai because it resembled the Japanese word for "dislike" or "disgusting." Instead, they named the port Karenko 花蓮港. After the ROC assumed control of Taiwan, it retained the Japanese kanji but shortened the name to Hualien 花蓮, which remains its official name today.

6. I want to include a note about my use of the term *Indigenous* in its capitalized form. While it is still common to see references to "aborigines" in Taiwan, that usage has fallen out of favor among Indigenous activists who have worked to shift the focus from primordialism to human rights (Friedman 2018, 80n1). Indigenous activists in Taiwan have selected their own terminology of *yuanzhumin* (Indigenous people) and *yuanzhuminzu* (Indigenous peoples) to connect themselves to a global identity of Indigenous peoples and its related international order (Simon 2023b, 9). Capitalization of *Indigenous* in the Taiwan context has been a somewhat contentious issue, with concerns about reifying Indigenous peoples as a single ethnic group and recognition that its use in North America is intended to convey respect for Native sovereignty. In this book, I capitalize the term for two reasons. The first stems from my consultations with Indigenous collaborators in Taiwan. Notably, the issue of capitalization does not arise in the Chinese language, with its use of characters. I explained the issue to my collaborators, and they expressed a preference that I capitalize the term in English, although they left it to my discretion. Second, capitalization connotes respect for Indigenous peoples' ongoing struggles and efforts toward sovereignty. In this sense, it is about political goals and aspirations: a prefiguring of Indigenous sovereignty and jurisdiction. Capitalizing the term has power in acknowledging Indigenous efforts to secure their sovereignties and futures in a space where colonial structures persist by changing form and through the creation of new institutions, like the ad hoc Chambers of Indigenous Courts.

7. Taiwan Constitutional Court 111 [2022] No. 17.
8. Interview, Taitung County, July 30, 2015.
9. Indigenous representatives on the Presidential Indigenous Historical Justice and Transitional Justice Committee succinctly summarized many of these senti-

ments in a joint declaration sent to Chinese President Xi Jinping in 2019 after Xi controversially vowed to reunify China and Taiwan (IHJTJ Committee 2019).

10. Taitung District Court 101 [2012] No. 8. See Lin (2017) for a description of the case and commentary on the proceedings.

11. In a 2003 case known as the "Tsou Leader Honey Incident" (*zouzu toumu fengmi shijian* 鄒族頭目蜂蜜事件), two Tsou men, a father and son, were charged with robbery after they confiscated wild honey that a Han Taiwanese man had taken from Tsou traditional territory without permission from the community (Chiayi District Court 92 [2003] No. 151). After the Supreme Court Procuratorate rejected an extraordinary appeal on the grounds that the case was "hard to handle," the Tsou men were convicted of ordinary robbery under Article 325 of the Criminal Code. Similarly, in a 2005 case known as the "Smangus Beechwood Incident" (*simakusi jumu shijian* 司馬庫斯櫸木事件), prosecutors charged three Tayan men from Smangus village with theft of forestry products under Article 52 of the Forestry Act for taking parts of a protected beech tree left behind by Forestry Bureau personnel, who had already extracted the most valuable parts of the tree, after it had fallen during a typhoon. After a saga of trials and appeals that lasted more than four years, in which the Tayan men were initially convicted in the lower courts, intervention from the Supreme Court ultimately led to their acquittal (Taiwan Supreme Court 98 [2009] No. 7210).

12. Interview, Taipei City, July 30, 2018.

13. Interview, Hualien City, October 24, 2017.

14. Interview, Taipei City, June 15, 2015.

15. Interview, Chiayi City, May 11, 2018.

16. Interview, Taitung City, October 2, 2018.

17. Quotations in this book come from these interviews, unless otherwise stated.

18. I examined a corpus of forty Taiwan court rulings from the preceding twenty years. My archival research covered a broad range of historical periods, from the Japanese colonial period to pending legislation, and encompassed various legal issues, from hunting of wildlife to territorial boundaries, as well as normative arenas such as Indigenous justice practices and international human rights.

19. There was also relative confusion about what I actually did in my law practice, because people assumed that "law" occupied the center of daily activities. In reality, law was relatively peripheral, even irrelevant. Although my tasks ostensibly fell within the discourse of law, this discourse rarely resolved disputes, or did so rarely enough that it was worthy of remark to colleagues ("We won on constitutional standing!"). Ordinarily, my days were consumed with tasks like sifting through hundreds of thousands of documents produced by opposing counsel intended to hide information, fighting to limit the scope of discovery to exclude potentially damaging documents, sending holiday cards to former clients to maintain my "book of business," worrying about clients unwilling to pay their high legal fees, dealing with a judge enraged by the lawyer who had argued just before I had, being enraged myself when the U.S. government produced a two-hundred-page fully redacted document with only the word *UNCLASSIFIED* at the top, asking for permission to

approach the bench only to find that the judge had been working on their personal bills the whole time, studying jury awards in a jurisdiction to determine if we should move the case to a more favorable venue, choosing among legal arguments and objections based on prior experiences with a judge, watching a young Department of Justice line attorney insist on a hearing time specifically to inconvenience my client but not realizing that it conflicted with the judge's regular golf tee time, watching my cocounsel intentionally forget to say "Doctor" to provoke a highly regarded expert witness and make them confuse their answers, negotiating an East African infrastructure deal funded by the World Bank where the contracting multinational corporation insisted on a broad force majeure clause based on a racist belief that "Africa was always falling into conflict," shopping for a black 7-series BMW sedan because that was what the law partners drove (I weakly attempted to buck the system by purchasing a black pickup truck), working not to win cases but to delay them because it would put such a financial strain on the small firms representing class action claimants that they would settle for cheap, and sobbing in a parking lot after the relative of a person who had been struck and killed by a train asked to keep a bloody dollar bill found next to the tracks, not realizing in their grief that their deceased relative's brain matter was spread all around us. From this perspective, the idea that law operated through an objective application of legal principles to fact sets, or that law always mattered, felt disconnected from reality.

20. Interview, Taipei City, June 18, 2015.

21. Anthropological work on institutions has typically focused on two kinds of institutions: social institutions and total institutions (see Hejtmanek 2016). Historically, anthropologists concentrated on what we might call social institutions, or organizing structures that shape the lives of people in nonindustrial societies (see Douglas 1986), such as economics, ecology, kinship, and politics. More recent work has focused on total institutions, which are spaces of living and work separated from wider society, under observation and control by authorities (see Goffman 1961). Foucault's (1977, 1994) work extended this framework, offering tools to analyze institutions that are not entirely totalizing but that are still formally organized and structured around disciplinary power. The account of institutions presented here builds on Foucault's insights, considering institutions as sites of knowledge and power. This model is particularly suited to the case of Taiwan's ad hoc Chambers of Indigenous Courts because the Judicial Yuan created the units with an explicit aim of generating knowledge about Indigenous cultures and rights and, for some legal actors, sweeping Indigenous peoples into the fold of the state system of law. Yet this framework also allows room for Indigenous persons and communities to challenge, subvert, and navigate these units to advance their own interests and goals in court proceedings.

1. BORN OF WOOD, BORN OF STONE

1. The wording of UN Resolution 2758 is crucial to understanding Taiwan's current international status. "*Recognizing* that the representatives of the Govern-

ment of the People's Republic of China are the only lawful representatives of China to the United Nations," the resolution states, it therefore moves "to expel forthwith the representatives of Chiang Kai-shek from the place which they unlawfully occupy at the United Nations and in all the organizations related to it." The resolution uses terms like *restore*, *expel*, and *unlawfully occupy*. The PRC has used these terms to argue that the resolution supports the one-China principle, which is the claim that there is only one sovereign state called China, with the PRC as its legitimate government, and that Taiwan is a part of China (Drun 2017). Representatives of the PRC, however, had a different understanding of the resolution at the time. In a 1971 conversation with Henry Kissinger, then assistant to the U.S. president for national security affairs, PRC prime minister Chou En-lai remarked that, if the resolution passed, "the status of Taiwan is not yet decided" (Lord 1971). According to this view, the resolution determined who represented China in the UN but did not address the status of Taiwan's government, nor did it explicitly prevent Taiwan from participating in the UN so long as it did not claim China's seat. In essence, while Chiang Kai-shek's representatives were dismissed from the UN, they were not permanently excluded. For some scholars, this suggests that there was, and is, no legal barrier to Taiwan's recognition as a state or to its participation in international organizations, only a political barrier maintained by the PRC (Drun and Glaser 2022).

2. Foreign courts have reached different conclusions about Taiwan's status as a "state," even when addressing the same underlying event. A notable example is the October 31, 2001, crash of Singapore Airlines flight SQ006 at Taiwan Taoyuan International Airport (then Chiang Kai-shek International Airport), which led to a series of civil lawsuits in Canada and Singapore. Although the facts and parties in the lawsuits were materially identical, the courts arrived at differing conclusions about Taiwan's status. In *Parent v. Singapore Airlines Ltd.*, the Superior Court of Quebec in Canada determined that Taiwan was a "foreign state" for purposes of Canada's State Immunity Act of 1982. *Parent and ors v Singapore Airlines Ltd and Civil Aeronautics Administration*, Decision of Superior Court of Quebec, 2003 IIJ Can 7285 (QC CS), ILDC 181 (CA 2003). By contrast, the Singapore High Court, in *Anthony Woo v. Singapore Airlines*, ruled that Taiwan was not a "foreign state" under Singapore's State Immunity Act of 1985. *Anthony Woo v. Singapore Airlines* [2003] SGHC 190. The divergence in rulings stemmed from differing interpretations of the respective ministries' refusals to issue certificates affirming Taiwan's status as a state, as well as contrasting views about the role of courts in matters of international relations. These differences highlight the complex and often contested nature of Taiwan's international status.

3. Taiwan Constitutional Court 111 [2022] No. 4.

4. Taiwan has been unable to ratify ILO No. 169 because its membership in the United Nations is blocked by the PRC. For the same reason, Taiwan has been unable to vote on the UNDRIP.

5. Interview, Taitung City, July 30, 2015.

6. Interview, Taitung City, July 30, 2015.

7. Scott Simon (2023b, xv) recounts a similar encounter with a Seediq shopkeeper, who told him, "You, too, are seediq," *seediq* meaning "human" in the Seediq language. Questions about the shopkeeper's meaning of *seediq* in this context served as a launching point for Simon's remarkably in-depth ethnographic study of the lifeworlds, teachings, political struggles, and relationships with nonhuman animals of Taiwan's Indigenous peoples.

8. My Truku friends shared a story about their ancestors' first encounters with Japanese authorities. When asked, "What do you call yourselves?" their ancestors responded, "We are Seediq (humans)." My collaborators recounted this story not only to reflect on the moment of first contact but also to emphasize the artificial nature of the classifications imposed by social scientists and used by colonial authorities.

2. ORDERS IN THE COURT

1. Interview, Hualien County, January 10, 2018.
2. Interview, Hualien County, January 10, 2018.
3. Interview, Hualien County, September 25, 2017.
4. Interview, Hualien City, September 18, 2018.
5. Interview, Tainan City, September 21, 2018.
6. Interview, Hualien City, September 19, 2018.
7. Taipei District Court 75 [1986] No. 26. While the court noted that there was no formal term for "Indigenous people" in Mandarin Chinese, there existed a long history of informal and often derogatory terms for Indigenous peoples, including *huana* (Taiwanese: "savage-barbarian") and, as mentioned earlier, "mountain compatriots" (*shandi tongbao* 山地同胞).
8. Chiayi District Court 92 [2003] No. 151.
9. Interview, Taitung County, April 19, 2018. This life history interview is also the source of the quotations that follow.
10. My thanks to Scott Simon for bringing this point to my attention.
11. The 1997 amendment states, in the relevant part: "The government shall, in accordance with the will of the ethnic groups, protect the status and political participation of aborigines" in the areas of education, culture, transportation, health, economics, and welfare. Simon and Awi Mona (2013, 104n4) observe that the official English version of the text translates the term *yuanzhuminzu* as "aborigines" instead of "Indigenous peoples," which fails to capture the important difference between Indigenous "people" and "peoples."
12. Interview, Tainan City, April 13, 2018.
13. Pingtung District Court 99 [2010] No. 11.
14. Kaohsiung High Court 101 [2012] No. 34.
15. Taiwan Supreme Court 102 [2013] No. 5093.
16. In 2018, the status of macaques and muntjacs was downgraded to "general wildlife," but unlicensed hunting is still punished (Qiu 2018).

17. Taitung District Court 102 [2013] No. 61.
18. Interview, Taitung City, June 1, 2016.
19. Hualien High Court 103 [2014] No. 17; Taiwan Supreme Court 104 [2015] No. 3280.
20. Taiwan Constitutional Court 110 [2021] Interpretation No. 803.
21. Interview, Taitung County, August 11, 2023.
22. Taiwan Supreme Court 111 [2022] No. 110; Taiwan Supreme Court 111 [2022] No. 111.
23. Hsinchu District Court 96 [2007] No. 4.
24. Taiwan High Court 96 [2007] No. 2092.
25. Taiwan Supreme Court 98 [2009] No. 7210.
26. Taiwan High Court 98 [2009] No. 565.
27. Personal communication, Taitung County, October 3, 2018. This event is also the source of the quotations that follow.
28. This reading of Samu is informed by Scott Simon's (2023a) analysis of the Seediq-Truku practice of "thinking with birds" as part of Indigenous hunters' cognitive apparatus.
29. Interview, Taipei City, July 31, 2016.
30. Personal communication, Taipei City, August 1, 2016.
31. Personal communication, Taipei City, August 1, 2016.
32. Other international instruments also emphasize the principle of human dignity. The International Convention on the Elimination of All Forms of Racial Discrimination and the Convention on the Elimination of All Forms of Discrimination Against Women refer to "the principles of the dignity and equality inherent in all human beings" and to "the dignity and worth of the human person and in the equal rights of men and women," respectively. The Convention Against Torture and Other Cruel, Inhuman or Degrading Treatment or Punishment recognizes "the inherent dignity of the human person," and the Convention on the Rights of the Child refers to "the dignity and worth of the human person." The Convention on the Rights of Persons with Disabilities acknowledges "the inherent dignity and worth and the equal and inalienable rights of all members of the human family."
33. For example, the scope of Indigenous peoples' rights to hunt and fish under the ICCPR has been examined in numerous cases, including *Apirana Mahuika et al. v. New Zealand*, Human Rights Committee View on Communication No. 547/1993 (adopted October 27, 2000); *Jouni Lansman et al. v. Finland*, Human Rights Committee View on Communication No. 1023/2001 (adopted March 17, 2005); *George Howard v. Canada*, Human Rights Committee View on Communication No. 879/1999 (adopted July 26, 2005); *Angela Poma Poma v. Peru*, Human Rights Committee View on Communication No. 1457/2006 (adopted March 27, 2009).
34. Taiwan Supreme Court 105 [2016] No. 984.
35. E.g., Taitung District Court 102 [2013] No. 93.
36. Interview, Hualien City, October 20, 2017.
37. Interview, Chiayi City, May 11, 2018.

38. Interview, Taipei City, July 7, 2015.
39. Interview, Taipei City, May 18, 2018.
40. Interview, Hualien City, June 20, 2018.
41. Interview, Hualien City, August 5, 2016.
42. Interview, Hualien City, September 27, 2018.
43. Interview, Hualien County, June 28, 2016.
44. Interview, Taitung County, July 27, 2016.
45. Interview, Hualien City, September 19, 2018.
46. Interview, Taipei City, December 15, 2017.

3. ETHEREAL PRESENCES OF THE AD HOC CHAMBERS

1. Interview, Taipei City, June 18, 2015; May 18, 2016; August 24, 2017.
2. Interview, Taipei City, August 24, 2017.
3. Other official descriptions of the Indigenous court units state that they would "consider the particularities of Indigenous matters and are based on respect for traditional customs, cultures, and values of Indigenous people"; that "the establishment of special Indigenous courts demonstrates judicial respect for multiculturalism and values and implements the concept of reform for the benefit of the judiciary, which will give Indigenous peoples the right to judicial protection more fully" (Judicial Yuan 2012b); that they would "protect the judicial rights of Indigenous peoples" (Judicial Yuan 2018a, 2); and that they were "based on respect for the traditional cultures and values of Indigenous peoples" (Council of Indigenous Peoples 2015).
4. Interview, Taipei City, August 11, 2016.
5. Judicial Assignment Measures, Article 23.
6. Interview, Hualien City, February 2, 2018.
7. Interview, Hualien City, October 24, 2017.
8. Interview, Hualien City, October 23, 2017.
9. Interview, Hualien City, August 5, 2016.
10. The statistical figures used in this paragraph are based on a report prepared by the Judicial Yuan describing the establishment of the ad hoc Chambers of Indigenous Courts (2018a, 5, 8–9, 28).
11. Interview, Chiayi City, May 11, 2018.
12. Interview, Taitung City, July 13, 2016.
13. Interview, Taichung City, November 21, 2017.
14. Interview, Taitung City, September 22, 2017.
15. Interview, Taitung City, July 13, 2016.
16. Interview, Hualien County, March 27, 2018.
17. Interview, Taipei City, May 18, 2016.
18. Interview, Taipei City, October 26, 2018.
19. Personal correspondence, Hualien City, April 16, 2018.
20. For a comparison, independent research by judges remains a contested issue in the United States. Rule 2.9(c) of the American Bar Association Model Code of

Judicial Conduct provides, for instance, that judges "shall not investigate facts in a matter independently, and shall consider only the evidence presented and any facts that may properly be judicially noticed." My thanks to Edith Beerdsen for drawing my attention to this point. The issue of judicial independent research did not appear to be a significant point of contention among the judges whom I encountered in the ad hoc Chambers of Indigenous Courts.

21. Interview, Hualien City, October 24, 2017.
22. Interview, Hualien City, February 2, 2018.
23. Interview, Hualien City, October 9, 2018.
24. Interview, Taipei City, October 26, 2018.
25. Interview, Taipei City, May 14, 2018.
26. Interview, Taipei City, October 11, 2017.
27. Official English translations of Taiwan codes frequently translate the term *jiancha* as "prosecutor" (see, e.g., Code of Criminal Procedure, Art. 3), although they may be more accurately described as "procurators," given their expansive powers. From the perspective of the United States, there is no precise equivalent of procurators in the U.S. legal system; procurators in Taiwan have extensive authority and perform the duties of both U.S. prosecutors and grand juries (Chiu and Fa 1994, 14). In conformity with official translations and other scholarship (e.g., Lewis 2009), I use the term *prosecutor* to refer to this class of legal actor.
28. Interview, Hualien City, September 13, 2017.
29. Interview, Taipei City, April 3, 2018.
30. Personal communication, Hualien City, March 26, 2018.
31. Interview, Taipei City, October 26, 2018.
32. Interview, Tainan City, April 13, 2018.
33. Interview, Hualien City, April 30, 2018.
34. Interview, Hualien City, October 9, 2018.
35. Interview, Taipei City, April 24, 2018.
36. Interview, Hualien City, October 24, 2018.
37. Interview, Taipei City, June 22, 2015.
38. Under Article 77–13 of the *Code of Civil Procedure*, court fees in civil lawsuits involving property rights are calculated using a progressive-decrease rate. This method divides the value of the claim into increments of a first NTD 100,000 unit and a decreasing additional fee for each NTD 100,000 unit of the claim. For litigation involving non-property rights, the filing party must pay a designated fee, presently NTD 3,000 for the court of first instance and NTD 4,500 for appeal to the court of second or third instance (Arts. 77–14 and 77–16).
39. Code of Civil Procedure, Art. 77–23.
40. Code of Civil Procedure, Art. 78. There is no statutory regulation of lawyers' fees in Taiwan, although the Taiwan Bar Association has set standards for fees related to service item charges, total charges, and hourly payments (e.g., a maximum hourly rate of NTD 12,000 for complicated cases) (Chiu and Sung 2015, 4). The Ministry of Finance Taxation Administration issued, for purposes of collecting taxes, the "Criterion of the Income and Expenses for the Professionals" in 2008,

which recommends a NTD 40,000 fee for civil cases in municipalities and regular cities and NTD 35,000 for civil cases in the country. Actual charges, however, are usually based on an agreement between the lawyer and her client and are typically higher than the Taxation Administration standard, but lower than the Taiwan Bar Association's maximum (Chiu and Sung 2015, 5).

41. Interview, Taichung City, July 29, 2016.
42. Interview, Taitung City, July 21, 2016.
43. Interview, Hualien City, September 19, 2018.
44. Interview, Taipei City, September 18, 2018.
45. Code of Criminal Procedure, Arts. 186–189; Code of Civil Procedure, Arts. 312–313–1.
46. Interview, Taipei City, April 24, 2018.

4. ONE COMMUNITY, TWO CONTROVERSIES

1. Interview, Hualien County, March 27, 2018.
2. Interview, Hualien County, September 25, 2017.
3. Interview, Hualien City, October 23, 2017.
4. Interview, Hualien City, October 23, 2017.
5. Personal communication, Hualien County, March 27, 2018.
6. Interview, Hualien City, October 13, 2017.
7. Personal communication, Hualien City, October 18, 2017.
8. Bruce Miller and Gustavo Menezes (2015, 412–13) similarly note the key role that expert witnesses and their reports can play in Indigenous cases and the impact of their exclusion.
9. Interview, Hualien City, October 20, 2017.
10. Interview, Hualien City, October 24, 2017.
11. Interview, Hualien City, October 24, 2017.
12. Interview, Taichung City, July 29, 2016.
13. Interview, Taichung City, July 29, 2016.
14. Interview, Hualien City, October 24, 2017.
15. I provide a few examples here of the concept of "culture" in ROC state laws related to Indigenous peoples. The Constitution provides that "the State affirms cultural pluralism and shall actively preserve and foster the development of aboriginal languages and cultures" (Additional Article 10.11). The Basic Law protects Indigenous peoples' rights to hunt wild animals, collect wild plants and fungus, collect minerals, and utilize water resources for "traditional culture, ritual or self-consumption purposes" (Art. 19). The Wildlife Conservation Act permits hunting for "traditional cultural or ritual hunting, killing or utilization" (Art. 21–1), and the Forestry Act allows the collection of forest products for "traditional living needs and activities" (Art. 15).
16. Pingtung District Court 106 [2017] No. 7.
17. Interview, Hualien City, October 24, 2017.
18. Interview, Taipei City, August 4, 2015.

19. Personal communication, Hualien City, October 22, 2018.
20. Personal communication, Hualien City, October 22, 2018.
21. Interview, Hualien City, October 22, 2018.
22. Interview, Hualien City, October 22, 2018.

5. HYBRID PRACTICES AND LEGAL INDIGENEITIES

1. Personal communication, August 7, 2018.
2. Interview, Taipei City, August 11, 2016.
3. Interview, Taichung City, July 8, 2015.
4. Interview, Taipei City, June 15, 2015.
5. Taiwan High Court 98 [2009] No. 565.
6. Interview, Taipei City, April 3, 2018.
7. Interview, Taipei City, August 5, 2016.
8. Interview, Hualien City, April 13, 2018.
9. See also Jeffrey Martin's (2019) work on Taiwan police officers balancing the duty to implement state law with Chinese moral norms, as well as Scott Simon and Awi Mona's (2015, 23) observations on how balancing figures into police officers' decisions about Indigenous hunting.
10. Interview, Taichung City, July 29, 2016.
11. Interview, Taichung City, July 29, 2016.
12. Interview, Hualien City, October 23, 2017.
13. Interview, Taipei City, August 4, 2015.
14. Interview, Chiayi City, May 11, 2018.
15. Interview, Taichung City, July 29, 2016.
16. Interview, Taipei City, August 4, 2015.
17. Interview, Taichung City, July 29, 2016.
18. Interview, Chiayi County, May 11, 2018.
19. Taipei District Court 101 [2012] No. 1139.
20. Interview, Chiayi County, September 21, 2018. The Tsou *kuba* meeting house is in an elevated building reserved for males to learn about Tsou culture and share knowledge. The Kuba Committee, composed of Tsou men from Dabang village, gathered in the *kuba* men's house to make decisions for the community.
21. Wang Tay-sheng's concept of "customary legislation" (*xiguan lifa* 習慣立法) draws on the idea that law is promulgated societal custom and refers to the enactment of laws that draw their normative content from customary practices rather than other statutes (Wu 2016, 230). Through this, Wang argues that Taiwan can shape its law with legal pluralism.
22. As a classification system used to represent and describe Indigenous life in Taiwan, the categories of habit, customary law, and customary legislation did not necessarily reflect how the Tsou community itself understood the customary rules surrounding their hunting practices. Further, such classification systems can exclude, marginalize, and misrepresent Indigenous groups and their practices.

23. Hualien District Court 105 [2016] No. 26 (emphasis added).

24. Povinelli's understanding of "recognition" may be brought into relief by comparing it to the work of philosopher Charles Taylor (1994), who argues that the "recognition" and preservation of bounded and delimited cultural identities can constitute part of the good life. Taylor appears to express optimism about the possibility of reconciliation through creating a regime of reciprocal dialogue oriented toward a fusion of horizons (Schaap 2003, 530), whereas Povinelli sees an incapacity of liberal states to grapple with alterity (Merlan 2018, 233). In Povinelli's view, inherent within liberal multiculturalism's logic of recognition are possibilities of derangement and rearrangement of the "other" as well as the "self."

25. Kaohsiung District Court 103 [2014] No. 1.

26. Personal communication, Kaohsiung City, July 28, 2016.

27. Kaohsiung High Court 105 [2016] No. 1.

28. Taiwan Supreme Court 108 [2019] No. 2454.

29. Taiwan High Court 107 [2018] No. 34.

30. Personal communication, Taipei City, August 31, 2018.

31. Interview, Taipei City, May 27, 2016.

32. Interview, Hualien City, September 22, 2017.

33. Personal communication, Hualien City, October 6, 2017.

34. Interview, Hualien City, March 30, 2018.

35. As Andrew Schaap (2003, 525) argues, "agonistic reconciliation" involves a form of political recognition that understands how "a relation of antagonism might turn out to be ethical and integrative." Under this approach, the point is not to achieve a common identity, but rather "to make available a space for politics within which citizens divided by the memories of past wrongs could debate and contest the terms of their political association" (Schaap 2003, 525).

6. BOUNDARY INSTITUTIONS AND BEYOND

1. See the Enforcement Act of Convention on the Elimination of All Forms of Discrimination Against Women (2011), Implementation Act of the Convention on the Rights of the Child (2014), Act to Implement the Convention on the Rights of Persons with Disabilities (2014), and Act to Implement United Nations Convention Against Corruption (2015).

2. Interview, Taipei City, August 4, 2015.

BIBLIOGRAPHY

Abas. 2009. "Court Repeals Guilty Verdict of Second Hearing of Beech Tree Case [櫸木案二審有罪法院撤銷原判決]." *Taiwan's Indigenous Peoples Portal* (blog). December 17. http://www.tipp.org.tw/news_article.asp?F_ID=16042&FT_No=1.

Abel, Richard L. 2010. "Law and Society: Project and Practice." *Annual Review of Law and Social Science* 6: 1–23.

Abel, Richard L. 2011. "Epilogue: Just Law?" In *The Paradox of Professionalism: Lawyers and the Possibility of Justice*, edited by Scott L. Cummings, 296–317. Cambridge University Press.

Abu-Lughod, Lila. 1990. "The Romance of Resistance: Tracing Transformations of Power Through Bedouin Women." *American Ethnologist* 17 (1): 41–55.

Albrecht, Don E., and Carol Mulford Albrecht. 2004. "Metro/Nonmetro Residence, Nonmarital Conception, and Conception Outcomes." *Rural Sociology* 69 (3): 430–52.

Alfred, Taiaiake. 1999. *Peace, Power, Righteousness: An Indigenous Manifesto*. Oxford University Press. Reprint, 2009.

Allee, Mark A. 1994. *Law and Local Society in Late Imperial China: Northern Taiwan in the Nineteenth Century*. Stanford University Press.

Allen, Stephen. 2005. "Establishing Autonomous Regimes in the Republic of China: The Salience of International Law for Taiwan's Indigenous Peoples." *Indigenous Law Journal* 4 (Fall): 159–217.

Allio, Fiorella. 1998. "The Austronesian Peoples of Taiwan: Building a Political Platform for Themselves." *China Perspectives* 18 (July–August): 52–60.

Anaya, S. James. 2000. *Indigenous Peoples in International Law*. Oxford University Press.

Andrade, Tonio. 2008. *How Taiwan Became Chinese: Dutch, Spanish, and Han Colonization in the Seventeenth Century*. Columbia University Press.

Apple Daily. 2017. "'Return to Me My Indigenous Hunters Tradition,' Supreme Court First Broadcast of Appeal [「還我原住民獵人傳統」最高院首度直播

非常上訴開庭]." February 9. https://tw.appledaily.com/new/realtime/20170209/1052226/.

Arpin, Isabelle, Marc Barbier, Guillaume Ollivier, and Celine Granjou. 2016. "Institutional Entrepreneurship and Techniques of Inclusiveness in the Creation of the Intergovernmental Platform on Biodiversity and Ecosystem Services." *Ecology and Society* 21 (4): 11–20.

Arvin, Maile. 2019. *Possessing Polynesians: The Science of Settler Colonial Whiteness in Hawai'i and Oceania*. Duke University Press.

Augé, Marc. 1998. *A Sense for the Other: The Timeliness and Relevance of Anthropology*. Translated by Amy Jacobs. Stanford University Press.

Awi Mona. 2007. "International Perspective on the Constitutionality of Indigenous Peoples' Rights." *Taiwan International Studies Quarterly* 3 (2): 85–139.

Awi Mona (Tsai Chih-wei), and Chia-yuan Huang. 2021. "Conflict and Reconciliation Between Civil Law and Indigenous Legal Traditions: The Case of Land Governance in Taiwan." In *Taiwan's Contemporary Indigenous Peoples*, edited by Chia-yuan Huang, Daniel Davies, and Dafydd Fell, 206–22. Routledge.

Awi Mona (Tsai Chih wei), and Scott Simon. 2011. "Imagining First Nations: From Eeyou Istchee (Quebec) to the Seediq and Truku of Taiwan." *Issues and Studies* 47 (3): 29–70.

Barclay, Paul. 2003. "'They Have for the Coast Dwellers a Traditional Hatred': Governing Igorots in Northern Luzon and Central Taiwan, 1895–1915." In *The American Colonial State in the Philippines: Global Perspectives*, edited by Julian Go and Anne L. Foster, 217–55. Duke University Press.

Barclay, Paul. 2005. "Cultural Brokerage and Interethnic Marriage in Colonial Taiwan: Japanese Subalterns and Their Aborigine Wives, 1895–1930." *The Journal of Asian Studies* 64 (2): 323–60.

Barclay, Paul. 2017. *Outcasts of Empire: Japan's Rule on Taiwan's "Savage Border," 1874–1945*. University of California Press.

Barclay, Paul. 2020. "Japanese Empire in Taiwan." *Oxford Research Encyclopedia, Asian History*.

Barth, Frederik. 1998 [1969]. *Ethnic Groups and Boundaries: The Social Organization of Cultural Difference*. Waveland Press.

Basso, Keith. 1990. "'Speaking with Names': Language and Landscape Among the Western Apache." In *Western Apache Language and Culture: Essays in Linguistic Anthropology*, 138–73. University of Arizona Press.

Bekhoven, Jeroen van. 2016. "Identity Crisis: Taiwan's Laws and Regulations on the Status of Indigenous Peoples." *Asia Pacific Law Review* 24 (2): 202–32.

Bekhoven, Jeroen van. 2018. "Unraveling the Double Oppression of Indigenous Peoples in Taiwan and Paraguay: The Rights of Land and Self-Government of Indigenous Peoples." PhD dissertation, National Taiwan University.

Bellwood, Peter. 1984. "A Hypothesis for Austronesian Origins." *Asian Perspectives* 26 (1): 107–17.

Bens, Jonas. 2018. "The Courtroom as an Affective Arrangement: Analysing Atmospheres in Courtroom Ethnography." *The Journal of Legal Pluralism and Unofficial Law* 50 (3): 336–55.

Bernstein, Anya. 2008. "The Social Life of Regulation in Taipei City Hall: The Role of Legality in the Administrative Bureaucracy." *Law & Social Inquiry* 33 (4): 925–54.

Boj Lopez, Floridalma. 2017. "Mobile Archives of Indigeneity: Building La Comunidad Ixim Through Organizing in the Maya Diaspora." *Latino Studies* 15: 201–18.

Borao Mateo, José Eugenio. 2009. *The Spanish Experience in Taiwan, 1626–1642: The Baroque Ending of a Renaissance Endeavor*. Hong Kong University Press.

Bourdieu, Pierre. 1977. *Outline of a Theory of Practice*. Translated by Richard Nice. Cambridge University Press. 1972.

Bourdieu, Pierre. 1990. *The Logic of Practice*. Translated by Richard Nice. Stanford University Press. 1980.

Brković, Čarna. 2015. "Management of Ambiguity: Favours and Flexibility in Bosnia and Herzegovina." *Social Anthropology/Anthropologie Sociale* 23 (3): 268–82.

Brković, Čarna. 2017. *Managing Ambiguity: How Clientelism, Citizenship, and Power Shape Personhood in Bosnia and Herzegovina*. Berghahn Books.

Brown, Melissa J. 2004. *Is Taiwan Chinese? The Impact of Culture, Power, and Migration on Changing Identities*. University of California Press.

Burns, Robert, Marianne Constable, Justin Richland, and Winnifred Sullivan. 2008. "Analyzing the Trial: Interdisciplinary Methods." *PoLAR: Political and Legal Anthropology Review* 31 (2): 303–29.

Butler, Judith. 1990. *Gender Trouble: Feminism and the Subversion of Identity*. Routledge.

Butler, Judith. 1993. *Bodies That Matter: On the Discursive Limits of "Sex."* Routledge.

Cain, Butler. 2021. "'To Deepen and Broaden Our Presence': Taiwan's Strategies for Participating in the International System." *China Currents* 20 (1).

Cattelino, Jessica. 2008. *High Stakes: Florida Seminole Gaming and Sovereignty*. Duke University Press.

Chang, Donatien Huei-tung. 2023. "The Challenge of the Legal System for Autonomous Hunting Management of Indigenous Peoples: Focused on Interpretation No. 803 of the Constitutional Court [原住民族狩獵自主管理法制的挑戰—以司法院大法官釋字第八〇三號解釋爲中心]." *Public Law* [公法研究] 2023 (3): 161–85.

Chang, Hung-chieh. 2018. "An Empirical Study on the Verdicts of Illegal Hunting for Protected Wildlife: Focus on Indigenous Culture Defences [非法獵捕保育類野生動物判決之實證研: 以原住民文化抗辯爲中心]." *Legal Aid and Society Review* 1: 31–69.

Chang, Tao-chou. 2016. "Confronting the Impact of National Participation in Trials on the Judicial Power of Indigenous Peoples [正視國民參與審判對於原住民司法權的影響]." *Tipslaw* [原住民族法學研究室] (February).

Chang, Wen-chen. 2014. "Courts and Judicial Reform in Taiwan: Gradual Transformations Towards the Guardian of Constitutionalism and Rule of Law." In *Asian Courts in Context*, edited by Jiunn-rong Yeh and Wen-chen Chang, 143–82. Cambridge University Press.

Chang, Wen-chen. 2018. "Institutional Independence of the Judiciary: Taiwan's Incomplete Reform." In *Asia-Pacific Judiciaries: Independence, Impartiality and Integrity*, edited by H. P. Lee and Marilyn Pittard, 330–53. Cambridge University Press.

Charlton, Guy C., Xiang Gao, and Da-wei Kuan. 2017. "The Law Relating to Hunting and Gathering Rights in the Traditional Territories of Taiwan's Indigenous Peoples." *Asia Pacific Law Review* 25 (2): 125–48.

Chau, Thompson. 2022. "For Many, Being Taiwanese Means Being Pro-LGBTQ+." *Nikkei Asia*, November 14. https://asia.nikkei.com/Life-Arts/Life/For-many-being-Taiwanese-means-being-pro-LGBTQ.

Chen, De-min. 2012. "On the Establishment of the Ad Hoc Chamber of Indigenous Courts by the Judicial Yuan [論司法院設置原住民族專業法庭]." *Legal Aid Quarterly* [法律扶助] 30: 25–26.

Chen, Jackie. 2000. "Talking About Taiwan—A Conversation Between Bo Yang and Tai Kuo-hui." *Taiwan Panorama*. https://www.taiwan-panorama.com/Articles/Details?Guid=7d4ac19d-0696-4295-9d86-3b724ac0659c&langId=3&CatId=11.

Chen, Thomas Chih-hsiung. 2012. "Legal Education Reform in Taiwan: Are Japan and Korea the Models?" *Journal of Legal Education* 62 (1): 32–65.

Chen, Yi-fong. 1998. "Indigenous Rights Movements, Land Conflicts, and Cultural Politics in Taiwan: A Case Study of Li-Shan." PhD dissertation, Louisiana State University.

Chen, Yu-jie. 2019. "Isolated but Not Oblivious: Taiwan's Acceptance of the Two Major Human Rights Covenants." In *Taiwan and International Human Rights: A Story of Transformation*, edited by Jerome A. Cohen, William P. Alford, and Chang-fa Lo. Springer.

The China Post. 2010. "Atayal Men Taking Beechwood Found Not Guilty." February 11. https://chinapost.nownews.com/20100211-131287.

Chiu, Fred Y. L. 2000. "Suborientalism and the Subimperialist Predicament: Aboriginal Discourse and the Poverty of State-Nation Imagery." *positions: east asia cultures critique* 8 (1): 101–49.

Chiu, Hungdah, and Jyh-pin Fa. 1994. "Taiwan's Legal System and Legal Profession." In *Taiwan Trade and Investment Law*, edited by Mitchell A. Silk, 21–37. Oxford University Press.

Chiu, Ju-na. 2005. "Closing the Gap in Labor Market—The Employment Policy for Indigenous Peoples in Taiwan." East Asian Social Policy Research Network Conference, University of Kent, June 30–July 2. http://www.welfareasia.org/2ndconference/presenter&paper2_fullpaper.htm.

Chiu, Tai-san, and Fu-mei Sung. 2015. "Cost and Fee Allocation in Taiwan Civil Procedure." http://www-personal.umich.edu/~purzel/national_reports/Taiwan%20(ROC).pdf.

Chou, Ching-yuan. 2009. "A Cave in Taiwan: Comfort Women's Memories and the Local Identity." In *Places of Pain and Shame: Dealing with "Difficult Heritage,"* edited by William Logan and Keir Reeves, 114–27. Routledge.

Chun, Allen. 1994. "From Nationalism to Nationalizing: Cultural Imagination and State Formation in Postwar Taiwan." *The Australian Journal of Chinese Affairs* 31 (January): 49–69.

Chun, Allen. 1996. "Fuck Chineseness: On the Ambiguities of Ethnicity as Culture as Identity." *boundary 2* 23 (2): 111–38.

Ciwang, Teyra, and Wan-jung (Wendy) Hsieh. 2023. "Carrying Historical Trauma: Alcohol Use and Healing Among Indigenous Communities in Taiwan." In *Indigenous Reconciliation in Contemporary Taiwan: From Stigma to Hope*, edited by Scott Simon, Jolan Hsieh, and Peter Kang, 121–44. Routledge.

Clifford, James. 1988. *The Predicament of Culture: Twentieth-Century Ethnography, Literature, and Art*. Harvard University Press.

Clough, Ralph N. 1993. "The Status of Taiwan in the New International Legal Order in the Western Pacific." Proceedings of the Annual Meeting, American Society of International Law, Cambridge University.

Cobo, José R. Martínez. 1972. *Preliminary Report: Study of the Problem of Discrimination Against Indigenous Populations*. United Nations Economic and Social Council. E/CN.4/Sub.2/L.566.

Cobo, José R. Martínez. 1986. *Study of the Problem of Discrimination Against Indigenous Populations*. United Nations Economic and Social Council. E/CN.4/Sub.2/1986/7.

Cohen, Amy J., and Bronwen Morgan. 2023. "Prefigurative Legality." *Law & Social Inquiry* 48 (3): 1053–82.

Colangelo, Anthony J. 2016. "A Systems Theory of Fragmentation and Harmonization." *New York University Journal of International Law and Politics* 49 (1): 1–61.

Comaroff, Jean, and John L. Comaroff. 1991. *Of Revelation and Revolution: Christianity, Colonialism, and Consciousness in South Africa, Vol. 1*. University of Chicago Press.

Comaroff, John L., and Simon Roberts. 1981. *Rules and Processes: The Cultural Logic of Dispute in an African Context*. University of Chicago Press.

Conklin, Beth A., and Laura R. Graham. 1995. "The Shifting Middle Ground: Amazonian Indians and Eco-Politics." *American Anthropologist* 97 (4): 695–710.

Cooter, Robert D., and Wolfgang Fikentscher. 1998a. "Indian Common Law: The Role of Custom in American Indian Tribal Courts." *American Journal of Comparative Law* 46: 287–337.

Cooter, Robert D., and Wolfgang Fikentscher. 1998b. "Indian Common Law: The Role of Custom in American Indian Tribal Courts, Part 2." *American Journal of Comparative Law* 46: 509–80.

Coulthard, Glen Sean. 2014. *Red Skin, White Masks: Rejecting the Colonial Politics of Recognition*. University of Minnesota Press.

Council of Indigenous Peoples. 2015. "Judicial Branch Sets Up Special Indigenous Courts [司法院設置原住民族專業法庭（股）]." Council of Indigenous Peoples. http://indigenous.hsinchu.gov.tw/zh-tw/Event/BulletinDetail/50862/?page=6.

Covenants Watch. 2016. *Shadow Report 2016 on Government's Response to the Concluding Observations and Recommendations*. https://en.covenantswatch.org.tw/portfolio/shadow-report-2016-on-governments-response-to-the-concluding-observations-and-recommendations/.

Dai, Xing-sheng. 2015. "Norms and Contemporary Actions of the Truku Snkreygan (Tongmen) [太魯閣族 Snkreygan 部落（銅門部落）的傳統規範與當代集體行動]." *Indigenous Literature* [原住民族文獻], October. https://ihc.cip.gov.tw/EJournal/EJournalCat/272.

Danapan, Paelabang (Sun Ta-chuan). 1991. "To Add Another Zero [再加一個零]." In *Drinking Once in a While [久久酒一次]*, edited by Paelabang Danapan, 174–76. Shanhai Culture Magazine [山海文化雜誌].

De Sousa Santos, Boaventura. 1987. "Law: A Map of Misreading. Toward a Postmodern Conception of Law." *Journal of Law and Society* 14 (3): 279–302.

deLisle, Jacques. 2011. "Taiwan: Sovereignty and Participation in International Organizations." Foreign Policy Research Institute E-Notes.

deLisle, Jacques. 2019. "'All the World's a Stage': Taiwan's Human Rights Performance and Playing to International Norms." In *Taiwan and International Rights: A Story of Transformation*, edited by Jerome A. Cohen, William P. Alford, and Chang-fa Lo, 173–206. Springer.

Democratic Progressive Party. 1999. *White Paper on Foreign Policy for the 21st Century*. Taipei, Taiwan. http://www.taiwandocuments.org/dpp02.htm.

Douglas, Mary. 1966. *Purity and Danger: An Analysis of Concepts of Pollution and Taboo*. Routledge.

Douglas, Mary. 1986. *How Institutions Think*. Syracuse University Press.

Drun, Jessica. 2017. *One China, Multiple Interpretations*. Center for Advanced China Research. https://www.ccpwatch.org/single-post/2017/12/29/one-china-multiple-interpretations.

Drun, Jessica, and Bonnie S. Glaser. 2022. *The Distortion of UN Resolution 2758 to Limit Taiwan's Access to the United Nations*. The German Marshall Fund of the United States. https://www.gmfus.org/news/distortion-un-resolution-2758-and-limits-taiwans-access-united-nations.

e'Akuyana, Yapasuyongu. 2009. "A Brief Discussion of the Ad Hoc Chambers of Indigenous Courts [淺談原住民族專業法庭]." *Judicial Reform Magazine* [司法改革雜誌] 74 (2009/10): 21–24.

Echo-Hawk, Walter R. 2010. *In the Courts of the Conqueror: The 10 Worst Indian Law Cases Ever Decided*. Fulcrum.

Engle, Karen. 2010. *The Elusive Promise of Indigenous Development: Rights, Culture, Strategy*. Duke University Press.

Everington, Keoni. 2017. "Taiwan Aborigines Can Now Legally Hunt for Food." *Taiwan News*, June 9. https://www.taiwannews.com.tw/en/news/3183918.

Executive Yuan. 2012. *Implementation of the International Covenant on Civil and Political Rights: Initial Report Submitted under Article 40 of the Covenant.* https://www.humanrights.moj.gov.tw/media/14393/541517201510.pdf?mediaDL=true.

Executive Yuan. 2016a. *Implementation of the International Covenant on Civil and Political Rights: Second Report Submitted under Article 40 of the Covenant.* http://covenantswatch.org.tw/wp-content/uploads/2017/01/ICCPR_Shadow-Report_final.pdf.

Executive Yuan. 2016b. *Republic of China Yearbook.* https://issuu.com/eyroc/docs/the_republic_of_china_yearbook_2016.

Executive Yuan. 2019. "Austronesian Forum Key Topic at Indigenous Committee Meeting Hosted by Premier Su." https://english.ey.gov.tw/Page/61BF20C3E89B856/249bcf83-e7b7-415d-a825-3cf855f77228.

Farmer, Paul. 2004. *Pathologies of Power: Health, Human Rights, and the New War on the Poor.* University of California Press.

Fassin, Didier. 2011. "Policing Borders, Producing Boundaries: The Governmentality of Immigration in Dark Times." *Annual Review of Anthropology* 40: 213–26.

Focus Taiwan. 2017. "Wang Guang-lu's Hunting Case, Supreme Court Rules Case Suspended Pending Interpretation [王光祿獵槍案 最高法院裁定停審並釋憲]." September 28. https://www.cna.com.tw/news/firstnews/201709285009.aspx.

Forsyth, Miranda. 2009. *A Bird That Flies with Two Wings: Kastom and State Justice Systems in Vanuatu.* ANU E Press.

Foucault, Michel. 1977. *Discipline and Punish: The Birth of the Prison.* Translated by Alan Sheridan. Vintage. Reprint, 1995.

Foucault, Michel. 1982. "The Subject and Power." In *Power: The Essential Works of Foucault, 1954–1984*, edited by James D. Faubion. The New Press.

Foucault, Michel. 1991. "Governmentality." In *The Foucault Effect: Studies in Governmentality*, edited by Graham Burchell, Colin Gordon, and Peter Miller, 87–104. Harvester Wheatsheaf.

Foucault, Michel. 1994. *The Birth of the Clinic: An Archaeology of Medical Perception.* Translated by A. M. Sheridan Smith. Vintage Books.

Freiberg, Arie. 2004. "Innovations in the Court System." Crime in Australia: International Connections, Australian Institute of Criminology International Conference, Melbourne, Australia, November 30.

French, Jan Hoffman. 2009. *Legalizing Identities: Becoming Black or Indian in Brazil's Northeast.* University of North Carolina Press.

Friedman, P. Kerim. 2018. "The Hegemony of the Local: Taiwanese Multiculturalism and Indigenous Identity Politics." *boundary 2* 45 (3): 79–105.

Friedman, Sara L. 2015. *Exceptional States: Chinese Immigrants and Taiwanese Sovereignty.* University of California Press.

Friedman, Sara L. 2021. "Aspirational Sovereignty and Human Rights Advocacy: Audience, Recognition, and the Reach of the Taiwan State." In *The Everyday Lives of Sovereignty: Political Imagination Beyond the State*, edited by Rebecca Bryant and Madeleine Reeves, 89–113. Cornell University Press.

Fujimura, Joan H. 1992. "Crafting Science: Standardized Packages, Boundary Objects, and 'Translation.'" In *Science as Practice and Culture*, edited by Andrew Pickering, 168–211. University of Chicago Press.

Gao, I-an. 2014. "Framing Health: Explanations of Disadvantages in Taiwanese Indigenous Health from the Perspective of the Government, the Media and the Experts." Master's thesis, Department of Political and Economic Studies, University of Helsinki.

Gao, Pat. 2015. "Promoting Indigenous Rights." *Taiwan Today*, February 1. https://taiwantoday.tw/news.php?post=23754&unit=12,29,33.

Gao, Xiang, Guy C. Charlton, and Mitsuhiko A. Takahashi. 2016. "The Legal Recognition of Indigenous Interests in Japan and Taiwan." *Asia Pacific Law Review* 24 (1): 60–82.

Gerber, Abraham. 2017. "Aborigines to Gain New Legal Aid Center." *Taipei Times*, July 27. http://www.taipeitimes.com/News/taiwan/archives/2017/07/27/2003675391.

Gershon, Ilana. 2019. "Porous Social Orders." *American Ethnologist* 46 (4): 404–16.

Gieryn, Thomas F. 1999. *Cultural Boundaries of Science: Credibility on the Line*. University of Chicago Press.

Goffman, Erving. 1959. *The Presentation of Self in Everyday Life*. Doubleday.

Goffman, Erving. 1961. *Asylums: Essays on the Social Situation of Mental Patients and Other Inmates*. Aldine.

Goodwin, Charles. 1994. "Professional Vision." *American Anthropologist* 96 (3): 606–33.

Government of Canada. 2018. "Canada and Taiwan Relations." https://www.international.gc.ca/country-pays/taiwan/relations.aspx?lang=eng.

Gozzi, Raymond, Jr. 1998. "Is Language a Game?" *ETC: A Review of General Semantics* 55 (2): 189–94.

Graham, Laura R., and H. Glenn Penny. 2014. "Performing Indigeneity: Emergent Identity, Self-Determination, and Sovereignty." In *Performing Indigeneity*, edited by Laura R. Graham and H. Glenn Penny, 1–31. University of Nebraska Press.

Green, Sarah F. 2005. *Notes from the Balkans: Locating Marginality and Ambiguity on the Greek-Albanian Border*. Princeton University Press.

Greene, J. Megan. 2016. "Understanding Taiwan's Colonial Past: Using History to Define Taiwan's 21st-Century Identity." In *Area Studies in the Global Age: Community, Place, and Identity*, edited by Edith W. Clowes and Shelly Jarrett Bromberg, 17–33. Northern Illinois University Press.

Greenhouse, Carol. 2005. "Nationalizing the Local: Comparative Notes on the Recent Restructuring of Political Space." In *Human Rights in the 'War on Terror,'* edited by R. A. Wilson, 184–208. Cambridge University Press.

Gustafsson, Karin M., and Rolf Lidskog. 2013. "Boundary Work, Hybrid Practices, and Portable Representations: An Analysis of Global and National Coproductions of Red Lists." *Nature and Culture* 8 (1): 30–52.

Gustafsson, Karin M., and Rolf Lidskog. 2018. "Boundary Organizations and Environmental Governance: Performance, Institutional Design, and Conceptual Development." *Climate Risk Management* 19 (2018): 1–11.

Guston, David H. 1999. "Stabilizing the Boundary Between US Politics and Science: The Role of the Office of Technology Transfer as a Boundary Organization." *Social Studies of Science* 29 (1): 87–111.

Guston, David H. 2000. *Between Politics and Science: Assuring the Integrity and Productivity of Research*. Cambridge University Press.

Guston, David H. 2001. "Boundary Organizations in Environmental Policy and Science: An Introduction." *Science, Technology, & Human Values* 26 (4): 399–408.

Hacking, Ian. 1999. *The Social Construction of What?* Harvard University Press.

Hale, Erin. 2020. "'Always Campaign Time': Why Taiwan's Indigenous People Back KMT." *Al Jazeera*, January 9. https://www.aljazeera.com/news/2020/1/9/always-campaign-time-why-taiwans-indigenous-people-back-kmt.

Hatfield, DJ. 2020. "Good Dances Make Good Guests: Dance, Animation and Sovereign Assertion in 'Amis Country, Taiwan." *Anthropologica* 62 (2020): 337–52.

Hatfield, DJ. 2022. "Registering Sonic Histories in a Multiply Occupied Place: Sound and Survivance in Mangoa'ay, Taiwan." In *Sonic Histories of Occupation: Experiencing Sound and Empire in a Global Context*, edited by Russell P. Skelchy and Jeremy E. Taylor, 148–69. Bloomsbury.

Hejtmanek, Katie Rose. 2016. "Institutions." In *Oxford Bibliographies*.

Herrera, Luz E. 2014. "Encouraging the Development of 'Low Bono' Law Practices." *University of Maryland Law Journal of Race, Religion, Gender & Class* 14 (1): 1–49.

Herzfeld, Michael. 1987. *Anthropology Through the Looking-Glass: Critical Ethnography in the Margins of Europe*. Cambridge University Press.

Hioe, Brian. 2016. "Two Days of Demonstrations Leading Up to Tsai's Apology to Taiwanese Indigenous." *New Bloom*, August 1. https://newbloommag.net/2016/08/01/tsai-apology-demonstrations-eng/.

Hioe, Brian. 2018. "Indigenous City Councilor's Swearing-In Ceremony Declared Invalid for Being Conducted in Amis." *New Bloom*, December 28. https://newbloommag.net/2018/12/28/ingay-tali-oath/.

Hirano, Katsuya, Lorenzo Veracini, and Toulouse-Antonin Roy. 2021. "Vanishing Natives and Taiwan's Settler-Colonial Unconscious." In *Indigenous Knowledge in Taiwan and Beyond*, edited by Shu-mei Shih and Lin-chin Tsai, 225–48. Springer.

Ho, Karen. 2009. *Liquidated: An Ethnography of Wall Street*. Duke University Press.

Hoekema, Andre. 2017. "The Conundrum of Cross-Cultural Understanding in the Practice of Law." *The Journal of Legal Pluralism and Unofficial Law* 49 (1): 67–84.

Horton, Chris. 2018. "As U.N. Gathers, Taiwan, Frozen Out, Struggles to Get Noticed." *New York Times*, September 21. https://www.nytimes.com/2018/09/21/world/asia/taiwan-united-nations-joseph-wu.html.

Hou, Hsiao-i, and Chia-kai Huang. 2012. "An Analysis of Taiwanese Aboriginal Students' Educational Aspirations." *Higher Education Studies* 2 (2): 79–99.

Hsiang, Cheng-chen, and Jason Pan. 2013. "Paiwan Man Wins Rifle Battle in Court." *Taipei Times*, December 18. http://www.taipeitimes.com/News/taiwan/print/2013/12/18/2003579289.

Hsiao, Alison. 2015. "Puyuma Protest Hunters' Arrest." *Taipei Times*, January 3. https://www.taipeitimes.com/News/taiwan/archives/2015/01/03/2003608362.

Hsieh, Hsing-en, and Mathew Mazzetta. 2024. "Supreme Court Overturns Bunun Man's Illegal Hunting Convictions." *Focus Taiwan*, March 14. https://focustaiwan.tw/society/202403140019.

Hsu, Ching-fang, Ivan Kan-hsueh Chiang, and Yun-chien Chang. 2020. "Pro Bono Is Pro, Low Bono Is Low: Qualitative and Quantitative Analysis of Lawyers' Legal Aid Participation." *NYU Law and Economics Research Paper Series* No. 19–24: 1–35.

Hsu, Hui-yen. 2015. "The Establishment of Indigenous Courts and the Right to a Fair Trial of Indigenous Offenders in Criminal Procedures." International Conference on the Prospect and Challenge of Indigenous Legal Institutions, Fuhua International Culture and Education Center in Taipei, Taiwan, May 30.

Hsu, Wen-hsiung. 1980. "From Aboriginal Island to Chinese Frontier: The Development of Taiwan Before 1683." In *China's Island Frontier: Studies in the Historical Geography of Taiwan*, edited by Ronald G. Knapp, 3–28. University Press of Hawaii and Research Corporation of the University of Hawaii.

Huang, Chih-huei. 2001. "The *Yamatodamashi* of the Takasago Volunteers of Taiwan: A Reading of the Postcolonial Situation." In *Globalizing Japan: Ethnography of the Japanese Presence in Asia, Europe, and America*, edited by Harumi Befu and Sylvie Guichard-Anguis, 222–50. Routledge.

Huang, Shu-min, and Shao-hua Liu. 2016. "Discrimination and Incorporation of Taiwanese Indigenous Austronesian Peoples." *Asian Ethnicity* 17 (2): 294–312.

Huteson, Greg. 2003. "Sociolinguistic Survey Report for the Tona and Maga Dialects of the Rukai Language." *SIL International*.

Hwai, Lee Seok. 2019. "Xi Jinping Says China 'Must Be, Will Be' Reunified with Taiwan." *The Straits Times*, January 2. https://www.straitstimes.com/asia/east-asia/xi-jinping-says-china-must-be-will-be-reunified-with-taiwan.

Indigenous Historical Justice and Transitional Justice Committee (IHJTJ Committee). 2019. "Indigenous Peoples of Taiwan to President Xi Jinping of China [台灣原住民族致中國習近平主席]." *Apple Daily*, January 8. https://gov.hackmd.io/s/SyKTh6bM4.

Jacobs, J. Bruce. 2019. "Myth and Reality in Taiwan's Democratisation." *Asian Studies Review* 43 (1): 164–77.

Jennings, Ralph. 2014. "Taiwan MPs Give Aborigines Greater Autonomy." *Voice of America*, January 20. https://www.voanews.com/a/taiwan-mps-aborigines-greater-autonomy/1833500.html.

Johnson, Giff. 2019. "Marshall Islands Back Taiwan." *RNZ*, September 19. https://www.rnz.co.nz/international/pacific-news/399121/marshall-islands-back-taiwan.

Johnson, Greg. 2014. "Bone-Deep Indigeneity: Theorizing Hawaiian Care for the State and Its Broken Apparatuses." In *Performing Indigeneity*, edited by Laura R. Graham and H. Glenn Penny, 247–72. University of Nebraska Press.

Juan, Shao-chiu, Tamara Awerbuch-Friedlander, and Richard Levins. 2016. "Ethnic Density and Mortality: Aboriginal Population Health in Taiwan." *Public Health Reviews* 37 (11): 1–8.

Judicial Yuan. 2012a. "Indigenous Courts [原住民法庭]." http://www.judicial.gov.tw/videonews/video8-5.asp.

Judicial Yuan. 2012b. "Judicial Yuan Designated 9 Courts or Special Divisions for Indigenous Peoples on January 1, 2013 [司法院指定9地院 102.1.1 設原住民族專庭或專股]." *Judicial Weekly E-paper*, October 11.

Judicial Yuan. 2012c. Letter no. 1010028460 to Taiwan High Court and Other Courts. On file with author.

Judicial Yuan. 2014. Letter no. 1030016783 to Taiwan High Court and Other Courts. On file with author.

Judicial Yuan. 2017. *Presidential Judicial Reform Conference Report* [總統府司法改革國是會議]. September 8.

Judicial Yuan. 2018a. *The Establishment and Implementation of the Indigenous Courts* [原住民族法庭設置沿革與施行成效]. Unpublished.

Judicial Yuan. 2018b. "Judicial Yuan Website." https://www.judicial.gov.tw/index.asp.

Judicial Yuan. 2020. "District Courts—Cases Commenced, Terminated, and Pending." https://www.judicial.gov.tw/juds/report/eg-10.htm.

Kafka, Franz. 1925. *The Trial*. Schocken Books. Reprint, 1999.

Kalt, Joseph P., and Joseph William Singer. 2004. "Myths and Realities of Tribal Sovereignty: The Law and Economics of Indian Self-Rule." Native Issues Research Symposium, Harvard University John F. Kennedy School of Government.

Kant, Immanuel. 1785. "Groundwork of the Metaphysics of Morals." In *Immanuel Kant: Practical Philosophy*. Translated by Mary J. Gregor. Cambridge University Press. Reprint, 1996.

Kauanui, J. Kēhaulani. 2008. *Hawaiian Blood: Colonialism and the Politics of Sovereignty and Indigeneity*. Duke University Press.

Kennedy, Brian L. 2003. "Walking the Fine Line in Taiwan's New Criminal Code." *American Journal of Chinese Studies* 10 (2): 111–17.

Kennedy, Brian L. 2007. "Changes to Taiwan's Legal Professions: Judges, Prosecutors and Attorneys." *American Journal of Chinese Studies* 14 (1): 5–24.

Kermode, Frank. 2000. *The Sense of an Ending: Studies in the Theory of Fiction*. Oxford University Press.

King, Michael S. 2003. "Applying Therapeutic Jurisprudence in Regional Areas—The Western Australian Experience." *E Law: Murdoch University Electronic Journal of Law* 10 (2).

Ko, Shu-ling. 2004. "Truku Delighted at Official Recognition." *Taipei Times*, January 15. http://www.taipeitimes.com/News/taiwan/archives/2004/01/15/2003087672.

Ku, Kun-hui. 2012. "Rights to Recognition: Minorities and Indigenous Politics in Emerging Taiwan Nationalism." In *Taiwan Since Martial Law: Society, Culture,*

Politics, Economy, edited by David Blundell, 91–129. Shung Ye Museum of Formosan Aborigines, University of California, and National Taiwan University Press.

Kuan, Da-wei. 2010. "Transitional Justice and Indigenous Land Rights: The Experience of Indigenous Peoples' Struggle in Taiwan." Bilateral Conference (Taiwan and Austria) for Justice and Injustice Problems in Transitional Societies. https://pdfs.semanticscholar.org/4215/5baf3d19d4ad9fffae09e630567l6a302bb3.pdf.

Kyōko, Matsuda. 2003. "Inō Kanori's 'History' of Taiwan: Colonial Ethnology, the Civilizing Mission and Struggles for Survival in East Asia." *History and Anthropology* 14 (2): 179–96.

Lai, Ping-yu. 2013. "Refuse to Relocate: Katipu, Taitung County Government, and Taitung City Office First Debates in Court [拒絕遷葬 卡地布與台東縣府、台東市公所法院首攻防]." Environmental Information Center [環境資訊中心], May 3. https://e-info.org.tw/node/85583.

Lamont, Michèle, and Virág Molnár. 2002. "The Study of Boundaries in the Social Sciences." *Annual Review of Sociology* 28: 167–95.

Latour, Bruno. 1993. *We Have Never Been Modern*. Translated by Catherine Porter. Harvard University Press.

Lee, Hsin-yin. 2021. "Indigenous Languages Indispensable Voice of Taiwan: President." *Focus Taiwan*, February 20. https://focustaiwan.tw/culture/202102200014.

Lee, I-chao, Chia-hui Chao, Yu-je Lee, and Lung-yu Chang. 2011. "Reflections on the Education and Employment of Indigenous Taiwanese." *World Transactions on Engineering and Technology Education* 9 (1): 60–67.

Lee, Liling. 2015. "Problem-Solving Courts for Taiwan Family Courts: Current Preface and Future Prospects in Domestic Violence." University of California, Berkeley, School of Law. http://digitalassets.lib.berkeley.edu/etd/ucb/text/Lee_berkeley_0028E_15848.pdf.

Legal Aid Foundation. 2018a. "Latest News [最新消息]." https://www.laf.org.tw/indigenous/index.php?action=news_detail&cid=5&id=20.

Legal Aid Foundation. 2018b. *Legal Aid Foundation (Taiwan) Annual Report*. https://www.laf.org.tw/en/publication.

Legal Aid Foundation. 2018c. "Make the Law Support Indigenous Peoples: Inauguration Ceremony of the Legal Aid Foundation Legal Center of Indigenous Peoples [讓法律成為原民的後盾－法律扶助基金會原住民族法律服務中心揭牌典禮]." Legal Aid Foundation, March 13. https://www.laf.org.tw/index.php?action=news_detail&p=5&id=5722.

Legal Aid Foundation. 2019. *Legal Aid Foundation (Taiwan) Annual Report*. https://www.laf.org.tw/en/index.php?action=report.

Legal Center of Indigenous Peoples (LCIP). 2018. Untitled Facebook image. August 12. https://www.facebook.com/LafIndigenous/photos/679131569114327.

Lewis, Margaret K. 2009. "Taiwan's New Adversarial System and the Overlooked Challenge of Efficiency-Driven Reform." *Virginia Journal of International Law* 49 (3): 651–726.

Lim, Benjamin Kang. 2011. "Timeline: Taiwan's Road to Democracy." Reuters, 2011. https://www.reuters.com/article/us-taiwan-election-timeline/timeline-taiwans-road-to-democracy-idUSTRE7BC0E320111213.

Lin, Chang-shun, and Luke Sabatier. 2022. "Constitutional Court Strikes Down Legal Clause on Indigenous Status." *Focus Taiwan*, April 1. https://focustaiwan.tw/politics/202204010022.

Lin, Chih-chieh. 2010. "Failing to Achieve the Goal: A Feminist Perspective on Why Rape Law Reform in Taiwan Has Been Unsuccessful." *Duke Journal of Gender Law & Policy* 18: 163–201.

Lin, Hui-zhen. 2023. "Were the Draft Indigenous 'Hunting Gun Management Measures' to Ensure Safety or Suppress Hunting Culture? [原住民《獵槍管理辦法》草案出爐，保障安全或壓抑狩獵文化？]" *The Reporter* [報導者], March 15. https://www.twreporter.org/a/taiwanese-indigenous-peoples-hunting-rifle-draft-regulation.

Lin, Meng-huang. 2013. "Vanishing Witness Testimony? Discussing the Judge's Trial Spirit Based on the Paiwan Uncle-Child Touching 'Alili' Incident [消失的證人證詞？—從排灣族舅公摸童「阿力力」事件談法官的審判靈]." *Judicial Reform Magazine* [司法改革雜誌] 95 (2013/04): 72–78.

Lin, Pei-hsi. 2016. "Firearms, Technology and Culture: Resistance of Taiwanese Indigenes to Chinese, European and Japanese Encroachment in a Global Context circa 1860–1914." PhD dissertation, Nottingham Trent University.

Lin, Yu-ying. 2017. "The Difficult Problem of Indigenous Crime—Starting from the Alili Case (Taiwan Taitung District Court 101, No. 8 and Taiwan Hualien High Court 101, No. 47) [原住民犯罪之難題—自阿力力案出發(臺灣台東地方法院 101 年度侵訴字第 8 號、臺灣高等法院花蓮分院 101 年度侵上訴字第 47 號刑事判決)]." *Judicial Aspirations* [司法新聲] 123: 78–96.

Lindberg, Kajsa, Lars Walter, and Elena Raviola. 2017. "Performing Boundary Work: The Emergence of a New Practice in a Hybrid Operating Room." *Social Science & Medicine* 182 (2017): 81–88.

Lo, Ching, and Dau-jye Lu. 2021. "Exploring the Governing Institutions of Wildlife Resources in an Indigenous Community: A Case Study of Taromak, Taitung, Taiwan [一個原住民部落的野生動物資源體制探索：以達魯瑪克爲例]." *Taiwan Journal of Indigenous Studies* [台灣原住民族研究] 14 (1): 89–126.

Lo, Shu-fen, Fang-tsuang Lu, An-chi O. Yang, Jia-ling Zeng, Ya-yu Yang, Yen-ting Lo, Yu-hsuan Chang, and Ting-hsuan Pai. 2023. "Metabolic Syndrome-Related Knowledge, Attitudes, and Behavior Among Indigenous Communities in Taiwan: A Cross-Sectional Study." *International Journal of Environmental Research and Public Health* 20 (3): 2547–57.

Lord, Winston. 1971. Nixon Presidential Materials, NSC Files, Box 1035, Files for the President-China Material, HAK visit to PRC, October 21, 1971, Memcons-originals. National Archives.

LRC (Law Reform Commission of Western Australia). 2005. *Aboriginal Customary Laws*, Discussion Paper Project No. 94 (December).

Ma, Wei-fen, Chia-ing Li, Ellen R. Gritz, Irene Tamí-Maury, Cho Lam, and Cheng-chieh Lin. 2017. "A Symbol of Connectedness Between the Self and the Tribal Home: Betel Quid in the Lives of Indigenous Taiwanese [連接自我與家鄉的信物—檳榔在台灣原住民族文化中的角色]." *The Journal of Nursing* [護理雜誌] 64 (3): 65–73.

Marchetti, Elena, and Kathleen Daly. 2004. "Indigenous Courts and Justice Practices in Australia." *Trends & Issues in Crime and Criminal Justice* 277: 1–6.

Marsden, David. 1994. "Indigenous Management and the Management of Indigenous Knowledge." In *Anthropology of Organizations*, edited by Susan Wright, 39–53. Routledge.

Martin, Jeffrey T. 2019. *Sentiment, Reason, and Law: Policing in the Republic of China on Taiwan*. Cornell University Press.

Martin, Steven Andrew. 2006. "Ethnohistorical Perspectives of the Bunun: A Case Study of Laipunuk, Taiwan." Master's thesis, Taiwan Studies, National Chengchi University.

Masau Mona. 1984. *The Atayal Culture* [泰雅族的文化]. Taipei: World College of Journalism.

Mazel, Odette. 2009. "The Evolution of Rights: Indigenous Peoples and International Law." *Australian Indigenous Law Review* 13 (1): 140–58.

Maziere, Christophe. 2011. "Taiwan Aboriginal Peoples in Global Perspective: An Interview with Monanung." YouTube, https://www.youtube.com/watch?v=4DASBsWk190.

McFadden, Patrick M. 1988. "The Balancing Test." *Boston College Law Review* 29 (3): 585–656.

McMillan, L. Jane. 2011. "Colonial Traditions, Co-optations, and *Mi'kmaq* Legal Consciousness." *Law & Social Inquiry* 36 (1): 171–200.

Merlan, Francesca. 2009. "Indigeneity: Global and Local." *Current Anthropology* 50 (3): 303–33.

Merlan, Francesca. 2018. *Dynamics of Difference in Australia: Indigenous Past and Present in a Settler Country*. University of Pennsylvania Press.

Merry, Sally Engle. 1988. "Legal Pluralism." *Law & Society Review* 22 (5): 869–96.

Merry, Sally Engle. 2000. *Colonizing Hawai'i: The Cultural Power of Law*. Princeton University Press.

Merry, Sally Engle. 2006. *Human Rights and Gender Violence: Translating International Law into Local Justice*. University of Chicago Press.

Meskill, Johanna. 1979. *A Chinese Pioneer Family: The Lins of Wu-feng, Taiwan, 1729–1895*. Princeton University Press.

Miller, Bruce Granville. 2001. *The Problem of Justice: Tradition and Law in the Coast Salish World*. University of Nebraska Press.

Miller, Bruce Granville. 2023. *Witness to the Human Rights Tribunals: How the System Fails Indigenous Peoples*. UBC Press.

Miller, Bruce Granville, and Gustavo Menezes. 2015. "Anthropological Experts and the Legal System: Brazil and Canada." *American Indian Quarterly* 39 (4): 391–430.

Miller, Clark. 2001. "Hybrid Management: Boundary Organizations, Science Policy, and Environmental Governance in the Climate Regime." *Science, Technology, & Human Values* 26 (4): 478–500.

Moore, Sally Falk. 1978. *Law as Process: An Anthropological Approach*. Routledge & Kegan Paul.

Moore, Sally Falk. 1986. *Social Facts and Fabrications: "Customary" Law on Kilimanjaro, 1880–1980*. Cambridge University Press.

Morphy, Howard. 2006. "Sites of Persuasion: Yingapungapu at the National Museum of Australia." In *Museum Frictions: Public Cultures/Global Transformations*, edited by Ivan Karp, Corinne Kratz, Lynn Szwaja, and Tomás Ybarra-Frausto, 469–99. Duke University Press.

Moser, Michael J. 1982. *Law and Social Change in a Chinese Community: A Case Study from Rural Taiwan*. Oceana.

Munsterhjelm, Mark. 2002. "The First Nations of Taiwan: A Special Report on Taiwan's Indigenous Peoples." *Cultural Survival Quarterly* 26 (2): 53–55.

Munsterhjelm, Mark. 2014. *Living Dead in the Pacific: Racism and Sovereignty in Genetics Research on Taiwan Aborigines*. UBC Press.

Nadasdy, Paul. 2002. "'Property' and Aboriginal Land Claims in the Canadian Subarctic: Some Theoretical Considerations." *American Anthropologist* 104 (1): 247–61.

Nader, Laura. 1972. "Up the Anthropologist: Perspectives Gained from Studying Up." In *Reinventing Anthropology*, edited by Dell H. Hymes. Vintage Books.

Nader, Laura. 1990. *Harmony Ideology: Justice and Control in a Zapotec Mountain Village*. Stanford University Press.

NCAO (National Cultural Assets Online). 2017. "Earth-Oxen Trench Yangmei Section [土牛溝楊梅段]." National Cultural Assets Online [國家文化資產網]. https://nchdb.boch.gov.tw/assets/overview/culturalLandscape/20150113000001.

NDHU (National Dong Hwa University). 2020. *The Current Situation of Indigenous Peoples' Hunting and Fishing Governance and the Development of Self-Management-Spatial Ecology and the Development of Autonomous Management in the Modern Hunting Grounds of the Taroko People in Hualien (109–111): Initial Report* [原住民族漁獵治理現況與自主管理的發展-花蓮太魯閣族近代獵場的空間生態學與自主管理的發展 (109–111)：期初報告書]. National Dong Hwa University (Hualien, Taiwan).

Nenozō, Utsushikawa, Mabuchi Tōichi, and Nobuto Miyamoto. 1935. *The Formosan Native Tribes: A Genealogical and Classificatory Study, Vol. 1* [壺湾高砂族 系統所厨 の研究 第一冊(本篇)]. Taihoku Imperial University. Reprint, 1988.

Nesper, Larry. 2007. "Negotiating Jurisprudence in Tribal Court and the Emergence of a Tribal State: The Lac du Flambeau Ojibwe." *Current Anthropology* 48 (5): 675–99.

Nesterova, Yulia. 2019. "Teaching Indigenous Children in Taiwan: Tensions, Complexities and Opportunities." *Global Studies of Childhood* 9 (2): 156–66.

Newman, Jess Marie. 2019. "'There Is a Big Question Mark': Managing Ambiguity in a Moroccan Maternity Ward." *Medical Anthropology Quarterly* 33 (3): 386–402.

The News Lens. 2015. "Tongmen Community Fired Guns to Block the Road but Declined to Prosecute. The Prosecutor Said: Understanding the Situation of Indigenous Peoples and Respecting Their Traditional Culture [銅門部落鳴槍封路不起訴，檢方：理解原住民族處境、尊重傳統文化]." October 20. https://www.thenewslens.com/article/26849.

Newton, Nell Jessup. 1998. "Tribal Court Praxis: One Year in the Life of Twenty Indian Tribal Courts." *American Indian Law Review* 22 (2): 285–353.

Niezen, Ronald. 2003a. "Culture and the Judiciary: The Meaning of the Culture Concept as a Source of Aboriginal Rights in Canada." *Canadian Journal of Law and Society* 18 (2): 1–26.

Niezen, Ronald. 2003b. *The Origins of Indigenism: Human Rights and the Politics of Identity.* University of California Press.

OED. 2022. *Oxford English Dictionary.* Oxford University Press.

Ong, Aihwa. 2006. *Neoliberalism as Exception: Mutations in Citizenship and Sovereignty.* Duke University Press.

Palemeq, Yedda. 2012. "No People Are an Island: On Taiwanese Indigenous Peoples in the Permanent Forum and the Austronesian Forum." In *Die indigenen Völker Taiwans: Vorträge zur Geschichte und Gesellschaft Taiwans*, edited by Songa Peschek, 123–42. Peter Lang.

Parker, John, and Beatrice Crona. 2012. "On Being All Things to All People: Boundary Organizations and the Contemporary Research University." *Social Studies of Science* 42 (2): 262–89.

Pecoraro, Fernando. 1977. *Essai de dictionnaire Taroko-Français.* EHESS.

Pence, Ellen. 1997. "Safety for Battered Women in a Textually Mediated Legal System." PhD dissertation, University of Toronto.

Perley, Bernard. 2011. *Defying Maliseet Language Death: Emergent Vitalities of Language, Culture, and Identity in Eastern Canada.* University of Nebraska Press.

Piechowiak, Marek. 1999. "What Are Human Rights? The Concept of Human Rights and Their Extra-Legal Justification." In *An Introduction to the International Protection of Human Rights*, edited by Raija Hanski and Markku Suksi, 3–14. Institute for Human Rights.

Povinelli, Elizabeth A. 2002. *The Cunning of Recognition: Indigenous Alterities and the Making of Australian Multiculturalism.* Duke University Press.

Pruitt, Lisa R. 2014. "The Rural Lawscape: Space Tames Law Tames Space." In *The Expanding Spaces of Law: A Timely Legal Geography*, edited by Irus Braverman, Nicholas Blomley, David Delaney, and Alexandre Kedar, 190–214. Stanford University Press.

Qiu, Li-rong. 2018. "Formosan Muntjac, Macaque and 8 Animals Will Receive a Downgraded Conservation Class, Arbitrary Hunting Will Still Be Punished [山羌、獼猴等8動物從保育類除名　任意獵捕仍將受罰]." *Newtalk.tw*, June 27. https://newtalk.tw/news/view/2018-06-27/129055.

Rai, Shirin M. 2010. "Analysing Ceremony and Ritual in Parliament." *The Journal of Legislative Studies* 16 (3): 284–97.

Richland, Justin. 2008. *Arguing with Tradition: The Language of Law in Hopi Tribal Court*. University of Chicago Press.

Richland, Justin. 2021. *Cooperation without Submission: Indigenous Jurisdictions in Native Nation–US Engagements*. University of Chicago Press.

Rifkin, Mark. 2011. *When Did Indians Become Straight? Kinship, the History of Sexuality, and Native Sovereignty*. Oxford University Press.

Rifkin, Mark. 2014. *Settler Common Sense: Queerness and Everyday Colonialism in the American Renaissance*. University of Minnesota Press.

Rigger, Shelley. 2002. "Nationalism versus Citizenship in the Republic of China on Taiwan." In *Changing Meanings of Citizenship in Modern China*, edited by Merle Goldman and Elizabeth J. Perry. Harvard University Press.

Riles, Annelise. 1998. "Infinity Within the Brackets." *American Ethnologist* 25 (3): 378–98.

Riles, Annelise. 2006. "Anthropology, Human Rights, and Legal Knowledge: Culture in the Iron Cage." *American Anthropologist* 108 (1): 52–65.

Ruckus. 2018. "RUCKUS Changes the World of Indigenous Communities in Taiwan." https://pt.commscope.com/resources/case-studies/taiwan-indigenous/.

Rudin, Jonathan. 2009. "Addressing Aboriginal Overrepresentation Post-*Gladue*: A Realistic Assessment of How Social Change Occurs." *Criminal Law Quarterly* 54: 447–69.

Rutherford, Danilyn. 2009. "Sympathy, State Building, and the Experience of Empire." *Cultural Anthropology* 24 (1): 1–32.

Sack, Robert D. 1993. "The Power of Place and Space." *Geographical Review* 83 (3): 326–29.

Sandberg McGuinne, Johan. 2014. "Official Definitions of Indigeneity." *Indigeneity, Language and Authenticity* (blog). https://johansandbergmcguinne.wordpress.com/official-definitions-of-indigeneity/.

Sapignoli, Maria. 2017. "'Bushmen' in the Law: Evidence and Identity in Botswana's High Court." *PoLAR: Political and Legal Anthropology Review* 40 (2): 210–25.

Schaap, Andrew. 2003. "Political Recognition Through a Struggle for Recognition?" *Social & Legal Studies* 13 (4): 523–40.

Schafferer, Christian. 2003. *The Power of the Ballot Box: Political Development and Election Campaigning in Taiwan*. Lexington Books.

Schubert, Gunter, ed. 2016. *Routledge Handbook of Contemporary Taiwan*. Routledge.

Scott, James C. 1985. *Weapons of the Weak: Everyday Forms of Peasant Resistance*. Yale University Press.

Scott, James C., John Tehranian, and Jeremy Mathias. 2002. "The Production of Legal Identities Proper to States: The Case of the Permanent Family Surname." *Comparative Studies in Society and History* 44 (1): 4–44.

Shan, Shelley. 2012. "Tilting Trains to Be Named 'Puyuma.'" *Taipei Times*, July 27. https://www.taipeitimes.com/News/taiwan/archives/2012/07/27/2003538762.

Shepherd, John Robert. 1993. *Statecraft and Political Economy on the Taiwan Frontier, 1600–1800*. Stanford University Press.
Shih, Cheng-feng. 1999. "Legal Status of the Indigenous Peoples in Taiwan." International Conference on the Rights of the Indigenous Peoples, Taipei, Taiwan, June 18–20. https://faculty.ndhu.edu.tw/~cfshih/deault2_99-06-18.htm.
Shih, Shu-mei. 2011. "The Concept of the Sinophone." *PMLA* 126 (3): 709–18.
Simon, Scott. 2002. "The Underside of a Miracle: Industrialization, Land, and Taiwan's Indigenous Peoples." *Cultural Survival Quarterly* 26 (2): 64–67.
Simon, Scott. 2009. "Indigenous Peoples and Hunting Rights." In *Confronting Discrimination and Inequality in China: Chinese and Canadian Perspectives*, edited by Errol P. Mendes and Sakunthala Srighanthan, 405–21. University of Ottawa Press.
Simon, Scott. 2010. "Negotiating Power: Elections and the Constitution of Indigenous Taiwan." *American Ethnologist* 37 (4): 726–40.
Simon, Scott. 2011. "Multiculturalism and Indigenism: Contrasting the Experiences of Canada and Taiwan." In *Politics of Difference in Taiwan*, edited by Tak-Wing Ngo and Hong-zen Wang, 14–33. Routledge.
Simon, Scott. 2012a. "Politics and Headhunting Among the Formosan Sejiq: Ethnohistorical Perspectives." *Oceania* 82 (2): 164–85.
Simon, Scott. 2012b. *Sadyaq Balae! L'autochtonie formosane dans tous ses états*. Presses de l'Université Laval.
Simon, Scott. 2013. "Of Boars and Men: Indigenous Knowledge and Co-management in Taiwan." *Human Organization* 72 (3): 220–29.
Simon, Scott. 2015a. "Making Natives: Japan and the Creation of Indigenous Formosa." In *Japanese Taiwan: Colonial Rule and Its Contested Legacy*, edited by Andrew D. Morris, 75–92. Bloomsbury Academic.
Simon, Scott. 2015b. "Real People, Real Dogs, and Pigs for the Ancestors: The Moral Universe of 'Domestication' in Indigenous Taiwan." *American Anthropologist* 117 (4): 693–709.
Simon, Scott. 2016. "From the Village to the United Nations and Back Again: Aboriginal Taiwan and International Indigenism [從部落到聯合國及再返回：台灣原住民與國際原住民主義]." *Taiwan Journal of Indigenous Studies* [台灣原住民族研究季刊] 9 (3): 49–89.
Simon, Scott. 2017. "All Our Relations: Indigenous Rights Movements in Contemporary Taiwan." In *Taiwan's Social Movements Under Ma Ying-jeou: From the Wild Strawberries to the Sunflowers*, edited by Dafydd Fell, 236–57. Routledge.
Simon, Scott. 2021. "The Limits of Indigenous Hunting Rights in Taiwan." *East Asia Forum*, June 30. https://www.eastasiaforum.org/2021/06/30/the-limits-of-indigenous-hunting-rights-in-taiwan/.
Simon, Scott. 2023a. "Thinking with Birds: The Cognition of Hunting in the Formosan Highlands (Taiwan)." American Anthropological Association Annual Conference, Toronto, Canada.
Simon, Scott. 2023b. *Truly Human: Indigeneity and Indigenous Resurgence on Formosa*. University of Toronto Press.

Simon, Scott, and Awi Mona (Chih-wei Tsai). 2013. "Human Rights and Indigenous Self-Government: The Taiwan Experience." In *Human Rights and the Third World: Issues and Discourses*, edited by Subrata Sankar Bagchi and Arnab Das, 99–122. Lexington Books.

Simon, Scott, and Awi Mona (Chih-wei Tsai). 2015. "Indigenous Rights and Wildlife Conservation: The Vernacularization of International Law on Taiwan." *Taiwan Human Rights Journal* [台灣人權學刊] 3 (1): 3–31.

Simon, Scott, and Awi Mona. 2023. "Between Legal Indigeneity and Indigenous Sovereignty in Taiwan: Insights from Critical Race Theory." *Social Inclusion* 11 (2): 187–97.

Simpson, Audra. 2014. *Mohawk Interruptus: Political Life Across the Borders of Settler States*. Duke University Press.

Simpson, Audra. 2016. "Consent's Revenge." *Cultural Anthropology* 31 (3): 326–33.

Simpson, Leanne Betasamosake. 2014. "Land as Pedagogy: Nishnaabeg Intelligence and Rebellious Transformation." *Decolonization: Indigeneity, Education & Society* 3 (3): 1–25.

Smith, Glenn. 2014. "Taiwan Indigenous Television Approaches 10 Year Anniversary." *Cultural Survival*, October 9. https://www.culturalsurvival.org/news/taiwan-indigenous-television-approaches-10-year-anniversary.

Smith, Linda Tuhiwai. 1999. *Decolonizing Methodologies: Research and Indigenous Peoples*. Zed Books.

Song, D. Y. M. 2000. "The Legal Profession in Taiwan." In *Yearbook Law & Legal Practice in East Asia, Volume 4 (1999)*, edited by Annie J. de Roo and Robert W. Jagtenberg, 141–50. Martinus Nijhoff.

Star, Susan Leigh, and James R. Griesemer. 1989. "Institutional Ecology, 'Translations' and Boundary Objects: Amateurs and Professionals in Berkeley's Museum of Vertebrate Zoology, 1907–39." *Social Studies of Science* 19 (3): 387–420.

Sterk, Darryl. 2020a. "Ecologising Seediq: Towards an Ecology of an Endangered Indigenous Language from Taiwan." *International Journal of Taiwan Studies* 4 (1): 54–71.

Sterk, Darryl. 2020b. *Indigenous Cultural Translation: A Thick Description of Seediq Bale*. Routledge.

Su, Kai-ping. 2017. "Criminal Court Reform in Taiwan: A Case of Fragmented Reform in a Not-Fragmented Court System." *Washington International Law Journal* 27 (1): 203–40.

Su, Yi-yuan (William). 2006. "The Effects of the Kyoto Protocol on Taiwan." *Sustainable Development Law & Policy* 6 (2): 51–56.

Sugimoto, Tomonori. 2018. "Settler Colonial Incorporation and Inheritance: Historical Sciences, Indigeneity, and Settler Narratives in Post–WWII Taiwan." *Settler Colonial Studies* 8 (3): 283–97.

Tagliarino, Nicholas K. 2017. "Avoiding the Worst Case Scenario: Whether Indigenous Peoples and Local Communities in Asia and Africa Are Vulnerable to Expropriation Without Fair Compensation." Annual World Bank Conference on Land and Poverty, Washington, D.C., March 20–24.

Tai, Hsing-sheng. 2015. "Cross-Scale and Cross-Level Dynamics: Governance and Capacity for Resilience in a Social-Ecological System in Taiwan." *Sustainability* 7 (2): 2045–65.

Tai, Hsing-sheng, Wu-long Jhuang, and Shyang-woei Lin. 2011. "Governmental Conservation Institutions, Socioeconomic Change and Indigenous Hunting: An Empirical Analysis of Institutional Interplay in a Truku Case [國家野生動物保育體制、社經變遷與原住民狩獵：制度互動之太魯閣族實證分析]." *The Taiwanese Political Science Review* [臺灣政治學刊] 15 (2): 3–66.

Taiwan Association for Human Rights. 2013. *The Hidden Face of Taiwan: Lessons Learnt from the ICCPR/ICESCR Review Process.* https://www.fidh.org/IMG/pdf/taiwan605u2013.pdf.

Taiwan Today. 2017. "Indigenous Languages Development Act Takes Effect." June 15. https://taiwantoday.tw/news.php?unit=2,6,10,15,18&post=116946.

Taiwan Today. 2022. "Taiwan Co-founds Indigenous Peoples Economic and Trade Cooperation Arrangement." March 30. https://taiwantoday.tw/news.php?unit=2&post=216957&unitname=Politics-Top-News&postname=Taiwan-co-founds-Indigenous-Peoples-Economic-and-Trade-Cooperation-Arrangement.

Taiwan Today. 2023. "Taiwan Ranks 7th Globally for Gender Equality." August 17. https://taiwantoday.tw/news.php?unit=10&post=240659.

Taiwan's Indigenous Peoples Portal (TIPP). n.d. "Katatipul [卡地布部落]." https://www.tipp.org.tw/tribe_detail3.asp?City_No=18&TA_No=5&T_ID=72.

Takisvilainan, Salizan. 2012. "Closed Refrigerator [封冰箱]." *Indigenous Literature.* https://blog.udn.com/salizan/6660349.

Takisvilainan, Salizan. 2013. "The Indigenous Peoples Basic Law [原住民族基本法]." *Indigenous Literature.* https://blog.udn.com/salizan/7212535.

Tali, Ingay. 2019. Facebook. February 12. https://www.facebook.com/IngayTali2018/.

Tamanaha, Brian Z. 2007. "Understanding Legal Pluralism: Past to Present, Local to Global." *St. John's University School of Law Legal Studies Research Paper Series,* no. 07–0080: 1–63.

Tang, Wen-zhang. 2013. "The Operation of the Aboriginal Courts [原住民族專業法庭目前之運作情形]." *Frontier* [原教前線] 53: 18–21.

Tavares, Antonio C. 2005. "The Japanese Colonial State and the Dissolution of the Late Imperial Frontier Economy in Taiwan, 1886–1909." *The Journal of Asian Studies* 64 (2): 361–85.

Taylor, Charles. 1994. "The Politics of Recognition." In *Multiculturalism: Examining the Politics of Recognition*, edited by Amy Gutmann, 25–73. Princeton University Press.

Templeman, Kharis. 2016. "Tsai Ing-wen's Pingpuzu Aborigines Challenge." *Ketagalan Media*, August 16. https://ketagalanmedia.com/2016/08/16/tsai-ing-wens-pingpuzu-aborigines-challenge/.

Templeman, Kharis. 2018. "When Do Electoral Quotas Advance Indigenous Representation? Evidence from the Taiwanese Legislature." *Ethnopolitics* 17 (5): 461–84.

Torres, Gerald, and Kathryn Milun. 1990. "Translating *Yonnondio* by Precedent and Evidence: The Mashpee Indian Case." *Duke Law Journal* 4 (September): 625–59.

Tsai, Grace Ying-fang. 2015. "Inheritance Dispute Resolution in Paiwan Tribes." *National Taiwan University Law Review* 10 (2): 289–358.

Tsai, Chih-wei (Awi Mona). 2019. "National Apology and Reinvigoration of Indigenous Rights in Taiwan." In *Taiwan and International Human Rights: A Story of Transformation*, edited by Jerome A. Cohen, William P. Alford, and Chang-fa Lo, 609–23. Springer.

Tsai, Ing-wen. 2016. "Presidential Apology to Indigenous Peoples." *Focus Taiwan*, August 1. http://focustaiwan.tw/news/aipl/201608010026.aspx.

Tsai, Ting-yi. 2022. "Specialised Indigenous Divisions in Taiwan's High Courts: Practices and Concerns." *Journal of Legal Anthropology* 6 (2): 76–92.

Tseng, Katherine, and Tai Wei Lim. 2018. "Gender Politics in Taiwan Compared with Hong Kong: A Survey of Socio-political Developments in the LGBTQ Community." In *Studying Hong Kong: 20 Years of Political, Economic and Social Developments*, edited by Tai Wei Lim and Tuan Yuen Kong, 93–115. World Scientific Publishing.

Tso, Tom. 1989. "The Process of Decision Making in Tribal Courts." *Arizona Law Review* 31: 225–35.

Tsukida, Naomi. 2011. "Seediq." In *The Austronesian Languages of Asia and Madagascar*, edited by Alexander Adelaar and Nikolaus P. Himmelmann. Routledge.

Tylor, Edward. 1871. *Primitive Culture: Researches into the Development of Mythology, Philosophy, Religion, Language, Art, and Custom*. Cambridge University Press. Reprint, 2010.

UNHRC (United Nations Human Rights Committee). 1994. CCPR General Comment No. 23: Article 27 (Rights of Minorities). CCPR/C/21/Rev.1/Add.5.

UNHRC Working Group (United Nations Human Rights Council Working Group on the Universal Periodic Review). 2013. *National Report Submitted in Accordance with Paragraph 5 of the Annex to Human Rights Council Resolution 16/21 New Zealand*.

United Nations. 1971. UN General Assembly Resolution 2758(XXVI).

United Nations Committee on Economic, Social and Cultural Rights. 2009. General Comment No. 21: Right of Everyone to Take Part in Cultural Life. E/C.12/GC/21.

Upton, J. Christopher. 2022a. "Courts of Being and Non-being: Taiwan's Indigenous Courts and Judicial Hybrid Practice." *Journal of Legal Anthropology* 6 (2): 25–51.

Upton, J. Christopher. 2022b. "From Thin to Thick Justice and Beyond: Access to Justice and Legal Pluralism in Indigenous Taiwan." *Law & Social Inquiry* 47 (3): 996–1025.

Upton, J. Christopher. 2023a. "Courts and Indigenous Reconciliation: Positivism, the A Priori, and Justice in Taiwan." In *Indigenous Reconciliation in Contemporary Taiwan: From Stigma to Hope*, edited by Scott Simon, Jolan Hsieh, and Peter Kang, 96–118. Routledge.

Upton, J. Christopher. 2023b. "Legal Indigeneities: Identity, Authenticity, and Power in Taiwan's Indigenous Courts." *International Journal of Taiwan Studies* 6 (1): 5–32.

Upton, J. Christopher. Forthcoming. "Codifying *Gaya*, Cultivating Hunters: Indigenous Hunting Self-Governance and Self-Discipline in Taiwan." *PoLAR: Political and Legal Anthropology Review*.

Vaihinger, Hans. 1935. *The Philosophy of 'As if': A System of the Theoretical, Practical and Religious Fictions of Mankind*. Translated by C. K. Ogden. Kegan Paul.

Van De Fliert, Lydia, ed. 1994. *Indigenous Peoples and International Organisations*. Spokesman.

Veracini, Lorenzo. 2011. "Introducing: Settler Colonial Studies." *Settler Colonial Studies* 1 (1): 1–12.

Wang, C. 2007. "Indigenous Basic Law in Line with U.N. Declaration: Official." *News Room Formosa*, September 30. http://newsroomformosa.blogspot.de/2007/09/indigenous-basic-law-in-line-with-un.html.

Wang, I-shou. 1980. "Cultural Contact and the Migration of Taiwan's Aborigines: A Historical Perspective." In *China's Island Frontier: Studies in the Historical Geography of Taiwan*, edited by Ronald G. Knapp, 31–54. University Press of Hawaii and Research Corporation of the University of Hawaii.

Wang, Jaw-perng. 2011. "The Evolution and Revolution of Taiwan's Criminal Justice." *Taiwan in Comparative Perspective* 3: 8–29.

Wang, Li-jung. 2004. "Multiculturalism in Taiwan: Contradictions and Challenges in Cultural Policy." *International Journal of Cultural Policy* 10 (3): 301–18.

Wang, Mei-hsia. 2008. "The Reinvention of Ethnicity and Culture: A Comparative Study of the Atayal and the Truku in Taiwan." *Journal of Archaeology and Anthropology* 68: 1–44.

Wang, Tay-sheng. 2015. "Legalization of Societal Customs in Taiwan [論台灣社會上習慣的國家法化]." *NTU Law Journal* 44 (1): 1–69.

Weinauer, Ellen M. 1996. "'A Most Respectable Looking Gentleman': Passing, Possession, and Transgression in *Running a Thousand Miles for Freedom*." In *Passing and the Fictions of Identity*, edited by Elaine K. Ginsberg, 37–56. Duke University Press.

Weitzer, Ronald. 1990. *Transforming Settler States: Communal Conflict and Internal Security in Northern Ireland and Zimbabwe*. University of California Press.

Wen, Zheng-yan. 2017. "Mining Rose Stones Is Stealing? Judge Cites Basic Law in Acquittal [採玫瑰石算偷竊？法官引原基法判無罪]." *FTV*, July 7. https://www.ftvnews.com.tw/news/detail/2017707N03M1?fbclid=IwAR30kLNAjAKoV_bxO-DtDksWqGn-GjisqOp5kQiF58Ygz358pye3XoCpKho.

White, Richard. 1991. *The Middle Ground: Indians, Empires, and Republics in the Great Lakes Region, 1650–1815*. Cambridge University Press.

Wilkinson, Maria. 2023. "The 'Citizen Judge Act' and Its Implications for Major Criminal Cases in Taiwan's Legal System." *Global Taiwan Brief* 8 (7): 9–11. https://globaltaiwan.org/wp-content/uploads/2023/04/GTB-8.7-PDF.pdf.

Wittgenstein, Ludwig. 1953. *Philosophical Investigations*. Translated by G. E. M. Anscombe. Blackwell.

Wolfe, Patrick. 2006. "Settler Colonialism and the Elimination of the Native." *Journal of Genocide Research* 8 (4): 387–409.
World Bank. 2003. *Implementation of Operational Directive 4.20 on Indigenous Peoples: An Independent Desk Review.* http://documents.worldbank.org/curated/en/570331468761746572.
Wu, Tzung-mou. 2016. "Western Legal Traditions for 'Laying Down Taiwan's Indigenous Customs in Writing.'" *Rechtsgeschichte—Legal History* 24: 222–33.
Xiang, Cheng-zhen. 2012. "9 District Courts Will Expand Next Year with Aboriginal Courts [9地方法院 明年增原民法庭]." *Liberty Times Net*, October 16. http://news.ltn.com.tw/news/society/paper/623027.
Xu, Jia-ning. 2017. "Invoking the 'Indigenous Peoples Basic Law': 5 People Found Not Guilty of Mining Rose Stones [援引《原基法》5人採玫瑰石無罪]." *China Times*, July 6. https://www.chinatimes.com/newspapers/20170706000357-260106?chdtv&fbclid=IwAR3hklyOdudNirdXbFIiAKd7XE5JkFGHYs8VljB2zfAU88Ae8awj9KK5YOs.
Yi, Ho. 2016. "A Clash of Cultures." *Taipei Times*, January 26. https://www.taipeitimes.com/News/feat/archives/2016/01/26/2003638073.
Zhang, Ming-zhe. 2017. "Indigenous People Declare Territorial Rights: Dissatisfied with Policy Delays, Dulan Tribe Declares Their Own Traditional Areas [Indigenous People Declare Territorial Rights: 不滿政策拖延 都蘭部落自行公告傳統領域]." *PTS News*, 2017. https://news.pts.org.tw/article/350978.
Ziaja, Sonya, and Christopher Fullerton. 2015. "Judging Science: The Rewards and Perils of Courts as Boundary Organizations." *Hastings Environmental Law Journal* 21 (2): 217–46.

CASE LAW

Taiwan

Chiayi District Court 92 [2003] No. 151 [臺灣嘉義地方法院92年度簡上字第151號]
Hsinchu District Court 96 [2007] No. 4 [臺灣新竹地方法院96年度易字第4號]
Hualien District Court 105 [2016] No. 26 [臺灣花蓮地方法院105年度原訴字第26號]
Hualien High Court 103 [2014] No. 17 [臺灣高等法院花蓮分院103年度原上訴字第17號]
Kaohsiung District Court 103 [2014] No. 1 [臺灣高雄地方法院民事103年度原重國字第1號]
Kaohsiung High Administrative Court 102 [2013] No. 109 [臺灣高雄高等行政法院102年度訴字第00109號]
Kaohsiung High Court 101 [2012] No. 34 [臺灣高雄高等法院101年度上更(一)字第000034號]
Kaohsiung High Court 105 [2016] No. 1 [臺灣高等法院高雄分院民事105年度原重上國字第1號]

Pingtung District Court 99 [2010] No. 11 [臺灣屏東地方法院99年度重訴字第11號]
Pingtung District Court 106 [2017] No. 7 [臺灣屏東地方法院106年度國字第7號]
Taipei District Court 75 [1986] No. 26 [臺灣臺北地方法院75年度重訴字第26號]
Taipei District Court 101 [2012] No. 1139 [臺灣臺北地方法院刑事101年度審訴字第1139號]
Taitung District Court 101 [2012] No. 8 [臺灣台東地方法院101年度侵訴字第8號]
Taitung District Court 102 [2013] No. 61 [臺灣臺東地方法院102年度原訴字第61號]
Taitung District Court 102 [2013] No. 93 [臺灣臺東地方法院102年原易字第93號]
Taiwan Constitutional Court 110 [2021] Interpretation No. 803 [臺灣憲法法庭110年釋字第803號]
Taiwan Constitutional Court 111 [2022] No. 4 [臺灣憲法法庭111年憲判字第4號]
Taiwan Constitutional Court 111 [2022] No. 17 [臺灣憲法法庭111年憲判字第17號]
Taiwan High Court 96 [2007] No. 2092 [臺灣高等法院96年度上訴第2092號]
Taiwan High Court 98 [2009] No. 565 [臺灣高等法院98年度上更(一)字第565號]
Taiwan High Court 107 [2018] No. 34 [臺灣高等法院107年度原上訴第34號]
Taiwan Supreme Court 98 [2009] No. 7210 [臺灣最高法院98年台上第7210號]
Taiwan Supreme Court 102 [2013] No. 5093 [臺灣最高法院102年度台上字第5093號]
Taiwan Supreme Court 104 [2015] No. 3280 [臺灣最高法院104年度台上字第3280號]
Taiwan Supreme Court 105 [2016] No. 984 [臺灣最高法院105年度台上字第984號]
Taiwan Supreme Court 108 [2019] No. 2454 [臺灣最高法院108年度台上字第2454號]
Taiwan Supreme Court 111 [2022] No. 110 [臺灣最高法院111年度台非字第110號]
Taiwan Supreme Court 111 [2022] No. 111 [臺灣最高法院111年度台非字第111號]

Other Jurisdictions

Angela Poma Poma v. Peru, Human Rights Committee View on Communication No. 1457/2006 (adopted March 27, 2009)
Apirana Mahuika et al. v. New Zealand, Human Rights Committee View on Communication No. 547/1993 (adopted October 27, 2000)
Anthony Woo v. Singapore Airlines [2003] SGHC 190
George Howard v. Canada, Human Rights Committee View on Communication No. 879/1999 (adopted July 26, 2005)
Jouni Lansman et al. v. Finland, Human Rights Committee View on Communication No. 1023/2001 (adopted March 17, 2005)

Parent and ors v Singapore Airlines Ltd and Civil Aeronautics Administration, Decision of Superior Court of Quebec, 2003 IIJ Can 7285 (QC CS), ILDC 181 (CA 2003), Canada; Quebec; Superior Court

CONSTITUTIONS, REGULATIONS, AND STATUTES

Taiwan

Act to Implement the Convention on the Rights of Persons with Disabilities (身心障礙者權利公約施行法) (August 20, 2014)
Act to Implement United Nations Convention Against Corruption (聯合國反貪腐公約施行法) (May 20, 2015)
Act to Implement the International Covenant on Civil and Political Rights and the International Covenant on Economic, Social and Cultural Rights (公民與政治權利國際公約及經濟社會文化權利國際公約施行法) (April 22, 2009)
Additional Articles of the Constitution of the Republic of China (Taiwan) (中華民國憲法增修條文) (May 1, 1991; last amended June 10, 2005)
Attorney Regulation Act (律師法) (January 11, 1941; last amended May 28, 2025)
Citizen Judges Act (國民法官法) (August 12, 2020)
Code of Civil Procedure (民事訴訟法) (December 26, 1930; last amended November 29, 2023)
Code of Criminal Procedure (刑事訴訟法) (July 28, 1928; last amended January 15, 2020)
Code of Ethics for Lawyers (律師倫理規範) (December 18, 1983; last amended July 3, 2022)
Constitution of the Republic of China (Taiwan) (中華民國憲法) (1947)
Court Organization Act (法院組織法) (October 28, 1932; last amended November 29, 2024)
Criminal Code of the Republic of China (中華民國刑法) (January 1, 1935; last amended May 28, 2025)
Development of National Languages Act (國家語言發展法) (January 9, 2019)
Draft Act Governing Indigenous Historical Justice and the Restoration of Indigenous Rights (原住民族歷史正義與權利回復法草案)
Draft Law on the Establishment of Tribal Public Corporations (部落公法人組織設置辦法草案)
Education Act for Indigenous Peoples (原住民族教育法) (June 17, 1998; last amended January 20, 2021)
Enforcement Act of Convention on the Elimination of All Forms of Discrimination Against Women (消除對婦女一切形式歧視公約施行法) (June 8, 2011)
Firearms, Ammunition, and Knives Control Act (槍砲彈藥刀械管制條例) (June 27, 1983; last amended January 3, 2024)
The Forestry Act (森林法) (September 15, 1932; last amended May 5, 2021)
Implementation Act of the Convention on the Rights of the Child (兒童權利公約施行法) (June 4, 2014; last amended June 19, 2019)

Indigenous Languages Development Act (原住民族語言發展法) (June 14, 2017)
Indigenous Peoples Basic Law (原住民族基本法) (February 5, 2005; last amended June 20, 2018)
Indigenous Peoples Employment Protection Law (原住民族工作權保障法) (October 31, 2001; last amended February 4, 2015)
Legal Aid Act (法律扶助法) (January 7, 2004; last amended July 1, 2015)
Measures for the Annual Assignment of Judges in Civil and Administrative Litigation Cases and Special Courts (各級法院法官辦理民刑事與行政訴訟及特殊專業類型案件年度司法事務分配辦法) (October 11, 2001; last amended August 2, 2019)
Mining Act (礦業法) (May 26, 1930; last amended June 21, 2023)
Name Act (姓名條例) (March 7, 1953; last amended May 29, 2024)
Regulations for Demarcating Indigenous Peoples Land or Tribal Land Area (原住民族土地或部落範圍土地劃設辦法) (February 18, 2017)
Regulations for Indigenous Peoples or Tribes Being Consulted, Obtaining Their Consent and Participation (諮商取得原住民族部落同意參與辦法) (January 4, 2016; last amended January 5, 2023)
Status Act for Indigenous Peoples (原住民身分法) (January 17, 2001; last amended January 3, 2024)
Use of Wildlife Management Measures for Indigenous Peoples' Traditional Cultural and Ritual Hunting and Killing Needs (原住民族基於傳統文化及祭儀需要獵捕宰殺利用野生動物管理辦法) (June 6, 2012; last amended June 9, 2015)
Wildlife Conservation Act (野生動物保育法) (June 23, 1989; last amended February 18, 2025)

Other Jurisdictions

American Bar Association, Model Code of Judicial Conduct (2020)
State of Alaska Rules of Civil Procedure (1959)

INTERNATIONAL DECLARATIONS AND TREATIES

Convention Against Torture and Other Cruel, Inhuman or Degrading Treatment or Punishment, June 26, 1987, 1465 U.N.T.S. 85
Convention Concerning Indigenous and Tribal People in Independent Countries (ILO No. 169), June 27, 1989, 1650 U.N.T.S. 383 (entered into force September 5, 1991)
Convention Concerning the Protection and Integration of Indigenous and Other Tribal and Semi-tribal Populations in Independent Countries (ILO No. 107), February 6, 1959, 328 U.N.T.S. 247 (entered into force June 2, 1959)
Convention on the Elimination of All Forms of Discrimination Against Women, December 18, 1979, 1249 U.N.T.S. 13

Convention on the Rights of Persons with Disabilities, May 3, 2008, 2515 U.N.T.S. 3
Convention on the Rights of the Child, September 2, 1990, 1577 U.N.T.S. 3
International Convention on the Elimination of All Forms of Racial Discrimination, January 4, 1969, 660 U.N.T.S. 195
International Covenant on Civil and Political Rights, March 23, 1976, 999 U.N.T.S. 171
International Covenant on Economic, Social and Cultural Rights, January 3, 1976, 993 U.N.T.S. 3
United Nations Declaration on the Rights of Indigenous Peoples, G.A. Res. 61/295, A/61/L.67 and Add.1 (September 13, 2007)
Universal Declaration of Human Rights, G.A. res. 217A (III), U.N. Doc A/810 at 71 (December 10, 1948)

INDEX

aboriginal courts, 247n2. *See also* ad hoc Chambers of Indigenous Courts (*yuanzhuminzu zhuanye fating*)

aboriginal languages and cultures, ROC Constitution on, 256n15

activists, Indigenous: advocating court institutions managed by Indigenous peoples, 162; on appellate judges, 151; Indigenous Peoples Basic Law and, 106, 120, 187; calls for court reform, 14–15; Council of Aboriginal Affairs and, 65; criticism of Lawyer Xu, 168–69; demonstrations, 1, 32, 113–15, 212; goal of recognition, 12, 14, 116; on how Indigenous case management in ad hoc chambers, 171; on human rights-based arguments, 120, 123; Indigenous hunting rights and, 98, 101, 221; Indigenous peoples term inclusion in ROC Constitution, 93–94; Ingay Tali and, 233; LCIP and, 233; on lower-court judges, 140; name rectification movement, 11, 68, 76–77; Paiwan Alili Incident and, 16; push for reforms on training programs, 131; redirecting levels of engagement, 21; on special interpreter program, 158; on specialized unit cases, 135; support of specialized Indigenous courts, 4, 12; Taitung Bunun Youth Group, 100; terminology of *yuanzhumin* and *yuanzhuminzu*, 248n6; on training of special prosecutors, 142–43; younger, 9

Act to Implement the Convention on the Rights of Persons with Disabilities, 258n1, 283

Act to Implement the International Covenant on Civil and Political Rights and the International Covenant on Economic, Social and Cultural Rights (Two Covenants Act), 116, 118–22, 184–85, 258n1, 283

Act to Implement United Nations Convention Against Corruption, 238, 258n1, 283

Additional Articles of the Constitution of the Republic of China (Taiwan), 12, 283

ad hoc Chambers of Indigenous Courts (*yuanzhuminzu zhuanye fating*), 1, 2; access to, 153–60; administrators of, 41; advocates for, 41; ambiguities and, 17, 41, 124, 136–37, 144; as attempt to bridge state understanding and Indigenous understanding of culture/territory/law, 3, 41–42; as boundary institutions, 36–40; conception of, 127; as courts of opportunity, 17; establishment of, 4, 41, 127–28, 128–29, 254n3, 254n10; global recognition and, 17; handling of disputes over Indigenous culture, territory, and natural resources, 41; as highly formalized and constrained spaces, 5; history, 41; in Hualien, 22–31; legal and normative orders of, 41; legal pluralism and, 32; legal representation, 145–49; local Indigenous laws as ignored in, 14; local

ad hoc Chambers *(continued)*
  perspectives on, 20; national identity construction and, 17; new configurations of, 3; obstacles to Indigenous persons and communities in accessing, 41; official language of, 16; Paiwan Alili Incident and, 16; personnel, 41, 137–45, 255–56n40; power of, 166–67; procedures of, 4, 16–17; purpose of, 17; role in mediating state-Indigenous divides, 42; as situated at intersection of Han Taiwanese/Indigenous social/legal worlds, 6, 12; structures of, 4, 41, 129–37; system of, 41, 149–52; term usage, 247n2; therapeutic potential of, 20; types of cases in, 135
adversarial systems, 18, 151, 224
advocacy, engagement through, 7
agonism, 224
agonistic reconciliation, 258n35
Alfred, Taiaiake, 236
alili cultural practice, 14–16
Alliance of Taiwan Aborigines, 65
American Bar Association, Model Code of Judicial Conduct, 254–55n20, 284
Amis (Pangcah), 54–55, 143, 10*map*; Hualien County and, 8; Hualien District Court dealing with, 26; hunting conventions, 83; as recognized Indigenous group, 68; LCIP and, 220; self-governance, 232; Taitung District Court dealing with, 26; wildlife protections case, 143
ancestral cemetery (Taitung County), relocation issue, 1, 2
ancestral knowledge, 228; Mangayaw and, 73–74; other knowledge forms and, 82; relying on, 86
ancestral spirits: hunting and, 99; invocation of, 173, 176, 177; Katratripulr case and, 1, 3; penance for Gaya violations and, 81
Andrade, Tonio, 46
Angela Poma Poma v. Peru, 253n33, 282
Anping, 50
Anthony Woo v. Singapore Airlines, 251n2, 282
Apirana Mahuika et al v. New Zealand, 253n33, 282

appeal cases: absolute right to appeal, 150; as de novo, 150; Dowmung Rose Stone Case and, 180–92; rates of reversal in, 151; Tama Talum appeal case, 26, 30, 106, 162, 165, 191–92
appellate court, procedures of, 150–51
Articles of Dowmung Hunters Self-Governance and Self-Discipline Convention (*tongmen buluo lieren zizhu guanli zilü gongyue tiaowen*), 84–86
as-if sovereignty, 228, 234–239
"Assessing the Feasibility of Setting Up a Special Indigenous Court" (*pinggu shezhi yuanzhuminzu zhuanye fating zhi kexingxing*), 127
assimilation, degrees of, 10–11
assimilationist policies, injustice of, 1
Atayal. *See* Tayan (Atayal)
Attorney Regulation Act, 147, 283
Australia: empowering Indigenous peoples and communities in, 22; Indigenous courts in, 19; Indigenous Peoples Economic and Trade Cooperation Arrangement, 14, 239
Austronesian-speaking peoples: colonialism of Taiwan and, 8, 44–59; indigeneity and, 10, 40; Indigenous peoples of Taiwan and, 40, 44; study of, 13
Awi Mona, 105, 148, 219, 237, 252n11, 257n9

Babuza, 68
Bamboo House Case (*tongmen zhuwu an*), 41, 166–79
Barclay, Paul, 51, 52, 62, 63
Barth, Fredrik, 5
Basay, 68
Beerdsen, Edith, 255n20
Beinan, 51
Bellwood, Peter, 8
betel nut: ceremonial uses of, 73; as cosmological median, 1; usage at courthouse, 169; usage by Han Taiwanese, 214; usage in Katratripulr community, 3
Biological and Toxin Weapons Convention, 238
born in the backwoods (*chushen qiongxiangpirang*), as court description, 89

boundaries: boundary metaphor, 5; cultural boundaries, 3, 5; of difference, 3; as divide between Indigenous peoples and colonizing society, 3; emergence of, 5; establishment and control of, 4; ethnic, 3; of identity, 3; Indigenous courts as institutions of, 36–40; intersections of, 5; legal, 3; linguistic, 3, 157–60; as negotiated and contested, 3; ontological (between what is and what isn't to create space for something), 3; power and, 4; racial, 3; as separating ROC state and Indigenous peoples, 4; spanning, 160–63; territorial, 3
boundary institutions, 1; bridging state-Indigenous divides in, 12, 27, 42; characteristics of, 6, 37; defined, 5, 37; Indigenous courts as, 36–40
boundary trenches, 43, 49, 62
boundary work theory, 3, 5, 37, 226; defined, 5; integration of, 37; multicultural policies and, 3; stability of relations in, 5
Brazil, indigeneity in constitutions of, 71
Buddhism, Indigenous cultural practices encountering, 82
Bunkiet, 51
Bunohon, 43
Bunun, 10*map*, 28, 54–55; cases in, 28; Hualien County and, 8; Hualien District Court dealing with, 26; hunting, 107–11, 233; hunting conventions, 83; identity of, 214–15; LCIP and, 220; muntjac deer hunting, 41, 80, 107–11; as recognized Indigenous group, 68; Samu (Bunun ancestral law), 107, 109–11, 233; shared memories of, 9; social connectedness and consensus of, 154–55; Taitung District Court dealing with, 26; Takisvilainan, Salizan, 241; Tama Talum appeal case, 26, 30, 98–101, 106, 162, 165, 191–92, 220
Bunun language, 30, 213, 214, 217, 218
Bureau of Pacification and Reclamation (*fukenju*), 51

Cairo Declaration, 56
camphor, 50–53, 62–63, 105

Canada: First Nations, 232; *George Howard v. Canada*, 282; Gladue (Aboriginal Persons) Courts, 19; Indigenous Peoples Economic and Trade Cooperation Arrangement, 14, 239; national court systems of, 127; *Parent and ors v. Singapore Airlines Ltd and Civil Aeronautics Administration*, 282
Capen Nganaen (Tao elder), 113
cartographic representations of Taiwan, 8
categorization, activities of, 4–5
Cattelino, Jessica, 235
Chemical Weapons Convention, 238
Chen, Judge, 182–91, 201, 204–5
Chen Shui-bian, 12, 94, 95, 104, 229
Chiang Kai-shek, 56–58, 60, 64, 65, 227, 251n1
Chiayi (city), 29*map*, 48
Chiayi County, Tsou in, 83
Chiayi District Court, 89, 249n11; ad hoc Chambers of Indigenous Courts in, 128; case law, 281
China, rejection of indigeneity, 71
Chinese Civil War, 93
Chinese cultural movements, use of Indigenous cultures and, 13
Chinese empires: efforts to control Taiwan, 40; Imperial Chinese law, 149
Chinese mainland: legal system brought by KMT from, 88–89; narrative of Taiwan's ties to, 8, 56
Chinese nationalism: decline of, 13; tensions between Taiwanese consciousness and, 12–13
Chinese settlements, Japanese protection of, 53
Chinese settlers, 45, 46, 48, 49, 51, 52, 60
Chou Ching-yuan, 55
Christianity, 228; incorporation into Indigenous cultural practices, 77, 82, 169, 173, 178; Indigenous peoples resistance to assimilation into Chinese culture and, 36; Spanish empire and, 47
CIP (Council of Indigenous Peoples). *See* Council of Indigenous Peoples (CIP)
Circle Sentencing (New South Wales), 19
Citizen Judges Act, 150, 283

civil law tradition, 38, 149, 222; constraints of, 17, 21, 121, 129, 198; principles of statutory construction in, 150, 205; stare decisis doctrine and, 119, 150

Civil Service Special Examination for Judges and Prosecutors (Judicial Officer Exam), 138, 142, 145

classification systems: imperial and colonial classification, 10; of Indigenous peoples, 9–10; Japanese classifications, 66–67

Cobo, José R. Martínez, 71

Code of Civil Procedure, 255nn38–40, 256n45, 283

Code of Criminal Procedure, 146, 256n45, 283

Code of Ethics for Lawyers, 148, 283

Cohen, Amy, 235

colonialism: ad hoc chambers as revealing geographies of, 37; behaviors accepted within, 4; ongoing colonization by ROC government, 4; divide between Indigenous peoples and colonizing society, 3, 227; as enduring structure and ongoing process, 4, 6, 44; Indigenous courts in colonial contexts, 6–7; multiple colonialisms, 3, 42, 44–59; new geographies of, 3; physical boundaries in, 61–63; recolonization, 60; relations of power in, 6; settler colonialism, 59–60; violence of, 61

comfort stations, 55

community (*buluo*), identifying with, 11

Constitutional Court (*xianfa fating*): as branch of national court system, 247n3; Indigenous status and, 69; interpretations invoking human dignity, 208; *pingpuzu* recognition path, 68; Tama Talum case, 191

constitutional multiculturalism: government efforts to strengthen, 2; government pursuit of, 4; movement toward, 227

Constitution of the Republic of China (Taiwan), 138, 283

Control Yuan (*jianchayuan*), as branch of ROC government, 247n3

Convention Against Corruption, 238

Convention Against Torture and Other Cruel, Inhuman or Degrading Treatment or Punishment, 253n32, 284

Convention Concerning Indigenous and Tribal People in Independent Countries (ILO No. 169), 72, 116–17, 251n4, 284

Convention Concerning the Protection and Integration of Indigenous and Other Tribal and Semi-tribal Populations in Independent Countries (ILO No. 107), 57, 89, 284

Convention on the Elimination of All Forms of Discrimination Against Women, 238, 253n32, 284

Convention on the Rights of Persons with Disabilities, 238, 253n32, 284

Convention on the Rights of the Child, 238, 253n32, 284

cooked savages (*shoufan*), 49–50, 51

Coulthard, Glen, 236

Council of Aboriginal Affairs. *See* Council of Indigenous Peoples (CIP)

Council of Indigenous Peoples (CIP): designation of Indigenous territories, 230; establishment of, 13, 65; funding from, 30; hunting conventions and, 87; Indigenous Languages Development Act, 157–58, 283; Indigenous Peoples Basic Law, 118–21; Indigenous Peoples Economic and Trade Cooperation Arrangement, 14; joint ruling on use of natural resources on ancestral territories, 111; Legal Aid Foundation and, 146; list of interpreters in Indigenous languages, 158; memoranda of understanding with Canada and New Zealand, 238; regulations issued by, 112; status issues, 69

Court Organization Act, 130, 132, 157, 283

court reforms, as establishing ad hoc Chambers of Indigenous Courts, 37, 127; Paiwan Alili Incident and, 14–17

courts of law: circulation of conceptions of, 41; Indigenous worldviews and, 3, 6, 21, 33, 39, 135, 196–97, 199, 206, 222; power of, 166–67; state authority and, 3; understanding and addressing Indig-

enous cultural and linguistic differences in, 4
Criminal Code of the Republic of China, 166, 168, 180, 181, 186, 191, 200, 206–7, 249n11, 283
cultural boundaries: ad hoc Chambers of Indigenous Courts and, 3; complexity of, 11; construction and negotiation of, 3; of Indigenous groups, 9; problems of translation and, 6; processes of making, 5
cultural erasure, 89
cultural pluralism, ROC Constitutions' affirmation of, 12
cultural practices: *alili* cultural practice, 14–16; disputes over, 123; Indigenous peoples as divided by practices of, 10; involving/affecting Indigenous women, 35; prosecution against Indigenous persons engaging in, 14; of Truku, 164
cultural rights, 11; risk in fighting for, 152
culture (*wenhua*): aboriginal cultures, 256n15; definitions of, 188–90; discrimination against, 1; Gaya defined as, 81; in Indigenous rights discourse, 188–89; integration of Indigenous perspectives on, 4, 7; as source of empowerment, 12
customary law, as category, 207–8, 257n22
customary legislation (*xiguan lifa*): as category, 207–8, 257n22; concept of, 257n21

Dabang village, 207, 257n20
Daly, Kathleen, 20, 22
Darwin Community Court (Northern Territory, Australia), 19
decolonization: Indigenous court units and, 4, 225, 226; Indigenous identities as means to promote, 12
defendants, Indigenous: critical roles of, 4, 32, 42, 78, 209, 218; involvement of, 7, 20, 38, 144, 151, 161, 201
deLisle, Jacques, 234–35
democracy: Indigenous court units initiative and, 4; recognition and principles of, 11; Taiwan's transition to, 44, 64–65, 153
Democratic Progressive Party (DPP): about, 94; Indigenous peoples and, 94, 229, 237; Indigenous Peoples Basic Law and, 103–104. *See also* Chen Shui-bian; Tsai Ing-wen's apology
demographics: of Han Taiwanese, 1–2; of Indigenous persons, 1
demonstrations, Tsai Ing-wen's apology and, 80, 113–15
De Sousa Santos, Boaventura, 32
Development of National Languages Act, 158, 233, 283
district courts (*difang fayuan*): ad hoc Chambers of Indigenous Courts in, 137; as branch of national court system, 136, 247n3; Indigenous cases in, 133–34; judges in, 142, 187–90, 200, 204. See also *specific district courts*
diversity, promotion of, 12–13
double jeopardy, 150
Douglas, Mary, 214
Dowmung village: about, 28; cases in, 30; communities in, 11
Dowmung Bamboo House Case, 32, 41, 153, 166–79
Dowmung community, 29*map*, 41; ad ho chambers and, 137; cases in, 28; drafting hunting convention, 83–88; Gaya and, 80, 81
Dowmung Rose Stone Case, 41, 179–92, 201
Draft Act Governing Indigenous Historical Justice and the Restoration of Indigenous Rights, 112, 283
Draft Law on the Establishment of Tribal Public Corporations, 112, 283
Dutch empire: Chinese migrants and, 60; departure from Taiwan, 48, 229; Dutch East India Company, 46, 47, 48, 229; efforts to control Taiwan, 40, 44; matchlock guns from, 96; resource extraction by, 60

economic issues, as matter of access, 41, 134, 156–57
Education Act for Indigenous Peoples, 94, 283
elders, Indigenous: as cultural brokers, 6, 7, 20, 33, 64, 78, 84, 132, 145, 172, 181, 190, 193, 201, 207, 223; Indigenous court

elders, Indigenous *(continued)*
units and, 18, 19, 38, 132, 155; Indigenous sovereignty and, 232; Katratripulr case and, 1, 3; LCIP and, 34; Paiwan Alili Incident and, 15–16
Enforcement Act of Convention on the Elimination of All Forms of Discrimination Against Women, 258n1, 283
ethnic boundaries: complexity of, 11; construction and negotiation of, 3, 5; ethnic representation among judges and, 138–39
evidence: adoption of US-style rules of, 151; in appeal cases, 150; of Chinese settlement on Taiwan, 45; gatekeepers of, 40; household registration records as, 67; judges and, 40, 203, 254–55n20; of ownership, 168; re-presentation of, 146; scientific evidence, 5, 33
Examination Yuan *(kaoshiyuan)*, 2016a, 247n2; as branch of ROC government, 247n3
exclusion: classification systems and, 257n22; negotiations of, 5
Executive Yuan *(xingzhengyuan)*, 65; as branch of ROC government, 247n3; name rectification movement, 76–77
experts: on cultural significance of Indigenous norms and practices, 2, 7, 32, 207; Indigenous court units and, 38, 131, 147, 156, 165, 194, 197, 201, 223, 226; Indigenous persons as expert witnesses, 64, 132, 145, 164, 181, 190, 193, 199

Firearms, Ammunition, and Knives Control Act, 95, 96, 100, 147, 207–8, 283
First Sino-Japanese War, 51
Forest Bureau Division Office, 85, 179
forest resources: cases related to, 135; rights of Indigenous peoples and, 14
Forestry Act, 95, 101–2, 105, 184, 200, 206–7, 208, 249n11, 256n15, 283
Forestry Bureau of the Council of Agriculture (Forestry and Nature Conservation Agency): Dowmung community and, 83, 84, 179; hunting self-governance pilot programs, 83, 230; Smangus community and, 102, 249n11

formal legal pluralism, defined, 17
The Formosan Native Tribes: A Genealogical and Classificatory Study Vol. 1, 54–55
Foucault, Michel, 34
French, Jan Hoffman, 33, 106
Friedman, Kerim, 13, 56
Friedman, Sara, 235
Fujian Province, 27, 46, 48, 50, 61
Fuxing community, 29*map*, 210, 211–15

Gaga (Tayan ancestral law), 102–3, 200–201, 215
gaps, between constitutional principles and implementation, 14
Gaya (Truku ancestral law): codifying oral tradition of, 34, 80, 84, 85, 86, 87; defined, 81; in Dowmung community, 80; Dowmung hunting convention and, 83–88; enforcement of, 81; Gaya groups, 81; as governing daily life, 82, 175, 176, 200; interpretation of norms of, 81, 82; intersections of, 82; moral and ethical issues, 81; penance for violations of, 81; in Dowmung Bamboo House Case, 32; role in wildlife hunting, 30–31, 41, 81–88; state law and, 32, 80–81, 86–87
gender equality, 238
General Bureau of Camphor Affairs *(naowu zongju)*, 51
George Howard v. Canada, 253n33, 282
Gladue (Aboriginal Persons) Courts, 19
global indigenism, 65
global issues: constructing indigeneity and ethnic categories in Taiwan, 9–10; enhancing global recognition, 37; human dignity as, 116–18; human rights law, 32; Indigenous courts in North America, 18–19; Indigenous recognition to enhance Taiwan's international standing, 3; Indigenous court units and global recognition, 4, 17; international human rights protections for Indigenous peoples, 41, 80; rise of global Indigenous movement, 115–16; Taiwanese legal system and, 41, 80; UNDRIP, 118
Goffman, Erving, 214
Goodwin, Charles, 185–86

government initiatives, supported by Indigenous politicians and activists, 4
Guangdong, 46, 61
guard-line system, 53

habit, as category, 257n22
Hakka, 2, 50, 52; categorization of, 11; cultural policies and, 13
Han Taiwanese, 180; assimilation into society of, 10–11; boundaries separating Indigenous peoples in Taiwan from, 9; case administration handled by, 130; as dominant in court units, 17, 133, 144; as dominant in society, 4, 20; improving communication between in courtroom, 2; interactions between Indigenous litigants/defendants and, 7, 42; judges at Katratripulr trial as, 3; judges in ad hoc Chambers of Indigenous Courts, 6, 7, 20, 134, 139, 182–91, 201, 204–5; lawyer in Katratripulr trial, 1; lawyers developing legal arguments based on human rights norms, 81; Lawyer Yang, 180–82; perspective of, 15; ROC government and, 94; stereotype of Indigenous persons, 135–36; techniques of judges, 42; understanding of being Indigenous, 78. *See also* Hakka; Hoklo
Hatfield, DJ, 235
Hawai'i, 8, 87–88, 221
healing, 11
high courts (*gaodeng fayuan*): as branch of national court system, 247n3; Indigenous cases in, 133–34; judges in, 87, 96, 120, 121, 131–32, 135–36, 136, 137, 139–40, 146–47, 156–57, 201, 204, 205, 239. *See also specific high courts*
Hirano, Katsuys, 60
Hla'alua, 10*map*, 68
Hoanya, 68
Hoekema, Andre, 32, 79
Hokkien language, 27, 50, 174, 177, 213
Hoklo, 2, 11, 27, 50, 52
Holy See, 4, 64
household registration records, 55, 67–69
Hsinchu (city), 29*map*
Hsinchu District Court, 102; ad hoc Chambers of Indigenous Courts in, 128;

case law, 281; Smangus Beechwood Incident, 102
Hualien City, 8, 22, 29*map*, 81
Hualien County: guard-line system, 53; Indigenous peoples in, 8–9, 140, 227
Hualien County Bar Association, 219
Hualien District Court, 1, 29*map*, 139–40; ad hoc Chambers of Indigenous Courts in, 22–31, 128, 133; Bunun case, 195, 217; case law, 281; criminal division, 29*map*, 134, 135, 139, 143, 202; Dowmung Bamboo House Case, 153, 166–79; Dowmung Rose Stone Case and, 180–81; Fuxing community flooding case, 212; Indigenous groups under, 26; judges of, 139–40, 158–59; Prosecutor's Office, 142–43, 168, 171, 179, 180, 231; summary proceedings, 152; Truku and, 139–40, 164–65; Truku forest products collection case, 208; Truku hunter case, 202–3. *See also specific high courts*
Hualien High Court, 1, 29*map*, 100; ad hoc Chambers of Indigenous Courts in, 22, 24–27, 30, 133; case law, 281; cases in, 25–26; Dowmung Bamboo House Case, 179; Dowmung Rose Stone Case and, 180–81, 190; judges of, 120, 139–40; Prosecutor's Office, 179; representations of Indigenous peoples and, 24–25; reviewing of appeals by, 26; Tama Talum appeal case, 100; Truku and, 139–40
human dignity principle, 206–8, 253n32
human rights: arguments based on, 32, 120–23; engagement with international orders of, 36; Indigenous court units initiative and, 4; international protections for Indigenous peoples, 80; recognition and, 11; Taiwan's adoption of international norms on, 237–38; Two Covenants Act and, 118–19
Human Rights Committee, 119
hunting, Indigenous: cases related to, 135; Chinese moral norms and, 257n9; conventions, 1; customary rules and, 257n22; discourse, 1; in Dowmung community, 30–31; Dutch traders' matchlock guns, 46–47; firearms, 1, 95–98, 107–8, 135; Gaya and, 30–31, 41,

hunting, Indigenous *(continued)* 81, 82; ICCPR and, 253n33; identification cards for, 21, 86; Indigenous Peoples Basic Law on, 256n15; lawyers dedicated to defending Indigenous persons in cases involving, 28; new regulation proposal, 98; rights of Indigenous peoples and, 14; role of Gaya in, 41, 81–88; self-governance and, 83, 230; Tama Talum appeal case, 26, 98–101, 106, 162, 165, 191–92

Huteson, Greg, 157

hybrid practices, 1, 6, 32, 37–38, 41–42, 198–208, 208–22, 222

identities: cultivation of Chinese identity by KMT, 89; national identity construction, 36–37; struggles with classification of, 9

Implementation Act of the Convention on the Rights of the Child, 258n1, 283

inclusion, negotiations of, 5

India, rejection of indigeneity, 71

indigeneity: Austronesian-speaking peoples and, 10; as central to ad hoc Chambers of Indigenous Courts, 44; challenging dominant narratives about, 6; circulation of conceptions of, 41; connections between sovereignty and, 42; countries rejecting of, 71; defining Gaya in, 77; disjunctions and discontinuities of, 206–8, 210–15; from global to local, 70–77; Han Taiwanese understandings of, 17; as influence on court units, 17; as legal and political category, 43–44; as legal term, 40, 44; performances of, 42, 197, 209–15, 222; ROC government and, 69; as self-identification, 40; shifting meaning of, 40; shifting perspectives on, 8–12, 40; sovereignty and, 42; state-centric approaches to, 20

Indigenous communities, 29*map*; building on ancestral lands, 21; Indigenous court units and, 6, 7; issuance of hunting identification cards, 21; roles of elders and members of, 6, 20; sovereignty making and, 42. *See also* Bunun; Pinuyumayan (Puyuma); Truku

Indigenous courts: community member involvement in, 20; debates over, 19–20; global innovations in, 6, 18–19, 18–22; scholarship on Indigenous-controlled courts, 7; as world-spanning institutions, 6. *See also* ad hoc Chambers of Indigenous Courts (*yuanzhuminzu zhuanye fating*)

Indigenous Historical Justice and Transitional Justice Committee, 65, 112, 234

Indigenous identities: assertions of, 6, 21, 208–22; as central to ad hoc Chambers of Indigenous Courts, 77–78; classification systems and, 9; compelling courts to recognize, 42; erasing of, 16; new configurations of, 3; openly acknowledging, 12; performances of, 209–15; recognition of, 14; ROC's turn to, 4

Indigenous justice practices, 6–7, 16, 32, 156, 196

Indigenous Languages Development Act, 157–58, 159, 283

Indigenous Peoples Basic Law (Basic Law), 118–21, 283; amendments to, 112, 230; as core Indigenous rights instrument, 136; in Dowmung Bamboo House Case, 172; in Dowmung Rose Stone Case, 181, 183, 184–85, 186–88, 191; efforts to implement, 111; foundation for, 229; on hunting, foraging, mineral collection and water resources, 96, 256n15; Indigenous status and, 66, 67; lawyers requiring knowledge of, 147; Legislative Yuan and, 204; passing of, 65, 95; poem about, 241; provisions of, 16; recommendation to amend laws to be consistent with, 128, 182; ROC Constitution and, 204–5; specialized units and, 16; UNDRIP and, 118

Indigenous Peoples' Day, 112

Indigenous Peoples Economic and Trade Cooperation Arrangement, 14, 239

Indigenous Peoples Employment Protection Law, 94, 283

Indigenous peoples, 1; boundaries separating Han Taiwanese from, 9; changing perceptions of, 89–90; colonization by ROC government of, 4, 88–90; cultural boundaries, 9; demographics, 1–2, 58–59; as diverse and divided, 10; efforts to elevate status of, 13; empowerment of, 12, 22; exclusion of, 166–67; formally recognized groups, 68; incorporation of perspectives into legal processes of, 42; interests of colonizing society prioritized over those of, 4; lawyers dedicated to defending, 28; legal protections in ROC law for, 41; linguistic boundaries, 9; measure to categorize and manage, 40; as non-Chinese people category, 13; oppressive governance practices, 9; as separated from ROC state, 4; social shift toward, 227; spatial distribution of, 10; state governance of, 7; stereotype of, 135–36; women's role as cultural brokers, 63; worldviews and perspectives of, 3, 6, 21, 33, 39, 135, 196–97, 199, 206, 222. *See also* Amis (Pangcah); Bunun; Paiwan; Pinuyumayan (Puyuma); Seediq; Tayan (Atayal); Truku

Indigenous recognition: complexity of, 11–12; court units oriented toward promotion of, 17; Indigenous court units initiative and, 2; multiculturalism and, 3; multiculturalism to advance, 3; opportunities for, 43; of plains-dwelling peoples, 10–11; possibilities and limitations for, 42; promotion of, 36–37

Indigenous reconciliation: capacities for, 7; Indigenous court units initiative and, 2, 4

Indigenous rights, 88–115; attitudes toward, 83; court units oriented toward promotion of, 17; developments in, 41; Indigenous court units initiative and, 4; movements for, 41, 64–65; new configurations of, 3; ROC's turn to, 4; struggles for, 3, 37

Indigenous sovereignty: Indigenous justice practices in relation to, 6–7; value of making space for, 42. *See also* sovereignty

Indigenous status in Taiwan: determinations of, 11; legalities of, 66–69

Indigenous worldviews, integration of, 3, 6, 21, 33, 39, 135, 196–97, 199–201, 206, 222

Indonesia, rejection of indigeneity, 71
Ingay Tali, 233–34
inquisitorial system, 150–51
Intellectual Property Court, 130
interlegality, 32
International Convention on the Elimination of All Forms of Racial Discrimination, 253n32, 284
International Covenant on Civil and Political Rights (ICCPR), 65, 285; in Dowmung Rose Stone Case, 185; first report on, 128; ratification of, 116, 118–21; Taiwan's incorporation of, 238; Thao community land reclamation case and, 203; use in Taiwan, 122–23
International Covenant on Economic, Social and Cultural Rights (ICESCR), 65, 285; in Dowmung Rose Stone Case, 185; ratification of, 116, 118–21; Taiwan's incorporation of, 238
interpretation: activities of, 4–5; court interpretation limits of, 21; of Gaya norms, 81; interpreter programs, 158–59; judges freedom in, 21; special interpreter program, 158–60. *See also* translations
interpreters: CIP list of, 158; critical roles of, 4; Indigenous court units and, 7; infrequent use of, 159; Legal Aid for Indigenous Peoples Program provision of free, 152
i-Tribe program, 233

Jacobs, Bruce, 60
Japanese empire, 60; aboriginal border, 62–63; annexation of Taiwan, 52; boundaries during, 62–63; Chinese migrants and, 60; colonial period, 11, 22; Dowmung during, 28; efforts to control Taiwan, 40, 44, 50; end of control of Taiwan, 56; First Sino-Japanese War, 51; household registration records, 55; invasion of Korea, 51; KMT process of erasing traces of, 89; relocation of Tastas community, 30; Spanish trading with, 47; Taiwan under rule of, 51–52, 90, 91, 92
Johnson, Greg, 149, 209, 221
Jouni Lansman et al. v. Finland, 253n33, 282

judges, 138–42; approaches to Indigenous issues, 26; deepening understanding of, 12; district court judges, 87, 120, 129, 130–32, 136–37, 139–40, 187–90, 190, 200, 204; evidence and, 40, 203, 254–55n20; high court judges, 87, 96, 120, 121, 131–32, 135–36, 136, 137, 139, 146–47, 156–57, 201, 204, 205, 239; with Indigenous status, 130; interpretation of laws, 21; interpretation of laws defining Indigenous status by, 4; judicial hybrid practices, 198–208; judicial reassignment and rotation, 140–42; knowledge disparity in specialized units, 139; lack of understanding of Indigenous social norms and legal rights, 14; perspective on Indigenous court, 20; redefining legal practices, 6; in specialized district courts, 130–31; therapeutic justice and, 20; training programs, 16–17, 26, 28, 130–31, 138, 139

Judicial Assignment Measures, 127–28, 132

Judicial Officer Exam, 138, 142, 145

judicial precedent tradition, absence of, 21

judicial reassignment and rotation, 140–42

judicial rights (*sifa quanyi*), securing, 16

Judicial Training Institute, 138, 142

Judicial Yuan (*sifa yuan*): advocating for natural law approach at presentations at, 206; balancing state-Indigenous interests, 201–2; as branch of ROC government, 247n3; court reforms, 198; creation of Indigenous court units, 2, 12, 16, 38–39, 65, 78, 125, 127–29, 254n10; Deputy Director Wu, 125–26, 137, 163; on ethnic representation among judges, 138–39; expectations of, 198, 222; facilitation of introductions by, 22; formal directives to district courts to create Indigenous court units, 127–28; fulfilling objectives for specialized units, 171, 188; funding for LCIP from, 222; goal of promoting respect for Indigenous peoples and cultures, 192, 194, 196, 197; goals for court units' future development, 162; goals in creating Indigenous court units, 38, 78; incorporation of Indigenous perspectives in application of state law, 79; Indigenous court units creation by, 2; Indigenous Peoples Basic Law and, 145; initiatives for access to legal representation for Indigenous communities, 146; integration of Indigenous worldviews, 3, 6, 21, 33, 39, 135, 196–97, 199, 199–201, 206, 222; on judges conducting visits to Indigenous communities, 156; Judicial Assignment Measures, 127–28; on Judicial Officer Exam, 145; key objectives for court units, 129, 250n21; officials from, 17; on ongoing process of ad hoc chambers, 160–61; powers of, 247n3; public pronouncements about, 136, 188; recognition of relationship between Indigenous peoples and the land, 176; on rotation of judges, 141–42; special interpreter program, 158–60; on therapeutic potential of court units, 20; training programs, 28, 131–32, 139, 142, 155, 198

justice: assimilationist policies and, 1; Draft Act Governing Indigenous Historical Justice and the Restoration of Indigenous Rights, 283; Han Taiwanese understandings of, 17; Indigenous Historical Justice and Transitional Justice Committee, 234; Indigenous justice practices, 6–7, 162; mobile ethnography of, 41, 165, 177; multiculturalism and social justice, 12–13; seeking, 11; therapeutic justice, 17, 20

Kalt, Joseph P., 231

Kanakanavu, 10*map*; as recognized Indigenous group, 68

Kant, Immanuel, 116, 206, 208, 236

Kaohsiung (city), 29*map*, 50

Kaohsiung District Court, 128, 151; ad hoc Chambers of Indigenous Courts in, 128; approaches of judges to Indigenous issues in, 26; Bunun flooding case, 151; case law, 281; Fuxing community flooding case, 211–12

Kaohsiung High Administration Court, 1, 2*fig.*, 209, 281

Kaohsiung High Court, 96, 151, 215

Katratripulr community: formation of, 11; Pinuyumayan of, 1–2
Katratripulr case, 1, 3, 33
Kavalan, 10*map*; Hualien County and, 8; Hualien District Court dealing with, 26; LCIP and, 220; as recognized Indigenous group, 68
Keelung (city), 29*map*, 50, 62
Ketagalan, 68
Kinmen District Court, 128
knowledge: ancestral knowledge, 82; bridging gaps in, 6; building knowledge about Indigenous peoples, 17, 20; determining legitimate forms of, 4
Koori Court (Victoria, Australia), 19
Kuba Committee, 207, 257n20
Kuomintang (KMT): under Chiang Ching-kuo, 58; under Chiang Kai-shek, 56–58, 60; Indigenous peoples' rights and, 92–93, 103–4; Indigenous Peoples Basic Law adoption, 103–4; Indigenous support for, 169; Sun Yat-sen, 233; Taiwan's transition to, 88–92

lands of Indigenous peoples in Taiwan: as ancestral territory, 31; colonial claims on, 175; colonization by ROC government of, 4; disputes over, 123; Dutch treaties and rights to, 47; Indigenous communities building on, 21; Japanese seizure of Truku lands, 52–53; under KMT government, 56–57; lawyers dedicated to defending Indigenous persons in cases involving, 28; recognition and claims to, 11–12. *See also* territory
language(s), 58–59; aboriginal languages, 256n15; Austronesian languages, 8, 45; bridging gaps in, 6; Bunun language, 30, 213, 214, 217, 218; calls for recognition for Indigenous, 4; code-switching, 215–19; in the courtroom, 158, 215–19; in court use of Indigenous languages, 16; discrimination against, 1; Hokkien language, 27, 50, 174, 177, 213; Indigenous languages banned, 57, 59; Indigenous peoples as divided by, 10; Mandarin Chinese as dominant in Indigenous court units, 6, 16, 17, 130, 159, 215–16, 218; Mandarin Chinese as mandatory language in schools, 57; Mandarin Chinese as the norm, 59; Mandarin Chinese usage by Indigenous persons, 9, 84, 85; Paiwan language, 216; Pangcah language usage, 133; preservation and fostering of development of Indigenous languages, 12; recognition of, 2; as source of empowerment, 12; special interpreter program, 158–60; spoken by Indigenous peoples in Taiwan, 45; Taiwan Indigenous Television and, 233; Tayan language, 215–16, 218; Truku language, 81, 84, 85, 87, 174, 177, 181; understanding and addressing differences of, 4. *See also* Indigenous Languages Development Act; linguistic boundaries
law(s): challenging dominant narratives about, 6; circulation of conceptions of, 41; conflicting laws protecting Indigenous people, 14; constraints of civil law tradition, 17; efforts to raise status of Indigenous peoples through, 13; Han Taiwanese laws as dominant in Indigenous court units, 17; hierarchies of law, 204–6; hybrid practices, 1, 32, 198–208, 222; integration of Indigenous perspectives on, 4, 7; local Indigenous laws, 14; natural law and human dignity, 206–8; obscurities of national laws protecting Indigenous peoples, 17; social context of, 31; state law diminishing Indigenous peoples, 16. *See also* Indigenous Peoples Basic Law; local Indigenous laws; national laws; ROC law(s); state legal system
lawyers: access to, 145–49; Code of Ethics for Lawyers, 148, 283; critical roles of, 4, 6; dedicated to defending Indigenous persons, 28; educational programs for, 28; fees, 255–56n40; Indigenous court units and, 7; with Indigenous status, 130; legal aid services, 147; non-Indigenous, 4; summary proceeding recommendations from, 152; training programs, 147. *See also* prosecutors

Legal Aid Act, 146, 284
Legal Aid for Indigenous Peoples Program, 146, 152, 168
Legal Aid Foundation (LAF): branches of, 147; educational programs for lawyers, 28; establishment of, 146; funding for LCIP from, 222; intervention of, 231; LCIP and, 24, 148. *See also* Legal Center of Indigenous Peoples (LCIP)
legal aid services: as inadequate for Indigenous peoples, 14; in Paiwan Alili Incident, 15
Legal Center of Indigenous Peoples (LCIP): establishment of, 148–49, 219, 233; funding for, 222; Hualien District Court and, 24; managing a broken system, 219–22
legal documents, form and aesthetics of, 84–85, 87
legal pluralism, 31–36, 79, 137, 155, 165, 257n21
legal process: conducted in language of Han Taiwanese society, 14; Indigenous cultural values and, 3; state definitions and, 3
Legislative Yuan (*lifayuan*), 65; as branch of ROC government, 247n3; Development of National Languages Act, 233; Indigenous Peoples Basic Law and, 204, 230; Indigenous representatives in, 90
lex specialis principle, 150, 183–84, 205
Li, Judge, 170–78, 173
Lin Chiang-yi, 13
linguistic boundaries: complexity of, 11; construction and negotiation of, 3; of Indigenous groups, 9; as matter of access, 41, 157–60; problems of translation and, 6. *See also* language(s)
local Indigenous laws: in conflict with state law, 28; Gaya as, 81; as ignored by national legal systems, 14; importance of, 80; state law and, 17
low bono services, 147, 148
Luilang, 68
Lungkiau, 46

Mabuchi Tōichi, 54
Mainlanders (*waishengren*), arrival of, 11

Makatau, 46, 48, 68
Manchuria, 47, 48, 55
Mandarin Chinese: defining Gaya in, 81, 85; as dominant in court units, 6, 16, 17, 130, 159; Indigenous persons knowledge of, 27; lack of term for Indigenous in, 89; as mandatory language in schools, 57; as official language of Taiwan courts, 157; resistance to, 6, 32, 177
Marchetti, Elena, 20, 22
marginalization: classification systems and, 257n22; as shared common experience, 73
Marsden, David, 73
martial law, 56, 57, 58, 227
Martin, Jeffrey, 257n9
Mashantucket Pequot Court, 18
Mātāriki Courts (New Zealand), 19
McMillan, Jane, 144
Measures for the Annual Assignment of Judges in Civil and Administrative Litigation Cases and Special Courts, 127, 132, 141, 284
Menezes, Gustavo, 256n8
Merry, Sally, 31, 79, 87, 165
methodology, 26–27, 34–36, 40–42, 125
Miaoli District Court, 128
Miller, Bruce, 15–16, 256n8
mineral resources: cases related to, 135; Dowmung Rose Stone Case, 41, 179–92, 201
Ming dynasty, 46, 47; efforts to control Taiwan, 44
Mining Act, 180, 181, 182, 183–84, 284
misrepresentation, classification systems and, 257n22
Missile Technology Control Regime, 238
mobile ethnography of justice, 41, 165, 177. *See also* site visits
Mona Ludaw, 53–54
Monanen Malialiaves, 59
Morgan, Bronwen, 235
mountain-dwelling peoples, 10–11, 48–57, 62–63, 66–67, 89–91, 189, 252n7
Mugua River, 28, 30, 167–68, 173, 178, 179, 231
multiculturalism: to advance Indigenous recognition, 3; to enhance Taiwan's

international standing, 3; politics of, 3; process and problems of, 12–14; to secure claim to sovereignty, 3
multiple colonialisms, 3, 36, 42, 226, 228, 237. *See also* colonialism
muntjac deer: hunting of, 41, 80, 107–11. *See also* Bunun
Murri Court (Brisbane, Australia), 19
Myanmar, rejection of indigeneity, 71

Nadasdy, Paul, 86
Name Act, 95, 284
name rectification movement (*zhengming yundong*), 11, 68, 76–77
Nantou (city), 29*map*, 48, 53
Nantou District Court, 128
Nanzhuang Incident, 51
National Bar Association Lawyers Training Institute, 145
national court system: addressing systemic disadvantages of Indigenous peoples in, 224; ad hoc Chambers of Indigenous Courts and, 130, 132, 137; ad hoc Chambers of Indigenous Courts as embedded in, 38, 241, 247n2; ad hoc Chambers of Indigenous Courts formation and, 38, 127; bridging state-Indigenous divides in, 194, 196; of Canada, 127; Constitutional Court (*xianfa fating*), 247n3; district courts (*difang fayuan*), 247n3; high courts (*gaodeng fayuan*), 247n3; Indigenous court units as within, 6–7, 37; Indigenous groups relying on justice outside of, 162; Indigenous peoples and, 2, 16, 21, 38, 80, 125, 129; Indigenous peoples' interests and rights through use of, 149; Indigenous persons' marginalized position in, 193; judges' understanding of ad hoc chambers' role in, 170–71; LCIP and, 222; levels of, 180, 188; overseeing of, 80; promoting respect for Indigenous peoples in, 228; reforms introduced to, 2; replication of ordinary court processes of, 152; re-presentation of standard forms applied in, 146; securing judicial rights of Indigenous peoples in, 228; struggles of the Indigenous persons and communities to navigate, 165; Supreme Court (*zhonghua minguo zuigaofayuan*), 247n3. *See also* Hualien District Court; Hualien High Court
national laws: Chiayi District Court on adhering to, 89; form of, 85, 87; interlegality with local Indigenous law, 32; obscurities of national laws protecting Indigenous peoples, 17; turning toward, 86–88
Native American tribal courts, 18
native Taiwanese (*benshengren*), indigeneity intersection with claims of, 11
natural law, 206–8
natural resources: disputes over, 41; lawyers dedicated to defending Indigenous persons in cases involving, 28
Navajo judicial system, 18
"New Partnership Between Indigenous Peoples and the Taiwan Government," 229
New Zealand: *Apirana Mahuika et al v. New Zealand*, 282; Indigenous courts in, 19; Indigenous Peoples Economic and Trade Cooperation Arrangement, 14, 239
Ngambra Court (Australian Capital Territory), 19
Niezen, Ronald, 65, 73, 212
Nobuto Miyamoto, 54
nonadversarial methods of dispute resolution, 18
Nuclear Non-Proliferation Treaty, 238
Nunga Court (South Australia), 19

Oceania: Austronesian-speaking peoples, 40; Taiwan's connections to, 8
Office of Pacification and Reclamation, 52
Ong, Aihwa, 235
ontological boundaries, construction and negotiation of, 3
Orchid Island, 68, 113

Paiwan, 9, 10*map*, 54–55; dispute resolution in, 233; Taitung District Court dealing with, 26; hunting conventions, 83; during Japanese colonial period, 11; Paiwan Alili Incident, 14–16, 20; as recognized Indigenous group, 68

Paiwan language, 216
Pangcah. *See* Amis (Pangcah)
Pangsola-Dolatok, 46
Papora, 68
Parent and ors v. Singapore Airlines Ltd and Civil Aeronautics Administration, 282
Pasifika (Youth) Court (New Zealand), 19
Pazeh/Kaxabu, 68
Peacemaker Courts, 18
Pecoraro, Fernando, 81
Penghu Islands, 29*map*, 45–46, 51
People's Republic of China (PRC), 66, 93, 234, 237, 239, 240, 240–41; claims on Taiwan, 4
Perley, Bernard, 209
Permanent Forum on Indigenous Issues (UN), 65
Philippines, 8; indigeneity in constitutions of, 71
Pingtung (city), 29*map*, 48, 62, 96; experts from, 207
Pingtung District Court: ad hoc Chambers of Indigenous Courts in, 26, 128; approaches of judges to Indigenous issues in, 26; case law, 281; Paiwan cemetery site visit, 176; Paiwan hunting case, 96
Pinuyumayan (Puyuma), 10*map*, 55; attire of, 1; betel nut usage by, 1; collaboration with Japanese, 51; connection to land, 90–93; cosmology of, 1; elders of, 1, 41, 74–75, 80; hunting conventions, 83; Hunting Festival (Mangayaw), 73–75; during Japanese colonial period, 11, 90, 91, 92; of Katratripulr, 1–2; as recognized Indigenous group, 68; Taitung District Court dealing with, 26; during transition to ROC, 41, 91–93
plains-dwelling peoples (*pingpuzuqun*), 10–11, 49, 51–52, 62, 67–69, 189
plea bargaining, introduction of, 151
pluralism, 17, 31, 31–36, 257n21. *See also* legal pluralism
Portuguese explorers, 44, 46
postcolonial contexts, Indigenous courts in, 6–7
Povinelli, Elizabeth A., 14, 40, 210–11, 258n24

power: attention to power relations, 39–40; boundaries embedded in relations of, 5; imbalances in, 17, 40, 69; in Indigenous court units, 6, 39; recognition and related dynamics of, 14; in relationship between colonizer and colonized, 4, 6, 32, 40; spatiality and, 155–56
prefigurative legality, 235
Presidential Office Indigenous Historical Justice and Transitional Justice Committee, 65, 112
problem-solving courts, 19
pro bono services, 147, 148, 180–81
process, in Indigenous court units, 6, 38–39
prosecutors, 255n27; as antagonistic toward Indigenous claims, 14, 142; appeals of not-guilty verdicts, 150, 179; critical roles of, 4; in Hualien District, 142–43, 179; Prosecutor-General Yen, 100; training of specialized, 142–43; training programs, 130, 131
Pruitt, Lisa, 154

Qauqaut, 68
Qing dynasty, 48, 51; administrative influence of, 52; boundaries during, 61–62; boundary strategy of, 53; Chinese migrants and, 60; efforts to control Taiwan, 44; Qing government, 48–50

racial boundaries, construction and negotiation of, 3
Rakaw (Dowmung elder), 31, 32, 153, 166–67, 217. *See also* Dowmung Bamboo House Case
Rangatahi Court (New Zealand), 19
raw savages (*shengfan*), 49, 51
recognition: Povinelli on, 258n24; Schaap on, 258n24, 258n35; Taylor on, 258n24
recolonization, 60. *See also* colonialism
registration system, ROC law and, 69
Regulations for Demarcating Indigenous Peoples Land or Tribal Land Area, 112, 284
Regulations for Indigenous Peoples or Tribes Being Consulted, Obtaining Their Consent and Participation, 112, 284

Republic of Taiwan, establishment of, 51
restoration of communities, Indigenous recognition and, 11–12
Richland, Justin, 21, 235
rights of Indigenous peoples: advocating for, 1; global issues influencing Taiwan's, 115–23; movements for, 16, 41; phases in development of, 88–115; state authorities restrictions on, 14
Riles, Annelise, 84–85
ritual practices, prosecution against Indigenous persons engaging in, 14
ROC Constitution: cultural pluralism and, 12; culture (term) in, 188; Dowmung Rose Stone Case and, 181, 184; Indigenous Peoples Basic Law, 204–5; Indigenous peoples term inclusion in, 93–94; as related to Indigenous peoples, 117, 136, 256n15; at top of legal system, 150, 204; violations of, 69
ROC government: arrival of, 11, 41; branches of, 247n3; control over Indigenous status, 73; Democratic Progressive Party (DPP) and, 94; efforts to control Taiwan, 44; efforts to raise status of Indigenous peoples through policies of, 13; Indigenous (legal term) under, 40, 66; loss of seat in UN, 3–4, 14, 44; multiculturalism in policy of, 12–14; official diplomatic relations, 4, 64, 239; sovereignty making and, 42; Taiwanese national identity and, 13; transition to, 41, 80, 88; use of Indigenous peoples and cultures to counter China's territorial claims, 10; use of Indigenous peoples' identities and rights by, 40. *See also* Control Yuan (*jianchayuan*); Executive Yuan (*xingzhengyuan*); Judicial Yuan (*sifa yuan*); Legislative Yuan (*lifayuan*)
ROC law(s): as applied by ad hoc chambers, 196; centrality of, 32; Chinese moral norms and, 257n9; concept of culture in, 256n15; educating Indigenous peoples as, 192; Gaya legitimacy and, 84, 86–87; incorporation of ICCPR and ICESCR into, 116; Indigenous (legal term) under, 40, 44; Indigenous customary legislation and, 207–8; Indigenous peoples and, 123–24; legal protections for Indigenous peoples in, 41; for protection of Indigenous peoples, 80; as rapidly changing, 38; reforms to, 30–31; registration system and, 69
ROC state: bridging divides separating Indigenous peoples and, 225; Bunun culture and, 217; engagement in sovereignty by, 42; framed as outsider, 177, 193; growing recognition of harms inflicted on Indigenous peoples by legal system, 162; as Han Taiwanese-controlled, 94; Indigenous sovereignty and, 236–37; LCIP and, 222; privileging of interests of, 88; pursuit of constitutional multiculturalism, 4; relations of power privileging interests of, 226; representation of Taiwan at UN meetings on Indigenous affairs by, 236–37; ROC law as privileging perspectives and interest of, 123; slow implementation of legislation supporting Indigenous self-governance, 231; sovereignty and, 118, 228; traditional territory as belonging to, 105; turn to multiculturalism, 3
Rodney King trial, 185–86
Rose Stone Case, 41, 179–92, 201
Rukai, 10*map*, 55; Indigenous language in, 157; as recognized Indigenous group, 68; Taitung District Court dealing with, 26
rule-crafting processes, 6, 33–36, 37, 123

Saisiyat, 10*map*, 51, 55; as recognized Indigenous group, 68
Sakizaya, 10*map*; Hualien County and, 8; Hualien District Court dealing with, 26; LCIP and, 220; as recognized Indigenous group, 68
Salizan Takisvilainan, 107, 241
same-sex marriage, 238
Samu (Bunun ancestral law), 107, 109–11, 233, 253n28
Schaap, Andrew, 258n24, 258n35
Scott, James, 217
Second Opium War, 50
Second Sino-Japanese War, 55

Seediq, 10*map*; categorization of, 11; guardline system, 53, 63; Hualien County and, 8; Hualien District Court dealing with, 26; LCIP and, 220; legal pluralism and, 155; as recognized Indigenous group, 68; Truku Name Rectification Campaign, 76–77; Wushe Incident, 53–54
self-determination: assertions of, 21; struggles for, 5, 221; value of making space for, 42
self-governance, 118; Amis, 232; hunting pilot program, 83, 230; legislation supporting, 231; Truku, 232
self-identification: as contested concept, 11; meaning of indigeneity and, 40; for understanding indigeneity at global level, 72
sentences, under summary proceedings, 151
Seqalu, 51
settler colonialism, 60. *See also* colonialism
Shimonoseki, Treaty of, 51
Simon, Scott, 53, 57, 73, 203, 232, 237, 253n28, 257n9
Simpson, Audra, 21, 175, 217, 236
Singer, Joseph William, 231
Sino-French War, 50
Siraya, 46, 48, 68
site visits, 20–21, 32, 156, 173–76. *See also* mobile ethnography of justice
Smangus Beechwood Incident, 101–3, 111, 131, 200–201, 249n11
Smangus community, 29*map*
social justice, multiculturalism and, 12–13
South China Sea, 29*map*
sovereignty: calls for recognition for Indigenous, 4; as contested, 3, 42; de facto, 229, 230–31; de jure, 229; de recto, 229; graduated sovereignty, 235; indigeneity and, 42; Indigenous Historical Justice and Transitional Justice Committee, 234; matter of, 229–30; multiculturalism to secure claim to, 3; new configurations of, 3, 239–41; rebuilding of, 11–12; reimagining, 42; restoration of, 12; self-governance, 230–34; Taiwan's enactment of state sovereignty, 5; types of, 229. *See also* as-if sovereignty; Indigenous sovereignty

Spanish empire: efforts to control Taiwan, 40, 44; in northern Taiwan, 47
spatiality: in Indigenous court units, 5, 38; Indigenous perspectives and, 4; as matter of access, 41, 154–56
specialized courts: ad hoc chambers as, 130–31; knowledge disparity of judges in, 139–40; programs for judges in, 131; types of, 19, 130
state-Indigenous relations: balancing interests in, 201–4; character of, 42; judges on, 21
state legal system: as broken system to be managed, 219–22; centrality of, 32; in conflict with local Indigenous law, 28; Indigenous cultural practices and, 17, 83; Indigenous peoples repurposing of state laws and knowledge, 87; as primary shaper of court units, 17; relationships between unofficial forms of law and, 31
State of Alaska Rules of Civil Procedure, 18, 284
Status Act for Indigenous Peoples, 66–69, 94, 284
Sugimoto Tomonori, 60
summary proceedings, 151–52, 161, 196
Supreme Court (*zhonghua minguo zuigaofayuan*): as branch of national court system, 247n3; Indigenous hunters' firearms case, 96; Smangus Beechwood Incident, 249n11; Tama Talum appeal case, 30, 191–92

Taichung (city), 29*map*
Taichung District Court, 199
Taichung High Court, 203
Tainan (city), 29*map*, 44, 46
Tainan High Court, 206, 207
Taipei (city), 29*map*
Taipei District Court, 204–5; approaches of judges to Indigenous issues in, 26; case law, 282; Indigenous cultural erasure in case in, 89; judges in, 205; Tayan forest burial case, 206–7; on terms for Indigenous people, 252n7
Taitung (city), 29*map*
Taitung County: Amis of A-tolan in, 232; ancestral cemetery in, 1; approaches of

judges to Indigenous issues in, 26; Bunun hunt, 107–11; Bunun Youth Group (*dongbuqing*), 100; cases in, 28; Christianity in, 36; Han Taiwanese in, 36; human rights norms in cases in, 120; Indigenous peoples in, 140, 227; Paiwan Alili Incident, 15; Paiwan in, 9; Pinuyumayan in, 73, 90–93; Tama Talam and, 99–100; Tastas people in, 28, 29*map*, 30. *See also* Bunun

Taitung District County, Indigenous communities and, 26

Taitung District Court: ad hoc Chambers of Indigenous Courts in, 128; ancestral cemetery relocation incident, 1; case law, 282; Paiwan Alili Incident, 15; Tama Talam case, 30, 99–100

Taitung District Prosecutors Office, 99–100

Taivoan, 46, 48, 68

Taiwan: Austronesian diaspora and, 45; cartographic representations of, 8; colonial efforts to control, 40; colonial history, 59–66; culturally diverse society status of, 12–13; development of heavy industry in, 55; independence of, 40, 44; indigeneity in constitutions of, 71; international standing of, 3, 17; names throughout history, 44–45; national identity of, 12–13; place on the world platform, 40; Qing ceded to Japan, 51; transition to democracy, 44, 153; transition to ROC rule, 41, 66, 80, 88, 91–93, 94; UN dismissal of, 44; unique position of, 42

Taiwan Bar Association, 256n40

Taiwan Camphor Bureau, 52

Taiwan Constitutional Court: case law, 282; rulings by, 11

Taiwanese identity: Indigenous court units initiative and, 4; as influence on court units, 17; ROC's crafting of distinct, 4, 66

Taiwan High Court, 102–3; case law, 282; language usage in, 215; Smangus Beechwood Incident, 200–201, 249n11

Taiwan Indigenous Television, 1, 227, 233

Taiwan Provisional Assembly, 57, 90

Taiwan Strait, 29*map*

Taiwan Supreme Court, 26, 30, 103, 106, 192; appeals to, 191; case law, 282; exclusion of, 128; ruling on Paiwan hunting case, 96; Smangus Beechwood Incident, 200; Tama Talum appeal case, 100, 191–92

Takau, 50

Takimi (Japanese), 30. *See also* Tastas community

Tama Talum, 26, 30, 98–101, 106, 162, 165, 191–92, 220

Tamsui, 47, 50

Tao, 10*map*, 55; as recognized Indigenous group, 68; Taitung District Court dealing with, 26

Taoyuan (city), 29*map*

Taoyuan District Court, 128

Taoyuan International Airport, 1

Taroko National Park, 195, 232

Tastas community, 28, 29*map*, 30

Tata Rara, 51

Tavares, Antonio, 51

Taxation Administration, 255–56n40

Tayan (Atayal), 10*map*, 54–55; categorization of, 11, 75–76; forest burial case, 206–7; guard-line system, 53, 63; hunting conventions, 83; as recognized Indigenous group, 68; role of Gaya in, 200–201; Smangus Beechwood Incident, 101–3, 111, 131, 200–201, 249n11

Tayan language, 215–16, 218

Taylor, Charles, 258n24

territorial boundaries: ad hoc Chambers of Indigenous Courts and, 3; construction and negotiation of, 3; disputes over, 41; territorial rights, 11

territory: ancestral territory, 181, 232; challenging dominant narratives about, 6; Dowmung Bamboo House Case, 31; integration of Indigenous perspectives on, 4, 7; state narratives of national ownership of Indigenous, 20–21. *See also* lands of Indigenous peoples in Taiwan

Thao, 10*map*, 203

therapeutic jurisprudence, 19–20

Toakas, 68

tongmenren (term), 11
training programs: Judicial Yuan and, 28, 131–32, 139, 142, 155–56, 198; for lawyers, 145, 147; specialized training for judges and prosecutors, 16–17, 26, 28, 130–31, 138, 139
translations: engagement through, 7; problems of cultural and linguistic, 6. *See also* interpretation; language(s); linguistic boundaries
Tribal Councils, 112
tribal public corporations, 112, 230
Trobiawan, 68
Truku, 10*map*; ancestral practices, 82; camphor, 52–53; categorization of, 11, 75–76; cultural practices of, 164; in Dowmung, 11, 28, 41, 164, 233; Dowmung Bamboo House Case, 41; Dowmung Rose Stone Case, 41, 179–92; elders of, 9; guard-line system, 53, 63; Hualien County and, 8; Hualian District Court dealing with, 26; hunting in, 41, 82, 232; LCIP and, 220; local Indigenous laws in, 30, 80; name rectification movement, 11, 68, 76–77; origin stories, 43; role of Gaya in, 30, 41, 81, 200, 232; self-governance, 232; social connectedness and consensus of, 154–55; in Taroko National Park, 195; Taroko National Park, 232; Truku War, 53; women's role in hunting, 82; Xincheng Incident, 52. *See also* Dowmung community; Dowmung Rose Stone Case
Truku language, 81, 84, 85, 87, 174, 177, 181
Tsai, Grace, 119
Tsai Ting-yi, 132–33
Tsai Ing-wen's apology, 12, 14, 41, 65, 80, 101, 112–15, 118, 230
Tsou, 10*map*, 55, 249n11; classifications systems of Indigenous life and, 257n22; elders of, 207; hunting conventions, 83; hunting self-governance pilot program with, 83; *kuba* meeting house, 257n20
Tsou Leader Honey Incident, 249n11
Two Covenants Act. *See* Act to Implement the International Covenant on Civil and Political Rights and the International Covenant on Economic, Social and Cultural Rights (Two Covenants Act)
Typhoon Ophelia landslide memorial, 231

UN Gender Inequality Index, 238
United Nations Declaration on the Rights of Indigenous Peoples (UNDRIP), 285; description of Indigenous peoples in, 72; Indigenous Peoples Basic Law and, 65, 103, 118; significance of, 116–17; Taiwan's inability to vote on, 251n4; Taiwan's treatment of, 116, 118
United Nations: *Angela Poma Poma v. Peru*, 282; Indigenous youth delegations at, 13–14; legal document form at conferences of, 84–85; Permanent Forum on Indigenous Issues, 65; ROC Constitution and Charter of, 119; ROC government as member of, 118, 237, 251n4; ROC government's loss of seat in, 3–4, 14, 44, 65, 250–51n1; Taiwan's dismissal from, 44, 64; UNDRIP, 65, 72, 103, 116–18, 251n4, 285
United States: Anglo-American adversarial system in state and federal courts of, 18; Native American tribal courts and, 18; Rodney King trial, 185–86; US Navy bypassing of Taiwan in WWII, 9
Universal Declaration of Human Rights, 116, 285
UN Permanent Forum on Indigenous Issues, Indigenous representatives and, 65
UN Working Group on Indigenous Peoples, 71–72
Use of Wildlife Management Measures for Indigenous Peoples' Traditional Cultural and Ritual Hunting and Killing Needs, 99, 189, 284
Utsushikawa Nenozō, 54

Veracini, Lorenzo, 60
vernacularization, 31, 173
village settlement policy, 53

Wang Li-jung, 12, 13, 89
Wang Tay-sheng, 207, 257n21

White, Richard, 63
"White Paper on Aboriginal Policy," 94, 95, 229
"White Paper on Foreign Policy for the 21st Century," 237–38
White Terror program, 56, 92, 95
Wildlife Conservation Act, 95, 96, 98, 99, 142, 147, 202, 256n15, 284
wildlife protections: conservation efforts, 82. *See also* hunting, Indigenous
witnesses, Indigenous: critical roles of, 4; in Dowmung Bamboo House Case, 172; in Dowmung Rose Stone Case, 181; importance in Indigenous cases, 6, 256n8; Indigenous court units and, 7, 132; legal procedures requiring use of Mandarin Chinese, 159; refusals to speak in Mandarin Chinese, 32; in Smangus Beechwood Incident, 201
Wittgenstein, Ludwig, 217
Wolfe, Patrick, 60
World Bank, 72
World War II: Japanese conscription of Indigenous men, 55; transfer of Taiwan after, 66; US naval bypassing of Taiwan in, 9
Wu, Deputy Director, 125–26, 137, 163
Wushe Incident (Musha Incident), 53–54, 63

Xi Jinping, 234, 240–41, 248n9
Xincheng Incident, 53
Xu, Lawyer, 168–72

Yang, Lawyer, 180–82, 183, 184–85, 189, 191
Yen Da-ho, 100
Yilan (city), 29*map*, 45, 53
yuanzhumin (Indigenous people), 10, 89, 93, 112, 115, 133, 248n6
yuanzhuminzu (Indigenous peoples), 89, 94, 189, 248n6, 252n11
yuanzhuminzu zhuanye fating (term), 2, 94, 247n2

Zhang, Judge, 195, 199, 200
Zheng Cheng-gong (Koxinga), 47–48, 50
Zhou, Lawyer, 178–79

Founded in 1893,
UNIVERSITY OF CALIFORNIA PRESS
publishes bold, progressive books and journals
on topics in the arts, humanities, social sciences,
and natural sciences—with a focus on social
justice issues—that inspire thought and action
among readers worldwide.

The UC PRESS FOUNDATION
raises funds to uphold the press's vital role
as an independent, nonprofit publisher, and
receives philanthropic support from a wide
range of individuals and institutions—and from
committed readers like you. To learn more, visit
ucpress.edu/supportus.

www.ingramcontent.com/pod-product-compliance
Lightning Source LLC
Chambersburg PA
CBHW020532030426
42337CB00013B/824